JAMES JOYCE AND THE MATTER OF PARIS

In *James Joyce and the Matter of Paris*, Catherine Flynn situates Joyce definitively in the cultural capital of modern Europe. Beginning with Joyce's underexamined first exile in Paris, she shows the significance for his writing of the time he spent there and of a range of French authors whose works inflected his experience in the city. With them and in response to the pressures of Parisian consumer capitalism, Joyce was able to conceive a new somatic aesthetic, in which the philosophically disparaged senses of taste, touch, and smell join to resist capitalism's efforts to manage and manipulate the desire it creates. This book discovers a revolutionary Joyce and reclaims the philosophical content and political depth of that revolution.

CATHERINE FLYNN is Associate Professor of English at the University of California, Berkeley. She is the editor of a forthcoming volume titled *The New Joyce Studies* (Cambridge). She is co-editor with Richard Brown of the *James Joyce Quarterly* special issue, "Joycean Avant-Gardes". Before studying literature, she practiced as an architect in Vienna, Austria, and Ireland.

JAMES JOYCE AND THE MATTER OF PARIS

CATHERINE FLYNN

University of California, Berkeley

CAMBRIDGE
UNIVERSITY PRESS

CAMBRIDGE
UNIVERSITY PRESS

University Printing House, Cambridge CB2 8BS, United Kingdom

One Liberty Plaza, 20th Floor, New York, NY 10006, USA

477 Williamstown Road, Port Melbourne, VIC 3207, Australia

314–321, 3rd Floor, Plot 3, Splendor Forum, Jasola District Centre, New Delhi – 110025, India

79 Anson Road, #06-04/06, Singapore 079906

Cambridge University Press is part of the University of Cambridge.

It furthers the University's mission by disseminating knowledge in the pursuit of education, learning, and research at the highest international levels of excellence.

www.cambridge.org
Information on this title: www.cambridge.org/9781108485579
DOI: 10.1017/9781108752053

© Catherine Flynn 2019

First published 2019

Printed and bound in Great Britain by Clays Ltd, Elcograf S.p.A.

A catalogue record for this publication is available from the British Library.

ISBN 978-1-108-48557-9 Hardback

Contents

v

Figures

Acknowledgments

This is a book about the evolution of Joyce's forms and ideas and it is maybe fitting that the book itself went through a series of developmental stages. I am deeply grateful to the people who inspired and supported me as the project evolved and as I learned to think at the scale of a book. It began as a comparative literature dissertation at Yale University where I was, and continue to be, indebted to Peter Brooks and Shoshana Felman for their early, crucial encouragement, to my dissertation advisers, Katie Trumpener and Carol Jacobs, whose different performances of breadth and depth instilled a sense of autonomy in me, and to Barry McCrea for vital, and ongoing, exchanges. During my time at Stanford, Alex Woloch helped me understand how to choose my way forward. I brought this book to completion in the English Department at Berkeley, where my colleagues' intellectual liveliness, rigor, and dedication continue to inspire me.

I want to express my gratitude to the individuals who offered constructive criticism along the way. For reading the manuscript perceptively when it was still in an amorphous state, I thank Paul Saint-Amour, Andrew Gibson, Tim Conley, and Doug Mao. For their incisive and helpful advice in departmental reviews, I am indebted to Elizabeth Abel, Eric Falci, Mark Goble, Lyn Hejinian, and Kent Puckett. I owe a great deal to Dan Blanton who repeatedly pushed me to produce more direct and forceful statements of my argument and to Maura Nolan for her wisdom in the most difficult phase of that process. At the stage of manuscript evaluation for Cambridge University Press, Jean-Michel Rabaté's expertise and advice was invaluable. I am very grateful to Rob Kaufman and Marty Jay for their careful reading and thinking.

I can also trace the manuscript's advances to conversations at a series of venues: the Berkeley English Consortium on the Novel, the Townsend Humanities Center, the Modernist Studies Association (where a panel with Doug Mao and Ravit Reichman was an important step toward the book), the American Conference for Irish Studies, and the American

Comparative Literature Association all advanced my thinking. Conversations at International Joyce Symposia, the North American Joyce Conferences, and the Zurich Joyce Foundation helped me see what I needed to do. Talks at the Dublin James Joyce Summer School, the Trieste Joyce School, the Southern California Irish Studies Consortium, and the Conference on Modernism at Dartmouth College allowed me to hone aspects of my argument.

I would like to thank Anthony Cascardi, Dean of Arts and Humanities at Berkeley, for his support at key moments. I also want to express my appreciation of the various chairs of the English department: Sam Otter, Katherine O'Brien O'Keeffe, Genaro Padilla, and Steve Justice. My progress on the book was greatly assisted by fellowships at Berkeley: a Humanities Research Fellowship; a Townsend Fellowship; a Global Urban Humanities Townsend Fellowship; a Committee on Research Faculty Research Grant; and an Institute of International Studies Grant. The Introduction to the Humanities Postdoctoral Fellowship at Stanford provided a safe and stimulating haven. I was grateful to receive a Whitney Humanities Graduate Fellowship and a Leylan Dissertation Fellowship at Yale.

Grateful acknowledgment is given here to the Beinecke Rare Book and Manuscript Library, Yale University, for permission to reproduce an image of Joyce's 1902 photopostcard. Grateful acknowledgment is also given to the National Library of Ireland for permission to quote from Joyce's "Paris and Pola Commonplace Book." Earlier versions of parts of Chapters 4, 5, and 6 have appeared in "'Circe' and Surrealism: Joyce and the Avant-Garde" in *Journal of Modern Literature* 34.2 (Winter 2011): 121–38, and in "*Finnegans Wake*'s Radio Montage: Man-Made Static, the Avant-Garde, and Collective Reading," in *Joycean Avant-Gardes*, eds. Catherine Flynn and Richard Brown, *James Joyce Quarterly* 52.ii (Winter 2015): 287–306. Thankful acknowledgment is given to the publishers for permission to use this material in the present work. Of the team at Cambridge University Press, particularly Lisa Sinclair, Senior Content Manager, and Karen Slaght, sharp-eyed copy-editor, but most especially Ray Ryan, Senior Acquisitions Editor, for his crucial support and his judiciousness in managing the editorial process, I am deeply appreciative.

Throughout this process, conversations with friends and colleagues have sustained, stimulated, and guided me. In the joyful spirit of the Joycean catalogue, let me gather them together here: Charlie Altieri, Valérie Bénéjam, Stephen Best, Erik Bindervoet, Mitch Breitwieser, Luca Crispi, Ronan Crowley, Kathleen Donegan, Enda Duffy, Nadia Ellis, Eric Falci,

Karen Feldman, Anne Fogarty, Anne-Lise Francois, Catherine Gallagher, Josh Gang, Luke Gibbons, Cecil Giscombe, Kevis Goodman, Andrea Halpin, Alisa Hartz, Robbert-Jan Henkes, Michael Iarocci, Donna Jones, Maria Kager, Marianne Kaletzky, Annette Lienau, Laura O'Connor, Erica Levy McAlpine, Zena Meadowsong, Niklaus Largier, Grace Lavery, Stephen Lee, Colleen Lye, Vicki Mahaffey, David Marno, Geoffrey G. O'Brien, Kristin Primus, Kent Puckett, Poulomi Saha, Debarati Sanyal, Fritz Senn, Namwali Serpell, Emily Setina, Victor Sheridean, Vincent Sherry, Sam Slote, David Spurr, Emily Thornbury, Rebecca Walkowitz, Ellen Woods, and Dora Zhang. Thomas O'Dogherty got his teeth into the manuscript at an early stage; both I and the book are the better for it. My three kind and clever brothers have supported me from the start. Fundamental to everything are my parents, whose insight, generosity, and wit form the bedrock of my life.

Introduction: The Matter of Paris

Charles Baudelaire writes, in the letter to his friend, Arsène Houssaye, which prefaces his 1869 *Le Spleen de Paris: petits poèmes en prose*:

> Which of us has not, in his moments of ambition, dreamed of the miracle of a poetic prose, musical, without rhythm and without rhyme, supple enough and rugged enough to adapt itself to the lyrical movements of the soul, the undulations of reverie, the sudden starts of consciousness? It was, above all, out of the exploration of huge cities, out of the intersection of the innumerable interrelations, that this obsessive ideal was born.[1]

For the spectacularly talented and innovative Baudelaire, this new literary form is a "haunting ideal," a "dream," a "miracle." It is clear that the generic contradiction of a form that is neither and both poetry and prose presents considerable challenges.[2] Furthermore, this paradoxical form gives expression to an almost impossibly mobile subject to which Baudelaire refers in a series of terms that cast doubt upon each other: *l'âme* (soul), *rêverie* (revery), and, most vaguely, *conscience*, a word that in encompassing conscience, consciousness, and awareness ranges from moral probity to the registration of events. This indefinite subject is engaged in varieties of motion – "lyrical movements," "undulations," "somersaults" – in response to a setting that is definable only in its innumerable heterogeneous interrelations, "du croisement de leurs innombrables rapports." To give

---

[1] "Quel est celui de nous qui n'a pas, dans ses jours d'ambition, rêvé le miracle d'une prose poétique, musicale sans rythme et sans rime, assez souple et assez heurtée pour s'adapter aux mouvements lyriques de l'âme, aux ondulations de la rêverie, aux soubresauts de la conscience? C'est surtout de la fréquentation des villes énormes, c'est du croisement de leurs innombrables rapports que naît cet idéal obsédant." Charles Baudelaire, *Baudelaire: Œuvres Complètes* (Paris: Éditions du Seuil, 1968), 146 (my translation).

[2] See Barbara Johnson, *Défigurations du langage poétique* (Paris: Flammarion, 1975). Also, the more recent Anne Elizabeth Jamison, "Any Where out of This Verse: Baudelaire's Prose Poetics and the Aesthetics of Transgression," *Nineteenth-Century French Studies* 29.3–4, Spring–Summer 2001, 256–86 and Debarati Sanyal, *The Violence of Modernity: Baudelaire, Irony and the Politics of Form* (Baltimore, MD: Johns Hopkins University Press, 2006).

expression to experience in the "ville énorme," the city without norms, Baudelaire would forsake the usual patterning of poetry, its rhythm and rhyme, and devise a mode that is, mysteriously, "musicale." Baudelaire announces his failure in the same letter: "Once I had begun to work, I found out that not only did I remain very distant from my mysterious and brilliant model, but that I was creating *something* (if it can be called "something") altogether different, an accident in which anyone else would find cause for pride, but which can only lead to deep humiliation for one who thinks the poet's greatest honor lies in having accomplished *exactly* what he had planned to do."[3] Proud and modest simultaneously, Baudelaire declares prose poetry to be the limit of his capacities as an artist. What he produces not only fails to conform to his ideal but lacks a definitive identity; it is "*something* (if it can be called something)."

It may seem strange to begin a book on James Joyce with a passage from Baudelaire. The claim of this book, however, is that Joyce took up Baudelaire's challenge at the beginning of his career and that he devised a series of responses to it over the course of his work, drawing not only on Baudelaire's poetic prose but also on a host of innovative forms by nineteenth- and twentieth-century French writers. Joyce's explorations of prose poetry led him to grapple with the material pressures of the modern city and to develop a new kind of thinking to respond to them, one in which the centered subject and the normative structures of writing and thinking fall away in new modes of writing that reject the fundamental categories of art.

On December 3, 1902, a twenty-year-old Joyce set off for Paris. Before he left, he approached W. B. Yeats with what he called a "book of prose essays or poems."[4] Accounts of their meeting vary but, in a manuscript intended as a preface to *Ideas of Good and Evil* (1903), Yeats records their subsequent discussion: "I asked him to come with me to the smoking room of a restaurant in O'Connell Street, and read me a beautiful though immature and eccentric harmony of little prose descriptions and meditations. He had thrown over metrical form, he said, that he might get a form

---

[3] Baudelaire, *Paris Spleen and La Fanfarlo* trans. and ed. Raymond N. MacKenzie (Indianapolis, IN: Hackett, 2008), 4. "Sitôt que j'eus commencé le travail, je m'aperçus que non seulement je restais bien loin de mon mystérieux et brillant modèle, mais encore que je faisais *quelque chose* (si cela peut s'appeler quelque chose) de singulièrement différent, accident dont tout autre que moi s'enorgueillirait sans doute, mais qui ne peut qu'humilier profondément un esprit qui regarde comme le plus grand honneur du poète d'accomplir *juste* ce qu'il a projeté de faire." Baudelaire, *Œuvres Complètes*, 146.

[4] Qtd. in Richard Ellmann, *James Joyce* (Oxford, UK: Oxford University Press, 1982), 102. Hence cited in abbreviated form as *JJ*.

so fluent that it would respond to the motion of the spirit. I praised his work but he said, 'I don't really care whether you like what I am doing or not. It won't make the least difference to me. Indeed I don't know why I am reading it to you'" (*JJ* 102). The patterns of Baudelaire's formulations live on in Yeats's record of Joyce's words as Joyce presents as his own Baudelaire's ambition for poetic prose, a form that banishes meter to become supple enough to adapt to the motions of consciousness.

Joyce's scornful response constitutes an unacknowledged substitution of one father figure for another. By December 1902, Joyce had read Baudelaire widely. But he was also acquainted with other radically experimental figures of late-nineteenth-century French literature, having read Émile Zola, Gustave Flaubert, and Joris-Karl Huysmans (*JJ* 59, 75). He read Arthur Symons' *The Symbolist Movement in Literature* shortly after its publication in 1899 (*JJ* 79), a volume that featured poetry by Paul Verlaine, as well as Gérard de Nerval, Arthur Rimbaud, Stéphane Mallarmé, and Maurice Maeterlinck. He discovered Verlaine's *Les Poètes maudits* in 1900 or 1901 (*JJ* 75) and then translated and rewrote poems by Verlaine. The "accursed poet" offers us a lens through which to view the young Joyce's persona, "dédaigneux par excellence," disdaining alike Yeats, the Dublin literary establishment, and conventional success.[5] Accordingly, Paris as a hothouse of literary innovation offered an attractive alternative forum for Joyce.[6]

In moving to Paris, Joyce followed an Irish tradition of migration: continental Europe offered an arena free of British colonial rule, and Paris, in particular, was associated with the appealing republican ideal of a culture of free and equal citizens. It was also an alluringly modern city. Christopher Prendergast writes of the notion of Paris as "the capital of the nineteenth century": "Describing Paris in this way had become something of a commonplace from the late eighteenth century onwards. Paris, in these accounts, was variously capital of the century, Europe, nations, the

---

[5] "[D]édaigneux par excellence," disdainful above all, is Verlaine's description of the *poète maudit*, Tristan Corbière. Paul Verlaine, *Les Poètes maudits* (Paris: Léon Vanier, 1888), 3.

[6] As Finn Fordham and Rita Sakr point out in the introduction to their collection of essays on Joyce's relation to Flaubert, Alexandre Dumas, Balzac, Hugo, and Zola, "At the dawn of the twentieth century, Joyce's quest for a 'style' drove him in the direction of French literature." Finn Fordham and Rita Sakr, *James Joyce and the Nineteenth-Century Novel* (Amsterdam: Rodopi, 2011), 11. Fordham and Sakr write that the "unfolding narrative of revolutionary politics, especially in the figure of Napoleon, travels through nineteenth-century literature and historiography"; for Joyce this not only recalls failed French promises to the Irish in 1798 but also "looks forward, with imaginatively subversive hope, at heroic and unheroic resistance in everyday life, art and language" (13).

earth and the universe. In his poem, 'Paris,' Vigny presented the city not only as 'le pivot de la France,' but as 'l'axe du monde.' Balzac, in his early essay 'Paris en 1831,' spoke of Paris as 'la capital du monde,' and 'sans égal dans l'univers.'"[7]

As portrayed in novels by Victor Hugo, Stendhal, and Flaubert, Paris is a place of glamor and opportunity, of intense struggle as men rise to glory or fail dramatically. In setting off for Paris with this ambition of poetic prose, Joyce turned a novelistic trope into artistic one: reimaging the conquest of the city as the conquest of an urban form. Paris and *prose poétique* allowed Joyce to fly by the nets of language, nation and religion and, more specifically, of Yeats and a literary movement engaged in reworking myth and folklore in the service of cultural nationalism. Yet if Joyce flew by those nets, he was caught in new ones: economic conditions that were not unique to Paris but powerfully embodied there, conditions present in Dublin life in a less-developed but insidious form. This book does not discount the important work Joyce scholars have done on issues of nationalism and postcoloniality, nor does it deny the importance of a wider range of references for Joyce, but it aims to show that Joyce's early encounter with Paris exposed him to an intense experience of consumer capitalism that informed his subsequent perceptions of Dublin and motivated the innovations of his writing.

This book claims that Joyce had three overlapping and equally important relations to Paris. The first is to the city as a center of literary influence. Moving to the source of this cultural capital begins in Joyce a second relation to Paris as a vivid instantiation of modern consumer capitalism. A collision with the experiential reality of urban modernity would also have occurred to Joyce if he had moved to London, yet the uniquely developed culture of display in Paris, which as we will go on to see includes goods of all kinds, including the human, was of profound significance for him. Accordingly, the third facet of his relation to Paris was as a locus of vivid sensory and sensual experiences; Paris was a primal scene of such richness and depth that he returned repeatedly to it in his writings. These three relations are inextricable from one another, although they shift in priority at various moments in his work. Joyce's achievement was to find a way to hold in suspension the relation between these three relations to Paris and to generate, in response, increasingly innovative forms. In these forms, Joyce both mimes and produces new versions of sensuality that include and open up imaginative possibilities for recasting experience.

[7] Christopher Prendergast, *Paris and the Nineteenth Century* (Oxford, UK: Blackwell, 1995), 6.

Arriving in Paris with little money and few contacts, Joyce was exposed to the full brunt of the city. Paris of 1902 was an environment of massive sensory stimulation. As we will see, the nineteenth-century transformation of Paris features explicitly in the "Circe" episode. From the beginning of his career, however, Joyce grapples with the experiential impact of the Parisian metropolis and, most particularly, of its streets. Over the second half of the nineteenth century, Paris had been transformed into a display case for an unprecedented proliferation of goods and people. In 1853, Baron Haussmann began a twenty-year plan of modernization of the city, involving construction, transportation, communication, and sewage.[8] Key to this modernization was the demolition of narrow, winding, and often dirty medieval streets and their replacement with long, broad boulevards culminating in monumental vistas. Open to sunlight all day long and lit by gas at night, the boulevards led to what David Harvey has called a new "extroverted form of urbanism in which the public life of the boulevard became a highlight of what the city was about."[9] These streets, the new department stores, and food markets such as Les Halles featured a new, overwhelming abundance: Paris, already the center of production and distribution in France, was made the hub of a national network of trains and subsequently was flooded with imported goods and raw materials, and with workers, shoppers, and tourists. Nineteenth-century Paris became, in Prendergast's terms, a "desire-producing machine,"[10] a "dream-machine."[11]

These dreams and desires associated with consumption increasingly supplanted recent desires for the transformation of society. The erasure of much of the medieval streets and faubourgs of Paris meant the breaking apart of the dense urban fabric that had supported the popular rebellions of 1830 and 1848. "Haussmannization" accompanied the new Empire that followed the collapse of a democratic, socialist movement. Following the February and June uprisings of 1848, Louis-Napoléon Bonaparte was elected President of the Second Republic, which began by declaring universal male suffrage and the right to work but became increasingly conservative and monarchist following national elections. At odds with the

---

[8] As T. J. Clark notes: "the new boulevards and open spaces displaced 350,000 people [...] by 1870, one fifth of the streets in central Paris were his creation; he had spent 80 million francs on sewers, and 2.5 billion francs of the city as a whole; at the height of the fever for construction, one in five Parisian workers was employed in the building trade." T. J. Clark, *The Painting of Modern Life: Paris in the Art of Manet and His Followers* (Princeton, NJ: Princeton University Press, 1984), 37.

[9] David Harvey, *Paris: Capital of Modernity* (New York: Routledge, 2006), 113.

[10] Prendergast, *Paris and the Nineteenth Century*, 28.   [11] Ibid., 34, 37.

assembly, Louis-Napoléon staged a *coup-d'état* and held a plebiscite for a new authoritarian republic and, in 1852, amidst overwhelming popular support, was proclaimed Emperor Napoleon III. In 1850, he had already announced his intentions for Paris in terms borrowed from the Sun King, Louis XIV: "open up new roads, open up popular quarters which lack air and light so that sunlight may penetrate everywhere among the walls of the city just as the light of truth illuminates our hearts."[12] If Louis XIV gloried in a divinely ordained radiance, a light that was then appropriated by the leaders of the French Revolution for "historical processes of a more secular kind," as Martin Jay notes, the failure of radical political hope after 1848 meant that "anything that might remotely be called the 'age of reason' had clearly passed."[13] Napoléon III's "light of truth" was now the increasingly pervasive light of capitalism.

This light brought not enhanced perception but perceptual confusion. Paris became, increasingly, the site of conflictual conditions: physical rationalization, experiential disorientation, and economic coordination. Prendergast writes of the deceptive legibility that accompanied its new form: "paradoxically, the clearer, cleaner and more uniform the city came to appear physically, the more opaque and mysterious it came to seem socially, as governed by a contingent and chaotic play of forces, transactions and interests, to which one could not attach a correspondingly clear description."[14] Yet underlying this social chaos was nonetheless an incipient and encroaching order: "if the city appears to resist intelligible representation and 'workable forms of visualization,' it may be that appearances are to some extent deceptive; that what truly controls the city (for example, increasingly powerful mobile capital) seeks to remain hidden, unlocatable, at once fluid and disoriginated."[15] T. J. Clark also contrasts this new perceptual confusion to the older, positive uncertainties of Paris that were swept aside by the advance of Haussmann and capitalism. The street was no longer an active social space, a place of unpredictable encounters and negotiations between members of various classes, but an arena of display without community: "the city was precisely a site of unfixity – uncontrol – in the previous social order; it was a horizon of

---

[12] Qtd. in Harvey, *Capital of Modernity*, 107.
[13] Martin Jay, *Reason after Its Eclipse: On Late Critical Theory* (Madison: University of Wisconsin Press, 2016), 29, 82.
[14] Prendergast, *Paris and the Nineteenth Century*, 11.   [15] Ibid., 15.

possible collective action and understanding, and all such horizons must be made invisible in societies organized under the aegis of the commodity."[16]

As a site of thwarted political hopes, Paris thus had something in common with turn-of-the-century Dublin; it was, however, a city in which commerce was highly developed and pronounced. Paris increasingly featured two aspects of commodity capitalism: the replacement of collective rational deliberation with the *ratio* of calculation, instrumentalization, and reification, and a powerful mobilization of the senses in a theater of goods and people. This constructed sensuality, which stimulates the individual pursuit of physical pleasure, embodies Max Weber's later prediction of a "mechanized petrification," in which only means are considered rational, and individuals, bent on self-preservation and control of nature, lack shared, substantive ends: "Specialists without spirit, sensualists without heart; this nullity imagines that it has attained a level of civilization never before achieved."[17] Paris, however, defies the sense of individual control Weber associates with such heartless sensuality. If the city dweller has been understood in terms of a blasé attitude and as practicing a visual mastery of the environment – think of Georg Simmel's characterization of the mutual glance that achieves sociation – Paris defies such categorizations and trades instead on ambiguities.

Nowhere is this more clearly illustrated than in the city's preponderance of prostitutes. As Alain Corbin's and Charles Bernheimer's works show, Parisian authorities' attempts to identify, classify, and contain *les filles de noces* failed, and the city became a place in which desire was inextricably bound up with exchange, and social relations were uncontrollably infiltrated by transaction.[18] From the mid-nineteenth century, the city was identified with a prostitution so pervasive and uncontrollable as to

---

[16] Clark, *Painting of Modern Life*, 49–50. Clark argues that Paris became a spectacle, not merely in the sense of handsome buildings and grand vistas, but in the more important sense of staging images for consumption. The city belonged to its inhabitants "now simply *as an image*, something occasionally and casually consumed in spaces expressly designed for the purpose [. . .] it was no longer part of those patterns of action and appropriation which had made up the spectator's everyday lives" (36). He sees the 1871 Commune as expressing Parisians' "recalcitrance" at this reshaping of the city (68–69).

[17] "No one knows who will live in this cage in the future, or whether at the end of this tremendous development entirely new prophets will arise, or there will be a great rebirth of old ideas and ideals, or, if neither, mechanized petrification, embellished with a sort of convulsive self-importance." Max Weber, *The Protestant Ethic and the Spirit of Capitalism*, trans. Talcott Parsons (New York: Routledge, 2005), 124.

[18] Alain Corbin, *Women for Hire: Prostitution and Sexuality in France after 1850*, trans. Alan Sheridan (Cambridge, MA: Harvard University Press, 1990) and Charles Bernheimer, *Figures of Ill Repute: Representing Prostitution in Nineteenth-Century Paris* (Durham, NC: Duke University Press, 1997).

be called "Paris-putain," the original title of Baudelaire's "Les Septs Vieillards."[19] Clark observes, "The literature of the 1860s is characterized, in fact, by a fear that the equivalence of Paris and prostitution might be too complete. 'We are on our way to universal prostitution' was Dumas's catchphrase in 1867."[20] Prendergast notes that Paris was the "cette grande courtisane" in Hugo's *Farragus*, an "image connoting glamor, excitement, the great cosmetic games of leisure and pleasure in the modern city," but a diseased prostitute in *La Cousine Bette*, a "vision of a corrupted, self-prostituting urban society."[21]

The pervasive presence of exchange is exemplified in two seemingly, but not actually, contradictory accounts of the Parisian boulevards, in the decade before Joyce arrived in the city, the declaration by a French journalist, Émile Bergerat, in 1892 that "on the boulevard, one can say everything, hear everything and imagine everything. It's the ideal forum of the free city" and the observation in 1900 by English author and journalist Richard Whiteing that the boulevard is "the distributive center of all of the flitting fancies of France."[22] The freedom of the boulevard here is the freedom of consumption. Whiteing suggests the manipulation of social space by economic transaction, in which the street as the space of collective self-determination is replaced by the boulevard as the site of commodity culture, as he continues: "You come here in the daytime for the sensation of the day. You get it of a surety, whatever else you may miss; and while you enjoy it, hot and hot, truth seems but a spoil-sport. The art of life is, after all, but an art of impressions; and this impression, while it lasts, is sure to be to your taste. The Boulevard asks no more. There will be something new tomorrow; and what you have is sufficient unto the day."[23] This sufficiency is, as Whiteing quietly admits, dependent both on the offerings of the moment and on the financial means to enjoy them; it is the sensation of an emphatic but passing "hotness," the enjoyment of which requires the suspension of other demands. Whiteing gives casual expression here to Walter Pater's aesthetics of sensation, characterized famously in the conclusion to *Studies in the History of the Renaissance*: "To burn

[19] Richard E. Burton, *Baudelaire in 1859: A Study in the Sources of Poetic Creativity* (Cambridge, UK: Cambridge University Press, 1988).
[20] Clark, *Painting of Modern Life*, 104.   [21] Prendergast, *Paris and the Nineteenth Century*, 136.
[22] Émile Bergerat, "Le boulevard," *L'Echo de la Semaine*, 9 October 1892 and Richard Whiteing, *The Life of Paris* (Leipzig: Tauchnitz, 1901), 196–97, qtd. in Vanessa Schwartz, *Spectacular Realities: Early Mass Culture in Fin-de-Siècle Paris* (Berkeley: University of California Press, 1999), 21.
[23] Richard Whiteing, *The Life of Paris* (London: John Murray, 1900), 182–83.

always with this hard, gem-like flame, to maintain this ecstasy, is success in life."[24] Yet in siting this aestheticism within the boulevard, Whiteing suggests its limits, associating Pater's eschewal of habit in favor of sensory vividness with an absence of social relation, a dependence on commercial fare, and a replacement of lasting verity with the transaction of the moment.

This passage by a relatively obscure, if commercially successful, journalist and novelist raises questions about art and thought in the city posed with considerably more intensity thirty years before by Baudelaire, questions with which Joyce grapples intensely. Baudelaire announces in his letter to Houssaye that his collection of prose poems fails to meet the challenge of representing urban experience; a particular moment in the prose poem "Le Confiteor de l'artiste," however, figures this immersive environment in metaphorical terms and dramatizes the collapse of art within it. Recasting within the natural world the innumerable relations and sensations of the city, the prose poem presents an overwhelming environment into which the self disappears. Baudelaire's artist announces this disappearance in parentheses, with amusing understatement: "So great a pleasure to let one's gaze swim [drown] in the immensity of the sky and the sea! [. . .] all these things think through me, or I through them (for, in the grandeur of reverie, the 'me' is quickly lost); they think, I say, but musically, pictorially, without arguments, syllogisms, deductions."[25] Cogitation is replaced here by the registration of endless, shifting sensations. Art – music and picture – is replaced by the sensual workings of the environment upon the person, "ces choses pensent, dis-je, mais musicalement et pittoresquement." The artist declares his own failure, announcing himself able only to produce "shrill and mournful vibrations" in response to this dynamic and seductive sensory stimulation, "l'énergie dans la volupté." Sensing his own demise yet unable to extricate himself, he declares: "Stop arousing my desires and my pride! The study of the

[24] "To burn always with this hard gem-like flame, to maintain this ecstasy, is success in life. Failure is to form habits: for habit is relative to a stereotyped world; meantime it is only the roughness of the eye that makes two persons, things, situations, seem alike. While all melts under our feet, we may well catch at any exquisite passion, or any contribution to knowledge that seems, by a lifted horizon, to set the spirit free for a moment, or any stirring of the senses, strange dyes, strange colours, and curious odours, or work of the artist's hands, or the face of one's friend." Walter Pater, *Studies in the History of the Renaissance* (Oxford, UK: Oxford University Press, 2010), 120.
[25] Baudelaire, *Paris Spleen* trans. MacKenzie, 7. "Grand délice que celui de noyer son regard dans l'immensité du ciel and de la mer! [. . .] toutes ces choses pensent par moi, ou je pense par elles (car dans la grandeur de la rêverie, le *moi* se perd vite!); elles pensent, dis-je, mais musicalement et pittoresquement, sans arguties, sans syllogismes, sans déductions." Baudelaire, *Œuvres Complètes*, 149.

beautiful is a duel, one that ends with the artist crying out in terror before being vanquished."[26]

Is this a diagnosis or a discovery? In an 1865 review of Baudelaire, Verlaine situates Baudelaire's failure in terms of the impact of consumption on consciousness. He declares that Baudelaire's "profound originality lies in his powerful representation of the essence of modern man; and by this phrase, modern man, I do not mean to designate moral, political and social man, for a reason which I will explain immediately. I mean here nothing but modern physical man, such as have made of him the refinements of an excessive civilization, modern man with his anguished, vibrating senses, his painfully subtle mind, his brain saturated with tobacco, his blood burned by alcohol – in a word, the biliary-neurotic par excellence."[27] Verlaine thus celebrates, in terms that speak of his own poetic agenda, the depiction of a subjectivity submerged in vivid and excessive stimulation.

Verlaine's review prompts us to read Baudelaire's scene in terms of consumption; we can also understand it in terms of an urban experience: the immersive seascape recalls the mobile being and innumerable intersections Baudelaire described in his letter to Houssaye. It also evokes the experience of the speaker of the prose poem "Les Foules," "Crowds," who delights in "immersing himself in the multitude as in a bath." This speaker celebrates this state, although again in figural, enigmatic terms: "The thing that people call love is so small, so restrained, so weak compared to this ineffable orgy, to this holy prostitution of the soul that gives itself entirely, all its poetry and charity, to the unexpected as it arises, to the unknown that turns up."[28] If Baudelaire's writing does not concern, to borrow Verlaine's phrase, moral, political, and social man, it undoes the categories

---

[26] Baudelaire, *Paris Spleen* trans. MacKenzie, 7. "Cesse de tenter mes désirs et mon orgueil! L'étude du beau est un duel où l'artiste crie de frayeur avant d'être vaincu." Baudelaire, *Œuvres Complètes*, 149.

[27] "La profonde originalité de Charles Baudelaire, c'est, à mon sens, de représenter puissamment et essentiellement l'homme moderne; et par ce mot, l'homme moderne, je ne veux pas, pour une cause qui s'expliquera tout à l'heure, désigner l'homme moral, politique et social. Je n'entends ici que l'homme physique moderne, tel que l'on fait les raffinements d'une civilisation excessive, l'homme, moderne, avec ses sens aiguisés et vibrants, son esprit douloureusement subtil, son cerveau saturé de tabac, son sang brûlé d'alcool, en un mot, le *bilio-nerveux* par excellence." Paul Verlaine, "Charles Baudelaire," *L'Art*, 16 February 1866. *Œuvres Posthumes de Paul Verlaine*, Vol. 2 (Paris: Messein, 1911), 8–9.

[28] Baudelaire, *Paris Spleen*, trans. MacKenzie, 22. "Il n'est pas donné à chacun de prendre un bain de multitude"; "Ce que les hommes nomment amour est bien petit, bien restreint et bien faible, comparé à cette ineffable orgie, à cette sainte prostitution de l'âme qui se donne tout entière, poésie et charité, à l'imprévu qui se montre, à l'inconnu qui passe." Baudelaire, *Œuvres Complètes*, 12, 13.

of the individual while situating the perceiving consciousness in suggestively mobile, open relations.

Baudelaire gives expression in "Le Confiteor de l'artiste" to the experience of an immersive environment that refuses a position outside of its own consumption, an environment that muddles thought, defies art, and awakens desire. The carefully crafted scene presents a collapse of rational thinking, as its speaker announces that the traditional discursive forms of reason – arguments, syllogisms, and deductions – fall away. The "Confiteor" also presents the collapse of what, since Kant, has been understood as the correct aesthetic relation: instead of maintaining a disinterested, contemplative spectatorial position, the artist's desire is awoken, and he merges with his subject, becoming as much the medium as the agent of the scene. Yet as the artist registers the effects of this intense sensation, he describes an augmented being. His thought is no longer limited by the self: it expands beyond the borders of his body, just as his body is the site of a thinking that is not his own, "things think through me, or I through them (for in the grandeur of reverie, the 'me' is quickly lost!)" In this displaced cognition, agency is not certain or singular; it is multiplied in an undefined, mobile, and cooperative coexistence. Baudelaire's enigmatic figuration refuses to specify this nonrational thinking.

What Baudelaire intuits and presents in enigmatic figuration is something that becomes a central and motivating preoccupation for Joyce. Joyce responds to the challenges the city presents to art, thought, and experience by developing, through increasingly innovative narrative forms, a sentient thinking. This is not to say that Joyce found his answer in Baudelaire but rather that he found it in Paris, and he developed it over decades of writing in which he drew not just on Baudelaire but also on a series of other French writers who had also developed innovative literary forms to negotiate new relations to the senses. The challenge that Baudelaire presented and the literary form he proposed provided Joyce with the problem and means to develop a new kind of thought in the modern city. Poetic prose's generic unspecificity, its mobile and undefined subjects and objects, its "musical, pictorial" workings, makes it a highly productive form for this exploration. The material thinking that Baudelaire figures, either as aspiration or as failure, is something that Joyce develops as an aesthetic that absorbs, counters, and evades the pressures of the city.

While the senses are harnessed in an unprecedented way by Paris the desire-machine, Joyce's early writing reveals that sensation nonetheless holds the possibility of an alternative to reification and instrumentalization. Instead of a distant, objective perception of a fixed reality to be appropriated and mastered, the senses – especially the "lower" senses of smell, taste, and touch – register a material coexistence. These intimate sensations, experienced without volition or control, trigger a sentient thinking, a reflection that does not separate itself from sensation but rather takes place through it, proceeding by incorporation and material relation. Sensations associated with erotic desire are central to this sentient thinking as Joyce grapples with the encroachment of exchange on the most intimate of interpersonal relations. Through devising new means to represent sensual encounters between men and women, Joyce explores an embodied aesthetic practice that undoes the subject and object positions of calculation and control by focusing on ongoing physical processes of sensation, absorption, digestion, and excretion.[29] These processes reveal individuals to be in the midst of multiple processes of formation and suggest new possibilities of co-being and creation. Rather than transactions, these relations are explorations of "the various joys we each feel" in which individuality and gender are undone.

Throughout these explorations, Joyce's works feature an ongoing discussion of aesthetics. This at first takes the explicit form of his Parisian aesthetic essay in which he defines art as that which banishes desire and repulsion and achieves a static comprehension. Yet, in Paris, Joyce goes on to pose a series of obscene questions about the relation of art to desire, the body, and its physical processes. Subsequently, as Joyce explores increasingly innovative narrative forms, aesthetic reflections feature in an informal mode, as characters consider the Thomistic aesthetic of integrity, harmony, and clarity, or the neoclassical aesthetic of the closed, timeless bodies of Greek statuary. Counter to these conceptions of art as essential beauty or as autonomous, Joyce conceives of the aesthetic as a shared practice that involves states and processes banned from traditional

---

[29] Critical texts in the current sensory turn in modernist studies focus predominantly on the relation of the senses of sight and hearing to new art forms, technologies, and processes of abstraction; see works such as Sara Danius' *The Senses of Modernism: Technology, Perception, and Aesthetics* (Ithaca, NY: Cornell University Press, 2002), Ulrike Maud's *Beckett, Technology and the Body* (Cambridge, UK: Cambridge University Press, 2009), Sam Halliday's *Sonic Modernity: Representing Sound in Literature, Culture and the Arts* (Edinburgh: Edinburgh University Press, 2013), Abbie Garrington's *Haptic Modernism: Touch and the Tactile in Modernist Writing* (Edinburgh: Edinburgh University Press, 2013), and Josh Epstein's *Sublime Noise: Musical Culture and the Modernist Writer* (Baltimore, MD: Johns Hopkins University Press, 2014). This book considers sensory modalities often understood to be of lesser importance in twentieth-century experience, along with bodily processes traditionally excluded from aesthetics. Read in this way, Joyce's work suggests a modernism that complicates sight and sound with the proximate senses and concrete somatic processes and, in doing so, offers new resources for reflection within the developing environment of urban modernity.

aesthetics: desire, the proximate sensory modalities, and the workings of digestion. This is an aesthetics of *aisthesis*, in the original Greek sense of gratifying sensory perception. It takes place not outside of the space of commerce or of social interaction but between people and even within them, becoming the model and the means for a new kind of intersubjective sociality.

In tracing Joyce's development of a sentient thinking, this book understands him as staging in literary texts a new kind of reflection. In doing so, it sees him as anticipating Judith Butler's recent observation: "Just as philosophy founders time and again on the question of the body, it tends to separate what is called thinking from what is called sensing, from desire, passion, sexuality, and relations of dependency. It is one of the great contributions of feminist philosophy to call those dichotomies into question and so to ask as well whether in sensing, something called thinking is already at work, whether in acting, we are also acted upon, and whether in coming into the zone of the thinking and speaking I, we are at once radically formed and also bringing something about."[30] This book situates Joyce's undoing of the dichotomies of thinking and sensing – and consequently of subject and object, male and female – within the context of aesthetics and urban modernity.

What is at stake in the sentient thinking developed in Joyce's embodied aesthetics is the contestatory power of art under capitalism. Art has been understood to derive that power through its refusal of and separation from the workings of a world dominated by the false rationality of capitalism. J. M. Bernstein describes this distance aptly in an essay on Theodor Adorno's *Aesthetic Theory*: "The dialectic of reason led to a rationalization of reason in which the sensory (the contingent, contextual, and particular) is first dominated and then repudiated as a component of reason, and the remnant, the sensory rump, dispatched into the harmless precinct of art and the aesthetic."[31] Art is thus the preserve of everything that refuses calculation, instrumentalization, and conceptual domination: the nonidentical, the variable, the sensuous. Yet, as Jay suggests, this understanding perhaps "cede[s] too much ground to the 'diseased' versions of reason – instrumental, formal, subjective – that Critical Theory had feared were now almost totally hegemonic in the modern world, and as a consequence

[30] Judith Butler, *Senses of the Subject* (New York: Fordham University Press, 2016), 15.
[31] J. M. Bernstein, "'The Dead Speaking of Stones and Stars': Adorno's Aesthetic Theory," in *The Cambridge Companion to Critical Theory*, ed. Fred Rush (Cambridge, UK: Cambridge University Press, 2004), 144.

betoken[s] a retreat into a beleaguered aesthetic sanctuary that had little chance of ever expanding its territory."[32]

This book argues that Joyce, in contrast, develops an aesthetic that is located in encounters between people. This embodied aesthetic entails a different relation between sense and intellect as these encounters focus on the "sensory rump," often literally. In doing so they manifest the arationality that Adorno identifies with art in its refusal of the rationality of capitalism. To borrow the terms that Terry Eagleton uses to describe Adorno's understanding of the workings of art, there is a "paratactic logicality about it, akin to those dream images which blend cogency and contingency, and it might thus be said to represent an arational reason confronting an irrational rationality."[33] This is another way of describing the mode of sentient thinking that Joyce develops after Baudelaire's musical, pictorial thinking, a thinking that begins in sensation but does not proceed through rational forms but rather through the material relations between words, phrases, and images, such as pun, distortion, and association, but also more literal material activities and processes such as, for example, lice, cheese mites, saliva, internal digestion, and excretion.[34]

This focus on a displaced cognition bears some resemblance to the central aim of certain recent New Materialist works. In their recent collection, for example, Diana Coole and Samantha Frost assemble essays with an "emphasis on materialization as a complex, pluralistic, relatively open process and [an] insistence that humans, including theorists themselves, be recognized as thoroughly immersed within materiality's productive contingencies."[35] Where New Materialism asserts the "agentic" capacity of matter over sovereign individuality, valorizing a vital materiality's opposition to human domination and control, Joyce looks for the new forms of cognition made possible by the unavoidable dismantling of the sovereign individual in urban modernity. While neo-materialist approaches would replace the assumption of a dominating Cartesian subject with a vision of the world of matter "as lively or exhibiting agency," their explorations of agentic matter, however, sideline human thought and

[32] Martin Jay, *Reason after Its Eclipse*, 112.
[33] Terry Eagleton, *The Ideology of the Aesthetic* (Oxford, UK: Oxford University Press, 1990), 351.
[34] For Rancière, the aesthetic regime of art presents "the idea of the power of thought outside itself, a power of thought that is its opposite." I argue that what Joyce develops is a mode of critical sensation that is made possible by an aesthetic situated in everyday life. Jacques Rancière, "From Politics to Aesthetics?" *Paragraph* 28.1, 13–25, at 17.
[35] Diana Coole and Samantha Frost, *New Materialisms: Ontology, Agency, and Politics* (Durham, NC: Duke University Press, 2010), 7.

knowledge.[36] This book argues that Joyce's sentient thinking, a thinking that evades the conscious intentions of the subject as it occurs through material and involuntary processes, offers new possibilities of awareness, pleasure, and intersubjectivity.

These possibilities of cooperative co-being would, of course, be dismissed by a strict Marxist, for whom sensory perception is necessarily alienated until after the abolition of the commodity form. This book argues however that the modes of perception and consciousness attached to Joyce's sentient thinking undo the categories of transaction and exchange associated with the commodity. This embodied cognition offers counterknowledge of a human reality of subjugation and imprisonment within capitalism and, at the same time, allows an awareness of generative, creative encounters that take place despite these conditions. If the city offers freedom and pleasure under the constraints of the commodity form, this sentient thinking registers various kinds of freedom and pleasure that occur alongside, within, and independently of it. Joyce explores embodied realizations of Stendhal's notion that art is "une promesse de bonheur."

The sentient thinking that Joyce develops through his encounters with Paris finds corroboration in the work of Walter Benjamin, the heterodox Marxist literary and cultural theorist and author of a series of works on commodity capitalism in nineteenth- and twentieth-century Paris. Critics have often noticed the congruence between the two figures' works. In the introduction to their collection of essays on Joyce and Benjamin, Maurizia Boscagli and Enda Duffy call them "the two most obsessive, and brilliantly insightful, urbanists of their generation."[37] Noting Joyce and Benjamin's common experience of Paris, Boscagli and Duffy speculate that "Paris may be the city in [Joyce's] fiction – and indeed, its aspect as Paris fiction in disguise needs further study."[38] As this book explores the relation of Joyce's fiction to Paris and to French literature, it uncovers an active relationship between Joyce and Benjamin. It shows, in fact, that Joyce lends Benjamin a form to explore the importance of the sensorium in contending with the structures of commodity capitalism. Joyce's influence upon Benjamin occurs in a constellation at the beginnings of Surrealism,

---

[36] Ibid.
[37] Maurizia Boscagli and Enda Duffy, *Joyce and Benjamin and Magical Urbanism* (Amsterdam: Rodopi, 2011), 10. Boscagli and Duffy point to Joyce and Benjamin's "sense of childlike wonder and fascination with *everything*," and surmise that "the enormous capacity on the part of each for such a broadband sympathy is what makes possible the sense of utopian possibility which animates even their most sardonic moments" (8).
[38] Ibid., 10.

through the textual link of the first Surrealist novel, by Louis Aragon, a member of the circle around the Shakespeare and Co. and Les Amis des Livres bookstores, which galvanized Walter Benjamin to embark on the *Passagen-Werk*.

In arguing for Joyce's influence on one of the most important cultural critics of the twentieth century, *James Joyce and the Matter of Paris* indicates the overlooked impact of the Anglophone literary modernist tradition on Critical Theory.[39] In tracing links between Joyce and Benjamin and between Joyce and French literature, it responds to recent calls for modernist studies to consider continuities and intersections across linguistic, national, artistic, and cultural boundaries. As early as 1931, Edmund Wilson observed the influence of French Symbolism on Joyce, remarking that English and American criticism fails to read him because of its disciplinary distance from "a literary revolution which occurred outside English literature."[40] Situating one of the most central modernists in relation to this literary revolution, this book argues that some of the most important roots of Anglophone modernism are French.

James Joyce and the Matter of Paris consists of two parts: the first deals with Joyce's period in Paris in 1902–03 and his working through of the discoveries he made there until he returned to Paris in 1920. The first chapter, "Paris Encountered: 1902–03 Writings," reads chronologically works that have been addressed primarily under the aspect of their later appearance in Joyce's published texts. It traces Joyce's movement from a poetry that resists sensation through the aesthetic essay to an exploration of an indiscriminate and ineluctable physical permeation, and argues that Joyce draws forms for this evolution from Baudelaire, Verlaine, and Zola as well as Pseudo-Aristotle, whose unsystematic, zetetic *Problems* understands the body and the mind as consubstantial, porous, and processual. The second chapter, "Paris Recognized: *Stephen Hero* and *Portrait*," argues that Joyce's Parisian experiences and writings inform his subsequent understanding and representation of Dublin life. The chapter traces a series of meetings between Stephen Dedalus and Emma Clery that culminate in a desublimated and unconscious aesthetic encounter in which Joyce reworks the synesthesia of Rimbaud's "Voyelles." The third chapter, "Paris

---

[39] In tracing the impact of Joyce's work on a Paris-based theoretician, this book takes an opposite approach to Geert Lernout in *The French Joyce* (Ann Arbor: University of Michigan Press, 1990), who describes and critiques the reception of Joyce by French theorists, such as Lacan, Derrida, and Cixous.

[40] Edmund Wilson, *Axel's Castle: A Study in the Imaginative Literature of 1870–1930* (New York: Farrar, Straus and Giroux, 2004), 20.

Digested: 'Lestrygonians'" claims that Joyce extends this singular exchange into an ongoing mode of permeable digestive being in the Ulyssean stream of consciousness by drawing on the interior monologue form pioneered by the post-Symbolist Edouard Dujardin.

The second half of this book examines Joyce's reinvigorated exploration of these issues following his move to Paris in 1920. The fourth chapter, "Paris Re-envisioned: 'Circe,'" argues that the visionary form of the episode is developed from proto-Surrealist visionary texts by Flaubert, Nerval, and Rimbaud. The Circean "exploding visions" present the hyper-developed and futile productivity that results from the ensnaring of desire by structures of profit and possession. The fifth chapter, "Paris Profanely Illuminated: James Joyce's Walter Benjamin," deviates from the trajectory of Joyce's own writing to explore the afterlife of the "Circe" episode in 1920s Paris: it shows Benjamin's development, via Aragon, of the exploding vision in his conceptions of the threshold experience, the image body space, and the dialectical image. The chapter goes on to argue that Benjamin's dialectical image, presented as a dynamic interpretive practice in his capacious, fragmentary, and challenging *Passagen-Werk*, offers a particularly useful methodology for readers of the *Wake*. The closing chapter, "Paris Compounded: *Finnegans Wake*," argues that Joyce's final work compels readers to engage in sentient thinking. Focusing on the absurd and scatological aesthetics of the early years of the *Wake's* composition, it argues that Joyce draws on Jarry's *philosophie de merde*. As Joyce presents ambiguous encounters between characters of various numbers, genders, and sexual orientations, he stages a *ville énorme* in a set of references so profoundly compacted and diverse that it calls for an ideal aesthetic community to read it.

In each of these chapters, close reading is a vital methodology. As Joyce's forms foreground the sensory minutiae of experience, larger, traditional novelistic containers of meaning such as plot and character break down. Action occurs at the granular level of the texts. Intellection takes place in minor textual artefacts, and accordingly, the particulars of these elements' presentation sustain extended readings. Joyce registers new kinds of interrelation through irregularities of syntax and grammar and atypical uses of seemingly trivial punctuation marks such as the ellipsis and the colon. As he forges an increasingly innovative aesthetic by reworking elements of his own and of Parisian writers' texts, subtle but momentous events occur at the scale of the phrase, the word, and even the letter.

This attention to the minutiae of Joyce's texts, I will attempt to show in the following chapters, allows us to see something much larger: the embeddedness of this most canonical of Anglophone modernists within a transnational literary field. Joyce's contention with the matter of Paris, the aesthetic challenge of a sensorially overwhelming experience of consumer capitalism that the primary site of European urban modernity thrust upon its inhabitants and visitors and that had been so generative for Parisian writers, led him to process the materials of Dublin using a disparate set of aesthetic practices associated with the French avant-garde. In tracing the development of Joyce's oeuvre, then, we will see modernism's itinerary through the great artistic capital of Europe or, put differently, the transmission of French aesthetic culture to the Anglophone world through the transformative medium of Joyce's work.

CHAPTER I

Paris Encountered
1902/03 Writings

A photograph of Joyce taken in Dublin in 1904 has become the dominant image of the author; handsome, cocky, on two well-planted feet, he looks confidently into the lens, seemingly aware of the magnitude of his future achievements and coolly wondering if Constantine Curran "would lend me five shillings." A very different Joyce appears in a photograph he had taken of himself two years before. At this moment, the twenty-year-old Joyce was living in the center of the Parisian Latin Quarter, in a cheap hotel on the Rue Corneille. For the photograph, which he had printed on postcards that he sent home to Dublin, he poses uncertainly in borrowed Rive Gauche clothes, turned slightly away and on the back foot. Joyce spent about four months in Paris: from December 3, 1902 to April 11, 1903, when he returned to Dublin at the news that his mother was dying. In retrospect, the brevity of this period makes it easy to overlook the seriousness of Joyce's intentions in moving to Paris and the fundamental importance of his writing there for his work as a whole. Joyce subsequently pushed this time in Paris offstage: the site of Stephen Dedalus's future in *A Portrait of the Artist as a Young Man* and of his past in *Ulysses*, the city barely appears in these works. Yet Paris forced the young Joyce to embark on a struggle with a question that would motivate all of his subsequent innovations: in an environment of sensory stimulation so intense that it overwhelms the intellect, what is art?

This chapter shows that Joyce's writing undergoes a massive evolution in this short period as he struggles with the problem of overwhelming sensory experience; in doing so, it initiates the methodology of this book, one of revealing the dialectical development of Joyce's literary strategies in response to sensory experience, itself the basic condition of urban modernity. That Joyce reworks this period in the evolving figure of Stephen Dedalus is well known. But a closer reading of his writings from this period along with an attention to Joyce's physical presence in the Paris of 1902 and 1903 reveals that the work he does there is seminal to his

Figure 1.1   Joyce in Dublin, 1904
Irish National Archives

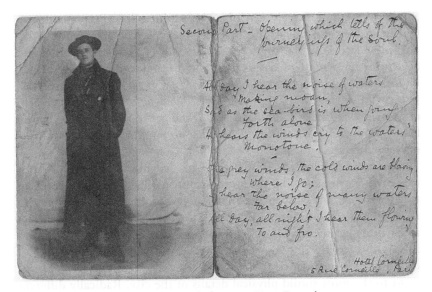

Figure 1.2   Photopostcard of Joyce in Paris, December 1902
Yale Beinecke Library

future writing. Over these months, Joyce's aesthetics change radically: from an art that would assert the autonomy of perceiving consciousness to an art that identifies with the powerful physical sensations of the modern urban environment.

Nineteenth-century French writers formed a literary context so attractive to Joyce that he moved to Paris at the age of twenty.[1] His flimsy plans to study medicine there were the pretext for a life lived on the Left Bank, the locale of the *poètes maudits* and the center of the most vibrant contemporary literary innovation. The "accursed poets," young, contrarian, and antibourgeois, provide a model for Joyce as he dismisses the Dublin literary establishment and resists all political factions. The rejection of community, socially accepted mores, and popular success animates Joyce's dramatically contrarian 1901 essay, "The Day of the Rabblement," which opens: "No man, said the Nolan, can be a lover of the true or the good unless he abhors the multitude, and the artist, though he may

---

[1] *JJ* 515. Verlaine was such a lastingly alluring figure for Joyce that he was recorded as reciting his poetry as late as 1918.

employ the crowd, is very careful to isolate himself."[2] Proponents of a rebellious lifestyle and artistic practice, they offer a precedent for his ongoing rejection of the comforts of home, of professional security, and of writing in service of a literary tradition and conventional values.[3] Baudelaire, another *poète maudit*, provides a powerful template for a Joycean artistic independence in the sparse dialogue of the first prose poem of *Le Spleen de Paris*, "L'Étranger": the "Stranger" declares that he has no family, no friends, no native land, and that he would love beauty, were she not "an immortal goddess."[4]

French writers led Joyce to Paris; Paris led him to dig deeper into these writers to adapt the technical resources they were developing to meet, register, and absorb the material pressures of the multisensory onslaught of the city. From Verlaine, Joyce took a poetic persona that melts into the material world; from Baudelaire, he took a prose form that mobilized fleeting syntactic patterns to express the motions of consciousness in the metropolis and, from Zola, a descriptive commitment to the most sordid physical details of the city. Radically different in other respects, what each of these sources offered was a fascination with the sensory impact of contemporary Paris and a commitment to devising new literary forms to address it. It was this same fascination that pushed Joyce in Paris to draw on the aesthetic theories of Aristotle, Thomas Aquinas, and G. W. F. Hegel to consider in philosophical terms the relation of sensation to thought and to devise a series of theoretical conceptions of what art is.

This chapter has three sections. The first looks at the three photopostcards Joyce sent shortly after his arrival in Paris, arguing that they constitute radically divergent efforts to respond to the sensuous appeal of the city. The poem on the postcard pictured in Figure 1.2, now known as Poem XXXV of *Chamber Music*, both figures and withdraws from the

---

[2] James Joyce, *Occasional, Critical and Political Writing*, ed. Kevin Barry (World's Classics; Oxford, UK: Oxford University Press, 2000), 50. Hence cited in abbreviated form as *OCPW*. The "Nolan" is Giordano Bruno, a sixteenth-century philosopher and cosmological theorist; as we will see in Chapter 6, he will recur both as an influential figure and a mask for more recent influences in Joyce's writing.

[3] The contradictory twenty-year-old Joyce bears a striking resemblance to Verlaine's portrait of himself as "Pauvre Lelian" in *Les Poètes maudits*, whose contrasting aspects of sentimentality and worldly debauch offer a precedent for Joyce's contradictions. Joyce's own trajectory in Paris is anticipated in Verlaine's progression from boarding school daydreaming to "draught beer drunk in the dive bars of this epoch [in which he] completed his melancholy study of the classics, all to a sketchy backdrop of brasseries and fast women." Paul Verlaine, *The Cursed Poets*, trans. Chase Madar (Copenhagen: Green Integer, 2003), 137.

[4] Baudelaire, *Paris Spleen*, trans. MacKenzie, 5.

invasive sensations of the city while a postcard in schoolboy Latin represents its streetwalkers in obscene terms. The second section traces, in the aesthetic essay and notes in the Paris section of "The Paris and Pola Commonplace Book," a striking progression in Joyce's theoretical account of the relation of art to sensation and to the involuntary processes of the body, a shift from an assertion of mastery to one of identification. The third section reads the short prose piece known as Epiphany 33, Joyce's representation of the movements of women on a Parisian boulevard, as setting against one another the opposing modes of cognitive mastery and passive sensuality in order to register and respond to the commercialization of sensory experience and desire. Having struggled to assert the autonomy of a perceiving consciousness, Joyce embarks on an art that identifies with the sensual, heralding his post-Parisian experiments.

The Photopostcards

On December 15, 1902, Joyce sent three copies of the photopostcard to Dublin. To John Francis Byrne, his friend from Belvedere College and the model for Cranly in *Stephen Hero* and *Portrait*, Joyce sent the postcard pictured in Figure 1.2, with a poem that he also sent to W. B. Yeats.

Second part – Opening which tells of the journeyings of the soul

> All day I hear the noise of waters
> Making moan,
> Sad as the sea-bird is when going
> Forth alone
> He hears the winds cry to the waters'
> Monotone.
>
> The grey winds, the cold winds are blowing
> Where I go;
> I hear the noise of many waters
> Far below,
> All day, all night I hear them flowing
> To and fro.

The blunt reader might remark that this isn't a very good poem. Yeats was not impressed: "I think it is not one of the best of your lyrics as a whole. I think that the thought is a little thin" (*Letters II* 23).[5] As a speaker's account of moving, like a bird, over a noisy seascape the poem indeed

---

[5] James Joyce, *Letters of James Joyce*, vol. I, ed. Stuart Gilbert (New York: Viking, 1966); vols. II and III, ed. Richard Ellmann (New York: Viking, 1966) are cited as *Letters I, II,* and *III.*

seems flimsy and even nonsensical. Yet, the poem is better understood as staging an encounter with sensation. Its "thought" is audition. As its speaker struggles with an environment of plangent sound, the poem presents this chaotic sound with emphatically metrical statements. As the sound becomes constant, increasing from "All day I hear" to "All day, all night I hear," the speaker's achievement is to be an unchanged auditor.

The poem and the photopostcard on which it is written mark Joyce's complex relation to Paris and to Parisian writing. Standing beside the poem in Latin Quarter clothing, Joyce identifies himself as a contemporary Parisian writer. The poem too cites a *poète maudit*, evoking Verlaine's famous "Chanson d'automne" from the collection *Poèmes saturniens* (1866) with its striking single line "Monotone," with its depiction of aimless motion "to and fro" like Verlaine's "Deçà, delà" and, above all, with its topic of solitary wandering.

Before he left Dublin, Joyce had translated Verlaine's "Chanson d'automne" as a poem of poetic vocation. To the right of Joyce's rendition is Symons' more literal translation:

Les sanglots longs	A voice that sings	When a sighing begins
Des violons	Like viol strings	In the violins
De l'automne	Through the wane	Of the autumn-song,
Blessent mon coeur	Of the pale year	My heart is drowned
D'une langueur	Lulleth me here	In the slow sound
Monotone.	With its strain.	Languorous and long.
Tout suffocant	My soul is faint	Pale as with pain,
Et blême, quand	At the bell's plaint	Breath fails me when
Sonne l'heure,	Ringing deep;	The hour tolls deep.
Je me souviens	I think upon	My thoughts recover
Des jours anciens	A day bygone	The days that are over,
Et je pleure;	And I weep.	And I weep.
Et je m'en vais	Away! Away!	And I go
Au vent mauvais	I must obey	Where the winds know,
Qui m'emporte	This drear wind,	Broken and brief,
Deçà, delà,	Like a dead leaf	To and fro,
Pareil à la	In aimless grief	As the winds blow
Feuille morte.[6]	Drifting blind.[7]	A dead leaf.[8]

[6] *Œuvres complètes de Paul Verlaine*, Vol. 1, *Poèmes saturniens* (Paris: Vanier, 1902), 33–34.
[7] Joyce, *Poems and Exiles*, eds. J. C. C. Mays and Seamus Deane (London: Penguin, 1992), 69.
[8] Arthur Symons, *The Symbolist Movement in Literature* (New York: Dutton, 1919), 403.

In Verlaine's poem, the human speaker loses distinction as the poem blurs sensation and expression. Verlaine's stanzas move from the invasive effects of the season, "Des violons/De l'automne," to the overflowing of memory prompted by a more abstract temporal marker – "quand sonne l'heure" – to the transformation of the speaker into matter in motion, "pareil à la/ Feuille morte," a preposition that stretches semantically from "like" to "the same as." The emphatic assonance performs the merging of the speaker with this powerfully sensuous environment. As the intricate sonic inter-twining in the third stanza of "Et je m'en vais/Au vent mauvais" unifies the speaker with the wind, "Chanson d'automne" becomes increasingly attenuated; a single sentence stretches over the first six-line stanza, and the second stanza continues into the third as the speaker loses distinct identity. The single-word line, "Monotone," along with the repeated vowel sounds, indicates the abandonment of differentiated speech and the ceding of individual boundaries. The sonic intertwining of persona and environ-ment presents an abdication of cognitive separation, albeit in superbly turned language that belies such a collapse.

Paul de Man understands Symbolism, despite the vagueness of the term, as a movement divided by alternative attitudes toward the relationship of consciousness to the object world. According to de Man, both Baudelaire and Yeats seek the unity of self and non-self and use the symbol as a vehicle for the unification of consciousness and the material world, although they court death in doing so as in this unification consciousness assumes the material world's inanimacy.[9] Mallarmé, contrastingly, holds that the poet must use the symbol to mediate between mind and "natural being," even if that attempt must fail because of the split nature of language itself.[10] We can see Verlaine's poetry, within this schema, miming an enthusiastic submission to immersion in the object world.

Joyce's translation of Verlaine's poem signals his fascination with this poetics of sensory transformation. Commenting on the translation, Marie-Dominique Garnier reads Verlaine's subject as "free of purpose and direc-tion – an early variation on the modern Ulyssean wandering subject adrift"[11] and sees Joyce's insertions of "voice," rhyming with Joyce, and "drifting blind" as a prophetic "crypto-autobiography of a wandering, yet

---

[9] Paul de Man, "The Double Aspect of Symbolism," *Yale French Studies* 74 (1988), 3–16, at 9.

[10] Ibid., 12.

[11] Marie-Dominique Garnier, "Verse after Verlaine, Rime after Rimbaud: Joyce and the 'poisondart' of *Chamber Music*," in *The Poetry of James Joyce Reconsidered*, ed. Marc C. Conner (Gainesville: University Press of Florida, 2012), 95.

sure-footed blind-to-be."[12] Joyce's translation is indeed "a narrative of literary exile," as Garnier suggests, yet it is better understood not as a divination of his life decades in the future but as an expression of Joyce's contemporary fascination with Verlaine, which is associated with his immediate ambition to move to Paris.[13]

Joyce's translation, crucially, asserts agency within this vagabond condition. He rewrites the poem as an aesthetic vocation, presenting not a vulnerable center of emotion and sensation, a heart wounded by "violins/Of the autumn-song" in Symons's translation (2/3), but an artistic sensibility responding to a human call: "A voice that sings/Like viol strings/Through the wane/Of the pale year/Lulleth me here" (1–5). Joyce's version resists the flow of the original with the emphatic interruption of the speaker's repeated exclamation, "Away! Away!"/"I must obey this drear wind" (13–15), announcing a consciousness of compulsion, a dutiful response to this lonely vocation. Instead of concluding with the speaker's identification with decomposing matter, the "Feuille morte" (16), Joyce's translation concludes with human attributes, "aimless grief/Drifting blind" (15–16), which the syntax prompts us to attribute to the dead leaf, rather than to the speaker, suggesting instead of a subjectivity submerged in matter a reassuringly anthropomorphized material world.[14]

In the Paris poem, entitled "Opening which tells of the journeyings of the soul," Joyce further questions Verlaine's aesthetic. The "soul" in this poem's title might seem an antiquated, self-ennobling gesture but it announces allegiance to an ordering *consciousness*, signaling a commitment to art as staging the conscious mastery of sensation. In contrast to the sensuous dissolution of Verlaine's persona, Joyce's speaker struggles to remain separate from the world around him. "Drifting blind" becomes the ongoing threat that Joyce's speaker faces, as the conclusion of Verlaine's poem – being carried randomly and passively by the wind – is expanded into a ceaseless threat posed by "the grey winds, the cold winds are blowing" and the "noise of many waters . . . flowing to and fro." Yeats' criticism of the poem as rote and passionless – "the poetry of a young man, of a young man who is practicing his instrument, taking pleasure in the

---

[12] Ibid., 96.   [13] Ibid.

[14] This reserve is visible in Joyce's "Drama and Life," in which he presents himself as an animating presence in this contemporary French scene: "Many feel like the Frenchman that they have been born too late in a world too old, and their wanhope and nerveless unheroism point on ever sternly to a last nothing, a vast futility and meanwhile – a bearing of fardels [. . .] Still I think out of the dreary sameness of existence, a measure of dramatic life may be drawn. Even the most commonplace, the deadest among the living, may play a part in a great drama" (*OCPW* 28).

mere handling of the stops" (*Letters II*, 23) – responds to a composition that draws heavily upon precedents yet refuses to identify with the full extent of their agenda.

Yeats recommends that Joyce write about Paris – "Impressions of books, or better still, of artistic events about you in Paris, bringing your own point of view in as much as possible, but taking your text from some existing interest or current event" (*Letters II*, 23). Yeats does so, however, in response to a poem that deliberately attempts not to address Paris or, more precisely, that figures an attempted refusal of the city. If in Dublin Joyce already resisted the full extent of Verlaine's poetics of sensual dissolution, the intense sensory concentration of Paris forced him to grapple with it in a new way. Despite its abstraction, the poem represents a salient feature of contemporary Paris: its discordant and plangently appealing soundscape. As recent sensory studies tell us, Paris was noisy, particularly for newcomers. Tracing the sonic cityscape of nineteenth- and early-twentieth-century Paris in guide books, ethnographies, and literary works, Aimée Boutin shows that Paris was a city filled with not just the noise of traffic but also with the cries of hucksters. Exploring how foreign visitors and provincial migrants were struck by the endless noise of nineteenth-century Paris, a din that was less audible to natives of the city, she focuses on the perception of the "shrillness, the incongruity, the discordance of peddlers' voices."[15] These hucksters were still in operation after the turn of the century, while the rest of the turmoil had only further intensified.[16] She opens her book with a nineteenth-century account of street noise by the American writer, John Sanderson:

> this unceasing racket – this rattling of the cabs and other vehicles over the rough stones, this rumbling of the omnibuses. For the street cries – one might have relief from them by a file and handsaw. – First the prima donna of the fish-market opens the morning: *Carpes toutes fraîches; voilà des carpes!* And then stand out of the way for the glazier: *Au vitriere!* Quavering down the chromatic to the lowest flat upon the scale. Next the iron-monger with his rasps, and files and augers [...] Beings set loose all at the same time, tuned to different keys. All things of this earth seek, at one time or another, repose – all but the noise of Paris. The waves of the sea are

[15] Aimee Boutin, *City of Noise: Sound and Nineteenth-Century Paris* (Urbana: University of Illinois Press, 2015), 4.

[16] Ibid., 2. A feature of an earlier, mercantile stage of capitalism, peddlers' increasing distance from modern forms of commerce was accompanied by their increasing insecurity: "Peddling was a precarious cover for begging; in other words, not commerce but charity. Peddling and pauperism were indissociable in nineteenth-century regulatory discourse" (8).

sometimes still, but the chaos of these streets is perpetual from generation to generation; it is the noise that never dies.[17]

This Paris finds figural representation in the plangent, endlessly unsettled seascape of Joyce's poem. The insistent noise of "making moan," "sad [...] cry" conveys an environment of skillful and plaintive supplication from which the speaker holds himself apart. Joyce's waterscape is endowed with all of the characteristics of the city: the ceaseless noise, the boundless matter, the endless motion, the inhospitality, the constant appeals.

Paris as a seascape and the Parisian street as a river of noise are common tropes in nineteenth-century literature. Prendergast notes that in the 1830s "Balzac mobilizes the routine comparison of Paris with the sea and the ocean, [...] in order to focus on his sense of its 'unfathomability.'"[18] William Paulson notes the impingement of city noise upon Frédéric's consciousness in Flaubert's *L'Éducation sentimentale* (1869): "'... all the noises of the night melted into a single murmur' (SE 60); '... the crowds made him dizzy ... in the midst of clouds of dust and a continuous din' (SE 75); '...distant sounds arose, mingling with the buzzing in his head' (SE 86); '... all those voices, through back by the houses, made a noise like the never-ending sound of the waves in a harbor' (SE 316)."[19] The noisy street, and indeed the street as a river of noise, features prominently in Baudelaire's poetry and prose poems. Ross Chambers writes of the Baudelairean "equivalence of streets and rivers": "Baudelaire's noise-filled streets are displaced rivers"; they take the "guise of 'fallen' rivers."[20] Chambers points to the "chaos mouvant," the moving chaos, of the street of "Perte d'auréole," "la rue assourdissante," the deafening street, of "Une Passante,"[21] and the street as a "rivière accrue," a flooded river, in "Les septs vieillards."[22] If in Flaubert's narrative, noise features as a realistic element of the city and an emblem of the incomprehensibility of its social world to its protagonist, Chambers argues for Baudelaire's "awakening to noise as the specific indicator of urban modernity and the crucial component of the city's atmosphere"; this awareness drives Baudelaire's development of a new poetics that "makes reading itself a direct experience of noise, and thus a directly disalienating (or consciousness-raising) encounter with an actual experience of alienation."[23]

---

[17] Ibid., 1.   [18] Prendergast, *Paris and the Nineteenth Century*, 11.
[19] William Paulson, "Flaubert's Sentimental Educations," in *Home and Its Dislocations in Nineteenth-Century France*, ed. Suzanne Nash (Albany: State University of New York Press, 1993), 94.
[20] Ross Chambers, *An Atmospherics of the City: Baudelaire and the Poetics of Noise* (New York: Fordham University Press, 2015), 11, 15, 16.
[21] Ibid., 7.   [22] Ibid., 15.   [23] Ibid., 9, 22.

Instead of a narrative setting or poetic model, in Joyce's poem noise is the antagonist. The poem counters this endless moaning, crying, blowing, and flowing with ordered patterns of sound.[24] An insistent meter opposes the uncontainable noise described in present participles: "All day I hear the noise of waters/Making moan" (1/2), etc. The emphatic contrast between the alternating iambic tetrameter and dactylic lines suggests a separation, a radical disjunction, between speaker and world, but if the first iteration holds the sound of the waters at a distance, "Making moan," any disjunction is undermined by the alternating presence of the speaker and waters in the dactyls: "Forth alone," "Monotone," "Where I go," "Far below," "To and fro." While the separation of the "soul" from this noisy seascape is figured in the image of the sea-bird, the bird is natural like the sea; it too is endlessly moving. The metrical, syntactical, and figural gestures of separation thus enact its impossibility. The poem gives voice to an intensifying alienation as the seascape progressively sheds its anthropologized behaviors and emotions: the "making moan" and "cry" of the winds to the waters shifts to a "grey" and "cold" "blowing" and "flowing" in the second stanza. Amidst this barrage of relentless and depersonalized sensation, the consciousness of the speaker is overwhelmed. No capacity for reflection remains. Hence, the thought is thin.

In representing "the journeyings of the soul," the poem evokes Joyce's announcement to Yeats, before departing for Paris, of his intentions to give representation to the "motion of the spirit." If that announcement was an unacknowledged echoing of Baudelaire's ambition for a poetic prose, this poem echoes Baudelaire's poem "Élévation" from *Les Fleurs du mal.* Attention to Baudelaire's poem shows, like Verlaine's "Chanson d'automne," how Joyce's Poem XXXV pushes these poets' figures to a greater degree of abstraction as he shrinks from the dissolution they embrace. If

---

[24] The soundscape of Joyce's poem contrasts with the aural qualities of his short prose piece on nighttime Dublin in the undated Epiphany 27, which he uses as a diary entry in the final section of *Portrait:* "Faintly, under the heavy summer night, through the silence of the town which has turned from dreams to dreamless sleep as a weary lover whom no caresses move, the sound of hoofs upon the Dublin road. Not so faintly now as they come nearer the bridge; and in a moment as they pass the dark windows the silence is cloven by alarm as by an arrow. They are heard now far away – hoofs that shine amid the heavy night as diamonds, hurrying beyond the grey, still marshes to what journey's end – what heart – bearing what tidings?" Robert Scholes and Richard M. Kain, eds., *The Workshop of Daedalus* (Evanston, IL: Northwestern University Press, 1965), 37. The prose poem presents a narrative of a sound, which is itself never given clear embodiment but is registered only in its motion, its advent, its presence and its departure, "faintly," "not so faintly," "now far away" and its effects on the speaker. The infernal quality of the hooves that render the air "cloven by alarm" is rendered erotic and glamorous as they "shine amid the heavy night as diamonds." The oneiric scene presents the enticing sound of motion away from a quietly sleeping city.

Baudelaire dramatizes in the prose poem "Le Confiteor de l'Artiste" the dissolution of the artist in the overwhelming sensations of a seascape, in "Élévation" this dissolution is not sensory but mundane. "Élévation" ironizes a poetic striving for independence from worldly conditions; Baudelaire's speaker identifies his soul as a bird soaring over waters, instructing it, somewhat problematically, to depart to a realm inaccessible to himself, trapped as he is within "these morbid miasmas" and "the ennuis and vast pains/Which burden hazy existence."[25] The spiritual separation from material realms collapses in the final stanza, where the soul takes on the lesser status of intellectual effort: "Happy is he who can with his vigorous wing/Soar up towards those fields luminous and serene,/He whose thoughts, like larks,/take flight each morning towards the sky."[26] This effort is a quotidian one, an ineffectual mental evasion of the conditions of reality through thoughts that are merely directed *towards* the skies. His ultimate achievement, declared in the final line of the poem, is a facility with "the language of flowers and mute things."[27] "Élévation" thus ends, bathetically, with a poet engaged in conventional, even commercialized expression and dumb, corrupting matter. These mute things are a duller form of the "miasmas morbides" from which the speaker initially asserts his soul's freedom.

If Joyce takes from Baudelaire the metaphor of the bird and uses the language of the soul in an attempt to access a nonmaterial register of being, he eliminates any ambiguity from this figure, ignoring the philosophical and material complications with which Baudelaire engages. Joyce's speaker asserts in a meager, repetitive manner its pure separation from the moaning waters. Under the pressure of these concealments and denials, this identification with the independent soul/bird becomes a thin and anguished assertion. The poem's perceiving consciousness finds itself in the crisis Baudelaire dramatized in "Le Confiteor de l'Artiste"; it struggles to maintain autonomy amidst the sensations of the environment, demonstrating that reflection is made almost impossible by sensation. The simple, emphatic form of the poem gives voice to this condition. If Yeats sees it as failing to meet the standard of Joyce's other poems, "I can remember that several of the other poems had more subject, more magical phrases,

---

[25] "ces miasmes morbides [. . .] les ennuis et les vastes chagrins/Qui chargent de leur poids l'existence brumeuse" (9, 13–14). Charles Baudelaire, *The Flowers of Evil*, trans. James McGowan (Oxford, UK: Oxford University Press, 1993), 17.

[26] "Heureux celui qui peut d'une aile vigoureuse/S'élancer vers les champs lumineux et sereins" (15–16). Ibid.

[27] "Le langage des fleurs et des choses muettes!" Ibid.

more passion" (*Letters II*, 23), this very lack of content and inspiration communicates the inglorious truth of a consciousness that can barely assert itself.

As a writer and as an individual, Joyce was overwhelmed by Paris. The second of the photopostcards he sent on September 15, to his family, "complained of a lack of money, of the condition of his health, of his uncertainty over accepting the job in the Berlitz School in Paris" (*Letters* 20 n.2). The emphasis on material needs is of a piece with his letters from this period, which are filled with lists of savings, outlays, potential earnings, and purchases both real and fantasized. On the sixth of December, he lists to his mother the small amounts he has spent on an alarm-clock, a bath, breakfast, lunch, and dinner. Reluctant to spend money on further sheets of paper, Joyce nonetheless fantasizes about buying a wardrobe, "twice as big as your wardrobe," that would cost almost three-quarters of his yearly rent.[28] His fantasy of surpassing his parents' lifestyle springs from an environment that awakened in him a desire for new possessions. "O, I have reveled in ties, coats, boots, hats since I came here – all imaginary!" he writes a couple months later to Stanislaus (*Letters II*, 27). The goods of Paris thus offer the promise of transformation, of self-realization not through writing but through consumption. As money distorts all topics, his letters grow increasingly pained and disabled. If it was a constant concern of the Joyce family, in these letters money becomes the medium through which all communication is made. On the day he sent the postcards, he writes to his mother with an uncharacteristic reticence that culminates in his avowal of an inability to write. In lieu of writing, he declares he will buy:

> I hardly know if I have anything to say. I received both your letters and see that I have alarmed you very much. My curious state has been followed by an equally curious weariness which is however painless. For instance I would prefer if you wrote and I read. [...] I also feel as if I should not seek to express but simply listen to people. I am afraid I shall not easily settle down. I should not like to live in Paris but I should like to divide my existence. I shall set you some music in a few days which I want you to

---

[28] But I am obliged to take coffee constantly through the day. This I find to my taste as the weather here is very severe sometimes going down to 7 or 9 degrees below zero. The wind too is very keen but there is neither fog nor rain. Tell Stannie to go to Eason's in Abbey St where I ordered and paid for a certain quantity of paper, and tell them to forward it to me [...] I intend next week to look around for a room at about 7£ or 8£ the year [...] There is magnificent Norman furniture in a shop here – heavy wooden presses with paneled doors 5£ for one about twice as big as your wardrobe and though I cannot buy these yet for my room I shall certainly get them as soon as I can when I have definitely settled myself in Paris for my medical course. (*Letters II*, 20)

learn. M Douce will give me 10^s/, the Express £1-1-0, and the Academy, I daresay, £1-0-0: that is £2-11-0. Could you get a set of teeth for that? Do not be offended please because I cannot write. Jim (*Letters II*, 21)

Joyce's intended purchase of dentures for his mother was also a response to his own experience. The gift would confer on May Joyce an ability to consume that he himself lacked. Herbert Gorman, in the biography he wrote in consultation with Joyce, presents his experience of the streets of 1902 Paris, one in which poor teeth and financial concerns converge with an overwhelming aroma of delicious food:

> As he tramped the vivacious streets, avoiding the rolling carriages driven by cochers in white hats, and smelled the freshly baked loaves of bread and observed the shopgirls munching their chaussons of pastry and sniffed the rich odor of steaming coffee and the heady fragrance of spiced beans and saw the great bowls of cooked vegetables in the crémeries, he comforted himself with the thought that it would be painful to eat anyway. For during this winter, Joyce suffered from ferocious toothaches, toothaches so intense that though he was ravenously hungry he dreaded the effect of the first mouthful.[29]

In this accumulation of scenes, Joyce's motion through the street enables both his refusal of the endless supply of goods on offer and an ongoing exposure to them. Joyce sees the food but he experiences more vividly the swirling, tantalizing odors that, impossible to shut out, heighten his desire.

This biographical context allows us to see the poem as strategically adopting a less-invasive sensory modality in order to assert a minimal separation from the environment. Street smells, as Gorman's account demonstrates, are situated at the extreme of a continuum of invasive sensations. The modality of hearing offers the illusive possibility, if not the reality, of physical separation. Sound also affords regulation and containment in the medium of poetry, making possible an active response to a sensation that threatens the individual's ability to maintain autonomy.

In the unavoidable sensory infiltration of the scene of the young Joyce in Paris, his body is invaded by impressions that profusely and chaotically provoke desire. Desire is restructured in this scene, leading to an ambivalent sensation of pleasure and pain. With the pleasure of delicious aromas comes the pain of desire unfulfilled due to poverty and bodily vulnerability. A scene of olfaction in *Ulysses* presents this painful conflict between pleasure and discomfort. Leopold Bloom observes: "Hot mockturtle vapor

---

[29] Herbert Gorman, *James Joyce* (New York: Farrar & Rinehart, 1939), 91.

and steam of newbaked jampuffs roly-poly poured out from Harrison's [...] A barefoot arab stood over the grating, breathing in the fumes. Deaden the gnaw of hunger that way. Pleasure or pain is it? Penny dinner. Knife and fork chained to the table."[30] The "barefoot arab" is a ragged, homeless child, the avatar of a starving Irishman in Paris. These inescapable sensations provoke an altered libidinal structure. Desire, in this environment, is not only the first step to pleasure but also the instigation of frustration and even pain.

This altered libidinal structure also features in the third of the photo postcards Joyce sent on September 15, which he sent to Vincent Cosgrave, a friend from University College Dublin with whom he had visited brothels. On this postcard, he discusses "the scorta (prostitutes) of Paris in dog-Latin" (*JJ* 115). The postcard is currently missing, but Ellmann refers to its content as "scatological" (*Letters II*, 41n.3). Ellmann notes Joyce's strikingly divergent occupations during this period: "He enjoyed some of the sexual pleasures of Paris, and he also attended vespers at Notre-Dame and St. Germaine l'Auxerrois" (*JJ* 131). Joyce's sometimes-less-than-reliable biographer Peter Costello tells us that, for Joyce, "having no money to spend in brothels, street-walkers ('Punks of the bankside, a penny a time,' as *Ulysses* says) had to suffice."[31] Costello quotes the lines from Stephen's interior monologue in "Scylla and Charybdis," in which he remembers the calls of prostitutes on the right bank of the river, just across the river from the Boulevard Saint Germain: "Cours-la-Reine. *Encore vingt sous. Nous ferons de petites cochonneries. Minette? Tu veux?*" (*U* 9:641–42); translated somewhat ingenuously by Gifford and Seidman as "Another twenty sous [one franc]. We will indulge in little nasty things. Pussy (darling)? Do you wish it?"[32] These calls are another kind of appeal in the street, along with the hucksters' cries. If these voices are figured in the poem's "noise of waters/Making moan," from which the speaker asserts distance in the ennobled figure of a hovering bird, their bodies are described in obscene detail in the postcard. Ellmann's representation of its content as "scatological" implies that it is preoccupied by their excretions, in (surely) olfactory observations that associate the women with the inescapably fragrant goods on the street as described in Gorman's biography. These goods join those as something simultaneously appealing

---

[30] James Joyce, *Ulysses*, eds. Hans Walter Gabler with Wolfhard Steppe and Claus Melchior (New York: Vintage, 1986). Hence cited as *U* with episode and line number. *U* 8:232–38.

[31] Peter Costello, *James Joyce: The Years of Growth 1882–1915* (New York: Pantheon, 1992), 205.

[32] Don Gifford and Robert Seidman, *Notes for Joyce: An Annotation of James Joyce's Ulysses* (New York: Dutton, 1974), 230 (Gifford's parentheses). *Minette* is translated more idiomatically as cunnilingus.

and repellant. The dog-Latin code is an attempt to express "offstage" this obscene sensation. It conveys an interest that Joyce can express only outside of the sphere of literary art.

The obscene postcard might suggest that the poem is a kind of evasion, an instance of art used as an alibi for an actual encounter with reality, but the poem stages, figuratively, a struggle with that reality, an attempt to assert independence within it. The contrast between Joyce's photopostcards, however, pained his friend Byrne, who saw the coded licentiousness of the card to Cosgrave and broke with Joyce when he returned to spend Christmas in Dublin (*JJ* 120). Instead of confirming Joyce as a Left Bank artist, the photopostcards register the challenges Paris presented to his art. Their collective failure calls for an art that can respond directly to the street, that can represent and master the unpredictable and chaotic sensations of the actual urban environment, that can deal with the desires it stimulates and come up with a form of thinking capable of contending with them.

The Aesthetic Essay and Notes: From an Aesthetics of Stasis to an Art of Motion

On returning to Paris after Christmas, Joyce composed two pieces that directly respond to this challenge: a theory of art that banishes desire and loathing and a prose depiction of the activities of redolent women on a Parisian boulevard. The prose piece is undated, but it exemplifies and moves beyond the values of the aesthetic essay as it wards against the lures of the city but also stages the power of the body in this setting. In the transition between these two pieces, Joyce poses a series of questions about the relation of art to desire, the body, and the body's material processes.

Joyce composed the aesthetic essay having embarked on a new regimen of daily and nightly visits to the Nationale Bibliothèque de Paris and the Bibliothèque Sainte-Geneviève, respectively half an hour and ten minutes from his hotel on the Rue Corneille. In *Ulysses*, Stephen thinks of "the studious silence of the library of Saint Genevieve where he had read, sheltered from the sin of Paris, night by night" (U 2:69–70). The essay can be read in a notebook Joyce purchased on his return to Paris, written in an even, legible hand and, as are many of the other entries, ostentatiously signed and dated.[33] The notebook records Joyce's new discipline: a

---

[33] The notebook is now known as "The Paris and Pola Commonplace Book" and is held at the National Library of Ireland (NLI MS.36, 639/02/A). See Luca Crispi's analysis, "A Commentary on

hand-drawn calendar heads the opening page, which bears an emphatic X on every day from mid-January to the 10th of April, the day before he hurriedly left for Dublin. Joyce's discipline in other realms is also attested to in the notebook: underneath the calendar on the opening page is Joyce's record of his finances, ordered into long columns of carefully written numbers under the headings "Received" and "Outlay."[34] The columns reveal not just the extent of Joyce's borrowings but also his desire to maintain control over them, numerically and aesthetically. This financial exercise is undertaken beside Joyce's serious scholarly and literary endeavors; over the page, the continued "Received" column faces a short poem by Ben Jonson and quotations from Aristotle. Rather than signifying radically disparate behaviors, the budgets, citations, and essay have a shared goal: the assertion of order and limits on material existence, both personal and aesthetic.

Joyce's aesthetic essay asserts that the purpose of art is beauty: "the apprehension of the beautiful [is] the end of all art, tragic or comic" (*OCPW* 103). In doing so, it radically departs from his declaration in Dublin in the 1900 lecture "Drama and Life" that the artist must "put life – real life – on the stage. [. . .] Life we must accept as we see it before our eyes, men and women as we meet them in the real world, not as we apprehend them in the world of faery" (*OCPW* 28). If Joyce takes a swipe here at Yeats he does so in allegiance with not only Henrik Ibsen but also Baudelaire.[35] Earlier in the lecture, he announces: "Human society is the embodiment of changeless laws which the whimsicalities and circumstances

James Joyce's National Library of Ireland 'Early Commonplace Book': 1903–1912 (MS 36,639/02/A)," in *Genetic Joyce Studies* 9 (Spring 2009). Where Joyce's notes are reproduced verbatim by Barry, I cite the *OCPW* – as Crispi notes, "Since [the commonplace book] was presumed to be lost until 2002, Herbert Gorman's 1939 'definitive biography' of Joyce was the source text for almost all the information scholars had about this manuscript [. . .] Gorman's transcriptions as they appeared in his published biography (and 3 pages of manuscript discussed below) have served as the source of all subsequent editions of Joyce's aesthetic texts in *The Workshop of Daedalus*, *The Critical Writings*, and the *Occasional, Critical, and Political Writings*"; otherwise, I cite the "Paris and Pola Commonplace Book."

[34] Joyce omits his everyday expenses from his "Outlay" (anticipating perhaps Bloom's omission of some of the events of "Circe" in the Ithacan budget), listing only his lodging and his payment of debts to two important creditors, Casey and "Casey *fils*." Listed together under the vague term "Received," his borrowings far outnumber his income from the *Express* and the *Irish Times* for whom Joyce writes some reviews; the positive column is then itself a list of arrears.

[35] As has been observed, in his lecture, Joyce refutes "boy orator" Arthur Clery's association of theater with moral elevation (*JJ* 70) and declares his interest in the work of Henrik Ibsen, whose plays he names and whose dialogue, from *Pillars of Society*, he quotes in conclusion: "'what will you do in our Society, Miss Hessel?' asked Rorlund – 'I will let in fresh air, Pastor.' – answered Lona" (*OCPW* 29). Joyce also implicitly invokes Verlaine in this lecture. As Ellmann observes, Joyce's opposition of drama to literature is inspired by the final line of Verlaine's poetic manifesto, "Ars poétique":

of men and women involve and overwrap [. . .] Drama has to do with the underlying laws" (*OCPW* 23–24), an echo of Baudelaire's statement, in the essay "The Painter of Modern Life," that the artist's task is "to distil the eternal from the transitory," that the artist is "the painter of the fleeting moment and of all that it suggests of the eternal."[36] This is not to equate Joyce's unchanging laws with Baudelaire's eternal truths – in both cases, these verities remain undefined – but rather to point to a shared artistic practice centered in an encounter with contemporary life and the subsequent mastery of that encounter in new abstracted and idealized forms.

In the aesthetic essay Joyce writes in Paris, however, he associates art not with truth but with beauty. This shift from truth to beauty suggests a defensive response to the libidinal effects of the city. Art is contrasted with "improper" art, which inspires "desire" and "loathing."[37] To develop this understanding of art, Joyce takes from Aquinas the notion that beauty causes the cessation of desire.[38] Kevin Barry notes that in the aesthetic essay "Joyce is adapting a Thomist definition of beauty: '*Ad rationem pulchri pertinet quod in ejus aspectu seu cognitione quietetur appetitus*': 'It appertains to the nature of beauty that, when it is seen or known, desire ceases.' (*Summa Theologica*, I 2ae, I)" (*OCPW* 311, n. 2). It is only later, in the small, sleepy town of Pola, far from the vivid streets of Paris, that Joyce

---

"With Verlaine's pronouncement, '*Et tout le reste est littérature*,' in mind, Joyce argued that drama was not to be confused with literature" (*JJ* 71).

[36] Charles Baudelaire, *Baudelaire: Selected Writings on Art and Artists*, trans. P. E. Charvet (Cambridge, UK: Cambridge University Press, 1972), 204, 394, 402.

[37] In *Portrait* when Stephen rehearses Joyce's aesthetic theory, he adds: "Desire urges us to possess, to go to something; loathing urges us to abandon, to go from something. The arts which excite them, pornographical or didactic, are therefore improper arts," James Joyce, *A Portrait of the Artist as a Young Man*, ed. Jeri Johnson (Oxford, UK: Oxford University Press, 2000), 172; hence cited in abbreviated form as *P*. When Garry Leonard argues that "Stephen's relentless attempt to outlaw arousal as a legitimate component of aesthetic contemplation must be placed within the psychological, historical, and sociological context of modernity and the modern metropolis," he effectively presents Joyce's motivation for the aesthetic essay in Paris, Garry Leonard, *Advertising and Commodity Culture in Joyce* (Gainesville: University Press of Florida, 1998), 176. Leonard writes that the "defining experience of modernism was that of living in a modern metropolis [characterized by] a nearly unmanageable assault of noise, illogical juxtaposition, relentless unpredictability, and enigmatic epiphanies [that] demands a strategy of delimitation" (185).

[38] In *Portrait*, Stephen is described as reading a slim compendium of Thomistic philosophy: "The lore which he was believed to pass his days brooding upon so that it had rapt him from the companionships of youth was only a garner of slender sentences from Aristotle's poetics and psychology and a *Synopsis Philosophiæ Scholasticæ ad Mentem Divi Thomæ, ad Utilitatem Discipulorum Redacta*" (*P* 148), which Aubert notes is still available in the Bibliothèque de Saint Geneviève, Jacques Aubert, *The Aesthetics of James Joyce* (Baltimore, MD: Johns Hopkins University Press, 2002), 100. O'Rourke comments, "there is no evidence that [Joyce in Paris] drew any evidence from the work; the only hint that he may have consulted it is the word 'slender.'" Fran O'Rourke, "Philosophy," in *James Joyce in Context*, ed. John McCourt (Cambridge, UK: Cambridge University Press, 2009), 329.

can embrace Aquinas's positive account of desire: his first entry in the same notebook, having arrived in Pola with Nora, is headed by Aquinas's "Bonum est in quod tendit appetitus," translated by Joyce as "The good is that towards the possession of which an appetite tends" (*OCPW* 105). In Paris, however, Joyce ignores Aquinas's Aristotelian eudaimonism. In the aesthetic essay, desire and its counterpart, loathing, are banished from "proper" art: "Desire is the feeling which urges us to go to something and loathing is the feeling which urges us to go from something: and that art is improper which aims at exciting these feelings in us whether by comedy or by tragedy" (*OCPW* 102).

Aquinas's aesthetic theory itself acts as a safeguard against an overwhelming environment. In *The Aesthetics of Thomas Aquinas*, Umberto Eco notes that Aquinas constructs his aesthetic theory to counter the pancalism of the sixth-century theologian Pseudo-Dionysius. Aquinas responds to a "Dionysian universe, coruscating with beauty, [in which] mankind risked losing its place, of being blinded and then annulled. This is why Aquinas began in the *Summa* to deal with issues in psychology, in a way which would transform the whole question. He introduced the problem of the psychological and subjective desire for beauty, not as a secondary matter, but as part of the very essence. The notion expressed in the words *visa placent* changed the picture. Aquinas's three formal characters of beauty – clarity, integrity, and proportion – modified it further, at least indirectly, because of their importance in his hylomorphic theory."[39] Aquinas's aesthetic theory thus, in contrast to Pseudo-Dionysius, conceives of the world not as an independent and overpowering locus of beauty but as a field in which the engagement of our higher abilities – disinterested contemplation and intellectual effort – allows us to realize the aesthetic qualities of things and in doing so to achieve higher states of tranquility and pleasure. When, in response to Joyce's statement in the notebook, "In regard then to that part of the act of apprehension which is called the activity of simple perception there is no sensible object which cannot be said to be in a measure beautiful" (*OCPW* 105), Barry quotes Pseudo-Dionysius' *Divine Names*, "there is nothing which does not partake in the beautiful and the good" (*OCPW* 313 n.18), he misapplies Pseudo-Dionysius' concept of a spontaneous, even uncontrollable worldly beauty to Joyce's use of Aquinas's mediated aesthetic possibilities.

[39] Umberto Eco, *The Aesthetics of Thomas Aquinas* (Cambridge, MA: Harvard University Press, 1988), 48.

Aquinas provides Joyce with a structured process of aesthetic perception. Drawing together references from various texts, Eco reconstructs the
different activities implied in Aquinas's "Pulcra sunt quae visa placent":
simultaneous but differentiated sensory perception, intellectual abstraction, and judgment according to the criteria of ontological perfection or
completeness.[40] It is only as a result of this effort that the thing "delivers
itself to aesthetic perception."[41] This intellectual effort leads to a sense of
peace in an order understood and delighted in. Joyce repurposes this
conscious and disinterested vision to devise an art that would allow the
perception of beauty. He does so not to offer an account of the beauty in
the world, as was Aquinas's concern, but to construct an alternative
aesthetic sphere within the world.

This shift responds to the outdated nature of Aquinas's theological
aesthetics. Although Aquinas's understanding of beauty is compelling, it
can no longer function in a secular, commercial environment. For Aquinas, beauty is about the relation of a thing's existence to its essence. As Eco
explains: "A thing may be said to 'be' in the act of combining its essence
with its existence, and this act involves a proportion, a concordance, a
harmony. This proportion, further more, is constitutive of beauty. Thus,
everything is beautiful insofar as it 'is,' because it 'is' on virtue of a
harmony of essence with existence."[42] God as the maker of natural world
has knowledge of its substance, which humanity cannot access, and
thus has a superior understanding of the perfection of a natural object's
being. The beauty we appreciate in natural things is perhaps based merely
on their accidental features. In an artisanal culture, the matter and form of
artifacts are organically related, and it is possible to have access to their
substance and to appreciate their beauty. However, in the modern city, the
problem of the loss of divinely ordained meaning is compounded by the
nature of goods in commodity culture. Individuals are far removed from
the category of maker or the context of fabrication; the commodity,
famously, erases its past and obscures its use, identifying itself instead with
a changing exchange value. Beauty, as understood by Aquinas, thus
becomes an unavailable category. Higher perceptions of the proportion
of essence to existence are replaced by crude encounters with goods that
are, on the one hand, merely available and, on the other, defined
by external monetary structures and interests. If we might imagine turn-
of-the-century Paris as an overwhelming world of beautiful things, and
perhaps at certain moments it was, it was also a place of mere profusion, of

[40] Ibid., 190.   [41] Ibid., 199.   [42] Ibid., 85.

a proffered, unstructured abundance that randomly moved individuals. The aesthetic that Joyce proposes is therefore to be understood in opposition to this sensory stimulation. Joyce fills the gap left by devout and artisanal culture with art, reconceiving of "the apprehension of the beautiful" as possible only through the mediation of the work of art.[43]

In adopting Aquinas's aesthetic vision, Joyce rejects its psychological and subjective aspects and devises a purely cognitive aesthetic vision. In the context of Paris, this rejection is necessary as these capacities have been mobilized by the world of commodity consumption. Through his aesthetics, Joyce constructs a separate realm to this world as he valorizes an objective, collective aesthetic perception: "All art, again, is static for the feelings of terror and pity on the one hand and the feeling of joy on the other hand are feelings which arrest us. Afterwards it will appear how this rest is necessary for the apprehension of the beautiful – the end of all art, tragic or comic – for this rest is the only condition under which the images, which are to excite in us terror or pity or joy, can be properly presented to us and properly seen by us. For beauty is a quality of something seen but terror and pity and joy are states of mind" (*OCPW* 103). Joyce departs here from Aquinas. Although the rest of what Joyce writes in some ways resembles Aquinas's "tranquilitas ordinis," the tranquility of desire,[44] this is not the sense of peace that *results from* the intellectual work of perceiving the beautiful but rather a sense of rest that must be established *before* the beautiful can be perceived. This rest, in Joyce's essay, is provided by art.

To address the specific problem of the movement from sensation to knowledge, or from matter to form, Joyce turns to Aristotle. His notes reveal an effort to assert the autonomy of the intellect, a dominance of the mind over the body, even while, at the same time, they show a fascination with the power of the senses. Aristotle's account of the sense of smell as lacking the precision associated with the other senses will become crucial in Joyce's depiction of the Parisian boulevard. This study of Aristotle also prompts in Joyce a new understanding of aesthetics: Joyce's exploration of beauty in Aristotle leads him to what are now known as the writings of Pseudo-Aristotle, a syncretic text that presents a vividly physical understanding of the mind and an account of being as dependent on a mobile and porous digesting and excreting body. This body will provide Joyce

---

[43] In *Portrait*, Stephen illustrates this difficulty by wavering between the perception of the essence of a basket and the artistic image conceived by the artist – aesthetic conception that evades problem of absence of divinely ordained essence.

[44] Eco, *Aesthetics of Aquinas*, 92.

with a crucial counterimage to the closed, autonomous body of neoclassical aesthetics.

As he explores the question of the separation of the intellect in sensory perception,[45] Joyce devotes several pages to notes from *De Anima* (On the Soul) and *Metaphysics*, as well as from *De Sensu* (On the Senses) and *Poetics*. As Jacques Aubert and Fran O'Rourke have shown, Joyce works from French translations of *De Anima* (and traditionally appended writings) by J. Barthélemy-Saint-Hilaire and, to a lesser extent, by Victor Cousin, and from a translation of *Metaphysics* by Barthélemy-Saint-Hilaire.[46] His notes reveal a desire to assert the sovereignty of the soul, as well as a fascination with the flesh. While Joyce commented later, "Everything, in his work, is defined with wonderful clarity and simplicity,"[47] for Aristotle, however, the relation of the soul to the body, and to the material world more generally, is a complex issue.[48] A large part of *De Anima* is devoted to aesthesis, or sense perception. Sense perception is necessary for intelligence, as it is the first stage in the assemblage of knowledge of the world.

Joyce's notes focus almost immediately on Aristotle's sections on the senses of smell and touch in Book II of *De Anima*.[49] For Aristotle, smell is a mysterious and inaccurate sense: "with smell and the object of the smell-faculty the situation is less well-defined than with what we have so far been discussing; for it is not clear what sort of thing smell is as it is clear with

---

[45] Following commentators, I will use *soul* and *intellect* interchangeably when referring to Aristotle's *psyche*.

[46] See Fran O'Rourke, *Allwisest Stagyrite: Joyce's Quotations from Aristotle* (Dublin: National Library of Ireland, 2005). Aristotle was much in the air in the late 1890s following new publications such as S. H. Butcher's 1895 critical edition of the *Poetics*. The UCD of Joyce's undergraduate years was permeated with Aristotle's thought. Felix Hackett, another friend of Joyce's, writes: "The university atmosphere around 26 St Stephen's Green (University College) was [...] peripatetic [...] in the philosophical sense" (qtd. in Jacques Aubert, *The Aesthetics of James Joyce* (Baltimore, MD: Johns Hopkins University Press, 1992), 6). Constantine Curran reports that in the first lecture in English Literature, "The lecturer was Father Darlington and his first words were from Aristotle's *Poetics*" (6). The biographer of Thomas A. Finlay, the Jesuit professor of "mental philosophy" at UCD, writes "The Aristotelian and Thomist current ran through the institution, and influenced those like James Joyce and Curran who did not follow any course in philosophy" (qtd. in O'Rourke, "Philosophy," 323).

[47] Letter to Stanislaus, qtd. in O'Rourke, *Allwisest Stagyrite*, 2.

[48] O'Rourke observes that "Aristotle's suggestion of the 'separated intellect' is among the most acutely disputed topics in the history of Aristotelian philosophy." *Allwisest Stagyrite*, 21. Aristotle himself declares: "the soul is not separable from the body" (II:1 431a).

[49] Joyce first notes the central claim of *De Anima*, from the first chapter of Book II (The first book is a survey and critique of previous discussions of the soul.): "The soul is the first entelechy of a naturally organic body" (NLI MS.36,639/02/A 2r). Hugh Lawson-Tancred defines entelechy as "intrinsic possession of end" (119) but also translates it as "actuality," Aristotle, *De Anima*, trans. Lawson-Tancred (New York: Penguin, 1987). Joyce also makes a note that procreation is "the most natural act for living beings" connecting them to "the eternal and divine" (NLI MS.36,639/02/A 2r).

sound and color. The reason is that we do not have this sense in an accurate way but worse than many animals. For man smells badly and perceives none of the smell-objects except the painful and pleasant ones, as his organ is not accurate."[50] Smell thus lacks the clarity possessed by sound and vision, a lack that comes with an absence of knowledge of the form of the thing smelled. The separation of the intellect in smell is thus uncertain, and Aristotle provides no clear answers.[51] If Joyce pursues the complexities of Aristotle's understanding of smell, he takes no notes on it.

From Aristotle's section on smell, Joyce takes notes on touch, showing an interest in the possibilities of a physically mediated thought: "Men who have tough flesh have not much intelligence" and "In the sense of touch man is far above all the other animals and hence he is the most intelligent animal."[52] Joyce's interest in the potential of touch leads him to an error of transcription in the sixth quotation, which he immediately corrects: "The flesh is the intermediary for the sense of ~~though~~ touch."[53] Joyce's fleeting error, as he begins to write "thought" instead of "touch," misidentifies thought as a sense, imagining the sensory body as a medium of thought. In doing so, it suggests a radical intertwining of the haptic and the cognitive, a thinking sensation that recalls Baudelaire's "things think through me, or I through them."

Yet this interest in the haptic is followed by an attention to Aristotle's discussion of the separateness of sense perception from its material object. Joyce's next citation is: "A sense receives the form without the matter"; this is followed by "The sensation of particular things is always true," suggesting Joyce's persistent interest in the authority of the senses, a theme taken up again in his later note "Error is not found apart from combination."[54] The separateness of the soul is at issue in the next quotation, from a section in III.5 on the intellect as active and passive: "That which acts is superior to that which suffers."[55] Joyce's citation falsely gives the impression that Aristotle denigrates sensation. For Aristotle, in all sensation, the one who senses is changed by the thing sensed: "perception is thought to be a kind of alteration, and nothing perceives that does not participate in soul."[56] Sensation is the actualization of the potential to become similar to the sensed object, a change in which the soul is passive; as Thomas Johansen summarizes, "In perception the agent is a sense-object and the

---

[50] *De Anima* II:9, 180.
[51] Thomas Johansen argues, with reference to *De Anima* and *De Sensu*, that smell "occupies a place between the contact senses [taste and touch] and the mediated senses [sight and hearing]." Johansen, "Aristotle on the Sense of Smell," *Phronesis* 41.1 (1996), 1–19, at 17. In other words, it is a sense that operates both through direct contact *and* through a mediating material.
[52] NLI MS.36,639/02/A 2r.   [53] Ibid.   [54] Ibid.   [55] Ibid.   [56] *De Anima* II:4, 166.

patient is a sense-faculty."[57] Yet the soul itself has an actualizing power in perception: "Such is, in effect, the intellect, which, on the one hand, can become all things, and which, on the other, can make all things. It is, in such a way, similar to light because light, in a certain sense, makes, from colors which are only potentiality, colors in reality."[58] The mind thus has an agency in sensation as it brings the world into actuality. Yet this activity is dependent upon a separation: thus Joyce's next quotation from the same section, "Only when it is separate from all things is the intellect really itself and this intellect separate from all things is immortal and divine."[59]

The seeming contradiction between a mind that is both separate from everything ("l'intelligence qui est separée, impassible, sans mélange avec quoi que ce soit") and also mixed with objects ("La science en acte se confond avec l'objet auquel elle s'applique") speaks to the complex definition of the embodied soul itself, an animating principle that is neither wholly empirical nor wholly conceptual.[60] Lawson-Tancred attributes this inconclusiveness to Aristotle's "intellectual honesty." He explains that Aristotle's concept of sense perception involves two different modes of behavior in "what for him is the single activity of *aesthesis*": the passive alteration of the sense faculty in sensation, by which "that which senses becomes like that which is sensed, having previously been unlike it" and, "in what is closer to an act of judgment", which we can think of as perception, "the reception of the Form of the percept without its Matter."[61] In this two-stage action of sensory perception – a process that underlies Aquinas's multistage account of apprehension – the mind is both passive and active, resembling but also separate from the objects it perceives. Joyce goes on to take Aristotle's words out of context to present a sovereign entity: "The soul is in a manner all that is."[62] Aristotle holds this to be so because the soul can become all things through sensing them while at the same time maintaining independence through recognizing their various forms. Yet in a modern context, Aristotle's account faces a similar problem to Aquinas's. The separation of the intellect in sense perception depends upon an essence or form that is stable and independent of matter, a possibility that has come under threat in Joyce's context. Without

[57] Johansen, "Aristotle on the Sense of Smell," 2.
[58] "Telle est, en effet, l'intelligence, qui, d'une part, peut devenir toutes choses, et qui, d'autre part, peut tout faire. C'est en quelque sorte une virtualité pareille à la lumière; car la lumière, en un certain sens, fait, des couleurs qui ne sont qu'en puissance, des couleurs en réalité. Et telle est l'intelligence qui est séparée, impassible, sans mélange avec quoi que ce soit, et qui par son essence est en acte." Barthélemy-Saint-Hilaire, qtd. in O'Rourke, *Allwisest Stagyrite*, 19 (my translation).
[59] NLI MS.36,639/02/A 2r.   [60] Ibid.   [61] Lawson-Tancred, *De Anima*, 78, 76, 77, 80.
[62] NLI MS.36,639/02/A 2v.

formal cause, there is only the blur of material sensation. Sensation thus offers the possibility of creating the world but at the risk of being submerged in it. The sense of smell is a modality that dramatizes this tension, as already for Aristotle its ability to discern essences was in doubt. We will see how smell plays a crucial role in the Epiphany that Joyce composes in Paris.

Aristotle lacks an overarching definition of art; the *Poetics* focuses on "Poetry in itself and of its various kinds, noting the essential qualities of each."[63] Rather than a conceptual structure, Aristotle's writing provides key words for Joyce's aesthetic essay. Shifting his focus from resolving the issue of sense perception to producing an account of art, Joyce turns to the *Poetics*, taking terms and phrases that he combines with Aquinas's *visio* and repeats in an incantatory manner to call into being a new kind of art:[64]

> All art, again, is static for the feelings of terror and pity on the one hand and the feeling of joy on the other are feelings which arrest us. Afterwards it will appear how this rest is necessary for the apprehension of the beautiful – the end of all art, tragic or comic – for this rest is the only condition under which the images, which are to excite in us terror or pity or joy can be properly presented to us and properly seen by us. For beauty is a quality of something seen but terror and pity and joy are states of mind. (*OCPW* 103)

The aesthetic essay transforms the central terms of the *Poetics*: tragedy and comedy refer not to dramatic works but to the contrasting affective tendencies of works in any artistic genre. Furthermore, pity and terror are intellectual states associated with stasis, rather than emotions that bring about catharsis. That these are at the same time both "states of mind" and "feelings" speaks to a residual uncertainty about the fundamental mechanisms of "proper" art and about the possibility of a state of mind independent of sensation.

Having assembled these phrases in the library, it is likely that Joyce composed the essay in the streets of Paris. In *Stephen Hero*, as in *Portrait*, Joyce ascribes all of the material he wrote on aesthetics in Paris to Stephen Dedalus in Dublin. He writes that Stephen composed the aesthetic essay while walking through the streets. He "perform[ed] preparative abstinences. His forty days were consumed in aimless solitary walks during which he forged out his sentences. In this manner he had his whole essay in his mind from the first word to the last before he had put any morsel of it on paper" (*SH* 74). The 500-word aesthetic essay that Joyce

---

[63] *Aristotle's Poetics*, trans. S. H. Butcher (New York: Hill & Wang, 1961), 49.

[64] As Joyce remarks to the dean in *Portrait*, "For my purpose I can work on at present by the light of one or two ideas of Aristotle and Aquinas ... I need them only for my own use and guidance until I have done something for myself by their light" (164).

composed in Paris, which he presents as the content of the aesthetic lecture
in *Stephen Hero*, is of a size and a style that befits a peripatetic mode of
composition (unlike the 3,000-word lecture). Stephen's mobile compositional practice takes place in a space of infernal temptation outside of the
sanctuary of the library: his performance of "preparative abstinences" over
"forty days" of "wandering in the desert" connotes the temptation of Jesus
in the Judean desert during which the Devil calls on a hungry Jesus to
worship him instead of God and, in a detail that recalls Gorman's depiction
of hungry Joyce "tramp[ing] the vivacious streets" of Paris, to turn stone into
bread.[65] This walking composition is Stephen's response to the intrusion of
his body into his thoughts: "In thinking or constructing the form of the
essay he found himself much hampered by the sitting posture. His body
disturbed him and he adapted the expedient of appeasing it by gentle
promenading" (*SH* 74). The regular rhythms of walking might indeed
undergird the insistent cadences of the aesthetic essay, which begins:

> Desire is the feeling which urges us to go to something and loathing is the
> feeling which urges us to go from something: and that art is improper which
> aims at exciting these feelings in us whether by comedy or by tragedy. Of
> comedy later. But tragedy aims at exciting in us feelings of terror and pity.
> Now terror is the feeling which arrests us before whatever is grave in human
> fortunes and unites us with its secret cause and pity is the feeling which
> arrests us before whatever is grave in human fortunes and unites us with the
> human sufferer. (*OCPW* 103)

Composed in the street, the aesthetic essay is as much a performative
response to Paris as a conceptual one; its rhythmically conjured phrases
are Joyce's means of resisting not only intellectually but also physically the
sensations of the city that unpredictably provoke the passive movements of
attraction and repulsion. In this "aimless, solitary" peripatetic composition,
the body is engaged in unobtrusive, almost automated motion rather than
troubling and unpredictable sensation. "Thinking and constructing" is a
physical activity in which fragments of language are repeatedly sounded in
order to "forge out" sentences.

The essay's patterned assertions regarding "proper" art exclude the
chaotic and desirous movement we can identify with the city street. As
Joyce states earlier, tragedy "arrests us" and "unites us" with the "secret

[65] "And Jesus being full of the Holy Ghost returned from Jordan, and was led by the Spirit into the
wilderness, being forty days tempted of the devil. And in those days he did eat nothing: and when
they were ended, he afterward hungered. And the devil said unto him, If thou be the Son of God,
command this stone that it be made bread. And Jesus answered him, saying, It is written, That man
shall not live by bread alone, but by every word of God." (*Authorized Version of the King James Bible*
Luke 4:1–4).

cause" of a grave situation and the character who undergoes it; this static communion of heightened cognition suggests that the space outside of the aesthetic realm is inhabited by unruly and uncomprehending individuals who have nothing in common but the experience of being moved haphazardly by desire and loathing. Comedy, also, opposes this motion as it prompts joy, "the feeling which the possession of some good excites in us," which "holds us in rest so long as we possess something." Joy, central to comedy, which Joyce understands as the "superior manner of art," offers a criterion for art in general: "according as this feeling of joy is excited by whatever is substantial or accidental, general or fortuitous, in human fortunes the art is to be judged more or less excellent" (*OCPW* 103). Artistic achievement thus depends on the exclusion of contingency from the aesthetic realm; superlative art enables a secure relation to a "substantial" and "general," although undefined, "good."

Similarly, the aesthetic essay announces but does not define the ultimate aim of art, beauty; Joyce's attempt to lend substance to this ultimate aim leads him in a surprising new direction. In the essay, he declares that comedy and tragedy arrest us but "Afterwards it will appear how this rest is necessary for the apprehension of the beautiful – the end of all art, tragic or comic" (*OCPW* 103). As discussed earlier, outside of a faithful or artisanal context the conceptual workings fall away from Aquinas' statement: "It appertains to the nature of beauty that, when it is seen or known, desire ceases." Joyce proceeds to investigate the relation of desire to beauty. In a series of quotations from Aristotle that follow the aesthetic essay, he uses one sentence to pose a question about the nature of desire. Enclosing a sentence from Aristotle's *Metaphysics* in square brackets, underlining the key words, and adding a question mark, Joyce asks: "[The object of desire is that which appears to us beautiful ... We desire a thing because it appears to us good.... (?) Met. XII. Cap 7.]"[66] Joyce's confusion is heightened by his translation of Cousin's "volonté" as "desire" rather than "will," which has the effect of collapsing the distinction Aristotle makes between desire and judgment as associated, respectively, with perceived good and actual good, although elsewhere Aristotle does associate desire with both actual good and perceived good: "Indeed, the object of desire is that which appears beautiful; and the primary object of the will is the good; for we desire a thing because we deem it good, more than we deem it good because we desire it."[67] As

[66] NLI MS.36,639/02/A 6v, Joyce's underlinings.
[67] "En effet, l'objet du désir est ce qui paraît beau; et l'objet premier de la volonté est le bien lui-même; car nous désirons une chose parce que nous la jugeons bonne, plutôt que nous la jugeons telle parce que nous la désirons" (Cousin, qtd. in O'Rourke, *Wisest Stagyrite*, 44); a more recent translation reads: "The primary objects of desire and of thought are the same. For the apparent good is the

Joyce translates Cousin's Aristotle, desire is associated with goodness. What power then can an art of substantial, general good, to use Joyce's terms, have to arrest desire? His essay is undermined.

This problem pushes Joyce toward an exploration of Aristotle's understanding of beauty. At the end of the page, Joyce notes three Aristotelian passages on beauty in, respectively, the *Poetics*, the *Metaphysics*, and *Problems*.[68] This exploration opens up radically divergent routes. The first undergirds the aesthetic essay and provides material for Joyce to amplify its rearticulation by Stephen in *Stephen Hero* and *Portrait*. Joyce does not note in full the reference to the *Poetics*, perhaps because he has studied the book already, but a part of Section 7 emphasizes the role of proportion: "in everything that is beautiful, whether it be a living creature or any organism composed of parts, these parts must not only be orderly arranged but must also have a certain magnitude of their own; for beauty consists in magnitude and ordered arrangement."[69] This notion finds expression in Joyce's notebook on March 25, when he writes: "Rhythm seems to be the first or ~~necessary~~ formal relation of part to part in any whole or of a whole to its part or parts, or of any part to the whole of which it is a part."[70] The second text, *Metaphysics*, supports the aesthetic essay's association of beauty with stasis: "Now since the good and the beautiful are different (for the former is always a property of action, but the latter extends to objects free from motion), those are mistaken who affirm that the mathematical sciences say nothing of beauty or goodness. [. . .] The main species of beauty are order, symmetry, definite limitation, and these are the chief properties that the mathematical sciences draw attention to."[71]

The third text, however, leads Joyce to a new, exploratory, and even comic mode of aesthetics and to the conception of an art that identifies with the body. *Problems* is no longer attributed to Aristotle, although it was at the time Joyce read it.[72] The book is concerned with the body's natural

---

object of appetite, and the real good is the primary object of rational wish. But desire is consequent on opinion rather than opinion on desire; for the thinking is the starting-point." www.classics.mit .edu/Aristotle/metaphysics.12.xii.html.

[68] NLI MS.36,639/02/A 9v "Poet: vii-4, Met: xiii-3, 1078 a36, Probl: xvii-1, 915, b36."

[69] Aristotle, *Poetics* 1450b, www.perseus.tufts.edu/hopper/text?doc=Perseus%3Atext%3A1999.01 .0056%3Asection%3D1450b.

[70] NLI MS.36,639/02/A 12v.

[71] *Metaphysics*, 1078a. Aristotle uses different words here for good and beautiful: "ἐπεὶ δὲ τὸ ἀγαθὸν καὶ τὸ καλὸν ἕτερον." www.perseus.tufts.edu/hopper/text?doc=Perseus%3Atext%3A1999.01 .0051%3Abook%3D13%3Asection%3D1078a.

[72] *Problems* combines concepts and passages from Aristotle's notes with writings by Hippocrates, Theophrastus, and other unidentified sources. E. S. Forster writes that its form was finalized at "a date certainly not much earlier than the first century BC, and probably a good deal later. Richter

processes and states of disequilibrium, its shifting qualities in relation to its surroundings. Presenting the body and mind, as well as the body and its environment, as naturally continuous states, it contrasts with Aristotle's emphasis on the separation of the intellect from all things and runs counter to Joyce's theory of stasis and containment.

Problems presents an understanding of beauty that is markedly different from the fixed, ordered notions of beauty in *Poetics* and in *Metaphysics*. The passage to which Joyce is directed is somewhat sober in comparison to the rest of the book, but it nonetheless communicates its almost comic emphasis on the varying conditions of perception: "Why do the asymmetrical look larger when standing by the side of others, than when they stand alone? Is it because symmetry implies unity, and to the greatest extent produces unity, but unity is indivisible, and the indivisible is smaller?"[73] In connecting symmetry with unity, or integrity, it recalls passages in *Poetics* that influence Aquinas's discussions of integrity, harmony, and clarity. Yet it relativizes issues that to this point Joyce has been dealing with in the abstract and absolute. One of the book's passages on beauty begins "Why does a horse enjoy and desire a mare, a man a woman [. . .]?" before moving to claim: "For it is not true that every living creature is equally beautiful, and desire is for beauty. So the more beautiful should be the more desirable. But rather in fact not every beauty is pleasant, nor is pleasure and beauty equally pleasant to all men; for instance, one man finds eating and drinking more pleasant, another sexual indulgence."[74] Providing a counter to the theological aesthetics of Aquinas, the passage links the topic of beauty to pleasure, resituating its definition within a contingent everyday environment, structured by individual embodiment.

Problems is a piecemeal text, inconclusive and multifaceted like the body it presents. The long work is unsystematic, moving from one topic to the next without argumentative connection. This is certainly due to the nature of the text as a compilation of writings by authors from the peripatetic school. The text's form of questions and answers is derived from the pedagogical practices at the Lyceum and Aristotle's zetetic mode, his tendency to proceed by inquiry. The text refuses conclusions, presenting

---

would put the date as late as the fifth or sixth century A.D." Forster, "The Pseudo-Aristotelian Problems: Their Nature and Composition," *The Classical Quarterly* 22.3–4 (July–October 1928), 163–65, at 65.

[73] Aristotle, *Problems, Vol. I*, Books XXII–XXXVIII, trans. W. S. Hett (Cambridge, MA: Harvard University Press, 1937), XVII:916a, 365.

[74] Aristotle, *Problems, Vol. I*, Books I–XXI, trans. W. S. Hett (Cambridge, MA: Harvard University Press, 1937), X:896b, 237.

sequences of questions and often laying out alternative, contradictory explanations, sometimes in question form, for the same phenomenon.

This mode of exploring multiple possibilities parallels *Problems'* representation of the body as acted upon by multiple mobile factors. The text presents thought and matter as consubstantial in a body through which disparate forces act and resist one another.[75] This imbricated, mobile soul must have been strikingly different for Joyce, who most recently had noted: "Only when it is separate from all things is the intellect really itself and this intellect separate from all things is immortal and divine."[76] If in Aristotle's *De Anima* any living body – whether plant, animal or human – is possessed of a principle of animation that governs the relation of part to whole, *Problems* is occupied not with essential being, the radiant clarity of entelechy, but with the body as dependent upon its relations to its surroundings, itself a shifting collection of aridities, humidities, moistures and temperatures. To characterize *Problems'* understanding of the body as humoral disguises the complexity of its representation of bodily workings. The four fundamental elements of heat, coldness, moisture, and dryness pass through the person in multiple, contingent directions and combinations, exacerbated or reduced by seasonal conditions, geography, diet, and activity.

Problems' fundamental principle is the necessity of excretion for the healthy functioning of both the body and the mind. Motion thus becomes an ideal: "a body should therefore be in such a condition as to remove the waste product as soon as it receives it, and be always in a motion and never quiescent. For what remains behind becomes putrid."[77] This concern with excretion comes, logically enough, with an attention to the motion of the fluids and vapors through the body. It considers the passage of phlegm, bile, marrow, sweat, semen, saliva, breath, and, more obscurely, temperature, air, fumes, and vapors throughout the body. This digestion and excretion facilitates other motions in the body, including the passage of thought. As Pseudo-Aristotle remarks, "when the soul moves naturally it does not sleep; for then it is particularly alive."[78] This lively motion of the

---

[75] The text is a fitting theoretical companion for the reader of Baudelaire and Verlaine. Baudelaire indeed named the first section of *Les Fleurs du mal*, "Spleen et Idéal," after the substance of bile, one of the four basic elements of the human body according to Greek humoral theory.

[76] NLI MS.36,639/02/A 2r.   [77] Aristotle, *Problems I*, 865b, 39–41.

[78] Aristotle, *Problems I*, XVIII:916b, 369. Joyce must have noticed the section titled "Problems connected with studiousness," which immediately follows the passage on beauty to which he was referred. Here coldness, due to external conditions or melancholy, hinders the person's digestion or "concoction" of breath, and they fail to concentrate on reading: "Why is it that in some cases, if men begin to read, they are attacked by sleep against their will, and that it makes others keep awake, even if they want to sleep, when they take a book? Is it because in those in whom movements of

brain originates not in the concatenation of logical statements but rather in the passage of air and fluid.

This focus on the motion through the body leads to one of the strangest questions in *Problems*, a question that has striking consequences for Joyce's thinking about art. The question concerns the proper creations of the body: "Why is it that, if a living creature is born from our semen, we regard it as our own offspring, but if it proceeds from any other part or excretion, we do not consider it our own? For many things proceed from decayed matter as well as from semen."[79] For Pseudo-Aristotle, excretion is constitutive of peripheral features of the body: for example, "Hair grows from waste product."[80] The fluid emitted by the brain also engenders lice: "Now the brain is moist; consequently the head is always most moist. This is obvious from the fact that most hair grows there. The dampness of the region is most liable to produce lice."[81] Pseudo-Aristotle's question thus inquires if parasites on the head are literal brain-children, offspring that we should consider our own.

Problems' focus on the status of waste prompts Joyce to consider the strange possibility of an artistic excretion. He does so in an interrogative aesthetics inspired by Pseudo-Aristotle's zetetic mode. He makes a list of eight inquiries that depart strikingly in tone and content from the aesthetic essay. The fifth question, "Why are not excrements, children and lice works of art?" is the most outré of the eight concrete and somatically oriented questions:

1. I desire to see the Mona Lisa. Is it therefore beautiful or is it good?
2. Spicer-Simson has made a bust of his wife. Is it lyrical, epical or dramatic?
3. Is a chair finely made tragic or comic?
4. Why are statues made white for the most part?
5. Why are not excrements, children and lice works of art?
6. If a man hacking in fury at a block of wood makes there an image of a cow (say) has he made a work of art?
7. Can a photograph be a work of art?
8. Are houses, clothes, furniture, etc. works of art?[82]

---

breath take place owing to the coldness which is either natural or due to melancholic humors, owing to which the waste product of breathing is unconcocted because of the coldness, in such men, when the mind is stirred but does not think with concentration, it is vanquished by the other movement which has a cooling effect, so they are more inclined to sleep?" Aristotle, *Problems I*, XVIII:916b, 369.

[79] Aristotle, *Problems I*, IV:878a, 119.   [80] Aristotle, *Problems II*, XXXI:957b, 185.
[81] Aristotle, *Problems I*, I:861a, 13.   [82] NLI MS.36,639/02/A 11v.

A sense of physical engagement with specific artworks is suggested by the first and second questions. Joyce poses the questions a thirty-minute walk from the Mona Lisa in the Louvre, a painting familiar to him from Walter Pater's *Studies in the History of the Renaissance* (1873). The first and second questions play on Joyce's declaration some pages earlier in the notebook that art is comprised of three modes of relation between the work of art, the artist, and the public.[83] Accordingly, the second question somewhat cheekily is asking if French sculptor Theodor Spicer-Simson made a bust of his wife for himself or for others, while the first directs an attitude of desire toward the Mona Lisa, which Pater calls "the seventh heaven of symbolical expression."[84] The implicit eroticism of this relation to art informs the second question: "Why are statues made white for the most part?"

The fifth question, however, moves beyond works of fine and practical art to consider matter that defies both canons of taste and commercial worth. In asking "Why are not excrements, children and lice works of art?" Joyce is concerned with physical entities that come from, pass through, or live off what passes through, the borders of the body. His subject matter analogously disrupts the authoritative scholarly tone he has maintained thus far in the aesthetic notes; the contrast between his subject matter and theoretical language creates a new comic effect. Children are less blessed little cherubs than excreta in a more repugnant sense, associated as they are with excrement and parasites. As the emissions of the body are considered to be artifacts, Aquinas's distinction between the natural and the artificial is overthrown. In contrast to an art of the beautiful defined by its exclusion of the body's contingent affects, here Joyce entertains the very opposite notion: the possibility that bodily emissions, whether of perspiration, mucus, excrement, or creatures of any kind, are art.

This possibility is supported by one of the next entries after the eight questions, in which Joyce quotes a Greek phrase from Aristotle's *Physics* and comments "This phrase is falsely rendered as 'Art is an imitation of Nature.' Aristotle here does not define art: he says only 'Art imitates Nature' and means that the artistic process is like the natural process" (*OCPW* 104).[85] Joyce might be misrepresenting Aristotle here, as Aristotle

---

[83] "There are three conditions of art: the lyrical, the epical and the dramatic. That art is lyrical whereby the artist sets forth the image in immediate relation to himself; that art is epical whereby the artist sets forth the image in mediate relation to himself and to others; that art is dramatic whereby the artist sets forth the image in immediate relation to others." *OCPW* 103.

[84] Walter Pater, *Studies in the History of the Renaissance*, ed. Matthew Beaumont (Oxford, UK: Oxford University Press, 2010), 67.

[85] The citation is from *Physics*, II.8:199a: "In general, art either imitates the works of nature or completes that which nature is unable to bring to completion. If, then, that which is in accordance with art is *for something*, clearly so is that which is in accordance with nature ... If the swallow's act

argues that art resembles nature by being "for something"; Joyce rejects the standard understanding of Aristotle's use of the term *mimesis*. Joyce does not provide further commentary on what this resemblance means. In the previous pages, he cited Aristotle's *Metaphysics*: "Nature, it seems, is not a collection of unconnected episodes, like a bad tragedy."[86] Nature, it is implied here, proceeds coherently and concisely, like a good tragedy. It is in combination with the ideas from Pseudo-Aristotle that Joyce produces the notion that artistic creations are like natural creations, or that the relation between artistic and bodily expression is not one of resemblance but of identity.

That Joyce poses the fifth question in the negative sense indicates his reservations. Pseudo-Aristotle himself draws distinctions in the ownership of excreta, discriminating between bodily emissions: semen "proceeds from what is our own [. . .] but excretions and putrefactions do not belong to us but are different and foreign to our nature. For one has no right to attribute to the body everything which is in it, since tumors appear in it which they remove and cast out. Speaking generally, everything which is unnatural is foreign; and many of the things that grow in the body are unnatural."[87] Pseudo-Aristotle's question distinguishes between that which belongs to the body and that which is processed by it. We are not the waste products we excrete; they merely pass through us.[88] Pseudo-Aristotle retains enough of Aristotle to have a continuous self, an essential being that persists amidst the various flows of matter. Despite the multiplicitous, teeming vision of the body it presents, creation in *Problems* is emphatically autochthonous – the natural produces the similar: "for from what is not corrupted there springs only something of the same type as the seed" – even as the text figures the illicit and abundant fertility of waste,

---

in making its nest is both due to nature and *for something*, and the spider's in making its web, and the plant's in producing leaves for its fruit, and roots not up but down for nourishment, plainly this sort of cause is present in things which are and come to be due to nature." John Hermann Randall explains this as art "brings that which is possible in materials to a realization, and thus completes nature." Aristotle, *Physics*, trans. John Herman Randall, Jr. (New York: Columbia University Press, 1962), 275–76.

[86] NLI MS.36,639/02/A 6v.   [87] Aristotle, *Problems I*, IV:878a, 119.

[88] "Is it, in the first place, because in the former case it proceeds from what is our own but in the latter from something foreign, such as purgation or excretion? Speaking generally, no part of an animal creates another animal except the semen. What is harmful and bad has no kinship with any thing, no more has anything foreign; for to be foreign or different or evil is not the same thing as being part of it. Now excretions and putrefactions do not belong to us, but are different and foreign to our nature. For one has no right to attribute to the body everything which is in it, since tumors appear in it which they remove and cast out. Speaking generally, everything which is unnatural is foreign; and many of the things that grow in the body are unnatural." Ibid.

foreign matter.[89] As we will see in Chapter 6, these deviant conditions are affirmed in *Finnegans Wake* through Joyce's development of Alfred Jarry's *philosophie de merde*.

In a short entry on the day after the comment on Aristotle, Joyce presents a new definition: "Art is the human disposition of sensible or intelligible matter for an aesthetic end" (*OCPW* 104). As with the aesthetic essay and the passage on the imitation of nature by art, Joyce signs with a flourish and the date, March 28. This embellishment signals a return to a willingness to own and display the fruits of his thinking, unlike the list of questions that is unsigned, divergent, and exploratory. In composing this new definition, Joyce articulates the influence of Pseudo-Aristotle in terms taken from to a more recent philosopher who develops Aristotle's concept of the embodied intellect in new ways. Barry notes that Joyce's definition of art "condenses Chapter 3, 'The Conception of Artistic Beauty,' in *Introduction to Hegel's Philosophy of Fine Art*, trans. Bernard Bosanquet, 46–106" (*OCPW* 311, n. 2). The *Introduction* is Bosanquet's translation of the first five chapters of Hegel's lectures on aesthetics in the 1820s.[90] In his new definition Joyce more than condenses Chapter 3 of the *Introduction*: The statement "Art is the human disposition of sensible or intelligible matter for an aesthetic end" assembles verbal fragments from a single page of Bosanquet's translation of Hegel. The work of art is "no natural product, but brought to pass by means of human activity"; art is the "*conscious* production of an external object" that "contain[s] an end"; it is "made *for* man and, indeed, to be more or less borrowed from the sensuous and addressed to man's sense."[91]

Hegel's theory of art places strict limits on the role of the physical. Hegel's key concept is that art, as beauty, reveals to consciousness the "most comprehensive truths of the mind."[92] Crucially, for Hegel, the sensuous serves to embody truth but it is merely the *impression* of the sensuous: "the sensuous must be present in a work of art, yet it must only appear as surface and *semblance* of the sensuous [. . .], liberated from the apparatus of its merely material nature."[93] That which affects the

[89] Aristotle, *Problems I*, IV:878a, 121.
[90] Joyce makes note of Bosanquet's *History of Aesthetic* on the same page as he notes the references to beauty in Aristotle. In the *History*, Bosanquet not only devotes a chapter to Hegel but also presents Hegel's aesthetic theory as the *nec plus ultra* of the understanding of art and beauty.
[91] Bernard Bosanquet, *A History of Aesthetic* (New York: Cosimo, 2005), 30.
[92] G. W. F. Hegel, *Introductory Lectures on Aesthetics*, ed. Michael Inwood, trans. Bernard Bonsanquet (New York: Penguin, 2004), 9.
[93] Ibid., 43 (Hegel's italics).

senses is thus both necessary to art and potentially fatal to it as it, as Hegel suggests when he presents a hierarchy of the senses inherited from Aristotle and Aquinas: "For this reason the sensuous aspect of art only refers to the two *theoretical* senses of *sight* and *hearing*; while smell, taste, and feeling remain excluded from being sources of artistic enjoyment. For smell, taste and feeling have to do with matter as such, and with its immediate sensuous qualities; smell with material volatilization in air, taste with the material dissolution of substance, and feeling with warmth, coldness, smoothness, etc."[94] The beautiful therefore is utterly separate from that which can be physically ingested or consumed. Accordingly Hegel contrasts the aesthetic mode, in which the artist actively and skillfully shapes sensible material, with a "purely sensuous apprehension," which he understands as the most basic sensory relation to the world, in which the individual is a passive sensorium played upon by the environment and a mind that "is itself impelled in a correspondingly sensuous form to realize itself in the things, and relates itself to them as *desire*."[95] This basic relation to the world of things offers, ahead of its time, a cogent account of the sensory power of Paris as experienced by Joyce.

Hegel's aesthetics provides Joyce with the concepts and terms for his new definition of art but there is an important redundancy in Joyce's phrase "sensible or intelligible matter." For Aristotle, "The things which exist are either sensible or intelligible."[96] For Hegel, these terms are never aesthetic alternatives: art makes sensible matter intelligible. If we might think of sensible and intelligible matter as respectively matter and ideas, this opposition contradicts Hegel's stipulation that art must always take a material form. Why should we expect Joyce to be precise in reading Hegel? It seems likely that Joyce turns to him, as he turned to Aristotle and Aquinas, as a master of aesthetics – Hegel's was the most powerful account of art in the nineteenth century – but that he again adopts phrases rather than faithfully adheres to a theory. Joyce's definition, "Art is the human disposition of sensible or intelligible matter for an aesthetic end," does not prescribe a material world placed in service to the intellect but rather names the sensible and the intelligible as equal, alternative, and possibly coordinated media for artistic practice.

As a response to the fifth aesthetic question, the disposition of the sensible connotes an art of the body and what passes through it. Hegel himself entertains an idea of an art of the body when he writes: "it is not only external things that man treats in this way, but himself no less, i.e. his

---

[94] Ibid. [95] Ibid., 41 (Hegel's italics). [96] Aristotle, *De Anima*, III.8:431b, 210.

own natural form ... It is only among cultivated men that change of the figure, of behavior, and of every kind and mode of self-utterance emanates from spiritual education."[97] After reading Pseudo-Aristotle, Joyce is willing to imagine, even if he retreats from it, a radically different form of "self-utterance." In his negative answer to the fifth question, he distinguishes between natural and artistic processes, and between natural and aesthetic ends.[98] Yet Joyce's pleonastic definition suggests the possibility that natural processes can serve aesthetic ends. The term "human disposition" undoes the distinction between artificial and natural: the artificial is not only that which is made but also potentially that which is merely altered by the body. The new definition thus retains the possibility of a somatic art. This entails, however, a reconception of the embodiment of truth, the aesthetic end of art. Joyce achieves this reconception in a depiction of women on a Parisian street.

The Epiphany

In a short piece of prose poetry, Joyce stages the physical sensations of a Parisian boulevard. The piece is now known as Epiphany 33, after its placement in a collection of Joyce's short prose writings in *The Workshop of Daedalus* by Robert Scholes and Richard Kain. The editors note: "A Parisian scene of 1902–3: Joyce attempts here to get at the essence of prostitution. Parts of this Epiphany turn up improved almost beyond recognition in *Ulysses* (43/42). (See also *MBK* 254.) This and the following Epiphanies all postdate Stephen's departure for Paris and thus were not used in *Stephen Hero* and *Portrait*."[99]

> They pass in twos and threes amid the life of the boulevard, walking like
> people who have leisure in a place lit up for them. They are in the pastry

---

[97] Hegel, *Introductory Lectures on Aesthetics*, 36.

[98] Joyce proceeds, under the heading of "Answers," to apply the new definition systematically (although out of numerical order) to four of the questions in a manner that shuts down the strange promise of the aesthetic questions. He begins with the fifth question: "5. Excrements, children and lice are human products – human dispositions of sensible matter. The process by which they are produced is natural and non-artistic; their end is not an aesthetic end: therefore they are not works of art. 7. A photograph is a disposition of sensible matter and may be so disposed for an aesthetic end but it is not a human disposition of sensible matter. Therefore it is not a work of art. 6. The image of the cow made by a man hacking in fury at a block of wood is a human disposition of sensible matter but is not a human disposition of sensible matter for an aesthetic end. Therefore it is not a work of art. 8. Houses, clothing and furniture are not necessarily works of art. They are human dispositions of sensible matter. When they are so disposed for an aesthetic end they are works of art" (*OCPW* 26).

[99] Scholes and Kain, *Workshop of Daedalus*, 43.

cook's, chattering, crushing little fabrics of pastry, or seated silently at tables by the café door, or descending from carriages with a busy stir of garments soft as the voice of the adulterer. They pass in an air of perfumes: under the perfumes their bodies have a warm humid smell . . . . No man has loved them and they have not loved themselves: they have given nothing for all that has been given to them.[100]

If these women are prostitutes, although it is not clear that they are, the short piece of prose recasts the obscene figures of the postcard in highly controlled form. These women enjoy what the city has to offer: they eat pastries, sport beautiful clothing, wear perfume. Functioning adeptly within the city, they do what Joyce, in his letters and Costello's biography, fantasizes of doing but fails to do.

The Epiphany devises new means to register and respond to the claims made upon the body and the mind by Paris. As we will see, it combines Zola's meticulous observation with the highly crafted language of Baudelaire's prose poems. Yet, crucially, although it uses the structure of the prose poem to present a "genus," in Zola's taxonomic sense, it refuses descriptive specificity in its representation of smell. In doing so, it resists the pornographic and the didactic as the aesthetic essay mandates, yet more importantly, it engages with and counters the environment it represents.

In writing the Epiphany, Joyce devises a particularly modern fulfillment of what Hegel calls "the highest, the absolute need of man," the expression of "that which he is and, generally, whatever is."[101] If Hegel's language here inhabits a male, idealizing philosophical mode, in the Epiphany Joyce exposes and undercuts gender hierarchies, as he exposes and undercuts a privileging of thought over sensation. The piece mobilizes the physical to counter an environment in which the sensory and the sensual have been brought under the regime of exchange. Needless to say, this is a piece of writing that engages the mode of semblance, rather than a natural process, yet it represents the body itself as expressing a different kind of truth, and it gestures toward this truth with a material mark-making. In doing so, it answers Hegel's call to "bring before the mind's eye a quite other and richer content and ampler individual creations than any abstract formula can dictate."[102] If for Hegel "everything spiritual is better than anything natural," the exigencies of the setting with which Joyce engages lead him to reject this hierarchy.[103] In doing so, he draws on the very overwhelming of cognition by sensation, which he struggled against in the poem and in the aesthetic notes.

[100] Ibid.   [101] Hegel, *Introductory Lectures on Aesthetics*, 35.   [102] Ibid., 31.   [103] Ibid., 34.

It would be apt that in representing Paris Joyce would have recourse to one of its central topoi: the figure of the prostitute was considered in the late nineteenth century to be representative of the city. There are certainly some indications that these women might be prostitutes: The skirts that swish "soft as the voice of the adulterer" suggest that the women's circulation is associated with illicit sexual relations. The description of their "walking *like* people who have leisure in a place lit up for them" (my italics) presents their movement as something other than an idle presence on the street. The awkward formulation that situates the women "in a place lit up for them" recalls the restriction placed on Parisian "free prostitutes," those not domiciled in licensed houses but allowed to solicit in public. William Acton, in his 1870 study, notes the condition printed on the reverse of the *carte* that bore periodic stamps testifying to the health of these "public women" that they appear only in the illuminated street: "They are forbidden to practice the calling during daylight, or to walk in the thoroughfares until at least half an hour after the public lamps are lighted."[104]

Most strikingly, the piece refers to the smell of their bodies. Alain Corbin relays early, distasteful accounts of the perception of the odor of prostitutes: "Excessive indulgence in coitus provoked a positive overflow of sperm into the woman's humors, putrefied the liquids, and engendered an intolerable stench. That was how prostitutes became *putains*. Juvenal had already made this claim; at the beginning of the eighteenth century, J.-B. Silva tried to find a scientific justification for this belief which in itself was enough to cause prostitutes to be considered dangerous women."[105] It is not clear, however, that these women's "warm humid" smell is an intolerable stench. In contrast with this ambiguous characterization, the intimate odor, perfume, and skirts of the women are redeployed without any ambiguity in a stage direction of the "Circe" episode of *Ulysses*: Bloom follows Zoe into Bella Cohen's brothel, "draw[n] by the odour of her armpits, the vice of her painted eyes, the rustle of her slip in whose sinuous folds lurks the lion reek of all the male brutes that have possessed her" (*U* 15:2015–17).

If Joyce banishes all ambiguity in his depiction of the red-light district of Dublin, he retains it in his account of the Parisian boulevard. The women's unclear status contributes to the Epiphany's realistic depiction

---

[104] William Acton, *Prostitution Considered in Its Moral, Social and Sanitary Aspects, in London and Other Large Cities and Garrison Towns: With Proposals for the Control and Prevention of Its Attendant Evils* (London: J. Churchill, 1870), 105.

[105] Alan Corbin, *The Foul and the Fragrant* (Cambridge, MA: Harvard University Press, 1988), 46.

of the city; Charles Bernheimer notes the problem of the unidentifiability of prostitutes in nineteenth- and early twentieth-century Paris. Describing efforts to combat the perceived pervasiveness of sex workers and the threat of contamination associated with them by registering the women and confining them to designated brothels, he notes Alexandre Parent-Duchâtelet's "campaign to register clandestine prostitutes, the so-called *insoumises* [literally 'unsubdued'], suspected of being the most highly syphilitic group of all."[106] Yet a more threatening category was perceived to exist: "The only class of prostitute Parent considers more dangerous than the *insoumises* consists of women who have made the construction of their social facades coincide so perfectly with what is publicly acceptable that the police administration cannot legally arrest them. These are the women Parent calls *femmes galantes, femmes à parties,* and *femmes de spectacles et de théâtres.*"[107] Bernheimer quotes Parent: "in public places and meetings, nothing can distinguish them from the most proper women; but, when they want to, they know how to affect a tone, a countenance, and a glance that are significant to those who look for this particular class."[108]

Bernheimer writes of these women as commercial rebels, "semiotic experts [. . .] turning their bodies into refined instruments to attract capital." By subtle performance, this kind of prostitute "exempts valuable capital-producing labor from male supervision and, by determining the semiotics of her availability, gains control over the public–private difference that is the basis of social formation."[109] As we will see, this heightened capacity with signification becomes translated in Joyce's Paris Epiphany into an intimate smell that is simultaneously a commercialization of sensory perception and an undoing of commercial calculation.

In composing a literary representation of the most intimate odor of prostitutes, Joyce follows the taboo-breaking precedent set by Émile Zola.[110] Before his move to Paris, Joyce had been reading Zola: "When a visitor remarked a book of Zola's in the sitting room and remonstrated

---

[106] Bernheimer, *Figures of Ill-Repute*, 25.   [107] Ibid., 27.   [108] Ibid.   [109] Ibid., 27–28.

[110] Alain Corbin, writing of the particular nineteenth-century concern with women's odors, remarks: "But there is one strange silence, probably reflecting a taboo: these erotic writings make no allusion to the seductive power of vaginal odors except for a few references to menstruation." Corbin, *The Foul and the Fragrant*, 45–46. Elsewhere he comments: "Baudelaire's poetry reflected both the movement of fashion toward heavy scents and a new significance attaching to sexual venality. The attractions of moist flesh, the poet's taste for animal perfumes, and perhaps even more, his repulsion at lack of intimate hygiene, transposed the effluvia and scrupulous toilette of the brothel into the domestic sphere. The judges never forgave this transfer of the erotic scene" (205). Suggestive of but not actually representing the smells of prostitutes' bodies, these scents are often the means to achieve transcendence in the evocation of exotic places or ideal realms. See for example, "Un Hémisphère dans une chevelure."

with Joyce's parents for allowing him to read it, they replied, 'Jim can read what he likes'" (*JJ* 75).[111] Zola's first novel, *La Confession de Claude* (1865), held certain appeal for Joyce as a semi-autobiographical work about a young man who falls in love with a prostitute. *Nana* (1880), his novel about a fantastically successful prostitute, was one of the most notorious depictions of nineteenth-century Paris. Zola's representation of Nana could well have structured Joyce's perception of the city. It is, more importantly, a foil against which to read Joyce's Paris Epiphany.

From the beginning, Nana's smell is associated with her allure as a performer in the Théâtre des Variétiés. The spectacle of her body is accompanied by a calculus of exchange that harnesses the olfactory. Bordenave, the manager of the theater, which he insists on calling "mon bordel,"[112] declares of Nana: "Does a woman need to be able to sing and act? Don't be stupid, my boy ... Nana has something else, dammit, and something that takes the place of everything else. I scented it out, and it smells damnably strong in her, or else I've lost my sense of smell ... You'll see, you'll see; she'll only have to appear and the whole audience will be hanging out their tongues."[113] Nana's permeating smell, associated with her own sexual arousal,[114] indeed "takes the place of everything else," collapsing the drama in which she appears and overwhelming any personal, moral, or intellectual resistance. Smell in this context takes on a new dimension of threat associated not only with disease but also, less explicitly but powerfully, with an inescapable involvement in a burgeoning environment of irresistible wares.

Described as the "Golden Beast, as blind as brute force, whose very odor corrupted the world," Nana is the apogee of Zola's depiction of a Paris rendered newly sensual by commerce.[115] This mingling of the commercial with private female odors appears in Zola's earlier novel about Les Halles,

[111] George Moore later referred to Joyce as "a sort of Zola gone to seed" (*JJ* 529).
[112] Émile Zola, *Les Rougon-Macquart: Nana*, La Bibliothèque électronique du Québec Collection, vol. 56, version 1.2, 10, 11, 62.
[113] Zola, *Nana*, trans. George Holden (New York: Penguin, 1972), 22. "Est-ce qu'une femme a besoin de savoir jouer et chanter? Ah! mon petit, tu es trop bête ... Nana a autre chose, parbleu! et quelque chose qui remplace tout. Je l'ai flairée, c'est joliment fort chez elle, ou je n'ai plus que le nez d'un imbécile ... Tu verras, tu verras, elle n'a qu'à paraître, toute la salle tirera la langue." Zola, *Nana*, 12. The ellipses are Zola's.
[114] "Little by little Nana had taken possession of the audience, and now every man was under her spell. A wave of lust was flowing from her as from a bitch in heat, and it had spread further and further until it filled the whole house." *Nana*, trans. Holden, 45–46. "Peu à peu, Nana avait pris possession du public, et maintenant chaque homme la subissait. Le rut qui montait d'elle, ainsi que d'une bête en folie, s'était épandu toujours davantage, emplissant la salle." Zola, *Nana*, 57.
[115] *Nana*, trans. Holden, 223.

Le Ventre de Paris (1873), where the bodies of the female vendors merge with the goods they sell. La Sariette, the fruit seller, "was eating some redcurrants, and what amused her was the way she was smearing her face with them. Her lips were bright red, glistening with the juice from the fruit, as if they had been painted and perfumed with some middle eastern cosmetic. A smell of plums rose from her skirts. Her loosely tied shawl smelt of strawberries."[116] The scent that diffuses from her lower body suggests that her sexuality is inseparable from her commercial activity; strikingly, this merging with merchandise is erotic for La Sariette.

Priscilla Parkhurst Ferguson writes that *Le Ventre de Paris* represents the "sensualization of the city" brought about by the new availability of flowers and foodstuffs on the streets of Paris. Les Halles was "a city within a city already importantly defined for contemporaries by materiality."[117] Brian Nelson writes: "Zola's preparatory work for *The Belly of Paris* inaugurated the 'naturalist' method he used systematically in his subsequent novels. His representation of society is informed by a vast amount of first-hand observation, note-taking and research [. . .] The originality of *The Belly of Paris* [. . . lies in] Zola's stylistic experiment with description, in his desire to test the limits of descriptive discourse."[118] This descriptive mode aims to master the "intense sensory concentration of the modern market," according to Ferguson.[119] She observes that, while Claude Lantier, the visual artist featured in *Le ventre de Paris*, attempts and fails to paint Les Halles, Zola "accomplishes what none of the others can do – render les Halles as a whole" because he is "able to convey the experience of all the senses."[120]

Zola's response to the stimulating urban environment thus contrasts starkly with Baudelaire's performed surrender to the flux of sensations, figured as a "holy prostitution of the soul." If, for example, Nana's smell erodes all cultural and intellectual forms, Zola's description contains her. Zola puts characters like Nana to work. While he writes in the name of "scientific realism" – Zola's subtitle for Rougon-Macquart series is "The Natural and Social History of a Family under the Second Empire" – he devises titillating scenes, such as that of Nana on stage or La Sariette at the fruit stall, in which women are erotic commodities observed by voyeuristic characters and narrators.

---

[116] Emile Zola, *The Belly of Paris*, trans. and ed. Brian Nelson (Oxford, UK: Oxford University Press, 2007), 206.
[117] Priscilla Parkhurst Ferguson, "The Sensualization of Flânerie," *Dix-Neuf: Journal of the Society of Dix-Neuviémistes* 16.2 (2012), guest ed. Aimée Boutin, 211–23, at 216.
[118] Zola, *The Belly of Paris*, ed. Nelson, ix/x.   [119] Ferguson, "Sensualization of Flânerie," 216.
[120] Ibid., 220–21.

While Zola represents Nana's presence in a space of culture visited by all members of respectable society, Joyce locates the women beyond the brothel or the theater in what we might think of as a more quotidian and ubiquitous theater of consumption. Joyce's depiction of these women locates them on the street; but, if the women's circulation is a kind of work, it does not look like work but rather like consumption. In this sense, the women might be the targets of the young Joyce's resentment, the happy counterparts to his own pained abnegation of pleasure as a poet and an impoverished city-dweller, holding himself separate from urban offerings. Yet the short piece raises issues more significant than personal frustration and resentment; Joyce represents an immersive environment of consumption. The ambiguity of the women's status, and the absence of any other figures other than the men who have provided them with material goods, suggests that their behavior is representative of the permeation of Parisian life by transactional relations.

Joyce draws upon Zola's scientific method and Baudelaire's poetic prose in depicting the women on the boulevard, yet the substance of the women's smell is drawn from a more recent text, which Joyce purchased in Paris in 1903 at the recommendation of George Moore.[121] Edouard Dujardin's novel *Les Lauriers sont coupés* presents the first-person narrative of Daniel Prince, a wealthy Parisian dandy erotically entangled with an "adventuress."[122] Léa is not clearly a prostitute or a kept woman but lives through marketing the possibility of her sexual availability. Prince's most intimate encounter with her is an encounter with the odors of her body; it follows, in a more longwinded fashion, the same trajectory of increasing physical intimacy as that of the Paris Epiphany:

> A warm profusion of things is here, and my beloved near me; a warmth, little by little is growing in her motionless body; a fervor permeates her body and mine caressed by hers. If she is unhappy, why does she refuse to

---

[121] The "Ulysses for Experts" group have cast doubt on Ellmann's claim that Joyce bought the novel when he was en route to Tours to hear an opera concert with a Siamese companion, but they agree that Joyce bought and read Dujardin's book during that first spell in Paris, based on the presence in Joyce's Trieste library of Dujardin's *L'Initiation au péché et à l'amour* (Paris: Mercure de France, 1912) and *La Source du fleuve chrétien* (Paris: Mercure de France, 1906), as well as Joyce's 1917 letter to Dujardin: "J'écris pour vous prier de vouloir bien me dire où je pourrais obtenir un exemplaire de votre roman *Les Lauriers Sont Coupés*. J'avais l'édition originale mais elle se trouve maintenant en Autriche d'où, étant sujet britannique, il ne m'est pas très facile de la ravoir" (*SL* 229); "I write to ask you to tell me please where I could obtain a copy of your novel, *Les lauriers sont coupés*. I had the original edition but it is now in Austria from where, because I am a British subject, I cannot recover it easily," Ibid.

[122] Edouard Roditi, review of *The Bays Are Sere and Interior Monologue*, by Edouard Dujardin, trans. Anthony Suter, *James Joyce Quarterly* 28.4 (Summer 1991), 1012–16, at 1012.

start a new life? . . . How grateful, comforting this warmth of her body and her perfume! A mixture of scents, subtly keen, blended together, all she is with all she has, by her blended; the perfume flows from all her body, from her clothes, a waft from the braided tresses of her hair, from her lips as well. She is asleep, my love-dear, in my arms, and I am ravished by her fragrance, that blended, subtle, intimate scent with which she impregnates her body, infused with her body's own perfume; I can distinguish it, her own, her body's own perfume, from all those mingled essences of flowers; yes, a tang of womanhood, the woman's mystic emanation at her hour of love, when sensually, with what ecstasy, at her man's bidding, the dark passion of her flesh is effused in an embrace, in love's orgiastic madness, a pale swoon of terrible delight! What joy, that to enjoy, as joy indeed . . .! She moved her head, half turns away; have I pressed her too closely? In a dream she whispers.

– What's come over you? Oh, I'm so tired! What time is it?[123]

Léa thus deploys her odors as enticement to and substitute for sexual exchange; Prince, consuming them in a proxy sexual act, is ravished by them.

When Joyce redeploys the Paris Epiphany in *Ulysses* the totality of the Parisian environment of consumption is emphasized. As the editors of *The Workshop of Daedalus* point out, its motifs are reworked in Stephen's memories of Paris as he walks along the strand in "Proteus": "In Rodot's Yvonne and Madeleine newmake their tumbled beauties, shattering with gold teeth *chaussons* of pastry, their mouths yellowed with the *pus* of *flan breton*. Faces of Paris men go by, their wellpleased pleasers, curled

---

[123] Edouard Dujardin, *Les lauriers sont coupés* (Paris: Librairie de la Revue Indépendante, 1888), 96–97; "ici le tiède énombrement des choses, et ma sainte amie, mienne; une chaleur, peu à peu, de son corps immobile; au long de son corps, en mon corps, tout en ce long qu'elle effleure, une chaleur croît; pourquoi ne veut-elle point, si elle est malheureuse de sa vie, la changer, et avec moi vivre? que doucement tiède est cette chaleur, et de son corps quel parfum monte! ce parfum, quel est-il? un mélange de parfums; si subtil et qui pénètre; elle-même a mélangé ces essences; et ce parfum monte de toute sa chair, il monte de ses vêtements, il les traverse, et s'issut de son corps vêtu; et de ses cheveux ensemble noués l'haleine s'épand; aussi de ses lèvres; princièrement, de ses lèvres (oh les moqueuses charmeresses) s'expire l'odorante exhalaison; baiserai-je ces lèvres, de mes lèvres les aspirerais-je? elle dort, la pauvre, entre mes bras amis; et des parfums d'elle je me grise; ce parfum mêlé, subtil, intime, dont elle a parfumé son corps, c'est qu'il se mêle au parfum même de son corps, et c'est lui, son corporel parfum, en l'admirable intensité des essences de fleurs conjointes; l'odeur, oui, victorieuse en cette haleine; de sa féminité l'odeur, en ces bouffées; elle; et le profond mystère de son sexe dans l'amour; luxurieusement, oh démonialement, quand sous la maîtrise virile les puissances de chair se délivrent, en le baiser, ainsi l'acre et terrible et pâlissante fumée d'elle; ah mourir de cette joie!. . . Elle remue sa tête, se tourne un peu; l'ai-je serrée trop fortement; quelle excitation avais-je? elle me parle, mi dormante:
– Qu'avez-vous? ah, je suis lasse. . . quelle heure est-il?"

conquistadores" (*U* 3:212–15).[124] Gifford notes that "Rodot's is a patisserie at 9 Boulevard Saint-Michel (c. 1902)."[125] The girls share a liberated lifestyle, meeting after a night out to take breakfast in a café. Their "tumbled beauties" are not instances of an eternal, ideal beauty but rather a multiple, fallen, and rumpled kind. This beauty is reconstructed through consumption: the girls recover by treating themselves to pastries, inflicting upon the confections the disorder that was visited on them the night before. The women are linked to the baked goods in the shared yellow of gold teeth and pastry, and also, more unpleasantly, in the yellow of the custard which is referred to as "*pus.*" Pleasurable involvement in consumption is thus linked with contamination and putrefaction. Leisured consumption is the ingestion of rotten matter, chewing with teeth that consumption has already rotted and which themselves are partly purchased. This circularity is also a feature of the women's clients, who circulate on the street as "wellpleased pleasers," a play on fashionable French style of facial hair, *favoris*.[126] Yet, more literally, these clients are themselves active in giving sexual satisfaction. In this self-feeding, self-sustaining environment, pleasure is coincident with commerce.

Instead of a Stephen idly reminiscing on Sandymount Strand, the speaker of the Epiphany observes the Parisian environment of pleasure in the present tense. In this scene, the women's activities are motivated by a desire for goods, an involvement that causes social distinctions, individual identity, and desire for men to disappear. Observing this scene, the speaker asserts moral and intellectual independence. Referring to the women only in the third-person plural, the Epiphany presents multiple, quasi-identical subjects: "They pass in twos and threes amid the life of the boulevard, walking like people who have leisure in a place lit up for them. They are in the pastry cook's, chattering, crushing little fabrics of pastry, or seated silently at tables by the café door, or descending from carriages with a busy stir of garments soft as the voice of the adulterer." The description presents the typical behavior of this genus, employing verbs in the present tense,

---

[124] The lines follow a couple of sentences from Joyce's *Giacomo Joyce*, which are nominally altered to refer to Paris: "Trieste is waking rawly: raw sunlight over its huddled browntiled roofs, testudoform; a multitude of prostrate bugs await a national deliverance. Belluomo rises from the bed of his wife's lover's wife: the busy housewife is astir, sloe-eyed, a saucer of acetic acid in her hand ..." (9). The passage in "Proteus" introduces an appealing array of smells of food: "Paris rawly waking, crude sunlight on her lemon streets. Moist pith of farls of bread, the froggreen wormwood, her matin incense, court the air. Belluomo rises from the bed of his wife's lover's wife, the kerchiefed housewife is astir, a saucer of acetic acid in her hand. In Rodot's [...]" (*U* 3:209–12).

[125] Gifford and Seidman, *Ulysses Annotated*, 54.   [126] Ibid., 54.

many of which are in the form of present participles – walking, chattering, crushing, descending – that create a sense of activity without issue or conclusion, an ongoing busyness that accomplishes nothing but the satisfaction of immediate desires; this consumption contrasts with action in the sense of traditionally masculine deeds that would be represented in punctual verbs. The other verbs in this section are forms of the verbs to have and to be, used as copulas, or verbs that register an ineffectual coming and going: "pass," "walking," "descending." The description thus creates the sense of ongoing, teeming, disordered sensuality.

Yet in composing the Epiphany, Joyce draws on the rhetorical, syntactic and sonic patterns of Baudelaire's *prose poétique* to produce a static art. He adheres to a configuration that Graham Chesters characterizes as an "initially narrative-descriptive mode then general reflection based on repeated experience," exemplifying a "homocentric vision in which the meaninglessness of things is overcome" (needless to say, these devices are employed by Baudelaire to his own complex effects).[127] The series of parallel incipits, "They pass ... They are ... They pass," presents an orderly account of these movements. The sonic features add to the sense of controlled aural patterning: "cook's, chattering, crushing [. . .] or seated silently," as well as: "like people who have leisure in a place lit up." The description is followed by the final, highly ordered sentence, which presents two seemingly axiomatic statements: "No man has loved them and they have not loved themselves: they have given nothing for all that has been given to them." This sentence of commentary engages a very different verbal mode, taking the negative form of the present perfect that turns the unspecified time of "has loved" and "have given" into a time of continuous absence. It locks the women, present before the eyes of the spectator and the reader, into a separate temporality, which underlines the judgment being passed on them. The parallelism of "No man has loved them and they have not loved themselves" presents the women as a kind of affective dead end. After the colon, a chiasmus, "they have given nothing for all that has been given them," comes as an explanation of this lovelessness. The final passive phrase emphasizes the women's inactive reception of material bounty, folding them into a materialistic world where they possess "all" while giving "nothing."

In contrast to these individuals who are consumed by consumption, the Epiphany presents an unmoved observer who fixes the women in

---

[127] Graham Chesters, *Baudelaire and the Poetics of Craft* (Cambridge, UK: Cambridge University Press, 1988), 166, 168.

judgment. We could say that the piece thus forms an example of Joyce's definition of tragedy, as it "arrests us before whatever is grave in human fortunes and unites us with its secret cause [...] and with its human sufferer." Yet while the chiasmus decries the domination of human relations by material interests, it too operates according to the logic of exchange as it condemns the women for not carrying out their part of transactions, "they have given nothing for all that has been given them." As the speaker judges them, he fails to articulate an alternative set of spiritual or intellectual values. Moreover, if the women are subject to insight and judgment as objects of vision, the modality of smell erodes this mastery. In representing the smell, the Epiphany of course masters it as it offers it for the reader's reflection. As Hegel makes clear, to articulate a sensation is to achieve freedom from it, to enter into an ideal relation toward it: "Art, by means of its representations, while remaining within the sensuous sphere, delivers man at the same time from the power of the sensuous."[128] The smell is also mastered formally in the crafted language of the Epiphany, as its repetitions create a sense of an increasingly penetrative perception: "They pass in an air of perfumes: under the perfumes their bodies have a warm humid smell . . . ." Crucially, however, if the Epiphany offers a speaker who dominates the scene through objective observation and reflection, this smell implicates the speaker as an embodied presence, a condition that undermines objective observation. The modality of smell, as we saw in Aristotle, lacks the clarity possessed by sound and vision, a lack that comes with a failure to extract the essence from the matter of the thing smelled: "For man smells badly and perceives none of the smell-objects except the painful and pleasant ones, as his organ is not accurate."[129] This smell is neither clearly painful nor pleasant. The perceiving consciousness at the center of the Epiphany thus fails to move from sensation to knowledge. The "secret cause" asserted by this speaker is not supported by the phenomena. The conclusion, "they have given nothing for all that has been given them," is not even accurate: the women have at least shared their smell. The final judgment provides merely a formal, rhetorical closure to the ellipsis, a mere assertion of autonomous insight. In representing the women's smell, the Epiphany undermines the judgment its speaker offers.

In contrast to the reductive effects of Zola's naturalist description, Joyce's representation of the smell in the Paris Epiphany must be understood in terms of its suggestive imprecision. Unexpectedly, a piece that

---

[128] Hegel, *Introductory Lectures on Aesthetics*, 54.   [129] Aristotle, *De Anima*, II.9:421a, 180.

seems aimed to master a sensory experience amplifies it. This lack of precision is not a shortfall of language, an inability to match word to object, but a refusal to use language to identify: the simultaneously positive and negative connotations of the adjectives "warm humid" confute the responses of desire and loathing. If it might be understood to refuse to name the smell out of decorum, this vagueness however gestures toward a range of possibilities that is potentially more disturbing than a single reference would be. The women's "warm humid smell" might be the scent of alluring flesh, of unwashed skin, of female sexual arousal, of male sexual traces, and of the "scatological" possibilities of Joyce's postcard to Cosgrave. This ambiguity undoes the means by which the women's value in a sexual market might be assessed.

This resistance to judgment is signaled by the ellipsis that follows the reference to the smell. Needless to say, ellipses often mark the omission of words that are superfluous. In *Nana*, ellipses signal the theater manager's eager and unerring anticipation of the profit Nana will generate; to repeat some of his words quoted above, "Don't be stupid, my boy. . . . Nana has something else [. . .] I scented it out, and it smells damnably strong in her, or else I've lost my sense of smell. . . . You'll see, you'll see."[130] In the Epiphany, the series of five periods brings the piece to a halt, rupturing the verbal artifice; the ellipsis thus indicates the disruption of clear articulation, the interruption of the abstracted temporality of generalization by a present-tense of experience which goes undefined. This mark-making replaces language with a material gesture that mimics the smell's uncontainability, as its five points suggest the diffusion of olfactory particles, infiltrating the sensorium of the figure who has until now been a spectator. Instead of providing support for a reassertion of a subject's cognitive power over an object, or for a consumer's evaluation of a good, it marks a mingling of bodies that undermines the emphasis on transactions between individuals in the economy in which the women move. In a surprising turn following Joyce's attempts to balance his budget in the notebook, where calculation is a means to assert control, the Epiphany undoes calculative judgment through gesturing toward an indiscriminate and ineluctable permeation.[131]

---

[130] Zola, *Nana*, 22.

[131] While Joyce uses ellipses in several early epiphanies to suggest the rhythms of dialogue and of suspense, the Paris Epiphany deploys in a commercial environment the use of the ellipsis to suggest a troublingly open body in a manner that resembles Epiphany 19: "The hole we all have . . . . here." Scholes, *The Workshop of Daedalus*, 29.

The Epiphany thus stages the power of the body in urban modernity. The most primitive sense, neglected in favor of the visual with the adoption of erect posture according to Sigmund Freud, features forcefully in this scene of consumption. The women's smell is not independent of commerce: the power of their smell is amplified by this commercial setting, as the preexisting ambiguity of the natural body is amplified by the uncertainties of exchange. The Epiphany shows us how the senses are harnessed in an unprecedented way in the physical space of consumption. It represents the ability of these conditions of consumption to erode the boundaries of the self and the autonomous workings of thought. Yet it also shows the body as escaping definition in this environment precisely through its sensible appeal. In contrast to the sense of vision, the modality of smell undoes the appearance of a clear division of subject and object. The physical interconnectedness of smell dissolves the fiction of the separate individual through which economic transactions operate. The redolent body illustrates the power of the proximate senses to retort to a setting in which cognition has been annexed by transactional calculation.

The smell of the women makes evident a new truth within the sensorially overwhelming conditions of urban modernity. This truth precisely opposes the discourses that normally are used to represent the smell of women's bodies: repressive discourses of hygiene and of class that present vocabularies for odors as signs of bodies that are to be debarred from social space. The "warm humid smell" does not allow either a social classification or a medical categorization; instead, this vague registration of odor reveals the women to be individuals with whom the embodied speaker has sensory and affective relations. In contrast to the taxonomic conclusion, the elliptical smell makes perceptible the shared inhabitation of social and commercial space. Instead of a purportedly objective view from a distance of a fixed or rather fixable reality, the modality of smell indicates an involved, coextensive, passive material existence. If these perspectives have been associated, traditionally, with male and female epistemologies, the terms in which the smell is described reveal an embodiment that undercuts gender difference, as they merely evoke the physical conditions necessary for any smell to leave the surface of the skin: warmth and moisture.[132]

---

[132] Thus, if Peter Brooks writes of Zola's *Nana*, "Sight may be inadequate to account for another's body – may in particular be inadequate to describe that inwardness of the woman's body that the male viewer and narrator feel to be essential, both the sign of difference and the essence of the otherness that he would like to understand," in Joyce's Epiphany the modality of smell undoes the oppositions of male viewer and female object, of understanding and embodiment. Peter

With this material coexistence that subverts traditional gender binaries, the Paris Epiphany belies Stephen's statement, in the manuscript, *Stephen Hero*, Joyce wrote after returning from Paris, that the epiphanies are "sudden spiritual manifestation[s]" (*SH* 216). Stephen's definition has been generally accepted by critics, even though its terms are strikingly disparate in nature: "By an epiphany he meant a sudden spiritual manifestation, whether in the vulgarity of speech or of gesture or in a memorable phase of the mind itself" (*SH* 216). This quasi-miraculous emanation of the spiritual from the merely, or basely, physical, is the opposite of what the Paris Epiphany actually achieves: the victory of the physical over the spiritual. Joyce indeed represents this victory in language and in doing so engages with Hegel's call for an art that "bring[s] before the mind's eye a quite other and richer content and ampler individual creations than any abstract formula can dictate."[133] If the Epiphany presents a truth in Hegel's terms, and thus ultimately asserts an ideal relation to its scene, this truth is radically at odds with Hegel's notion of the human being as, essentially, spiritual. Joyce devises a particularly modern fulfillment of what Hegel calls "the highest, the absolute need of man," the expression of "that which he is and, generally, whatever is" as the Epiphany expresses an ineluctable and emancipating sensuality.[134]

At this moment of olfaction, the Paris Epiphany is better understood as a comedy rather than a tragedy, as defined in the aesthetic essay. It is joyful rather than grave, to use Joyce's terms again, in its fascination with the shared possession of the "substantial, general good" of embodiment and the ability of this physical being to undercut an environment that operates according to transactional exchange. As Joyce indicates the potential of sensation that resists intellectual containment, he stages a version of what Baudelaire's speaker announces: "toutes ces choses pensent par moi, ou je pense par elles," "All these things think through me. Or I through them."[135] No longer objects, no longer separate, the women are joined with the speaker in their expression of a physical truth.

This sentient thinking is dependent upon the women's flaunting of their smell. Deliberately deploying the expression of their bodies, they are *femmes galantes* who evade identification, or women engaged in physical artistry, presenting a contemporary affirmative response to the Pseudo-

---

Brooks, *Body Work: Objects of Desire in Modern Narrative* (Boston, MA: Harvard University Press, 1993), 161.
[133] Hegel, *Introductory Lectures on Aesthetics*, 31.   [134] Ibid., 35.
[135] Baudelaire, *Baudelaire: Œuvres Complètes*, 5.

Aristotelian fifth aesthetic question. The Epiphany identifies with this practice that breaches decorum, as it constructs and ironizes a speaker who would objectify them. Complicit with the women in their unidentifiability as it refuses to specify their smell, the Epiphany presents its own unreadable materiality in the ellipsis. The Epiphany's alternate, opposed, and almost simultaneous gestures of judgment and identification present it too as capable of transformation.

Over the course of these four months in Paris, Joyce's aesthetic aims have shifted profoundly: from an imperative to control, define, and exclude, seen both in the poem "I hear the noise of many waters" and in the essay on aesthetics, to a curiosity about the aesthetic potential of the body in the Epiphany. With this shift, Joyce moves from a writing that is predicated upon the refusal of the urban environment to one that registers, contends with and avails of its effects. In the physical co-being that the Epiphany evokes, there is something like the sensual dissolution of Verlaine's personae, but it is devised in opposition to an environment of commercialized consumption. This depiction of porous boundaries has some of the transformative energies associated by Zola with the commodified woman but, instead of the spectacle of a female object for a male voyeur, the Epiphany undercuts its own observation with an identification of the physical interrelation of its persons. While Baudelaire identifies with the prostitute in a sacred openness to the urban crowd as he artfully stages an overwhelmed persona, Joyce redeploys this openness in opposition to materialistic calculation. If gender is the salient feature of the transactional relations associated with the boulevard, the material nature of the body becomes the means by which the objectification of bodies is resisted; intimate physical conditions undermine the identifying features of transaction: male and female, subject and object.

As this prose poem registers the sensual experience of the city street, an ironic distance is born. Joyce stages a narrator who fails to maintain the independence required to judge the world he encounters, and concomitantly, a distance opens between knowing and sensing, between conscious discrimination and aesthetic experience. As we will see, this irony is given fuller expression in *Portrait*, in which the pressures of sensual desire and the aesthetic potential of a sensory engagement that eludes conscious control form the poles of Joyce's aesthetic exploration. The encounter between a male sensorium and a female source of sensory stimulation will recur, in evolving form, in Joyce's work, as he progressively develops the potential of sensual encounters in a series of new narrative forms. Beginning with the Paris Epiphany, it is the means of an interrelation achieved despite and amidst material concerns.

CHAPTER 2

Paris Recognized: Stephen Hero and Portrait

After rushing away from Paris in 1903, Joyce intended to return with Nora Barnacle in 1904. Before their elopement, he wrote to her: "I do not like the notion of London and I am sure you won't like it either but it is on the road to Paris and it is perhaps better than Amsterdam. [. . .] Perhaps I may be sent straight to Paris, I hope I will. [. . .] Sometimes this adventure of ours strikes me as almost amusing. It amuses me to think of the effect the news of it will cause in my circle. However, when we are once safely settled in the Latin quarter they can talk as much as they like" (*Letters II*, 57). Despite Joyce's fantasy of a bohemian life on the *rive gauche*, the availability of postings for Joyce as a language teacher led the couple on an unexpected, alternative trajectory from Dublin to Pola to Trieste. However, as this chapter aims to demonstrate, the importance of Paris endured for Joyce. His encounter with the French metropole shaped his subsequent perception of Dublin, allowing him to recognize in his native city the pervasive distortion of social relations by commodity capitalism. He continued to develop the aesthetic project he conceived in Paris, although he concealed its Parisian origins.[1]

On his return to Dublin in 1903, Joyce began a semi-autobiographical novel he titled *Stephen Hero*. He continued to work on it after his move to Trieste in 1904. In 1907, he began to rework the material as *A Portrait of the Artist as a Young Man*, bringing it to completion in 1914.[2] The sprawling manuscript of *Stephen Hero* is generally passed over by critics,

---

[1] With his 1904 poem, "The Holy Office," Joyce blasts the Dublin literary establishment with a "Katharsis-Purgative" conceived from his Parisian reading of Aristotle and Pseudo-Aristotle. Joyce, *Poems and Exiles*, 103. In *Portrait*, Joyce presents his Parisian aesthetic theory and questions as the work of Stephen in Dublin: "I have a book at home, said Stephen [to Lynch], in which I have written down questions which are more amusing than yours were. In finding the answers to them I found the theory of aesthetic which I am trying to explain" (*P* 180).

[2] Hans Walter Gabler, "The Genesis of *A Portrait of the Artist as a Young Man*," in *Critical Essays on James Joyce's A Portrait of the Artist as a Young Man*, eds. Philip Brady and James R. Carens (New York: G. K. Hall, 1998), 83.

who turn instead to the concise, controlled, and completed *Portrait*. The further Joyce progressed through *Stephen Hero* and *Portrait* and the closer Stephen Dedalus comes to setting off for Paris, the further Joyce himself was from his own time there. But because of this *Stephen Hero* helps us to understand *Portrait*'s fundamental concerns and to see how Joyce developed the aesthetic possibilities he conceived in Paris. Read together, *Stephen Hero* and *Portrait* reveal the evolution of Joyce's conception of art as he struggles with the deformation of intimate relations by the forces of the modern city.

If the represented scene is now Dublin, Joyce views it through the lens of Paris. In a 1904 letter to Nora, shortly after their momentous encounter of June 16, Joyce describes Grafton Street:

> The street was full of a life which I have poured a stream of my youth upon. While I stood there I thought of a few sentences I wrote some years ago when I lived in Paris – these sentences which follow – 'They pass in twos and threes amid the life of the boulevard, walking like people who have leisure in a place lit up for them. They are in the pastry cook's, chattering, crushing little fabrics of pastry, or seated silently at tables by the café door, or descending from carriages with a busy stir of garments soft as the voice of the adulterer. They pass in an air of perfumes. Under the perfumes their bodies have a warm humid smell' – While I was repeating this to myself I knew that that life was still waiting for me if I chose to enter it. It could not give me perhaps the intoxication it had once given but it was still there and now that I am wiser and more controllable it was safe. It would ask no questions, expect nothing from me but a few moments of my life, leaving the rest free, and would promise me pleasure in return. (*Letters II*, 49)

As Joyce repeats his description of Paris in Dublin, he recognizes the vitality of the boulevard on the streets of the Irish capital. Only, he writes, his increased maturity prevents his loss of control in the "intoxication" that the city offers. Paris, then, reveals Dublin to be an erotically charged modern city.[3] In quoting the Paris Epiphany to Nora, Joyce omits its final line, withholding the Epiphany's judgment of the women as motivated only by material gain; the pleasures of the street, he writes here, are bought

---

[3] Jean-Michel Rabaté sees Joyce as identifying the vitality of Paris in Dublin and Trieste: "The sensuous pleasure taken in contemplation of the night crowds on Grafton Street has to be relayed by an even more sensual awareness of these Parisian prostitutes [...] the glitter of Dublin's most fashionable area is transformed into a more salacious Parisian evocation, which later [in *Giacomo Joyce*] encompasses Trieste." Jean-Michel Rabaté, "Joyce the Parisian," *Cambridge Companion to James Joyce*, ed. Derek Attridge (Cambridge, UK: Cambridge University Press, 2004), 50–51.

with time rather than money.[4] Yet in *Stephen Hero* and *Portrait,* Joyce explores the distortion of intimate relations by exchange. The transactional relations staged in the Paris Epiphany are central to relations between the sexes in Dublin, not only in prostitution but also in bourgeois society. In *Stephen Hero,* Stephen explicitly describes his relationship with the respectable Emma Clery as tending toward the sale of a "corporeal asset." This chapter traces how, in a series of encounters between Stephen and Emma, Joyce explores the enmeshment in transaction of the senses and desire, the central problem with which he grappled in his Paris writings. It shows how these encounters culminate in the final chapter of *Portrait* when Stephen and Emma cross paths in the colonnade of the museum library and their bodily sensations and expressions become the occasion and medium of an aesthetic exchange.

  Portrait's ostensible aesthetic achievement is the theory that Stephen, in the book's final chapter, delivers in a formal tone to his friend, Lynch. Based on the aesthetic essay Joyce composed in Paris, Stephen's theory defines art as static rather than kinetic and as invested in a beauty of essences, characterized via Aquinas by integrity, harmony, and radiance. Yet, instead of Stephen's progressive intellectual mastery of the senses leading to the crowning achievement of the aesthetic theory (as most critics have assumed), *Portrait* presents the humbling of his mind in a new interpersonal aesthetic relation. As I will attempt to show, even though Stephen rehearses this aesthetics of stasis in both *Stephen Hero* and *Portrait,* the Parisian questions are central to a somatic art in which he engages at the end of *Portrait.* This alternative relation contrasts profoundly with Aquinas's requirements for beauty. It concerns neither the spirit nor an essential being but the body and its excretions in an aesthetic practice associated with the derogated senses of touch, smell, and taste, and motivated by affects banned in Joyce's aesthetic theory. Thus Stephen, who critics often note barely writes anything, is actually engaged in innovative artistic work.[5] It is a desublimated and unconscious aesthetic

---

[4] In his letter to Nora, Joyce describes their relationship as sacred, "I thought of all this and without regret I rejected it. It was useless for me; it could not give me what I wanted. You have misunderstood, I think, some passages in a letter I wrote you and I have noticed a certain shyness in your manner as if the recollection of that night troubled you. I however consider it a kind of sacrament and the recollection of it fills me with amazed joy" (*Letters II,* 49).

[5] In *Ulysses,* Stephen mocks his own writerly ambitions, "Books you were going to write with letters for titles. Have you read his F? O yes, but I prefer Q. Yes, but W is wonderful. O yes, W. Remember your epiphanies written on green oval leaves, deeply deep" (*U* 3:139–41).

practice that is embodied in the moment and, crucially, in collaboration with Emma.

This somatic art suggests a new answer to an old problem in *Portrait*. Readers have often observed that Stephen is ironized in *Portrait*, "especially in the passages on aesthetics" as James Naremore observes.[6] Irony "is the tone of the last chapters, even to the point when Stephen bravely, flamboyantly utters his famous artistic manifesto."[7] Understanding exactly what this new answer is requires looking beyond *Portrait*'s explicit aesthetics of control and containment, what Ezra Pound celebrates as "a clear hardness, accepting all things, defining all things in clean outline."[8] "We can be thankful for clear, hard surfaces," Pound continues, "for an escape from the softness and mushiness of the neo-symbolist movement, and from the fruitier school of the neo-realists, and in no less a degree from the phantasists who are the most trivial and most wearying of the lot."[9] Pound associates this macho hardness with the influence of Flaubert, from whom, he writes, Joyce adopts the dictum of impersonality. In his preoccupation with masculine solidity, Pound overlooks the embodied aesthetics of *Portrait* that, at times subtle, at times crass, shares the interests of the troublingly soft and mushy poetry of Arthur Rimbaud. As the scene in the colonnade engages the faculties of smell and excretion, Joyce draws on Rimbaud's synaesthetic poem, "Voyelles," to devise a somatic aesthetic in which conscious articulation is replaced by the unconscious expression of unconsciously processed material. Joyce thus stages a performance art, in which the artwork is supplanted by an ephemeral excretion. This performance of a kinetic and physical relation forms the beginnings of a sentient thinking.[10]

---

[6] James Naremore, "Style as Meaning in 'A Portrait of the Artist,'" *James Joyce Quarterly* 4.4 (Summer 1967), 331–42, at 338.

[7] Ibid., 334.

[8] Ezra Pound, "The Non-Existence of Ireland," *The New Age* XVI.17 (25 February 1915), reprinted in *Pound/Joyce: The Letters of Ezra Pound to James Joyce, with Pound's Critical Essays and Articles about Joyce* (New York: New Directions, 1970), 32.

[9] Ibid., 33.

[10] In tracing this trajectory from *Stephen Hero* to *Portrait*, this chapter does not discuss *Dubliners*. In an essay forthcoming in *The New Joyce Studies: Twenty-First Century Critical Revisions* (Cambridge, UK: Cambridge University Press, 2021) I argue that in *Dubliners* Joyce draws on the naturalist writings of Zola and Henri René Albert Guy de Maupassant to present a social world ensnared in materialistic concerns. If the senses feature in these stories, they do not lead to a realization of a shared and incalculable embodiment but rather exemplify individuals' immersion in an oppressive materiality and the trammeling of their thoughts by calculation.

Parisian Stephen

One of the final passages of *Portrait* presents Stephen's dream of departure for Paris:

> The spell of arms and voices: the white arms of roads, their promise of close embraces and the black arms of tall ships that stand out against the moon, their tale of distant nations. They are held out to say: We are alone. Come. And the voices say with them: We are your kinsmen. And the air is thick with their company as they call to me, their kinsman, making ready to go, shaking the wings of their exultant and terrible youth. (*P* 213)

Joyce inserted the short piece, originally an undated epiphany, into the manuscript of *Stephen Hero*, writing "Departure for Paris" in blue crayon underneath it.[11] Scholes and Kain write: "This is a crucial Epiphany. In it we see Joyce beginning to clothe himself in the Daedalian myth."[12] Rather than the Greek myth, however, the prose fragment evokes a band of rebellious angels taking flight, in joyous abandonment of the native and respectable, an association of bold individualists like the *poètes maudits* whose influence attracted Joyce to Paris. This foreign, diabolical affiliation suggests the Luciferian *non serviam* that is so crucial a mode for Stephen Dedalus.

Stephen in *Stephen Hero* and *Portrait* is already a post-Parisian figure. David Weir remarks on Stephen's Parisian roots: "Stephen Hero, we know, has read Rimbaud, and while Stephen Dedalus may or may not have, Joyce did endow his character with certain traits that recall those of the major nineteenth-century French poets. Stephen has the lice of Baudelaire and the wanderlust of Rimbaud; his concept of the artist as 'invisible, refined out of existence' is Mallarmeán, but his own verses turn out to be vaguely Verlainean. [. . .] the character of Stephen Dedalus owes a great deal to the *general* turn-of-the-century image of the artist as a rebel in conflict with society, but this image is in turn one which the legendary reputations of Baudelaire and Rimbaud did much to foster."[13] These French traces have also been detected by other critics. Scarlett Baron has shown that Stephen's concept of the artist has more to do with Flaubert

---

[11] James Joyce, *Stephen Hero*, ed. Theodore Spencer, rev. John J. Slocum and Herbert Cahoon (London: Paladin, 1991), 240. Hence cited in abbreviated form as *SH*.

[12] Scholes and Kain, *Workshop of Daedalus*, 40.

[13] David Weir, "Stephen Dedalus: Rimbaud or Baudelaire?" *James Joyce Quarterly* 18.1 (Fall 1980), 87–91, at 87.

than with Mallarmé.[14] Ellmann remarks: "What other hero in the novel has, like Stephen Dedalus, lice? Yet the lice are Baudelairean lice, clinging to the soul's as well as the body's integument" (*JJ* 6).

I would like to add another source to this list. In embodying Joyce's Parisian discovery of the power of matter to counter the concepts of the spirit, Stephen echoes the persona who speaks in the final section of Rimbaud's *Une Saison en enfer*: "I who called myself magus or angel, free from all morality, I am thrown back to earth, with a duty to find, and rough reality to embrace! Peasant!"[15] Stephen's contradictory Dedalian status of soaring soul and fallen body gives voice to Joyce's struggle to form an aesthetic that responds to the material world, having initially eschewed it. As we will see, Joyce uses Rimbaud's poetry in conceiving Stephen's somatic art, produced not from a lofty spirit or a corrupted moral being, as Baudelaire's lice who are bred from hypocritical remorse, but from the waste that passes through the body.

This somatic art is subtle and interactive. Contrastingly, on the strand at the end of "Proteus," Stephen engages in an art of excretion that is explicit and solitary. Having reminisced on his Paris experiences in a figurative street where the shells are "Wild sea money" (*U* 3:19),[16] Stephen releases and orders the effluents of his body in exhalation, micturition, and rhinotillexis, mimicking with nonverbal vocalization the wind, the tide, and seaspawn and seawrack: "His mouth moulded issuing breath, unspeeched: ooeeehah: roar of cataractic planets, globed, blazing, roaring, wayawayawayawayaway" (*U* 3: 402–04); "Better get this job over quick. Listen: a fourworded wavespeech: seesoo, hrss, rsseeiss, ooos. Vehement breath of waters amid seasnakes, rearing horses, rocks. [. . .] And, spent, its speech ceases." (*U* 3:456–59); "He laid the dry snot picked from his nostril on a ledge of rock, carefully. For the rest let look who will" (*U* 3:500–01).[17]

---

[14] Scarlett Baron, '*Strandentwining Cable*': *Joyce, Flaubert, and Intertextuality* (Oxford, UK: Oxford University Press, 2012).

[15] Rimbaud, *Rimbaud: Complete Works, Selected Letters*, trans. Wallace Fowlie (Chicago, IL: University of Chicago Press, 1966), 209. "Moi! moi qui me suis dit mage ou ange, dispensé de toute morale, je suis rendu au sol, avec un devoir à chercher, et la réalité rugueuse à étreindre! Paysan!" (208)

[16] Stephen recalls reading in Paris Aristotle's *De Sensu* and *De Anima*, which Joyce studied there in 1903. He remembers drinking in "the bar MacMahon" with the socialist Patrice Egan, son of Kevin Egan, the Fenian expatriate (based on Joseph Casey and his son, with whom Joyce became friends in 1902). Stephen's memories of his behavior in Paris are somewhat self-mocking: "My Latin quarter hat. God, we must simply dress the character. [. . .] Just say in the most natural tone: when I was in Paris, *boul'Mich'*, I used to" (*U* 3:174–79).

[17] This last action is the cleverest of the three. Stephen's comment comes from Ecclesiastical Law of the Church of England: Number 37 of the tenth-century *Elfric's Canons* requires, on Good Friday, that housel, or Eucharists, consecrated on Thursday are to be mixed with "unhallowed wine

It might seem that it is only in solitude in this alternative environment, divorced from the modern urban context, that Stephen is able to embrace a material flux. In a Trieste notebook from 1919–1920, Joyce notes of Stephen: "He dreaded the sea that would drown his body and the crowd that would drown his soul."[18] But if Stephen aligns sea and street in "Proteus" as he replies in the affirmative to the fifth aesthetic question, there is already a more subtle and important moment of physical artistry in *Portrait*, one in which he is involved in an interaction that counters, if not the crowds, the underlying social conditions of the city.

Emma's Body as a Corporal Asset

In *Stephen Hero*, in harsh terms that evoke the speaker's judgment of the women on the boulevard in the Paris Epiphany, Stephen registers the smell of Emma's body as an empty lure: "He submitted himself to the perfumes of her body and strove to locate a spiritual principle in it: but he could not" (*SH* 161). When he encounters her on the street a little later, he responds to her appeal offensively, by jangling the money in his pocket: "She leaned a little more towards him and the same expression of tender solicitude appeared in her eyes. The warmth of her body seemed to flow into his and without a moment's hesitation he put his hand into his pocket and began to finger out his coins. – I must be going in, she said. – Good night, said Stephen smiling" (*SH* 193). Stephen's gesture of readiness to purchase shatters her growing tenderness toward him. Yet if his gesture implies that Emma is offering herself for sale, it is a defensive response to the threat her genuine appeal poses to his autonomy. He calls on his sovereignty as a consumer to assert his physical and spiritual independence.

In a subsequent conversation with Lynch, Stephen expresses his belief that women in Dublin society use their bodies as objects of trade. His logic evokes and extends the materialistic logic of the Paris Epiphany to all of Ireland: "A woman's body is a corporal asset of the State: if she traffic with it she must sell it either as a harlot or as a married woman or as a working

---

mingled with water," prayed over and then "Let him put a part of the housel into the chalice, as it is however usual; then let him go silently to the housel; and for the rest let look who will" (John Johnson, *A Collection of All the Ecclesiastical Laws, Canons, Answers, or Rescripts, with Other Memorials Concerning the Government, Discipline and Worship of the Church of England* (London: Robert Knaplock and Samuel Ballard, 1720), 404). The canon dismisses the question of what happens to the rest of the consecrated hosts, effacing the possibility of the body of Christ as waste material. In "Proteus" the waste is Stephen's body, walking away, in a corrupted ritual.

[18] Scholes and Kain, *Workshop of Dedalus*, 95.

celibate or as a mistress. But a woman is (incidentally) a human being: and a human being's love and freedom is not a spiritual asset of the State [...] The woman in the black straw hat gave something before she sold her body to the State; Emma will sell herself to the state but give nothing" (*SH* 207). The "State" here would seem to be the institutions of prostitution, marriage, and religious orders, although prostitution was not legal in Ireland, and the notion that in marriage women sell their bodies to the State seems nonsensical. Stephen's quasi-economic pronouncement ignores the material vulnerability of the women of Dublin, accusing them of self-objectification.

If Stephen is not entirely to be relied upon here as an observer of Dublin sociology, Emma Clery's name nonetheless signals an association with commerce: Clery's was one of Dublin's largest department stores. Opened in 1853 by McSwiney, Delany and Co. on Sackville Street, Dublin's main street (now O'Connell Street), it was bought in 1883 by Michael J. Clery. Initially named the "Palatial Mart," the store was an expression of a vast commercial ambition. As Joseph Connell notes: "Housed in a purpose-built building, the department store was designed to eclipse European outlets of the time."[19] Clery's supports a commercialized erotics in *Ulysses*: in the effort to increase her appeal, Gerty McDowell buys a fashionable ribbon for her "coquettish little love of a hat" at Clery's (*U* 13:156).[20] Emma has also the first name of one of nineteenth-century French literature's most famous female consumers of love and commodities.

Against the transactional nature of sexual relations between men and women, Stephen proposes the ideals of love and freedom, "spiritual" modes of relation that cannot be sold: "Love gives and freedom takes" (*SH* 207). If there were any doubt that Joyce's text ironizes Stephen's lopsided and misogynistic account of women's sexuality, Stephen explicitly collapses these ideals in a statement that combines an attitude of sexual acquisitiveness with a gender-based division of labor: "I like a woman to give herself. I like to receive" (*SH* 207). Stephen here declares, to the louche Lynch, his desire to be a consumer released from the imperative to pay, a freedom that ignores, or even takes advantage of, the stark gender asymmetries of turn-of-the-century Dublin. The "I" of this maxim is

---

[19] Joseph E. A. Connell, *Dublin Rising: 1916* (Dublin: Worldwell Limited, 2015).

[20] Gerty's own lack of success on the marriage market is given allegorical form as she reflects: "at last she found what she wanted at Clery's summer sales, the very it, slightly shopsoiled but you would never notice, seven fingers two and a penny" (*U* 13:159–61).

fundamentally compromised: an individuality founded on self-regarding entitlement and predicated on the category of woman as a generic object. This self-regard is intensified in the second sentence of the statement, which even lacks an object, let alone another subjectivity: "I like to receive."

The seemingly rapacious Stephen, however, has recently made an unsuccessful bid to receive freely Emma's love: "Just to live one night together, Emma, and then to say goodbye in the morning and never to see each other again!" (*SH* 203). Emma's tearful response indicates the text's sympathy for her disappointed hopes and the social cost for her of forsaking conventional social roles. In the absence of marriage or a night of passion, when Stephen and Emma next cross paths, courtesy masks frozen antagonism. Emma's politeness to Cranly shuns Stephen:

> One evening during the examinations Stephen was talking to Cranly under the arcade of the University when Emma passed them. Cranly raised his ancient straw hat (which he had once more resurrected) and Stephen followed suit. In reply she bowed very politely across Stephen at his friend. Cranly replaced his hat and proceeded to meditate in the shade of it for a few minutes.
> – Why did she do that? he said.
> – An invitation, perhaps, said Stephen. (*SH* 220)

Stephen and Emma's relationship thus ends in an impasse in *Stephen Hero*. Stephen's refusal of exchange offers no means of transcending it. As we will see, the configuration of bodies in this cold encounter prefigures the scene in the library colonnade in the final chapter of *Portrait*: male friends stand in the entry space of a center of learning through which a woman passes. These bodies, in contrast to those in the library colonnade, remain politely within their bounds.

The Dark Flows of the Red-Light District

In *Portrait*, schoolboy Stephen's desire is prompted by Emma's enticing gestures and beautiful clothing; her allure is figured as a lively sea that carries him, passive and joyful: "His heart danced upon her movements like a cork upon a tide. He heard what her eyes said to him from beneath their cowl and knew that in some dim past, whether in life or in revery, he had heard their tale before. He saw her urge her vanities, her fine dress and sash and long black stockings, and knew that he had yielded to them a thousand times" (*P* 58). Despite this, or rather because of this, Stephen refuses to yield. The next day, he writes a poem about "E. C.," which is described in the text as a somewhat clichéd abstraction that feeds Stephen's narcissism: "There remained no trace of the tram itself nor of the trammen nor of the horses: nor did he and she appear vividly. The verses told only of the night and the balmy breeze and the maiden lustre of the moon [. . .] he went into his mother's bedroom and gazed at his face for a long time in the mirror of her dressingtable" (*P* 59). Later, after he has become a client of the brothels of Mecklenburg Street, Stephen hears Fr. Arnall's hellfire sermon and feels shame at how he has used her in fantasy.[21] His only other actual exchange with her in *Portrait* arrives in its final chapter; it comes as the culmination of and the solution to Stephen's sensual encounters with commodified female bodies.

In *Portrait*, alluring female odors are first associated with the prostitutes who attract Stephen as a client: "He would pass by them calmly waiting for a sudden movement of his own will or a sudden call to his sinloving soul from their soft perfumed flesh" (*P* 86). This sensory appeal is spatialized and abstracted the first time Stephen wanders, unknowingly, into the brothel district. The passage presents a brutal intensification of the lure Stephen associated with Emma's body in *Stephen Hero*, expanding its scale from that of a personal encounter to the "dark presence" of a threateningly invasive environment:

> His blood was in revolt. He wandered up and down the dark slimy streets peering into the gloom of lanes and doorways, listening eagerly for any sound. He moaned to himself like some baffled prowling beast. He wanted to sin with another of his kind, to force another being to sin with him and to exult with her in sin. He felt some dark presence moving irresistibly upon him from the darkness, a presence subtle and murmurous as a flood filling him wholly with itself. Its murmur besieged his ears like the murmur of some multitude in sleep; its subtle streams penetrated his being. His hands clenched convulsively and his teeth set together as he suffered the agony of its penetration. He stretched out his arms in the street to hold fast the frail swooning form that eluded him and incited him: and the cry that he had strangled for so long in his throat issued from his lips. It broke from him like a wail of despair from a hell of sufferers and died in a wail of furious entreaty, a cry for an iniquitous abandonment, a cry which was but the echo of an obscene scrawl which he had read on the oozing wall of a urinal. (*P* 83–84)

---

[21] "The image of Emma appeared before him, and under her eyes, the flood of shame rushed forth anew from his heart. If she knew to what his mind had subjected her or how his brutelike lust had torn and trampled upon her innocence! Was that boyish love? Was that chivalry? Was that poetry? The sordid details of his orgies stank under his very nostrils" (*P* 97).

A vivid and even excessive figurality presents the instrumentalization of Stephen's desire in the red-light district, a social context regulated by exchange. His decision to use prostitutes is elided in this metaphorical language of physical interpellation. As Stephen is invaded by a "presence subtle and murmurous as a flood filling him wholly with itself," this experience is a heightened version of the effects of Emma's body upon his in *Stephen Hero,* where "the warmth of her body seemed to flow into his." These figural flows revive the language of Joyce's Paris poem, "All day I hear the voice of many waters." In contrast to the poem's speaker, who flies above the noisy waters that extinguish thought, Stephen submits to the "subtle streams," becoming the agonized observer of obscure forces flowing through his body and mind. In this "penetration," the harnessing of Stephen's desire places him in a traditionally female role. His response is a passive, involuntary one: he becomes a conduit for the lowest language of the city, the lewd graffiti of a public bathroom. In a meeting of sensation and physicalized expression, which will be reworked in the colonnade scene, "the dark presence moving irresistibly upon him from the darkness" is met by the "inarticulate cries and the unspoken brutal words rush[ing] forth from his brain."

Stephen's wandering into the brothel district occurs immediately after his failure to meet his emotional and relational needs with socially sanctioned material means. Following his receipt of prize money for an exhibition essay and exam, he sets up a family commonwealth and loan bank and initiates a "swift season of merrymaking" (*P* 82). Yet when the money runs out, Stephen is left even worse. "He had tried to build a breakwater of order and elegance against the sordid tide of life without him and to dam up, by rules of conduct and active interest and new filial relations, the powerful recurrence of the tides within him. Useless. From without as from within the waters had flowed over his barriers: their tides began once more to jostle fiercely above the crumbled mole" (*P* 82). Socially acceptable procurements, ordered expenditure, and the regulation of relations by money bring Stephen no closer to his family and to personal fulfillment; they are merely the brief containment of relentlessly mobile materialistic urges. The same watery figuration as that of the brothel district describes these forces within and without. The "fierce longings of his heart" (*P* 82) find no answer in an environment that lacks any meaningful structure other than the pressure of material concerns. To answer these longings is to turn away from respectable society but in doing so to turn toward the most extreme expression of those conditions.

The figural language used to depict the conditions of Mecklenburg Street finds full articulation in Fr. Arnall's hellfire sermon of the following chapter of *Portrait*, where "Hell is a strait and dark and foulsmelling prison" (*P* 100). If the references to "sin" and "hell" in the preceding passage situate Stephen's desire in the discourse of religious turpitude (Stephen's cries are like "a wail of despair from a hell of sufferers"), the language of religious damnation is repurposed to offer a radicalized vision of urban conditions; this hell is a paradoxical environment in which the exercise of choice leads to the loss of individual definition. Arnall, similarly, defines sin as the preeminence of will over spirit, the favoring of material desire over intellectual independence: "It is a base consent to the promptings of our corrupt nature to the lower instincts, to that which is gross and beast-like; and it is also a turning away from the counsel of our higher nature, from all that is pure and holy" (*P* 107).

This base and degraded state is figured in terms of a dark viscosity. As James R. Thrane has shown, Joyce draws Arnall's hellfire sermon from Giovanni Pinamonti's 1693 *Hell Opened to the Christians*. The line in Pinamonti is indeed: "1stly. Thither, as to a common sewer, all the filth of the earth shall run after the fire has purged it on the last day."[22] While sin is conceived of by Dante, after Aquinas, as an excess of carnality, a mortal weight that results from the denial of the spirit, Pinamonti and Joyce figure the body of the damned as deprived of form. In this, however, Joyce goes beyond the brief instances in Pinamonti, elaborating specifically on Pinamonti's description of the unbounded matter of the soul as a "jellylike mass of liquid corruption" (*P* 101). Most striking in Joyce's adaptation of Pinamonti is the emphasis he places on smell: "millions of fetid carcasses massed together in the reeking darkness, a huge and rotting human fungus" (*P* 101).[23] This emphasis on smell underlines the unbounded condition of this material hell in which individual definition is lost. In contrast to Pinamonti's Hell, which is a place of self-consciousness,

---

[22] Pinamonti, Giovanni Pietro, *Hell Opened to Christians: To Caution Them from Entering into It: Or, Considerations on the Infernal Pains, Proposed to Our Meditation to Avoid Them: And Distributed for Every Day in the Week*, ed. T. Richardson and Son (Derby: Richardson and Son, 1845), 19.

[23] Thrane corroborates these observations: "Joyce does not always copy his model's order, scale, and emphasis in detail, even in the morning sermon. His taunting devils are far more explicit and display a moral fastidiousness unknown to Pinamonti's. His elaboration upon the reek of the 'jellylike mass of liquid corruption' is matched or surpassed elsewhere, but not in his model's relatively squeamish analysis of hell's stench. The lack of any mitigating reference to heaven and the divine love by Arnall is not truly Ignatian." James R. Thrane, "Joyce's Sermon on Hell: Its Source and Its Backgrounds," *Modern Philology* 57.3 (February 1960), 172–98, at 188.

memory, and reflection on past sins and occasions neglected, the souls of the damned in Arnall's sermon do not think. Instead, they are a mass that lacks volition and even consciousness; this figures the consequences of a will that has submitted to external material forces.

Trembling Joy: Emma's Wild and Languid Smell and Rimbaud's Black Vowel

If these encounters reveal a volition that has been harnessed by transactional relations, the scene in which Stephen and Emma cross paths in the colonnade of the museum library stages relations that occur independently of the will. This sensual interchange occurs independently both of transaction and of social relation; the passive response to the ingress of external forces is recast as an aesthetic experience. Occurring in the porous boundary space of the library colonnade, the scene opposes the aesthetics of stasis that Joyce committed to paper in the reading room of the Bibliothèque Sainte-Geneviève. This scene is kinetic with desire. The significance of this encounter becomes clear to Stephen only gradually and retrospectively:

> She had passed through the dusk. And therefore the air was silent save for one soft hiss that fell. And therefore the tongues about him had ceased their babble. Darkness was falling.
> *Darkness falls from the air.*
> A trembling joy, lambent as a faint light, played like a fairy host around him. But why? Her passage through the darkening air or the verse with its black vowels and its opening sound, rich and lutelike? (*P* 196)

The indented and italicized line is of unclear status; we must look carefully to see that Stephen has spoken aloud this "verse with its black vowels and its opening sound, rich and lutelike." Stephen reflects a little later that "his music had flowed desirously" in response to Emma's "wild and languid smell" (*P* 196). A number of critics have noted, and Stephen himself later realizes, that the line is a distorted quotation of Thomas Nash's "A Litany in Time of Plague," which originally featured as a song in Nash's play *Summer's Last Will and Testament* (1600). The original line is in a central stanza:

> Beautie is but a flowre,
> Which wrinckles will deuoure,
> Brightnesse falls from the ayre,
> Queenes haue died yong and faire,

> Dust hath closde Helens eye.
> I am sick, I must dye:
> Lord, have mercy on vs.[24]

Written during the period of intermittent bubonic plague epidemics, Nash's "Litany" is not a carpe diem but a poem enthralled with death. The refrain "I am sick, I must dye," registers the capturing of the will by mortality, in a relentless focus on last things. The poem is concerned not merely with the effects of the plague but with the constancy of mortality in history – the deaths of everything from plants to royal figures to literary characters. In the scene in *Portrait*, Nash's line seems to find a milder referent in Stephen's observation that "darkness was falling."

The italicized line, however, conceals a reference to another, more recent poem, one that is also enthralled with death, although it omits all reference to an afterlife. Stephen also cites Rimbaud's celebrated 1871 sonnet, "Voyelles," a poem fascinated with the body's excretions and smells. Changing Nash's "Brightnesse falls from the ayre," to "Darkness falls from the air," Stephen sounds Rimbaud's "black vowel," A:

> A noir, E blanc, I rouge, U vert, O bleu: voyelles,
> Je dirai quelque jour vos naissances latentes:
> A, noir corset velu des mouches éclatantes
> Qui bombinent autour des puanteurs cruelles,
> Golfes d'ombre; [. . .]   (1-5)[25]

> Black A, white E, red I, green U, blue O: vowels,
> I will tell one day of your latent births:
> A, black velvet corset of sparkling flies
> That hum around cruel stenches,
> Gulfs of shadow; [. . .]

Joyce adopts Rimbaud's nonexplicit, synesthetic aesthetic and his interest in nonclassical aesthetic modalities to produce an aesthetic of the body and the body's emissions. Already in *Stephen Hero*, "Voyelles" is a crucial tool for Stephen's reworking of his artistic practice:

> He sought in his verses to fix the most elusive of his moods and he put his lines together not word by word but letter by letter. He read Blake and Rimbaud on the value of letters and even permuted and combined the five vowels to construct cries for the primitive emotions. To none of his former fervors had he given himself with such a whole heart as to this fervor; the

[24] *The Works of Thomas Nash*, Vol. III, ed. Ronald B. McKerrow (Oxford, UK: Oxford University Press, 1905), 283.
[25] Rimbaud, *Complete Works*, 120 (my translation).

monk now seemed to him no more than half the artist. He persuaded himself that it is necessary for an artist to labor incessantly at his art if he wishes to express completely even the simplest conception and he believed that every moment of inspiration must be paid for in advance. [. . .] Isolation is the first principle of artistic economy. (*SH* 37)

Stephen here embarks upon an emphatically materialist aesthetic practice, turning to the sonic components of language to construct expressions of basic affects. His efforts center on an identification of letters with physical experience. The letters William Blake drew in his notebook around the year 1800 are simultaneously graphemes and drawings of individual bodies; they explore a mode of inscription that is a representation of various kinds of embodiment.[26] These letters suggest the possibility of words spelled by ensembles of human bodies, although Stephen here, in *Stephen Hero*, is emphatically solitary. In the colonnade scene with Emma in *Portrait*, Stephen engages in a performance that is closer to Rimbaud's "Voyelles," in which letters are understood as basic vocalizations associated with colors.

In "Voyelles," Rimbaud undertakes a fundamental reconception of poetic composition that ignores the semantic level. As language becomes typographic and sonic material, the poem muddles the sensory modalities, mixing smell with sight and hearing. Later, Rimbaud summarized his aim in the poem: "with instinctive rhythms, I prided myself on inventing a poetic language accessible some day to all the senses."[27] Rimbaud's synesthetic writing explicitly lacks a theoretical foundation; its nonexpository condition is both announced and deflected by the poem's speaker: "I will tell one day of your latent births." That these paradoxical "naissances latentes" are associated with the "golfes d'ombre" does much to create a connotation of female sexual organs, although with these "puanteurs cruelles" other orifices too have their moment. Rimbaud's scenario is thus hostile to traditional aesthetics in several ways: its scenario of flies buzzing around cruel stenches defies any conventional sense of beauty, conjuring

---

[26] William Blake, David V. Erdman, and Donald K. Moore, *The Notebook of William Blake: A Photographic and Typographic Facsimile* (Oxford, UK: Clarendon Press, 1973).

[27] In the "Alchimie du verbe" section of *Une Saison en Enfer*, Rimbaud revisits the intention of his poem, "Voyelles," with a gibe at the inherent problem of translation: "I invented the color of the vowels! – *A* black, *E* white, *I* red, *O* blue, *U* green. – I regulated the form and movement of each consonant, and, with instinctive rhythms, I prided myself on inventing a poetic language accessible some day to all the senses. I reserved translation rights" (193). "J'inventai la couleur des voyelles! – *A* noir, *E* blanc, *I* rouge, *O* bleu, *U* vert. – Je réglai la forme et le mouvement de chaque consonne, et, avec des rythmes instinctifs, je me flattai d'inventer un verbe poétique accessible, un jour ou l'autre, à tous les sens. Je réservais la traduction" (192).

affects of desire and loathing that anticipate Joyce's Paris Epiphany. "Voyelles" disturbs the normal relation between text and meaning, confounding its readers and forcing them to sound its vowels successively and repeatedly in another kind of humming; in doing so, it associates aesthetic experience with physical activity.

The scene in the colonnade in *Portrait* recasts Rimbaud's synesthetic presentation of the first letter of the alphabet as a momentary interpersonal relation, one that is enacted unthinkingly and understood only retroactively. To see this, as well as the full significance of Rimbaud's poem for Joyce, we must follow the continuation of the passage:

> A trembling joy, lambent as a faint light, played like a fairy host around him. But why? Her passage through the darkening air or the verse with its black vowels and its opening sound, rich and lutelike?
>
> He walked away slowly towards the deeper shadows at the end of the colonnade, beating the stone softly with his stick to hide his revery from the students whom he had left: and allowed his mind to summon back to itself the age of Dowland and Byrd and Nash.
>
> Eyes, opening from the darkness of desire, eyes that dimmed the breaking east. What was their languid grace but the softness of chambering? And what was their shimmer but the shimmer of the scum that mantled the cesspool of the court of a slobbering Stuart. And he tasted in the language of memory ambered wines, dying fallings of sweet airs, the proud pavan, and saw with the eyes of memory kind gentlewomen in Covent Garden wooing from their balconies with sucking mouths and the pox-fouled wenches of the taverns and young wives that, gaily yielding to their ravishers, clipped and clipped again. (*P* 196)

To contemplate the possible sources of his "trembling joy" – Emma's movement through the colonnade of the library or the verse that he has uttered – Stephen consciously calls to mind images from Renaissance England of desirous gazes that are both dark and bright, figured as "the shimmer of the scum." This contradictory glittering filth evokes the lines from Rimbaud's "Voyelles": "A, black velvet corset of sparkling flies/That hum around cruel stenches/gulfs of shadow." The imageries disappoint Stephen, however; despite their lascivious content, they are distant and visual: "he saw with the eyes of memory."

> The images he had summoned gave him no pleasure. They were secret and inflaming but her image was not entangled by them. That was not the way to think of her. It was not even the way in which he thought of her. Could his mind then not trust itself? Old phrases, sweet only with a disinterred sweetness like the figseeds Cranly rooted out of his gleaming teeth.

It was not thought nor vision though he knew vaguely that her figure was passing homeward through the city. Vaguely first and then more sharply he smelt her body. A conscious unrest seethed in his blood. Yes, it was her body he smelt: a wild and languid smell: the tepid limbs over which his music had flowed desirously and the secret soft linen upon which her flesh distilled odour and a dew. (*P* 196)

Stephen thus rejects as inadequate to the experience and the desires of the present moment his practice of literary historical association, specifically related to the modality of vision. He questions in turn his conscious rational processes: "Could his mind then not trust itself?" This lapse of faith in reasoning is the explicit consequence of his utterance of the italicized line, which occupies a border zone between conscious and unconscious deliberation, observation and citation, accuracy and inaccuracy. As in the brothel district, where Stephen's "blood was in revolt," here, too, in response to Emma's passage, a "conscious unrest seethed in his blood." Instead of an intellectual, formally separate practice, Stephen realizes that his conscious will has been circumvented while he has been engaged in an embodied aesthetics (a "music") driven by sensation and desire. Stephen takes up the role of the flies in "Voyelles," as his sounding of the words "Darkness falls from the air" employs repeatedly the vowel A that Rimbaud associates with their compulsive closeness. Rather than a punishing taste for cruel stenches, however, he displays an appreciation of bodily odors that are indeed intimate but also artful.

Stephen realizes he has been involved in a bilateral aesthetic exchange. The "trembling joy [that] played like a fairy host around him" oscillates between two sources – her "passage" and the "verse with its black vowels" – which are now given substantiation in "a wild and languid smell, the tepid limbs over which his music had flowed desirously and the secret soft linen upon which her flesh distilled odor and a dew" (*P* 196). Joyce's conception of the emanations of Emma's body and Stephen's melodious words is indebted to the porous, mobile body of Pseudo-Aristotle's *Problems*. The Pseudo-Aristotelian notion of digestion is based on Aristotle's account of becoming as a realization of potential: "Concoction, then, is the production of a mature form out of passive material by the action of a body's natural heat. For a thing becomes fully mature when it has been concocted."[28] This unconscious, physical action is a breaking-down and reassemblage of multiple elements to produce a useful reduction, in the

---

[28] Qtd. in Stephen Toulmin and June Goodfield, *The Architecture of Matter* (New York: Harper & Row, 1962), 87.

digestion of food, and the creation of excretion; it brings with it the odd implication that excrements are a realization of matter's potential. Emma's smell is rendered in an elevated register – "dew" is a particularly delicate rendering of bodily secretions, pairing the action of her body with the condensation caused by twilight. Crucially, this dew and odor are "distilled." Her flesh's release of odor and moisture is the counterpart to Stephen's exclamation of verse, which is also the product of a kind of digestion. While Stephen rejects the phrases he consciously recalls, figuring them as food that lingers, rotting, in the mouth, the lines from Nash and Rimbaud have been swallowed, digested, and expressed unconsciously. His exclamation is the concoction of these elements into a new phrase by the heat of his desire for Emma. Literary and bodily expressions thus meet on the surface of her body.

This scene thus develops as an aesthetic possibility the penetrative female odor that featured in the Paris Epiphany. If we read there of the Parisian women that "under the perfumes their bodies have a warm humid smell," Emma's smell is given a more intriguing, paradoxical characterization, "wild and languid," combining the uncontrolled and vital with the peaceful and sensuous. This scene overturns Joyce's rejection of the fifth aesthetic question in Paris: "Excrements, children, and lice are human products – human dispositions of sensible matter. The process by which they are produced is natural and non-artistic; their end is not an aesthetic end: therefore they are not works of art" (*OCPW* 104). Instead of a deliberate artwork, Stephen's and Emma's bodies produce ephemeral and spontaneous emissions, dispositions of sensible matter that have aesthetic status. Together, they are engaged in performance art *avant la lettre*. In their exchange, Joyce reconceives the dramatic mode of art, which he originally defined in the Paris notebook as art in which "the artist sets forth the image in immediate relation to others" (*OCPW* 103). In *Portrait*, Stephen gives a fuller articulation of this mode: "The dramatic form is reached when the vitality which has flowed and eddied round each person fills every person with such vital force that he or she assumes a proper and intangible aesthetic life" (*P* 180). In contrast to the "life" on Grafton Street, which Joyce recognized from the boulevards of Paris, the scene in the colonnade is a realization of aesthetic life. Rather than a concrete and saleable work of art or a self-alienated "corporal asset" as Stephen understands the bodies of Dublin women in *Stephen Hero* (*SH* 207), vitality, "proper and intangible," flows through and between Emma's and Stephen's persons as an ephemeral expression that is given freely. This crafted waste offers a comic alternative to calculated transactions. It is easily overlooked, passes swiftly, and achieves nothing outside of itself. This immediate dramatic relation occurs not on a stage but in a public space. The curved and column-lined colonnade forms the location for this performance, as an intermediary space between Kildare Street and the library. Despite the architectural formality of this location, it is a linear space that is more like a street than a stage; there is no audience for this dramatic art but the individuals who, unconsciously, perform it.[29]

If Emma and Stephen are both passive in this aesthetic relation, there is an obvious asymmetry: Stephen is engaged in words, Emma in matter. Yet Stephen's words are materialized. Any hierarchy perceived between Stephen's and Emma's media of engagement assumes a primacy of language over matter. Furthermore, if the declaration "Darkness falls from the air" describes the situation in multiple ways (referring to the incipient twilight, the smell of Emma's body, Rimbaud, Nash), it is none of Stephen's conscious doing. There is perhaps a more significant asymmetry in the scene in that we have access to his consciousness, not to hers. If Stephen achieves retrospective understanding of what has occurred, there is no sign of Emma's awareness of it. The encounter thus lacks in subjective terms the mutuality suggested by the meeting of their physical expressions. This asymmetry however has an important aspect: Stephen's aesthetic capacity depends upon being touched by the creations of Emma's body. This situation recasts his repellent earlier assertion: "I like a woman to give. I like to receive"; now this gift, given freely if unconsciously, is the constitutive condition of his aesthetic practice, divorced from his will. Stephen no longer has a transparent relation to his own creative processes. Instead of an art that springs from cognitive mastery, a Thomistic perception of essence, Stephen's expression is born from sensual connection in which discernment of the relation of part to whole is replaced by an unconscious experience of connection.

---

[29] I examine here how Joyce's focus on materiality allows him to conceive of experiential and aesthetic possibilities within a social world mapped and regulated by capitalist exchange. These possibilities resonate with but are not identical to New Materialist concerns, for example, Jane Bennett's exploration of an "energetic vitality of things" in "heterogenous groupings" of human and nonhuman power or Diana Coole and Samantha Frost's "emphasis on materialization as a complex, pluralistic, relatively open process and [...] insistence that humans, including theorists themselves, be recognized as thoroughly immersed within materiality's productive contingencies." See Jane Bennett, *Vibrant Matter: A Political Ecology of Things* (Durham, NC: Duke University Press, 2010), 5, xvii, and Diana Coole and Samantha Frost, *New Materialisms: Ontology, Agency, and Politics* (Durham, NC: Duke University Press, 2010), 7.

An Aesthetics of Desire

Instead of an essence that is perceived through intellectual effort, this aesthetic is associated with digestion and excretion; Stephen, indeed, anticipates this association in subtle ways in his version of Joyce's Parisian aesthetic theory. Shortly before the scene with Emma, Stephen expounds the aesthetic theory to Lynch, who responds crudely while pointing out its lacunae: "But you have not answered my question, said Lynch. What is art? What is the beauty it expresses?" (*P* 174). The scene in the colonnade presents new answers to these questions, and it does by staging a developed form of Lynch's desirous and even coprophilic relation to art. In response to Stephen's illustration of his vision of art as an impersonal, intellectual, and static mode of truth, "You would not write your name in pencil across the hypothenuse of a rightangled triangle," Lynch replies, "No [. . .] give me the hypothenuse of the Venus of Praxiteles" (*P* 174).

> – You say that art must not excite desire, said Lynch. I told you that one day I wrote my name in pencil on the backside of the Venus of Praxiteles in the Museum. Was that not desire?
> – I speak of normal natures, said Stephen. You also told me that when you were a boy in that charming carmelite school you ate pieces of dried cowdung. (*P* 172).

Situating Stephen and Lynch's discussions of art in classical and Hegelian aesthetics, Valérie Bénéjam sees Stephen and Lynch as occupying opposing positions: "In contrast to Stephen's refined aesthetics, Lynch plays the part of the uneducated Barbarian."[30] However, pointing to the history of amorous physical responses to the unprecedentedly realistic statue of the Venus of Praxiteles, she argues: "for all his admiration for the backside of the statue, Lynch is not such an uncouth ignorant lout. On the contrary, even though he might not be aware of it, he belongs to a tradition which Stephen, for all his culture and confidence, does not seem to know."[31] Although she reads the aesthetic discussion in *Portrait* without comparing it to Joyce's Parisian writings, Bénéjam intuits that some crucial shifts and qualifications occur in Stephen and Lynch's conversation: "Indeed, Lynch displays quite a devastating irony, when you come to appreciate its blunt

---

[30] Valérie Bénéjam, "Stephen and the Venus of Praxiteles: The Backside of Aesthetics," in *Cultural Studies of James Joyce*, ed. R. Brandan Kershner (Amsterdam: Rodopi, 2003), 63.
[31] Ibid., 71.

and laconic quality rather than embrace Stephen's patronizing vision of him."[32]

Lynch laughs at his own past deeds, yet they set a precedent for *Portrait*'s aesthetic developments. While Stephen's asserted relation to art is theoretical and abstracted, Lynch's is bold and concrete. If he is perhaps a crass and lusty simpleton, his coprophagy responds to several of the Parisian aesthetic questions, particularly the fifth, "Why are not excrements, children and lice works of art?" It anticipates Stephen's savoring of Emma's "secret soft linen upon which her flesh distilled odor and a dew" (*P* 196). Similarly, Lynch's signing of his name on the buttocks of the beautiful statue anticipates Stephen's melodious touch of Emma's "tepid limbs." In his personal, desirous response to the artwork, Lynch actively asserts a dramatic relation to statue of Venus; his gesture answers the question Joyce posed in Paris: "Spicer-Simson has made a bust of his wife. Is it lyrical, epical or dramatic?"[33] Lynch explores the possibilities of Joyce's dramatic mode, wherein "the artist sets forth the image in immediate relation to others," albeit in a brashly appropriative manner.

It is precisely this appropriative gesture that is refused in the momentary touch of Stephen's music on Emma's flesh. The exchange in the colonnade evades not only possession but also volition. In this, it is directly opposed to the aesthetic theory Stephen has articulated to Lynch shortly before the encounter. Stephen associates the aesthetic mode with conscious deliberation rather than unconscious physical response: "The desire and loathing excited by improper aesthetic means are really unaesthetic emotions not only because they are kinetic in character but also because they are not more than physical. Our flesh shrinks from what it dreads and responds to the stimulus of what it desires by a purely reflex action of the nervous system" (*P* 173). Stephen's response to Emma is an unconscious desirous response to her body, which is itself engaged in unconscious artistic practice.

As Stephen and Emma engage in parallel, if asymmetrical, processes that are more and less literal versions of digestion and excretion, Joyce literalizes the aesthetic process Stephen described in *Stephen Hero*. Having mentally rehearsed the new definition of art Joyce developed in Paris, "art was the human disposition of intelligible or sensible matter for an aesthetic end" and his tripartite division of art into lyric, epic and dramatic (*SH* 81), Stephen conceives of aesthetic practice as a twofold operation: "The artist, he imagined, standing in the position of mediator between the world of his

[32] Ibid., 75.   [33] NLI MS.36,639/02/A.

experience and the world of his dreams – ~~a mediator, consequently gifted with twin faculties, a selective faculty and a reproductive faculty~~. To equate these faculties was the secret of artistic success: the artist who could disentangle the subtle soul of the image from its mesh of defining circumstances most exactly and ~~re-embody~~ it in artistic circumstances chosen as the most exact for it in its new office, he was the supreme artist" (*SH* 82, Joyce's strikethrough). Theodor Spencer, in an introductory essay to *Stephen Hero*, notes: "Joyce evidently went through the manuscript with a red or blue crayon in his hand and slashed strokes beside, under or across certain phrases, sentences and paragraphs. Presumably he did not like them and intended to change them or get rid of them" (*SH* 25). Yet genetic studies of Joyce's compositional practices have shown that his practice of striking through was a gesture of reappropriating earlier material.[34] These marks thus suggest not his rejection of these phrases but his increased interest in them. Passing over the idealist terms associated with this twofold aesthetic practice – "dreams," "soul," "the supreme artist" – Joyce seizes on the passage's physical terms: "selective" and "reproductive faculty," and, most crucially, "re-embody."

Stephen's theories of art in *Stephen Hero* anticipate the embodied aesthetics of Leopold Bloom's sentient thinking, which we will explore in the next chapter. In doing so, they incorporate many of the activities and ideas that Cranly models in a flawed and partial manner in *Stephen Hero*, just as Lynch provides a model for Stephen's aesthetics in *Portrait*. In this version of the aesthetic essay, Stephen declares that aesthetic apprehension is akin to digestion:

> It is almost impossible to reconcile all tradition whereas it is by no means impossible to find the justification of every form of beauty which has been adored on the earth by an examination into the mechanism of aesthetic apprehension whether it be dressed in red, white, yellow or black. We have no reason for thinking that the Chinaman has a different system of digestion from that which we have though our diets are quite dissimilar. The apprehensive faculty must be scrutinized in action. (*SH* 217)

In citing this racialized traditional variety, Stephen invokes and departs from Hegel's "The Conception of Artistic Beauty," which was such a crucial text for the evolution of Joyce's conception of aesthetics in Paris: "How often we hear it said that a European beauty would not please a Chinese or even a Hottentot, in as far as the Chinaman has quite a

---

[34] See, for example, James Joyce, *The Finnegans Wake Notebooks at Buffalo*, eds. Vincent Deane, Daniel Ferrer, and Geert Lernout (Turnhout, Belgium: Brepols Publishers, 2001).

different conception of beauty from the Negro, and the Negro in turn from the European, and so forth."[35] For Hegel, these differences are not equivalent conceptions of beauty; rather, "those extra-European peoples" have not yet achieved the production of the beautiful, which is the expression of truth in physical semblance. In contrast to this cultural hierarchy, Stephen posits a mutually unappealing yet equally valid array of cultural conceptions of the beautiful, understood as the products of a single "apprehensive faculty." Likening the action of this faculty to that of the digestive system, this aesthetic theory is centered in the human body, understood as equipped with standard functions. The various forms of beauty are the necessarily different end-products that result when different kinds of raw matter are fed into a standard "mechanism." In this account, aesthetics is closer to ingestion, digestion, and excretion than to cognition.

In contrast to a selective and discerning mode of consumption, this ingestion proceeds indiscriminately. Cranly displays a constant desire to eat, and his mental activity is also omnivorous: "His receptiveness was not troubled by any nausea; he received everything that came in his way and it was purely instinctive of Stephen to perceive any special affinity in so indiscriminate a vessel. He was fond of leading a philosophical argument back to the machinery of the intellectual faculty itself and in mundane matters he did likewise, testing everything by its food value" (*SH* 129).[36] Cranly thus understands thought as a mechanical process for the benefit of the whole being. A better sense of what the "food test of ideas" consists of is suggested when it is turned on Stephen's aesthetic theory: "Cranly's method in argument was to reduce all things to their food values (though he himself was the most impractical of theorists) and Stephen's conception of art fared very badly from such a method. Stephen held the test of food values an extreme one and one which in its utter materialism suggested a declination from the heights of romanticism" (*SH* 213). Cranly's food test of ideas is, explicitly here, an unselective and physical processing of material, utterly opposed to Stephen's romanticism, which "sees no fit abode here for its ideals and chooses to behold them under insensible figures" (*SH* 83).[37] If Stephen's theory of art fails this test, a few pages later

---

[35] Hegel, *Introductory Letters on Aesthetics*, 49–50.

[36] In *Portrait*, Cranly's eating of figs during a conversation on faith bothers Stephen: "Don't, please. You cannot discuss this question with your mouth full of chewed fig" (*P* 202).

[37] Stephen defines romanticism in opposition to classicism in *Stephen Hero* as modes of, respectively, symbolic and material expression: "The romantic temper [. . .] sees no fit abode here for its ideals and chooses therefore to behold them under insensible figures. [. . .] The classical temper on the other hand, ever mindful of limitations, chooses rather to bend upon these present things and so to

in the manuscript Stephen absorbs Cranly's mode of thinking when he likens aesthetic apprehension to digestion. When Stephen's subsequent rehearsal of the aesthetic essay includes a Thomistic multistaged process of perception, its stages are inflected by the processes of eating. Aquinas's sequence of selection, dissection, and synthesis now suggests the biting, chewing, and digesting of food: the mind "divides the entire universe into two parts, the object, and the void which is not the object"; it "considers the object in whole and in part"; it "makes the only logically possible synthesis" (*SH* 217–218).

This synthesis is expressed as physical excretion, announced with an incongruous detail at the climax of Stephen's rehearsal of the aesthetic theory in *Portrait*: "The aesthetic image in the dramatic form is life purified in and reprojected from the human imagination. The mystery of aesthetic like that of material creation is accomplished. The artist, like the God of creation, remains within or behind or beyond or above his handiwork, invisible, refined out of existence, indifferent, paring his fingernails" (*P* 181). Scarlett Baron traces Stephen's characterization of the artist to Gustave Flaubert's 1857 letter to Mlle Leroyer de Chantepie concerning *Madame Bovary*: "The artist in his work must be like God in creation, invisible and all-powerful; you can sense him everywhere but you cannot see him."[38] Baron draws our attention to Joyce's awkward adaptation of Flaubert's *impersonnalité* in Stephen's previous sentence: "The personality of the artist, at first a cry or a cadence or a mood and then a fluid and lambent narrative, finally refines itself out of existence, impersonalizes itself, so to speak" (*P* 180–81). Joyce's artistic process obviously entails the refinement of the details of his own biography; as I show here, it also entails the progressive reworking of particular scenes in order to develop a physical aesthetic. This reworking leads Joyce to stage, in the colonnade, the refinement out of existence of the artist as a controlling personality. Instead of a God-like intellect, the artist is physically and unconsciously engaged in a desublimated and collaborative art. The fingernails that obtrude in Stephen's account of an artist who is preeningly free of any effort of creation are a material that Pseudo-Aristotle understands as constituted by the body's excretion of waste product.[39]

---

work upon them and fashion them that the quick intelligence may go beyond them to their meaning which is still unuttered" (*SH* 213).

[38] Qtd. in Baron, *"Strandentwining Cable"*, 90.

[39] Baron suggests that this detail is a symptom of a "network of homoerotic suggestion" in *Portrait*, linking the covert homosexuality of the time with the concealment of the artist figure in Stephen's formulation. Ibid., 97–100. See also Timothy Dean, "Paring His Fingernails: Homosexuality and

The scene in the colonnade suggests that they figure an alternative creative labor that occurs outside of conscious volition, cogitation, and assertion.

A Sentient Thought

In reworking an aesthetics that is modeled on Aquinas, Joyce devises an embodied thinking. It is important to recall that Thomistic aesthetics is an account of an intellectual process: Aquinas is not concerned with a theory of art but rather with the perception of the beauty of the world. This perception involves an intellectual abstraction in which the perceived object is judged according to the criterion of ontological perfection: beauty is the conformity of existence to essence and, accordingly, the perception of beauty is the understanding of a divine order.[40] The aesthetic Joyce develops in the scene in the colonnade offers a powerful alternative to this, in a thinking that is concerned not with intellectual discernment of essence but with deviant generation.

This generation is figured immediately after Stephen realizes what has occurred between him and Emma:

> Yes, it was her body he smelt: a wild and languid smell: the tepid limbs over which his music had flowed desirously and the secret soft linen upon which her flesh distilled odor and a dew.
>
> A louse crawled over the nape of his neck and, putting his thumb and forefinger deftly beneath his loose collar, he caught it. He rolled its body, tender yet brittle as a grain of rice, between thumb and finger for an instant before he let it fall from him and wondered would it live or die. There came to his mind a curious phrase from Cornelius a Lapide which said that the lice born of human sweat were not created by God with the other animals on the sixth day. But the tickling of the skin of his neck made his mind raw and red. The life of his body, illclad, illfed, louseeaten, made him close his eyelids in a sudden spasm of despair: and in the darkness he saw the brittle bright bodies of lice falling from the air and turning often as they fell. Yes; and it was not darkness that fell from the air. It was brightness.

Joyce's Impersonalist Aesthetic," in *Quare Joyce*, ed. Joseph Valente (Ann Arbor: University of Michigan Press, 1998), 241–72.

[40] Stephen describes the stages of aesthetic perception in similar terms: "Your mind to apprehend that object divides the entire universe into two parts, the object, and the void which is not the object. [...] What then? Analysis then. The mind considers the object in whole and in part, in relation to itself and to other objects, examines the balance of its parts, contemplates the form of the object, traverses every cranny of the structure. [...] After the analysis which discovers the second quality the mind makes the only logically possible synthesis and discovers the third quality. This is the moment which I call epiphany. [...] we recognize that it is *that* thing which it is. Its soul, its whatness, leaps to us from the vestment of its appearance." (*SH* 217–18)

> *Brightness falls from the air.*
> He had not even remembered rightly Nash's line. All the images it had
> awakened were false. His mind bred vermin. His thoughts were lice born of
> the sweat of sloth. (*P* 196–97)

Stephen despairs here of the failure of his memory and the consequent
misdirection of his thoughts.[41] His shame is an Icarian shame, a fall from
artistic supremacy into a base materiality. But it also accompanies a new
freedom, embodied in the louse. Stephen's louse is not a rhetorical figure
of moral deficiency, as implied by Ellmann's observation that his lice are
"Baudelairean lice" (*JJ* 6). In "Au Lecteur," the opening poem of *Les Fleurs
du mal*, Baudelaire declares that he shares a moral hypocrisy with the
reader, "we feed our tame remorse/As beggars take to nourishing their lice"
(3–4).[42] Stephen's louse is literally nourished by his body, which, illfed
and illclad, resembles a beggar's body.[43] This is a deviant fecundity in
more ways than one. Cornelius a Lapide adapts for a Christian context
Pseudo-Aristotle's notion that lice are born of human sweat to assert that
lice were "not created by God with the other animals on the sixth day." As
we saw in Chapter 1, Pseudo-Aristotle holds that the body expels foreign
matter in its excretions and that this foreign matter breeds lice.[44] The louse
produced by Stephen's body is thus not only a retort to the Thomistic
aesthetics of radiant being, as it escapes a divine order, but also to sovereign
individuality, as it evades an individual will.[45] While creation in *Problems* is

---

[41] Stephen's mistake here would qualify as a member of the fourth category of Tim Conley's
taxonomy of error: an error of empirical fact. Tim Conley, *Joyce's Mistakes: Problems of Intention,
Irony, and Interpretation* (Toronto: University of Toronto Press, 2003), 12. Conley refers to it as
one of Joyce's many misquotations, understanding them as a "dramatic principle in his fiction"
(153), an "aesthetics of error," which demands readerly interaction (15). Fritz Senn understands
errors as generative, calling them "Portals of Stimulation": "Errors are unsettling, irritating and
therefore dynamic. A point reiterated here is that falls and disasters and mundane fumbles can
release energies. They motivate repair efforts," Fritz Senn, "Joyce's Erroneous Cosmos," in *Errears
and Erroriboose: Joyce and Error*, ed. Matthew Creasy. *European Joyce Studies*, 20. (Amsterdam:
Rodopi, 2011), 23–42, at 24.

[42] Baudelaire, *The Flowers of Evil*, trans. James McGowan (Oxford, UK: Oxford University Press,
1993), 5; "Et nous alimentons nos aimables remords,/Comme les mendicants nourrissent leur
vermine" (4).

[43] In "Scylla and Charybdis," Stephen translates Mallarmé's "Hamlet, ou le distrait," as the "absent
minded beggar," a term that he applies to himself in "Circe" (*U* 9:125).

[44] "Hair grows from waste product," (Aristotle, *Problems II*, XXXI:957b, 185). The fluid emitted by
the brain also engenders lice: "Now the brain is moist; consequently the head is always most moist.
This is obvious from the fact that most hair grows there. The dampness of the region is most liable
to produce lice" (Aristotle, *Problems I*, I:861a, 13).

[45] Rabaté notes that for Joyce "lice embody the stubborn resistance of nature or the body to ideas." Jean-
Michel Rabaté, *The Politics of Egoism* (Cambridge, UK: Cambridge University Press, 2001), 86. Rabaté
traces the reference to Aristotle in this passage, noting that "the Latin text confirms the importance of
the Aristotelian opposition between actual form and potentiality: *pulices, mures aliique vermiculi, non*

emphatically autochthonous – the natural produces the similar – "for from what is not corrupted there springs only something of the same type as the seed" – here creation is foreign to the self, an uninvited and uncontrolled flourishing of alien matter.[46]

This rebellious productiveness is figured in Stephen's image of "brittle bright bodies of lice falling from the air and turning often as they fell": these lice are Luciferean in their brightness but they rebel not through the affirmation of an independent will but rather through the weight and irregularity of their bodies. This is a rebellion as much against individual volition as it is against God's will. The twisting bodies of the lice figure a new kind of thought that occurs in the mobility of a materialized language. Language here is not a stable container of thought but a substance that responds to changing conditions. This aberrant vitality features in the phrase that Stephen misquotes, "Darkness falls from the air." If he castigates himself for deforming the line from Nash's poem, he still hasn't realized that it now contains the black vowels of Rimbaud, as it expresses the physical sensations of the darkening twilight and the smell of Emma's body. His "mind bred vermin," he thinks. The exclamation is his physical brainchild – to return to our discussion of the Pseudo-Aristotle question that prompted Joyce's fifth aesthetic question[47] – although it is better understood as an excretion than a child. Stephen's error here is a material aesthetic expression that defies truth, correctness, and intention. His "mind" is a displaced cognition in which physical sensations and materialized language are concocted by desire.

This mind, and the spiraling lice produced by it, bring us back to the humming flies of Rimbaud's "Voyelles": multiple, decentered, and driven by desire. Rimbaud's poem presents, in Rancière's characterization, a "body of utterance, the sensory network over which the first disagreement of look and lips is distributed into themes and registers where bodies and voices join and separate."[48] Yet if "Voyelles" is a "poem machine," as

---

fuerunt hoc sexto die creata formaliter, sed potentialiter, et quasi in seminale ratione.' The reason why this passage has stuck in Stephen's mind is probably that lice are seen here as a debased version of the *logos spermatikos* dear to Stoician philosophy" (95). Rabaté tracks the multiple appearances of lice in Joyce's work, noting that, in *Finnegans Wake*, Shem is a "dirty parasite and a snobbish Parisian: 'Let him be Artalone the weeps with his parisites peeling off him' (418.1–2)" (99).

[46] Aristotle, *Problems I*, IV:878a, 121.

[47] "Why is it that, if a living creature is born from our semen, we regard it as our own offspring, but if it proceeds from any other part or excretion, we do not consider it our own? For many things proceed from decayed matter as well as from semen." Aristotle, *Problems I*, IV:878a, 119.

[48] Jacques Rancière, *The Flesh of Words: The Politics of Writing*, trans. Charlotte Mandell (Stanford, CA: Stanford University Press, 2004), 48. Rancière reads the poem as reconfiguring the family romance of Rimbaud's relationship with his mother.

Rancière describes it, Joyce's scene in the colonnade situates these independent workings of language and sensation within and between human bodies, shifting the focus from the art work as an object to an embodied and collaborative aesthetic experience.

In tracing Stephen and Emma's relations, this chapter has argued for Joyce's replacement of a Thomistic aesthetics of *integritas, consonantia,* and *claritas* with a desublimated and unconscious aesthetic practice, instanced here in the transient expression of digested material. The exchange in the library colonnade is an exemplar of art rather than a theory of it, a turning away from conscious cognition to investigate new possibilities of embodiment. In *Stephen Hero,* after Rimbaud inspires Stephen to use the "five vowels to construct cries for the primitive emotions" (*SH* 37), Stephen rejects the mode of aesthetic theorization: "The treatises which were recommended to him he found valueless and trifling; the Laocoön of Lessing irritated him. He wondered how the world could accept as valuable contributions such fantas fanciful generalizations. What finer certitude could be attained by the artist if he believed that ancient art was plastic and that modern art pictorial[?]" (*SH* 38). The scene in the colonnade rejects theoretical generalization in favor of an exploration of the particular, the contingent, and the fleeting. It also contradicts Lessing's distinction between ancient and modern art as plastic and pictorial, mobilizing as it does the modalities of touch and smell and the faculty of digestion to stage an encounter between permeable bodies.[49] It does so in order to elude the calculus that regulates a social world mapped and regulated by capitalist exchange and to explore instead new experiential and aesthetic possibilities.

The distorted phrase that Stephen utters is a singular instant of what we might call sentient thinking. The involuntary process of distorted recall and association that he belatedly observes here is given full scope in a Bloomian sentient thinking that is situated not in the library colonnade but in the street, traversing and evading the categories that commerce would place on life. But this moment of somatic aesthetics, this peculiar,

---

[49] The scene also undermines Lessing's more famous aesthetic distinction that the "succession of time is the province of the poet just as space is that of the painter." Gotthold Ephraim Lessing, *Laocoön: An Essay in the Limits of Painting and Poetry,* trans. Edward Allen McCormick (Baltimore, MD: Johns Hopkins University Press, 1984), 91. The exchange between Stephen and Emma indeed unfolds over time, as it is retrospectively pieced together by Stephen. Yet this retrospection yields a version of what Lessing understands as painting's sensually immediacy, a vivid presentation of the most "suggestive" moment in an encounter between bodies, rather than the representation of a succession of actions over time that he holds to be the task of poetry (99).

early performance art, is the undeclared culmination of *Portrait*'s struggle with transactional sensations. If, in *Stephen Hero*, Stephen observes that none of his classmates is interested in his theories, that his "fine talk" of beauty, rhythms, and aesthetic to them is an attempt to mask that "really all art was rot: beside it was probably immoral" (*SH* 38), here Stephen and Emma meet in a new kind of relation, characterized by pleasure and freedom, skirting the categories of immorality and rottenness in a fleeting and deviantly beautiful exchange.

CHAPTER 3

Paris Digested: "Lestrygonians"

The first chapter of *Portrait* appeared in *The Egoist* in February 1914. Immediately under it appears a short essay titled "The Bourgeois" by Bastien von Helmholtz, a pseudonym of Ezra Pound.[1] It was Pound who had sent the first chapter of *Portrait* to Dora Marsden for publication in her magazine (having written gruffly to Joyce, "your novel is damn fine stuff [...] Confound it, I cant usually read prose at all").[2] Pound begins his essay by citing a journalist's claim that Yeats was wrong to attack the bourgeoisie because Yeats himself was middle class. He then counters that "bourgeois" is a pejorative term coined not by aristocrats but by artists:

> The bourgeoisie is a state of mind. It is a term of opprobrium, used by the bohemian, or the artist in contempt of the citizen. The bourgeoisie is digestive. The bourgeois is the lineal descendant of the 'honest citizen' of the Elizabethan. The 'honest citizen' was the person who was so overjoyed when he found out that Ben Jonson had made him a cuckold. [...] The bourgeois is, roughly, a person who is concerned solely with his own comfort or advancement. He is, in brief, digestive. He is the stomach and gross intestines of the body politic and social, as distinct from the artist, who is the nostrils and the invisible antenna. [...] It has become a term of contempt. It has replaced the term '*épicier*'[grocer], or rather it has not replaced that term of contempt, for '*épicier*' was used by the aristocracy as a term of contempt, whereas 'bourgeois,' as a discourtesy, has come from the artist.[3]

Pound's corporeal metaphors come with an implicit hierarchy: While artists are the perceptive organs of smell and hearing in this body politic, the bourgeoisie are the less-attentive organs of the stomach and gross intestines, devoted to the business of extraction and, implicitly, the by-production of things other than works of art. Yet, as our exploration

---

[1] Ezra Pound/Bastien von Helmholtz, "The Bourgeios" [*sic*], *The Egoist* I.3 (February 2, 1914), 53–54.
[2] *Pound/Joyce*, ed. Read, 24. [3] Ibid., 53.

of Stephen and Emma's encounter in the final chapter of *Portrait* has shown, digestive processes need be no less sensitive, nor aesthetically pleasing, than sensory processes. As we have seen, while Stephen's sense of smell and hearing are of crucial import in his encounter with Emma in the colonnade of the museum library, they are combined with a kind of concoction and excretion to constitute a more compelling engagement with his world than the artworks specified by his aesthetic theory.

It seems likely that Joyce read Pound's article. It seems unlikely that Joyce needed Pound to conceive of a way of extending his exploration of an aesthetic practice that takes place outside of the conventionally defined sphere of art. Yet Pound's bourgeois offers a useful account of the figure who comes after Stephen: in developing the bourgeois Bloom, Joyce takes up the outcast of the outcasts, the accursed of the accursed poets. As an entrepreneur, a canvasser for advertisements, Bloom indeed lives off the mechanisms of commerce.[4] We can readily see him as the stomach and gross intestines of society. If digestion allows Stephen a mode of relation that evades transactional exchange and the demands of a masculinist will, this mode is fully developed in Bloom, an honest citizen whose art is situated within the functioning of the city. Tracing Bloom's engagement in a somatic art allows us to take seriously the characterization made of him by the canny scrounger, Ned Lenehan: "He's a cultured allroundman, Bloom is, he said seriously. He's not one of your common or garden ... you know ... There's a touch of the artist about old Bloom" (*U* 10:581–83). In calling Bloom "old Bloom," Lenehan signals the complex sociality of Bloom's position, simultaneously communicating affection, familiarity, and derision for an ordinary person engaged in extraordinary activities, an urban insider who has outsider status not just because of his Jewish background but also because of his atypical engagement with his surroundings. At first glance a clichéd and approximate construction, the phrase "touch of the artist about" communicates a haptic, subtle, and

---

[4] Bloom, as Matthew Hayward has specified, occupies a somewhat subordinated position: he is "an advertisement canvasser employed solely by Freeman's Journal Ltd in order to solicit advertisements for *The Evening Telegraph*, one of the company's titles" a position with "no decisive control over the advertisement's puff ('par') or its positioning [...] no say in the placement of the ads he collects; neither is he free to engage in space brokering or 'farming,' by which method independent agents bought newspaper space wholesale before selling it on to individual advertisers at a profit." Matthew Hayward, "The Bloom of Advertising: Joyce's 'Notes on Business and Commerce' and *Ulysses*," *Dublin James Joyce Journal* 5 (2012), 49–65, at 49.

immersed aesthetic practice.[5] As this chapter will attempt to show, Bloom's somatic art engages the lower sensory modalities of touch, taste, and smell, as well as the digestive functions, to form an ongoing response to the relations of the street.[6] Bloom is indeed a digestive system but one that operates within and against the larger system of society.

That this system is digestive is vividly illustrated in "Lestrygonians," the lunchtime episode of *Ulysses*. The episode is often seen as a "baseline" episode of the novel: William Schutte writes, "'Lestrygonians' is as close to a 'typical' Bloom episode as we have. Unlike 'Calypso' and 'Lotus Eaters,' it is not much affected by Joyce's need to establish themes and relationships."[7] The episode thus allows the exploration of the basic concerns of the middle section of the novel, as it presents Bloom's thoughts and sensations while he moves through the city streets. In the schemas he provided to Gilbert and Linati for the episode, Joyce combines the domains of the natural and the sociopolitical: the "organ" of "the esophagus" and the "technic" of "peristalsis" are grouped with the "symbol" of "the constables" and the "art" of "architecture."[8] As digestive processes are thus brought together with law-enforcement and the built environment, the schemas suggest that the streets of Dublin, and indeed the episode itself, are a digestive tract through which Bloom moves.[9]

This digestive tract is, perhaps obviously, rapacious. Lyn Childress shows that in composing "Lestrygonians," Joyce paid particular attention

---

[5] Abbie Garrington's *Haptic Modernism: Touch and the Tactile in Modernist Writing* (Edinburgh: Edinburgh University Press, 2013), offers a fascination account of synesthesia in *Ulysses*, in the form of Bloom's "caressing look" (86). While she understands Bloom's hapticity as self-regarding, writing of "that necessity which plagues Leopold Bloom throughout his Dublin day: sexual self-touching" (74), and of Bloom's "morbid fascination with the penetration of the skin" (94), I will explore touch as the first stage of engagement with a porous body and of implication in intersubjective relations.

[6] Ellmann traces Bloom's origins to Joyce's involvement in a fistfight over a woman's honor in Stephen's Green: "Joyce was said to have been dusted off and taken home by a man named Alfred H. Hunter, in what *Ulysses* would call 'orthodox Samaritan fashion.' Hunter was rumored to be Jewish and to have an unfaithful wife, two disparate points that became important later" (*JJ* 161–62). This event is clearly of key significance in Joyce's conception of the distant acquaintance who comes to Stephen's assistance in Nighttown. For a recent synopsis of information, see Terence Killeen, "Fitz-Epsykure: The Further Adventures of Alfred and Marion Hunter," *James Joyce Online Notes*, www.jjon.org/jioyce-s-people/hunter.

[7] William Schutte, "Leopold Bloom: A Touch of the Artist," *James Joyce Quarterly* 10.1 (Fall 1972), 118–131, at 120.

[8] *Ulysses*, ed. Johnson, 737.

[9] Karen Lawrence writes that "Lestrygonians" explores the incorporation of power structures by the individual and the formation of the self through the internalization of the environment, as figured in the act of eating. Karen Lawrence, "Legal Fiction or Pulp Fiction in 'Lestrygonians,'" in *Ulysses-En-Gendered Perspectives: Eighteen New Essays on the Episodes*, ed. Kimberly Devlin and Marilyn Reizbaum (Columbia: University of South Carolina Press, 1999), 100–110.

to Victor Bérard's translation of the episode in *Les Phéniciens et l'Odyssée*, which uses physiological terms to render the description of the enclosed bay of Lamos, in which the Lestrygonian giants consume Odysseus' men (in Book 1:8): "The image that Bérard creates in his translation of Homer is one where Ulysses' men enter a mouth and pass through *du goulet*, 'a narrow strait' into an empty hollow that resembles the pit of a stomach [...] Bérard turns the geographical description into a metaphor for the human body with men as food."[10] Bérard's translation thus naturalizes the Lestrygonians' consumption of Odysseus' men, as the giants' predation is figured, merely, as the proper workings of the body. Joyce takes up the figure of digestion as a metaphor for the workings of the modern city to point to their brutality but also to indicate the means of countering them.

That "Lestrygonians" might offer a critique of society as inherently exploitative has been argued by critics. John Mood specifically links the act of eating to that of domination when he writes that the episode presents the "cannibalism of civilization, chewing up men to produce buildings, cities, whole cultures."[11] Roy Arthur Swanson writes that the episode plays on the popular etymology of the Lestrygonians as "rock-harvesters," which helps it to "allegorize the cannibalistic life cycle" of man, church and state.[12] Yet the episode presents the absorption of traditional forms of power by commercial processes. Many of the food terms in "Lestrygonians" indicate how aristocratic titles become adopted to add extra value to commercial goods: "Curly cabbage *à la duchesse de Parme*"; or reveal that elevated social status is coterminous with extravagant consumption: "The *élite. Crème de la crème*. They want special dishes to pretend they're" (*U* 8:877–84). The dissolution of earlier forms of social organization by commerce finds expression in the opening lines of the episode: "Lozenge and comfit manufacturer to His Majesty the King. God. Save. Our. Sitting on his throne sucking red jujubes white" (*U* 8:3–4). The jujubes that the King sucks wear away in his mouth, resembling the phrase "God. Save. Our.," a remnant of an earlier formulation in the process of erosion. The King becomes an ideal brand-patron and then a consumer

[10] Lynn Childress, "'Les Phéniciens et l'Odyssée': A Source for 'Lestrygonians,'" *James Joyce Quarterly* 26 (1989), 259–69, at 261.
[11] John Mood, "Gulliver and the Lestrygonians: A Heterodox View of the Social Relevance of Literature," *Midwest Quarterly: A Journal of Contemporary Thought* 16 (1975), 409–24, at 419.
[12] Roy Arthur Swanson, "'Lestrygonians,' a Pale 'Proteus'?" *Modern Fiction Studies* 15.1 (Spring 1969), 73–86.

among many others. In this new scenario, everyone is consuming and, because of that, being consumed.

Michael Groden observes that "Lestrygonians" was one of the episodes Joyce edited most heavily following his move to Paris in 1920. Joyce's insertions emphasize the Homeric connection and include these food terms and many others.[13] As we will see in the next chapter, the interest in Homeric adaptations in the Parisian literary scene pushed Joyce to make his own more explicit. However, if Joyce's composition of *Ulysses* was affected by his move to the city, the initial style was already profoundly influenced by the work of an obscure, third-generation French Symbolist.

Shortly before he left Paris in 1903, Joyce purchased Édouard Dujardin's 1887 novel, *Les Lauriers sont coupés*. In a later dedication to Dujardin, Joyce described himself as "le larron impenitent," the unrepentant thief (*JJ* 520). He remarked in 1931: "In the wooden horse borrowed from Dujardin I put the warriors I stole from Victor Bérard."[14] Jean-Michel Rabaté reads this statement as part of Joyce's cultivation of Parisian approval: "he attempted to become more French than the French."[15] Ellmann notes the skepticism of Parisians following the publication of *Ulysses*: "In August of 1923 [Joyce] obtained, thanks to Adrienne Monnier, a copy of the scarce book and brought it to his friend. Larbaud was convinced and soon began to persuade his incredulous countrymen that Dujardin, whom they considered merely a relic of the symbolist movement, was in fact the inaugurator of the latest literature" (*JJ* 520). Critics have directed attention away from Joyce's consistent attribution of the interior monologue to Dujardin and turned to more august influences, beginning with Freud and Tolstoy (Mary Colum), and Dostoyevsky, Poe, and Browning (André Gide).

Passed over and often, perhaps justifiably, laughed at by critics, Dujardin's novel displays not just the challenges of modern urban experience but the difficulty of representing it. Yet the *monologue intérieur* that Dujardin pioneered to present the thoughts of a bourgeois Parisian consumer offered Joyce the means to realize a fully operative mode of prose poetry that would give expression to experience in an immersive urban environment.

---

[13] Michael Groden, *Ulysses in Progress* (Princeton, NJ: Princeton University Press, 1977), 123, 180–85.

[14] Qtd. in Rabaté, "Joyce the Parisian," 58. Ellmann notes Joyce's remarks: "'in that book,' he said, 'the reader finds himself established, from the first lines, in the thought of the principal personage, and the uninterrupted unrolling *(deroulement ininterrompu)* of that thought, replacing the usual form of narrative, conveys to us what this personage is doing or what is happening to him" (*JJ* 519–20).

[15] Rabaté acutely describes Dujardin's novel as "an undistinguished piece of prose revery, even if it indeed 'invents' a continuous stream-of-consciousness technique" (58).

Reading Dujardin's novel alongside the "Lestrygonians" episode shows the striking similarity of everyday bourgeois consumption in Dujardin's 1887 Paris and Joyce's 1904 Dublin. If Dujardin's main character, Daniel Prince, often pays tribute to Paris as the city of lights, his life in the city is an immersion in consumption, and indeed in the clichés of consumption, possible for a man of means in any modern European city.[16] The following scene in a restaurant illustrates the closeness of Dujardin's novel to Bloom's stream of consciousness in the middle phase episodes of *Ulysses*. As he takes lunch, Prince puzzles over the lyrics of songs by Eugène Scribe for Giacomo Meyerbeer's highly successful grand opera, *Robert-le-Diable* (1831), and the comic opera, *Le Châlet* (1831):

> Now for the chicken; a wing this time; not so tough; some bread; not a bad bird at all; this is a good place to dine; next time Leah and I dine together at her flat I'll order dinner at that place in Rue Favert; it's cheaper there than the smart restaurants, and better. The wine here is nothing special; you have to go to an expensive restaurant to have proper wine. *Le vin, le jeu, − le vin, le jeu, les belles, − voilà, voilà...* [Wine, cards − wine, cards, and women − that's it, that's it...] but what has wine got to do with cards or cards with women? Of course I can see that men have to be a little drunk to make love, but cards? This chicken was remarkable and the watercress admirable. Ah, pleasant sensation this towards the end of a good meal! Where do the cards come in? ... *le vin, le jeu, − le vin, le jeu, les belles...* Woman, charming woman, so dear to M. Scribe. No, that's not in *Le Châlet* but in *Robert-le-Diable*; devil take it! That's Scribe too. The three together always, a triple passion ... *Vive le vin, l'amour et le tabac. Voilà, voilà, le refrain du bivouac.* [Long live wine, love, and tobacco. This is the refrain of the military camp.] Tobacco, too, of course; I was forgetting it. How should one pronounce them, *taba-c* and *bivoua-c* or *taba* and *bivoua*? Mendès, in the Boulevard des Capucines used to pronounce *dompter, dom-p-ter, dom-ter* is right, of course. *L'amour et le tabac ... le refrain du bivouac...* The solicitor and his wife are going. How absurd, silly, idiotic of me to let them slip off like that! − Waiter![17]

---

[16] For example, also in Trieste and Zurich in the years 1914–1920, although that is outside of the ambit of this book. See John McCourt's, *The Years of Bloom: James Joyce in Trieste: 1904–1920* (Madison: University of Wisconsin Press, 2000).

[17] Dujardin, *We'll to the Woods No More*, 33–34, 28–29, translation altered, Dujardin's ellipses.

> "Au poulet; c'est une aile; pas trop dure aujourd'hui; du pain; ce poulet est mangeable; on peut dîner ici; la prochaine fois qu'avec Léa je dînerai chez elle, je commanderai le dîner rue Croix-des-petits-champs; c'est moins cher que dans les bons restaurants, et c'est meilleur. Ici, seulement, le vin n'est pas remarquable; il faut aller dans les grands restaurants pour avoir du vin. Le vin, le jeu, − le vin, le jeu, les belles, − voilà, voilà... Quel rapport est entre le vin et le jeu, entre le jeu et les belles? je veux bien que des gens aient besoin de se monter pour faire l'amour; mais le jeu? Ce poulet était remarquable, le cresson admirable. Ah, la

Here, closely assembled, are a striking number of Bloomian concerns. Bloom, too, is preoccupied with the consumption of food and wine, "Nice quiet bar" (*U* 8:822), "Not logwood that" (*U* 8:820), "Nice wine it is" (*U* 8:851). He muses on the procurement of luxuries for his beloved, "Could buy one of those silk petticoats for Molly, colour of her new garters" (*U* 8:1061–62). He reflects on terms and popular sayings, "Born with a silver knife in his mouth. That's witty, I think. Or no. Silver means born rich. Born with a knife. But then the allusion is lost" (*U* 8:684–86). "Why do they call that thing they gave me nutsteak? Nutarians. Fruitarians. To give you the idea you are eating rumpsteak. Absurd" (*U* 8:538–40). He adds to his consideration of an issue further relevant terms, "That is how poets write, the similar sounds. But then Shakespeare has no rhymes: blank verse. The flow of language it is" (*U* 8:64–65). He observes the connections between physical conditions and bodily states, "Tastes fuller this weather with the chill off" (*U* 8:820–21); "Taste it better because I'm not thirsty" (*U* 8:851). He notes the onset of pleasure, "Mild fire of wine kindled his veins. I wanted that badly" (*U* 8:854). He is visited by the ear-worms of Meyerbeer's grand operas, "*Lacaus esant* tara tara. Great chorus that. *Taree tara*. Must be washed in rainwater. Meyerbeer. *Tara: bom bom bom*" (*U* 8:623–24). He struggles to remember the words of popular texts, "*Their lives*. I have it. *It grew bigger and bigger and bigger*" (*U* 8:782–83). He puzzles over language, "*A cenar teco*. What does that *teco* mean? Tonight perhaps" (*U* 8:1051–52). He bungles haphazard encounters, "Tea. Tea. Tea. I forgot to tap Tom Kernan" (*U* 8:371–72).

Taken out of context, these fragments of course fail to do justice to the complexity of the Lestrygonian stream of consciousness. Yet this chapter aims to show that Dujardin's form is the means through which Joyce achieves an extended version of Stephen's sentient thinking and, in doing so, develops a response to the problem of experience in the modern city. In the singular exclamation, "Darkness falls from the air," Stephen unconsciously combines Nash and Rimbaud; in "Lestrygonians," Bloom's stream

---

tranquillité du dîner presque achevé. Mais le jeu... le vin, le jeu, – le vin, le jeu, les belles... Les belles, chères à Scribe. Ce n'est pas du Châlet, mais de Robert-le-Diable. Allons, c'est de Scribe encore. Et toujours la même triple passion... Vive le vin, l'amour et le tabac... Il y a encore le tabac; ça, j'admets... Voilà, voilà, le refrain du bivouac... Faut-il prononcer taba-c et bivoua-c, ou taba et bivoua? Mendès, boulevard des Capucines, disait dom-p-ter; il faut dom-ter. L'amour et le taba-c... le refrain du bivoua-c... L'avoué et sa femme s'en vont. C'est insensé, ridicule, grotesque, les laisser partir... – 'Garçon!'"

Édouard Dujardin, Les Lauriers sont coupés (Paris: Librairie de la Revue indépendente, 188), 27–28.

of consciousness features an ongoing series of phrases that blend into and flow on from one another. If Stephen responds to Emma's physical expression, Bloom responds to individual women, who consciously and unconsciously offer him their bodily expressions, and also to the ongoing stimulation of the urban environment.

I use here the term "stream of consciousness" in preference to "interior monologue," despite the fact that Dujardin's term often features in critical reception. The stream of consciousness, in contrast to the interior monologue, suggests not an internal, solitary, and deliberate verbal performance but rather a continuous, spontaneous, and irregular flow of both physical and verbal events of which the individual is aware. My reading of the stream of consciousness, however, departs from much of preceding critical discussions: I understand it as Joyce's means of giving full expression, in an urban setting, to the porous, processual body of Pseudo-Aristotle's *Problems*.[18] If the individual in *Problems* retains an entelechy, in the Ulyssean stream of consciousness, individuation is put in question. It is this undermining of sovereign individuality that offers a means of resistance to the reigning principles of exchange. As the site of the stream of consciousness, Bloom is not an unthinking instrument of economic relations but rather is engaged in a critical mode of response, even while he is subject in an ongoing way to those relations.

That the stream of consciousness stages a creative, processual mode of thinking that, in resisting formal articulation, acts within and against an urban environment has not been a consensus view among critics. Ellmann writes of Joyce's "construction of character by odds and ends, by minutiae" (*JJ* 358) and argues that the stream of consciousness is a result of the isolation of Joyce's characters: "their basic anxieties and exaltations seemed to move with slight reference to their environment. They were so islanded, in fact, that Joyce's development of the interior monologue to enable his readers to enter the mind of a character without the chaperonage of the

---

[18] In recent years, the topic has fallen away as a central preoccupation among Joyce scholars. Works focused on the form date from earlier decades: Erwin R. Steinberg, *The Stream of Consciousness and Beyond in Ulysses* (Pittsburgh, PA: University of Pittsburgh Press, 1973); K. E. Robinson, "The Stream of Consciousness Technique and the Structure of Joyce's *Portrait*," *James Joyce Quarterly* 9.1 (Fall 1971), 63–84; Shiv K. Kumar, "James Joyce," in *Bergson and the Stream of Consciousness Novel* (New York: New York University Press, 1963). More recent engagements include Gabriel R. Ricci, "Finding in Favor of the Stream of Consciousness," in *The Tempo of Modernity* (New Brunswick, NJ: Transaction Publishers, 2012) and Doris Bremm, "Stream of Consciousness Narration in James Joyce's *Ulysses*: The Flâneur and the Labyrinth in 'Lestrygonians,'" in *The Image of the City in Literature, Media, and Society: Selected Papers, 2003 Conference, Society for the Interdisciplinary Study of Social Imagery*, ed. Will Wright and Steven Kaplan (Pueblo, CO: Society for the Interdisciplinary Study of Social Imagery, 2003).

author, seems a discovery he might have been expected to make" (*JJ* 358).
This chapter disputes Ellmann's claims: the form of "Lestrygonians" is not
a product of isolation but rather an ongoing register of interaction with the
physical, social, and economic world. In this way, the stream of consciousness can never be a "synthetic" method of establishing character, as
Ellmann claims, but is, rather, accretive and open-ended. If *Ulysses* min-
imizes scenes of interpersonal drama, it is in the service of the representation of the experience of the city street and of the staging of a mode that
counters it.

Franco Moretti comes closer to this reading when he sees the stream of
consciousness as the "inexhaustible transmitter of the capitalist metropolis"
that offers an "open present, where the various developments are still all
equally possible."[19] He understands the stream of consciousness as presenting not an islanded subjectivity, as Ellmann does, but indeed the
absence of the subject: "simple, fragmented sentences, where the subject
withdraws to make room for the invasion of things; paratactical paragraphs, with the doors flung wide, and always enough room for one more
sentence, and one more stimulus."[20] Moretti thus sees in Bloom an
"innocent passivity" in "the world – the truly *grand* world – of *consumption.*"[21] Moretti is right that this passivity and constant openness to
stimulation puts off any movement toward realized action: *Ulysses* does
not feature political intervention. Yet to expect Bloom to take political
action against consumer capitalism is to ask for a lot. Moretti's critique is
also predicated upon the assumption that a meaningful response could
only take the form of outwardly visible action. Instead, we can understand
Bloom as resisting the invasive forces of consumption in ongoing activities
and processes that take place at a small scale. Moretti focuses, following
Simmel, on the modality of vision, understood as a detached mode of
relation to the world: "a glance then on again. It is the metropolitan
way."[22] Yet Bloom's material and linguistic processing of "this invasion
of things" is a counterdigestion of forces that pass through him. It is
through what Moretti calls the "withdrawal of the subject," which
I would put as an undoing of the mode of sovereign individuality through
which consumption operates, that the stream of consciousness offers an
alternative mode to the objectification and calculation of transactional
relations.

[19] Franco Moretti, *Modern Epic: The World-System from Goethe to García Márquez*, trans. Quintin
Hoare (New York: Verso, 1996), 135, 139.
[20] Ibid., 135.   [21] Ibid., 143.   [22] Ibid., 136.

Dujardin's Succession of Short Phrases

To achieve this, Joyce avails of the problems of Dujardin's interior monologue as much as its achievements. In his subsequent book on the interior monologue, Dujardin called *Les Lauriers* a Symbolist novel, celebrating his innovation as importing techniques of Symbolist poetry to narrative: "In my opinion, I salute the interior monologue as one of the manifestations of this glittering entrance of poetry into the novel, which is the mark of the epoch."[23] Dujardin writes: "It has become impossible for us to call a work poetic in which reasoning intervenes and which does not emanate directly from the depths of the subconscious."[24] It is easy to question Dujardin's assumption here of the possibility of an artistic sensibility that arises from a private mental space, that evades reason, and that can be given verbal expression.[25] Yet this dissociation of poetry from reasoning speaks directly to Joyce's project of a musical and pictorial thought. Dujardin presents the preverbal, prerational state as one of sensation, where *sensibilité* means physical sensitivity rather than emotional character or temperament, although it encompasses the flux of emotion. He points to philosopher and essayist Jules de Gautier as showing that "poetry consisted in a sort of recovery of primitive language which was nothing but the 'extension and exteriorization in a sonic medium of the nervous vibration identified with the reality of physiological emotion,' man transmitting to man 'in an entirely adequate fashion,' his 'state of sensitivity.'"[26]

Dujardin's theory of the interior monologue comes long after his novel, yet *Les Lauriers* is indeed focused on sensation, to the extent that its main

[23] My translation. "Quant à moi, je salue dans le monologue intérieur une des manifestations de cette entrée fulgurante de la poésie dans le roman, qui est la marque de l'époque." Edouard Dujardin, *Le Monologue intérieur, son apparition, ses origines, sa place dans l'œuvre de James Joyce et dans le roman contemporain* (Paris: Messein, 1931), 224.

[24] My translation. "Il nous est devenu ... impossible d'accorder la qualité poétique a une œuvre ou intervient le raisonnement et qui n'émane pas directement des profondeurs du subconscient" Qtd. in King, 103. Qtd. in C. D. King, "Edouard Dujardin and the Genesis of the Inner Monologue," *French Studies* 9 (1955), 101–15, at 103.

[25] "La beauté de la forme dramatique n'est pas, comme l'ont cru quelques réalistes, de reproduire la conversation que deux personnes auraient pu avoir dans la réalité; elle est de faire jaillir de leur subconscient les choses qui y sont enfermées et qui dans la réalité ne seraient jamais montées jusqu'a leurs bouches" (qtd. in King, 102); "The beauty of the dramatic form is not, as the realists have believed, to reproduce the conversation that two characters could have had in reality; it is to make spring forth from their subconscious things that are enclosed therein, which in reality would never have reached their mouths."

[26] "la poésie consistait en une sorte de reprise du langage primitif lequel n'était que 'le prolongement et l'extériorisation dans le milieu sonore de la vibration nerveuse identifiée avec la réalité même de l'émotion physiologique,' l'homme transmettant alors à l'homme 'd'une façon entièrement adéquate' son 'état de sensibilité." Qtd. in King, 104.

character's thoughts are dominated by it. However Dujardin's novel presents a bathetic version of the heightened sensibility that modern man is given by consumption. If, as Verlaine describes, Baudelaire contends heroically with the agitation and hypersensitivity produced by overstimulation, Dujardin's protagonist (a term that ascribes him perhaps too much agency) operates in a decidedly unheroic mode. Prince's sensorium and intelligence are palliated and numbed rather than overstimulated by what he consumes, and he is awkward, calculating, and fixated on trivia. In this sense, Dujardin's is a significant, if uninspiring, achievement: the depiction of the deformation of an average mind by consumption.

If they lack the drama of Baudelairean agon, Dujardin's character's thoughts are nonetheless determined by the rhythm and scale of their environment. They are bite-sized. According to Dujardin, the "succession of short phrases" are inspired by the Wagnerian leitmotif:

> We deliberately set poetry on the Schopenhauerian throne of music. And it is that which is understood when one says that Symbolism, liberating poetry from intellectual servitude, restores to it its musical value. Just as a page of Wagner is a succession of undeveloped motifs, every one of which expresses a movement of the soul, the interior monologue is a succession of short phrases, every one of which also expresses a movement of the soul, with the resemblance that they are not linked one to the next in a rational order but in a purely emotional order, outside of all intellectual arrangement.[27]

Yet, in contrast to this Schopenhaurian music, this nonrational movement of the soul, this expression of unity in multiplicity, Dujardin's novel presents a caricatured, misdirected version of the nonverbal and nonconceptual: a subjectivity consumed by an environment of consumption. In the scene in the restaurant cited earlier, Prince thinks while chewing, and although he derives some pleasure from the food, his thoughts do not yield any insight. His thoughts, in fact, are a by-product of his eating and drinking. They take the form of assessments of what he is consuming: "pas trop dure," "mangeable," "on peut diner ici," "pas remarquable," "remarquable," "admirable." They focus on how best to consume, as he

---

[27] "Délibérément, nous assîmes la poésie sur le trône schopenhauerien de la musique. Et c'est ce qu'on entend lorsque l'on dit que le symbolisme, libérant du servage de l'intellectualisme la poésie, lui a restitué sa valeur musicale. [...] De même que le plus souvent une page de Wagner est une succession de motifs non développés dont chacun exprime également un mouvement d'âme, le monologue intérieur est une succession de phrases courtes dont chacune exprime également un mouvement d'âme, avec cette ressemblance qu'elles ne sont pas liées les unes aux autres suivant un ordre rationnel mais suivant un ordre purement émotionnel, en dehors de tout arrangement intellectualisé." Qtd. in King, 108, 110.

struggles over the pronunciation of Scribe's libretto and ponders its logic: "Faut-il prononcer taba-c et bivoua-c, ou taba et bivoua?"; "Le vin, le jeu, les belles, /Voilà, mes seuls amours! [...] Quel rapport est entre le vin et le jeu, entre le jeu et les belles?" In Scribe's lyrics, "Voilà" is an indication of preference; in Prince's thoughts, it is not an exclamation of insight but rather marks his fuller recall of words that pervade his consciousness and interrupt his thoughts.[28]

Prince's character is defined by his failure to answer the question that is prompted by the sonic associations of the word, wine: "Il faut aller dans les grands restaurants pour avoir du vin. Quel rapport est entre le vin et le jeu, entre le jeu et les belles?" "You must go to expensive restaurants to have proper wine. What is the connection between wine and cards, between cards and women?" He reflects, before becoming distracted by new sensations, "I can see that men have to get a little drunk to make love but cards? This chicken was remarkable." Returning to the question, he remarks "Et toujours la même triple passion ... Vive le vin, l'amour et le tabac," "Always the same triple passion... Vive wine, love and tobacco." As he fails to separate women from a shifting array of exciting stimulants, desire, for Prince, is the desire to consume. He thus names, unconsciously, his own domination by consumption.

Prince's brief sensations, his fragmentary memories of texts, and the thoughts closely associated with them are reconceived by Joyce as a process of thinking that occurs through physical processes. In a context where consecutive and independent articulation is no longer possible, the short phrases of Dujardin's interior monologue suggest a space for reflection. These bite-sized phrases, prompted by immediate sensory experiences and sonic associations, allow Joyce to develop a sentient thinking that counters the subsumption of the individual by consumption. This is illustrated in an early scene in "Lestrygonians" in which Bloom both considers forced consumption and experiences the imposition of the instruction to consume. The key difference is that Prince repeats, but Bloom distorts.

---

[28] Sarah Hibberd observes that "Scribe and his collaborators were complying opportunistically with the bourgeois public's demand for pure entertainment; the operas were thus titillating rather than challenging or engaging." Sarah Hibberd, *French Grand Opera and the Historical Imagination* (Cambridge, UK: Cambridge University Press, 2009), 6. She defines the genre of grand opera as involving a variety of amusements: "four or five acts, medieval or Renaissance setting, tragic ending, choruses of people in conflict, dramatically integrated ballet, mix of characters from different social backgrounds; impressive orchestral effects; melodramatic situations, tableaux; large scene complexes with embedded numbers; techniques and vocal styles influenced by French, Italian and German opera" (2).

Bloom's Osmosis

If you cram a turkey, say on chestnut meal it tastes like that. Eat pig like pig. But then why is it that saltwater fish are not salty? How is that? His eyes sought an answer from the river and saw a rowboat rock at anchor on the treacly swells lazily its plasterboard.
Kino's.
11/-
Trousers (U 8:85–92)

Here Bloom explores one of the consequences of eating, namely the permeation of the eater by the substance ingested. The particular process he considers is not entirely natural; it is an effect of a particular act of industrial management, the force-feeding of turkeys, which might be analogous to the preparation of the individual by the advertising industry. Immediately after this image of domination, Bloom offers an image of resistance: a fish that is not salty, despite swimming in the sea. A little later in the episode, Bloom recalls that he himself was called "mackerel" when a boy (U 8:405), and here his reaction to the advertisement is analogous to the process of osmotic regulation in fish. Bloom's linguistic and economic reflection provides a kind of counterforce to this environment, allowing him to process it, or digest it, as it fills him in the attempt to turn him to its own purposes. Yet, crucially, Bloom responds not with an independent and resistant rationality but with a conscious processing of received linguistic fragments that nonetheless yields insights.[29]

If Stephen, in Stephen Hero, thinks of aesthetic production as a twofold operation in which the artist engages a "selective faculty and a reproductive faculty," Bloom's selective faculty is not discriminating but proceeds according to proximity and association. Following his question of why some marine fish are not salty, "His eyes sought answer from the river." In this process, he engages with the environment in uncontrolled manner, as the trail of asyntactical words illustrates: "saw a rowboat rock at anchor on the treacly swells lazily its plasterboard." Bloom's glance is caught by an advertisement for Kino's clothing store fixed to this rowboat on the River Liffey. This sighting is an instance of the infiltration of the urban

---

[29] Bloom's thoughts here parallel Jane Bennett's, who invokes Friedrich Nietzsche and Ralph Waldo Emerson: "eating appears as a series of mutual transformations in which the border between inside and outside becomes blurry: my meal is and is not mine; you both are and are not what you eat," Jane Bennett, Vibrant Matter: A Political Ecology of Things (Durham, NC: Duke University Press, 2010), 49, yet Bloom's observation of this intermixing also includes the commercial environment that surrounds him and against which his material thought processes unfold.

dweller by a constant stream of sensory appeals. This infiltration is emphasized by a pun: *Kino* means cinema in German. The text of the Kino's
poster moves through Bloom like the images that saturate the audience in a
movie theater.

The sight of the advertisement prompts commercially oriented inquiries: "Wonder if he pays rent to the corporation," and "How can you
own water really?" which are followed by a series of distorted quotations,
puns, and clichés beginning with "flowing in a stream, never the same," a
distortion of Heraclitus' maxim, as quoted by Plato, "Heraclitus, I believe,
says that all things go and nothing stays, and comparing existence to
the flow of a river, he says you could not step twice into the same river"
(*U* 8:93–97).[30] But this notion blends into "which in the stream of life we
trace," a blurred citation of Edward Fitzball's libretto for the 1845 grand
opera *Maritana*, "Some thoughts none other can replace/Remembrance
will recall;/Which in the flight of years we trace,/Is dearer than them all."[31]
Bloom's spontaneous and inaccurate reproduction of the third line of this
passage replaces time with space and certain memory with constant
motion. The "stream of life," which replaces "flight of years," also warps
the cliché that "life is a dream," the translated title of a Spanish-language
play by Pedro Calderón de la Barca, *La vida es sueño* (1635). The "stream
of life" here is modern life, constantly prey to influences of all kinds: "All
kinds of places are good for ads" (*U* 8:95–96).[32]

Bloom's stream of consciousness contends with the erosion of individual
identity, memory, and stable ideation by the constant infiltration of the
urban environment. With this technique, Joyce develops both his representation of the body as a site of the confluence of forces and, associated
with that body, the possibility of a sentient thinking. Bloom's sentient
thinking resists passive material determination by the constant stream of
sensory appeals through generating instead a vital mobility. His repetitions
evolve toward an insight not through deliberate, formal, and rational

---

[30] Plato, *Cratylus* 402a.   [31] Gifford and Seidman, *Ulysses Annotated*, 100.

[32] Jennifer Wicke reads the Kino scene as a "passage that seems almost fortuitously to muse on the
constitutive power of advertising language," and, as part of her argument for the centrality of
advertising for high modernism, equates "the flow of advertising experience" with the stream of
consciousness, Jennifer Wicke, *Advertising Fictions: Literature, Advertisement and Social Reading*
(New York: Columbia University Press, 1988), 140; "The Kino's ad Bloom sees 'creates' his
subsequent stream of thoughts; it also suggests that advertising language is the only stream to
swim in, now" (141). My reading here, however, resists this determination and univocality along
material lines suggested by Wicke herself in another passage: "Bloom is established as a [...]
transformer station for everyday language. Bloom receives the signals that the culture is sending out,
and he makes his own mix of them [...] Bloom will continue to be an alembic filter of
advertisement" (129, 130).

cogitation but through spontaneous processes of connection and elaboration. His attunement to physical and mental processes is crucial to these processes, as the verbal terms of his awareness are transformed in pun, association, and sonic distortion. Precisely because it is closely related to his sensations, this procession of phrases allows Bloom's thinking to separate itself not just from received texts but also from preformed thoughts. This process responds to and relies upon an ineradicable openness.

Joyce does not merely employ the form pioneered by Dujardin to present Bloom; Joyce causes its particulate, absorptive mode to structure Bloom's own view of himself. Rather than understanding himself as a discrete, atomistic individual, Bloom is aware that he is constantly processing foreign thoughts and matter. His observation "Never know whose thoughts you're chewing" (U 8:717–18) signals his awareness that the mind is not a unified field in which original thoughts unfold but a physical locus in which ideas and formulations are processed, just as various kinds of food are combined and digested in the stomach.[33] That this is an aesthetic practice is suggested later when Bloom understands the production of poetry in terms of what the body has ingested:

> For example one of those policemen sweating Irish stew into their shirts you couldn't squeeze a line of poetry out of him. Don't know what poetry is even. Must be in a certain mood.
> *The dreamy cloudy gull*
> *Waves o'er the waters dull.* (U 8:545–50)

Italicized and offset from the rest of Bloom's thoughts, the rhyming lines visually perform the separation of the bird from the waters over which it flies. Unknowingly, Bloom parodies Joyce's Paris poem, "All day I hear the noise of waters": the separation of the comically lyrical "dreamy cloudy" gull in Bloom's poem is undone by this figural language, borrowed from the seascape itself. This comically awkward dissolution of the independent bird suggests the impossibility of separating oneself from context, or at least the futility of a literary project that would assert that separation. In contrast to this vaporous independence, Bloom offers his own poem, focused on the stomach:

> *The hungry famished gull*
> *Flaps o'er the waters dull.*

---

[33] This reading has something in common with Michael Tratner's, who, while focusing on the various social strata represented in *Ulysses*, sees Joyce's view of society as "radically pluralistic," composed of characters who are "merely a nexus through which social tides flow." Michael Tratner, *Modernism and Mass Politics: Joyce, Woolf, Eliot, Yeats* (Stanford, CA: Stanford University Press, 1995), 198.

That is how poets write, the similar sounds. But then Shakespeare has no rhymes: blank verse. The flow of language it is. (*U* 8:62–65).

Yet Bloom's poetic composition lacks the grace of his stream of consciousness. In fact, his own "flow of language" suggests that the stream of consciousness is a kind of poetry, which takes the form not of the metrical and rhythmic ordering of language, which he attempts briefly here, but fragmentary sonically and associatively related responses to what he experiences. We might call it, after Baudelaire, a poetic prose. In contrast to the first couplet, the stream of consciousness offers a genuine independence, as it functions within, rather than attempts to evade, the traffic of the city.

Eating Molly's Mumbled Words

Retrospective attributions of causality in a narrative are somewhat dubious; that caveat aside, we might see Bloom's observation "Never know whose thoughts you're chewing" as made possible by the encounter that forms his most potent memory in *Ulysses*: his erotic exchange with Molly on Howth Head.[34] Before we turn to examine it, it is useful to consider briefly the impasse of Prince's relations with his beloved, herself a part-time performer, and the focus of his fears of infidelity through much of *Les Lauriers*. Prince's relationship with Léa is defined by his failure to distinguish himself from the subject-position of the consumer. Throughout the novel, he struggles to avoid acting as if he has purchased Léa's body with his gifts and the money he gives in response to her reports of financial crises. Chavainne, his canny acquaintance, tells him to alter his method, "or you'll never get anything."[35] Prince rejects this with the idea that he is pursuing something more meaningful than "stupidly spending the night

---

[35] Dujardin, *We'll to the Woods No More*, 11; "Changez votre système, mon ami, ou vous n'obtiendrez rien" (Dujardin, *Les lauriers sont coupés*, 13).

[34] Luca Crispi notes the scene's foundational importance in *Ulysses*: "The first version of this momentous scene is in 'Lestrygonians' and it is also already present in the episode's earliest surviving document, its Rosenbach manuscript, which Joyce wrote in mid-1918. This particular story remained virtually unchanged until its appearance in *Ulysses* two and a half years later, which indicates that it is one of the primal stories in the book," Luca Crispi, *Joyce's Creative Process and the Construction of Characters in Ulysses: Becoming the Blooms* (Oxford, UK: Oxford University Press, 2015), 168. Crispi connects the setting of this scene to Oliver St. John Gogarty's description of lying in the sunshine under rhododendrons on moss and bracken on Howth Head, "the most happy day I ever wish to spend" (qtd. 168/9).

[35] Dujardin, *We'll to the Woods No More*, 11; "Changez votre système, mon ami, ou vous n'obtiendrez rien" (Dujardin, *Les lauriers sont coupés*, 13).

with absurd one-night-girls."[36] However, the proof he desires that their relationship is one of love rather than of transaction is sex. In his fantasies, he imagines demonstrating his nobility by refusing to take Léa's body in return for the money he has given her.[37] His intention to demonstrate his love by distancing himself from a relation of exchange is predicated upon the physical rights he sees as afforded by the money given her. Ironically, his money buys him the illusion of their purity, and a pose of nobility, which he nonetheless constantly undoes with his expectation of sexual intimacy.[38] Prince cannot resist bringing everything to account but Léa is constantly one step ahead of him, delaying sweetly in order to extend his payments.

If Prince is occupied by attempts at noble consumption, Bloom's mode of engagement with the world is inaugurated in an encounter with Molly that, through shared eating, defies a transactional relation. In contrast to Stephen and Emma's somatic aesthetics, which occurred in the absence of any deliberation, at the picnic at Howth, Bloom and Molly's aesthetic exchange is a consciously shared practice that consummates their relationship. In contrast to the passively expressed products of Emma's body that prompted Stephen's verbal exclamation, Molly deliberately shares with Bloom a partially digested substance, initiating Bloom into a somatic aesthetics. As opposed to the asymmetry of words and scent in Stephen and Emma's encounter, here Molly's chewing of the seedcake is figured as "mumbled," an obscure language that she puts in Bloom's mouth (*U* 8:908). Stephen experienced a "trembling joy" at their unconscious exchange; Bloom's joy is emphatic in this mutual, deliberate exchange.

Molly and Bloom's eating kiss recovers a primary relationality obscured by transactional relations. Her gesture reveals to him his implication in a "world of flesh" and the attendant discontinuity and obscurity of his own

---

[36] My translation. "bêtement faire la noce avec d'absurdes filles d'une nuit" (13).

[37] "I might pass the night in your arms, dear, but – . . . I give you back your body. Goodbye [. . .] nothing easier, nothing simpler; and so she will understand why I don't take advantage of my rights over her, how truly I love her . . ." (83); "Je puis rester ici cette nuit . . . Je vous rends votre corps . . . Adieu [. . .] rien de plus facile et de plus naturel. Elle comprendra enfin pourquoi je renonce mes droits à l'avoir, et combien je l'aime" (79–80).

[38] "It's very nice of you, Leah says. She comes back; I have pleased her; a bit expensive it was; still she will be kind now, show her appreciation; this way, too, I feel less compunction about staying the night, in fact she owes it to me" (144); "'Vous êtes gentil' dit Léa. Vers moi elle revient; je lui ai fait plaisir; ce me coûte encore un peu cher; mais elle sera contente de moi et sera amiable; et puis j'ai ainsi moins de scrupules à rester cette nuit, plus de droits" (137–38).

self, "Kissed, she kissed me. Me. And me now" (*U* 8:916–17).[39] While syntactical reorganization is a feature of Joyce's style from *Portrait* onward, here it takes on a new significance. It is associated with a heightened awareness of physical events, with a surrendering of individual agency, and with a new grammar of coexistence, where subject and object are no longer functional units. In this idiosyncratic syntax, "Ravished over her I lay, full lips full open, kissed her mouth," we can guess that it is Molly's mouth that is open and full-lipped, but this is not clear, as "full lips open" would most correctly qualify the subject of the sentence, Bloom (*U* 8:906). In this subversion of grammatical sense, subject and object drop away as key units of meaning. Accordingly, the sense of words is contradicted: Bloom is "ravished" as he lies over Molly, submitting in what might otherwise be a position of dominance.

Molly's sharing of the seedcake with Bloom comes with the softening of borders, specifically the borders that define the body, language, and ownership as Molly and Bloom become more than one body and less than two bodies. More precisely, counting does not apply. Their eating kiss belongs to neither of them and to both of them, as they simultaneously touch and are touched at once.[40] The lived synesthesia of the doubled proximate senses of taste and touch intensifies this flouting of individual boundaries. Their kiss continues the dissolution of the seedcake, which has already lost its definition in Molly's mouth in a savory process suggested by the bilabial nasals and sibilants of Bloom's description: "Mawkish pulp her mouth had mumbled sweet-sour of her spittle" (*U* 8:907–8). An unusual sentence performs the resistance of this sharing to calculation: "Joy: I ate it: joy" (*U* 8:908). Here, Bloom's report of eating the mush is surrounded by the naming of an emotion. The chiasmus suggests that Bloom is enveloped, even as he takes something into his mouth. Passive reaction and object of action blur.

---

[39] Butler uses this phrase in "Alterities of the Flesh in Irigaray and Merleau-Ponty," in *Senses of the Subject*: "Consider that the phenomenological counter to Cartesianism that Merleau-Ponty articulates is in part a refusal of that perceptual distance postulated between the reflecting subject and the world of objects. In breaking apart this distinction, the perceiving 'I' acquires a flesh that implicates him or her in a world of flesh" (161–62). For Butler, the subject as flesh is primarily an intersubjective being: "finding its primary sociality in a set of relations that are never fully recoverable or traceable" (168).

[40] According to Michel Serres, in *The Five Senses: A Philosophy of Mingled Senses* (London: Continuum, 2009), touch is the paradigmatic sense. Contact of the skin with itself leads to consciousness, where body is the site of the nonsite, of plurality.

The use of the colon as a kind of permeable punctuation takes on particular significance here. Fowler, in his 1926 *Dictionary of Modern English Usage*, writes that the colon "is not now a stop of a certain power available in any situation demanding such a power, but has acquired a special function, that of delivering the goods that have been invoiced in the preceding words; it is a substitute for such verbal harbingers as *viz, scil., that is to say, i.e., &c.*"[41] According to the grammatical conventions of the 1920s, then, the colon no longer merely signals a short pause, it manages an exchange. It is a signal that what has been promised in a preceding statement will be delivered in specific form in the following list, the grammatical equivalent of the bill of lading. Yet it is this very function that is undermined in the phrase: "Joy: I ate it: joy." Nothing is sufficiently particularized to allow it to take the role of the good that has been invoiced. The sentence presents us with a subverted inventory, a description that is not exhaustive, closed, or calculable.[42]

Molly initiates Bloom into a somatic aesthetic, an art that is concerned not with sublimation but with consciously shared embodiment, an art that consists of sensory perception, *aesthesis*. Unlike Stephen's encounter with Emma, Bloom's experience with Molly is not a culmination but an induction. Seeded by Molly, Bloom's stream of consciousness takes the place of Stephen's dark vowels. In the stream of consciousness, too, the conscious will is sidelined by a spontaneous and unconsciously produced sonic play, but rather than a singular, crystalizing expression, it takes the form of an ongoing processing. Bloom's habitual mode of thinking is intimately related to, even initiated by, this consciously celebrated moment of permeation and coexistence. Karen Lawrence sees this moment as figuring the penetrative capacity of the stream of consciousness: "The mollification of the seedcake stands as the symbol of the fluidity and liquidity of identifications that mark Joyce's text."[43] Lawrence sees Bloom's memory as overshadowed by his contemporary experiences, as

---

[41] H. E. Fowler, *A Dictionary of Modern English Usage* (Oxford, UK: Oxford University Press, 1926), 569.

[42] Mark Osteen celebrates the kiss as emblematic of *Ulysses*'s potentially infinite circulation: "the mutual kiss is erotic commerce, manifesting the ceaselessly circulating gift economy. The kiss is owned by both and neither; in it each person is at once rejuvenated individually and liberated from the self and submerged into the process of exchange" Osteen, *The Economy of Ulysses: Making Both Ends Meet* (Syracuse, NY: Syracuse University Press, 1995), 440.

[43] Lawrence, "Legal Fiction or Pulp Fiction in 'Lestrygonians,'" in Karen Lawrence, *Who's Afraid of James Joyce?* (Gainesville: University of Florida Press, 2010), 131.

he is situated within a world of hostile exchanges and physical exigencies.[44] Yet, as she points out, it is the "consubstantiality"[45] that follows Bloom's ingestion of bread soaked in wine in Davy Byrne's pub that triggers his memory of Howth Head, "Glowing wine on his palate lingered swallowed. Crushing in the winepress grapes of Burgundy. Sun's heat it is. Seems to a secret touch telling me memory. Touched his sense moistened remembered" (*U* 8:897–99). This lived aesthetic practice continues through Bloom's encounters in that world of hostile exchanges and physical exigencies.

An Aesthetic of Open Bodies

That this is an aesthetic practice is emphasized by the immediate turning of Bloom's thoughts from the picnic on Howth Head to art. "Me. And me now," Bloom muses, just before the countertop of Davy Byrne's bar reminds him of Greek statues. The porous human body is contrasted with discrete and impervious representations of the human form:

> His downcast eyes followed the silent veining of the oaken slab. Beauty: it curves: curves are beauty. Shapely goddesses, Venus, Juno: curves the world admires. Can see them library museum standing in the round hall, naked goddesses. Aids to digestion. They don't care what man looks. All to see. Never speaking. I mean to fellows like Flynn. Suppose she did Pygmalion and Galatea what would she say first? Mortal! Put you in your proper place. Quaffing nectar at mess with gods golden dishes, all ambrosial. Not like a tanner lunch we have, boiled mutton, carrots and turnips, bottle of Allsop. Nectar imagine it drinking electricity: gods' food. Lovely forms of women sculpted Junonian. Immortal lovely. And we stuffing food in one hole and out behind: food, chyle, blood, dung, earth, food: have to feed it like stoking an engine. They have no. Never looked. I'll look today. Keeper won't see. Bend down let something drop. See if she. (*U* 8:919–32)

Bloom's inquiry builds upon two of the aesthetic questions Joyce posed in Paris: "Why are statues made white for the most part?" and "Why are not excrements, children and lice works of art?" As he expresses curiosity about Greek statuary and the organs of excretion, Bloom questions, albeit in an

---

[44] Lawrence suggests that Molly fills a foundational role when she describes her as "a nourishing, yet not devouring, mother" (130). "It is shortly after this that we lose Bloom's interior monologue for a while as he goes to the urinal [. . .] this suddenly externalized view reminds us of the fact that the moment of oral exchange is a memory only, made more vivid and painful because of the ten years that have elapsed since full carnal intercourse has occurred between the Blooms" (130–31).

[45] Ibid., 129.

informal way, a central tenet of eighteenth-century aesthetics: the taboo on body openings.[46] Gotthold Ephraim Lessing remarks with horror on open mouths in *Laocoön: An Essay on the Limits of Painting and Poetry* (1766), a text that Joyce read in Paris in 1903, "Simply imagine Laocoön's mouth forced wide open, and then judge! [. . .] The wide-open mouth, aside from the fact that the rest of the face is thereby twisted and distorted in an unnatural and loathsome manner, becomes in painting a mere spot and in sculpture a cavity, with the most repulsive effect."[47] In his *Geschichte der Kunst des Alterthums*, or *History of Ancient Art*, (1764), Johann Winckelmann presents a catalogue of aesthetic regulations; crucial among them are the closed mouth, small, flat nostrils, the absence of any protrusions, and the exclusion of any signs of having eaten. Winckelmann explicitly attributes the beauty of the Belvedere Torso to the liberation of Hercules' deified body from the necessities of eating and digestion: "His body is nourished by no mortal food or coarse particles; he lives on the food of the gods, and he seems only to taste, not to eat, and altogether without being filled."[48] The unbroken line that results from such a taboo on digestion yields the "beautiful contour" celebrated by Winckelmann, or, as received by Bloom, "curves are beauty."

The closed body of the classical Greek statue is attributed the power to heal a subjectivity and a society riven by the division of labor and scientific knowledge in Friedrich Schiller's *On the Aesthetic Education of Man* (1795). Schiller describes the Juno Ludovisi as a "ganze Gestalt," a whole form, one that is "eine völlig geschlossene Schöpfung," a completely self-contained or, more literally, "closed" creation that lives entirely independently, "in sich selbst." This self-containment is most forcefully represented when the statue is described as existing outside of space itself: "The whole figure reposes and dwells in itself, a creation completely self-contained, and, as if existing beyond space, neither yielding nor resisting; here is no force to contend with force, no frailty [weak point] where temporality might break in."[49] The statue is thus removed from the effects of time,

---

[46] See Winfried Menninghaus' "Disgusting Zones and Disgusting Times: The Construction of the Ideally Beautiful Body" in Winfried Menninghaus, *Disgust: The Theory and History of a Strong Sensation* (Albany: State University of New York Press, 2003), 51–102.

[47] Lessing, *Laocoön: An Essay on the Limits of Painting and Poetry*, trans. Edward Allen McCormick (Baltimore, MD: Johns Hopkins University Press, 1962), 17.

[48] Qtd. in Franco Cirulli, *The Age of Figurative Theo-humanism: The Beauty of God and Man in German Aesthetics of Painting and Sculpture (1754–1828)* (New York: Springer, 2015), 40.

[49] Schiller, *Briefe über die aesthetische Erziehung des Menschen*, ed. and trans. Elizabeth Wilkinson and L. A. Willoughby (Oxford, UK: Clarendon Press, 1967), 109. "In sich selbst ruhet und wohnt die ganze Gestalt, eine völlig geschlossene Schöpfung, als wenn sie jenseits des Raumes wäre, ohne

which is understood as physical penetration, "wo die Zeitlichkeit einbrechen könnte." The goddess thus presents an absolute equilibrium, a plenitude that does not overflow but that also allows no ingress. This unity, self-sufficiency, and independence from the environment takes on connotations of economic independence: the goddess is freed from all effort and work.

Schiller's aesthetic employs a concept of divinity fitted to the modern world: a godhead identical with its artistic representation. Independent of every goal, duty, and material need, the goddess offers a counterpoint to the individuals defined and deformed by their roles in social and material exigencies. Whereas formerly, Schiller writes, society was structured organically, the disjunctive and arbitrary nature of modern society is increasingly apparent. Traditions oppose laws, and religious and public duties conflict. Instrumentalized by political and economic mechanisms greater than his own purview, the individual becomes a fragment, "ein Bruchstück," confused and alienated even from himself.

This fragmentation of a previously cohesive society, and consequently of the human being, begins with a new relation to sense experience. The advent of the scientific revolution, "empirical knowledge, and more exact modes of thought,"[50] "die erweiterte Erfahrung und das bestimmte Denken,"[51] brings about the separation of knowing subject and known object. This disassociation accompanies a process of disaggregation that restructures all of society, "eine strengere Absonderung der Stände und Geschäfte." This social division is itself centered on a hierarchical separation of individuals into knowing subjects and passive objects, into individuals who are distinguished by their respective emphases on thinking or feeling.[52]

Schiller's exemplum of the true work of art provides a solution to the world of fragments: the individual, once exposed to the unified form of the statue, becomes aesthetic man, no longer a fragment but free to follow reason and respond to material needs in a balanced, holistic manner. As Schiller declares: "All the other forms of perception divide a man, because

---

Nachgeben, ohne Widerstand; da ist keine Kraft, die mit Kräften kämpfte, keine Blösse, wo die Zeitlichkeit einbrechen könnte." Schiller, *Über die aesthetische Erziehung des Menschen*, ed. Klaus L. Berghahn (Stuttgart: Philipp Reclam, 2000), 108.

[50] Schiller, *Aesthetische Erziehung*, trans. Wilkinson and Willoughby, 35.

[51] Schiller, *Aesthetische Erziehung*, 33.

[52] "Ewig nur an ein einzelnes kleines Bruchstück des Ganzes gefesselt, bildet sich der Mensch selbst nur als Bruchstück aus . . ." (33–34); "Everlastingly chained to a single little fragment of the Whole, man himself develops into nothing but a fragment." Ibid., 35.

they are exclusively based either on the sensuous or on the intellectual part of his being; only the perception of the beautiful makes something whole of him, because both his natures must accord with it."[53] That this forms the means of restoring social cohesion is somewhat tenuous; as Martin Jay observes, "Schiller's aesthetic state is no more than a regulative ideal whose complete fulfillment is tantalizingly out of reach."[54] On an individual scale, this model of aesthetic education depends, paradoxically, on the premise that the individual is fundamentally opposite in his or her workings to the Juno Ludovisi – that he or she is possessed of the capacity to absorb the self-containment of the statue, to internalize and reorganize his or her being according to its independence.

Bloom draws, in somewhat bathetic terms, on this notion of the salutary visual absorption of Greek statuary in his thought that they are "aids to digestion." Yet this understanding of the curative powers of Greek art is part of his ongoing exploration of an art that is physically continuous with the everyday world and a means through which to make sense of it. Bloom indeed resolves to visit the library museum and is later observed by Buck Mulligan looking at a statue's bottom, "O, I fear me, he is Greeker than the Greeks. His pale Galilean eyes were upon her mesial groove. Venus Kallipyge" (U 9:614–16). But rather than perversity, or Lynch's lusty appropriation of the statue of Venus, Bloom here is engaged in an ongoing aesthetic practice that is directly opposed to that of Schiller and Winck-elmann. If the taboo on bodily openings in neoclassical aesthetics is part of a response to the split between thinking and feeling that imagines an impervious body, a formal etiquette that is never ascribed such psycho-logical and social ends, Bloom's open borders allow him to engage with various and fragmentary influences, in an inconclusive, interactive, and material manner that constitutes an integration of thinking and feeling. This aesthetic practice takes place within the world of work and pleasure, as "man the fragment" is replaced by the body as a site of the digestion of an endless series of fragments.[55] Bloom's encounter with Molly shows us that this lived aesthetic involves not an inert statue, nor an open female body, but rather a shared practice between and within bodies that dissolves conventional social divisions of gender and individuation.

[53] Schiller, *Aesthetische Erziehung*, trans. Wilkinson and Willoughby, 138.

[54] Martin Jay, *Marxism and Totality: The Adventures of a Concept from Lukács to Habermas* (Berkeley: University of California Press, 1986), 51.

[55] In this sense, the Hely's sandwichboard men are instances of "man the fragment" in Schillerian terms: ossified, inert fragments identified purely by commercial language, distinguished only by their parcel of the labor they share.

This is a practice, however, rather than an achieved state. Bloom's joyful experience with Molly is contingent upon foregoing appropriative relations and departing from the secure definitions of a possessive individualism. Bloom's dissimilarity to a clearly bounded and unchanging self is marked in the observation that prefaces his reflections on the statues: "Me. And me now," Bloom muses, as he returns from his reminiscence to the present day. Here, as his past and present selves are juxtaposed and contrasted, the particularity of the term "Me," initially emphasized by the full stop, is undermined by the capitalized "And," which begins the next sentence. These two beings form the corollary of the self that is experienced as porous. This self is not continuous over time, an atomic unit that continues unchanged and hard-set, but rather one that shifts according to context and influence. Yet, although James Maddox writes sadly of "the ultimate nullity of the individual ... the self seems to consist *only* of its manifestations, its serial incarnations, with no underlying sense of endurance," this is a positive state, despite Bloom's sadness at this moment.[56] Just as Bloom and Molly's kissing-eating is an exemplary transcendence of narrowly construed self-interest, Bloom's awareness of himself as temporary is accompanied by his expanded understanding of being as constituted by porousness and interpermeation.

Mity Cheese Digests All but Itself

While at the picnic at Howth, Bloom and Molly consciously celebrate their physical continuity through an activity that is both osculation and ingestion, Bloom observes this continuity even in the most aggressively avaricious corners of society. Thinking of eating lunch, Bloom: "pushed in the door of the Burton restaurant. Stink gripped his trembling breath: pungent meatjuice, slush of greens. See the animals feed. Men, men, men. Perched on high stools by the bar, hats shoved back, at the tables calling for more bread no charge, swilling, wolfing gobfuls of sloppy food, their eyes bulging, wiping wetted moustaches" (*U* 8:650–56). Lingering warily at the threshold of the Burton, Bloom resembles Homer's Odysseus, who having cautiously refused to enter the bay of Lamos, watches the giants "spearing my people like fish and collecting them to make their loathsome meal."[57] The Burton's customers are the historical and economic

---

[56] James Maddox, *Joyce's Ulysses and the Assault upon Character* (New Brunswick, NJ: Rutgers University Press, 1978), 64.

[57] Homer, *The Odyssey*, trans. T. E. Lawrence (London: CRW Publishing, 2004), 178.

instantiation of the human beings Bloom contrasts with the statues of Juno and Venus, "we stuffing food in one hole and out behind: food, chyle, blood, dung, earth, food: have to feed it like stoking an engine." Brutal embodiments of consumption, the customers' behavior implies that existence is divided into the opposing roles of predator and victim: "Every fellow for his own, tooth and nail. Gulp. Grub. Gulp. Gobstuff. He came out into clearer air and turned back towards Grafton street. Eat or be eaten. Kill! Kill!" (U 8:701–03). In the men's "Table talk," chewing and swallowing are conflated with business and money-making: "I munched hum un thu Unchster Bunk un Munchday" (U 8:692–93). Here, eating distorts the sentence "I met him at the Ulster Bank on Monday" not only in terms of its sounds ("hum" instead of "him," and "Unchster" instead of "Ulster") but also in terms of sense: "met" becomes "munch," and "Monday" becomes "Munchday." In this way, social interaction and the working week are distorted by predation.

Yet despite their individual focus on gain, or rather because of it, the men become indistinguishable in this desire to accumulate, "Men, men, men. Perched on high stools by the bar, hats shoved back, at the tables calling for more bread no charge, swilling, wolfing gobfuls of sloppy food." Bloom registers this scene largely through the modality of smell: the "stink" of ill-prepared food, the "smells of men," the "reek of plug, spilt beer, men's beery piss," the "stale of ferment" (U 8:670–71). This smell that invades Bloom's body illustrates the inseparability of human bodies, despite their competitive consumption.

In addition to this miasmic continuity, Bloom perceives another, more active kind of physical connection. While the scene presents us with images of aggressive consumption, it counters this consumption with a shared eating in the form of microbial action: "A pallid suetfaced young man polished his tumbler knife fork and spoon with his napkin. New set of microbes" (U 8:656–58). The absence of punctuation draws the utensils together, as the man's microbes join those already upon them, undermining the possession he attempts to assert. This microbial permeation also features when Bloom, immediately on leaving Burton's, imagines a communal kitchen that would feed everyone in Dublin for free. Despite this munificence, self-interest and greed persist and desperate, competitive consumption ensues, "Have rows all the same. All for number one" (U 8:713–14). Yet Bloom again pictures these greedy eaters as closer than they realize: "Rub off the microbes with your handkerchief. Next chap rubs on a new batch with his" (U 8:712–13). The bacteriological dissolution of individual boundaries is paralleled by a breakdown of syntax and punctuation as Bloom imagines the people who will gather to eat at the kitchen: "John Howard Parnell example the provost of Trinity every mother's son don't talk of your provosts and provost of Trinity women and children cabmen priests parsons fieldmarshals archbishops"(*U* 8:706–08).[58] The sentence is particularly disunified, mixing abbreviated comments ("example"), a proper name, song lyrics ("Don't talk of your Provost," from Alfred Graves' "Father O'Flynn"), verbal formula ("women and children") and professional and vocational titles ("priests parsons fieldmarshals archbishops"). It is now that Bloom's characterization of mental activity appears, "Never know whose thoughts you're chewing" (*U* 8:717–18); this context aligns thought with microbial action.[59]

This microbial action is given further articulation in Bloom's selection of cheese for lunch. After turning away from Burton's, Bloom goes to Davy Byrne's where, as he surveys the food on offer, a dense passage associates meat-eating with his repressed conjugal problems, his son Rudy's death, his friend Dignam's death, advertising language, and the regulation of society by religious consumption rituals. Bloom distinguishes between meat and cheese: "Peace and war depend on some fellow's digestion. Religions. Christmas turkeys and geese. Slaughter of innocents. Eat drink and be merry. Then casual wards full after. Heads bandaged. Cheese digests all but itself. Mity cheese. – Have you a cheese sandwich?" (*U* 8:752–56). Critics have pointed out that while meat is associated with religious ritual, domination, and war, cheese offers a more peaceable, vegetarian option. What goes unexplored is the mode of operation of cheese: "Cheese digests all but itself. Mity cheese." The 1922 edition has "Mighty cheese";[60] Gabler corrects the phrase, restoring Joyce's original pun on cheese mites as capable of vigorous microbial activity. Bloom thus eats a food that eats back.

---

[58] This looseness is also present at the level of punctuation and syntax: while there are commas in the 1922 edition of the text, Hans Walter Gabler prints the passage without commas in his 1984 edition and notes that the copulas were deleted at level B. Gabler, *Ulysses: A Critical and Synoptic Edition I* (Garland, 1984), 358.

[59] Frank Budgen claims to have offered inspiration to Joyce with his response to Joyce's remark: "'Fermented drink must have had a sexual origin,' said Joyce to me one day. 'In a woman's mouth, probably. I have made Bloom eat Molly's chewed seed cake.' I told him I had just read a German book in which was described a tribal orgy on a South Sea island. The drink was prepared by the women of the tribe. They chewed a certain herb and spat the pulp into a huge crock out of which the men then drank." Budgen, *James Joyce and the Making of Ulysses and Other Writings* (London: Oxford University Press, 1972), 108. If this primitive ritual is evoked in the individuals' partaking not only of the communal soup but also of the microbes, Joyce's achievement is not to imagine the reinstitution of primitive rituals but the communal nature of existence, even under capitalism.

[60] *Ulysses*, ed. Johnson, 163.

In choosing a substance that breaks down the distinction between aggressor and victim, Bloom's choice of cheese constitutes an interest in peaceful, transformative permeation. If society is a body that digests people, cheese provides a metaphor for an unusual kind of political agency: an active and ongoing transformation of the conditions of existence that occurs at a microscale. The minute parasites of Bloom's mity cheese are pervasive and creative. In choosing cheese, Bloom posits a form of resistance that avails of the penetrability of matter, just as his digestion of the elements he encounters allows him to make an active response to the verbal and material fragments that enter him. While Stephen's louse is a parasite that feeds on the waste matter excreted by his body, these mites work on everything that they contact, they eat everything but themselves. Cheese is not the host of mites; its flavor is produced by them. It lives through their activity (as well as that of molds, yeasts, and bacteria). Cheese thus emblematizes Bloom himself, enlivened by the processes of the stream of consciousness: the distortions of phrases in sonic play, pun, and association, in the ongoing active and depersonalized digestive processing of personal, cultural, and economic conditions.

Mrs Breen's Open Purse

"Lestrygonians" ends with Bloom at the threshold between the commercial, social world and the realm of pure, traditional art, a moment which emblematizes the episode's interrelation of digestion, aesthetics, and expanded being. Bloom rushes to the museum to avoid Blazes Boylan, whom he has glimpsed approaching, while, in an additional evasive maneuver, he searches through his pockets: "Busy looking [...] I am looking for that. Yes, that. Try all pockets" (U 8:1185–88). As the narration shifts into the third-person narration, the ruse becomes a depersonalized action: "His hand looking for the where did I put found in his hip pocket soap lotion have to call tepid paper stuck" (U 8:1191–92). In handling these objects, Bloom is in fact is repeating the behavior of Josie Breen who, at the beginning of the episode, rummages in her handbag for an anonymous postcard bearing the message U.P. that has disturbed her husband's already fragile mental state. Bloom mimics her gesture, unconsciously but tactically. His truncated question as he watched her search, "What is she?..." is here adapted to accompany his own search: "Where did I? [...] His hand looking for the *where did I put* found in his hip pocket soap" (U 8:1189–91).[61]

---

[61] Bloom's search produces a flyer, a handkerchief, a newspaper, a purse, a potato, and, finally, this bar of soap.

Unconsciously, then, in redeploying her gesture to ward off Boylan, Bloom identifies himself with a beleaguered woman.

Like Bloom's picnic with Molly on Howth Head, Bloom's encounter with Mrs Breen centers on baked goods. The confections in this scene communicate, however, that this is an environment of evaluative consumption: "Wait till I show you. Hot mockturtle vapour and steam of newbaked jampuffs rolypoly poured out from Harrison's. The heavy noonreek tickled the top of Mr Bloom's gullet. Want to make good pastry, butter, best flour, Demerara sugar, or they'd taste it with the hot tea. Or is it from her?" (*U* 8:231–35). Here, Bloom isn't sure what he is smelling, a situation that associates her with the ambiguous women in the Paris Epiphany but separates her from the prostitutes in *Portrait* whom Stephen chooses according to "a sudden call to his sin-loving soul from their soft perfumed flesh" (*P* 86). Josie Breen is a former friend of Molly's, with whom Bloom flirted before they married; "Josie Powell that was, prettiest deb in Dublin," Bloom declares in "Circe" (*U* 15:441–42). Here, Bloom registers her aging face and her worn-out clothes, but he immediately observes and distances himself from an evaluating gaze: "Lines around her mouth. Only a year or so older than Molly. See the eye that woman gave her, passing. Cruel. The unfair sex" (*U* 8:268–69). While the speaker of the Paris Epiphany critically describes the women on the boulevard as identically glamorous and subjectively empty consumers or courtesans, here Bloom considers the subjective distortions caused to women by their situation in a competitive materialistic environment. While she searches inside her tattered handbag, Bloom's eye falls upon items of dubious worth: "chipped leather. Hatpin," "Soiled handkerchief," and "Pastille that was fell" (*U* 8:239–44). The syntax of the last phrase is repeated when Bloom notices traces of pastry on her dress and sugared flour on her cheek and thinks: "Rhubarb tart with liberal fillings, rich fruit interior. Josie Powell that was. In Luke Doyle's long ago. Dolphin's Barn, the charades. U.p: up. Change the subject" (*U* 8:273–75). Rather than dwelling on her status in a market of women as appetizing goods, or on the sad ending of her career on the marriage market, he chooses to deflect their attention.

If Bloom later mimics Josie Breen's gesture of searching through her handbag, here he changes the subject in a manner that suggests his mind has the disorder of the handbag's interior. He produces a muddled creation that resists the values and calculations of consumption. Asking if she ever sees "Mrs Beaufoy," he replaces the name of an old acquaintance, Mina Purefoy, with that of a writer, "Philip Beaufoy I was thinking" (*U* 8:276–78). Uttering "Beau" instead of "Pure," Bloom produces an anomalous creation who is both a pregnant woman and a man whose fiction Bloom has associated with pleasurable defecation.[62] We might read this amalgamated creature as representing the creative power of Bloom's stream of consciousness. In this processing of linguistic fragments, as in the other instances of behaviors, sensations, microbes, and gestures, individuation and gender distinctions are eroded. Everything here is contagious, or rather infectious, although those terms misleadingly imply an initial physical purity that is contaminated rather than an ongoing circulation in an open-ended, creative being.

Bloom's encounter with Josie Breen shows that he is neither a judgmental observer nor a calculating consumer but rather a porous body and mind. If Mrs Breen's handbag is, perhaps too obviously, a symbol for the vagina, we might understand it instead in terms of the Rimbaudian opening, which we saw in Chapter 2 plays such a key role for Stephen at the end of *Portrait*: the ambiguous "Golfes d'ombres," the "gulfs of shadows," around which glittering flies buzz. Motivated more by concern than by desire, Bloom produces distorted words, although he too is an opening, a place of shifting, disordered abundance. This openness is radically opposed to the self-contained forms mandated by Schiller and Winckelmann. If the closed body of eighteenth-century aesthetics was understood as restoring unity to the individual, this openness allows an expanded understanding of being in which individuals are linked, even while they are fully immersed in a commercial environment. The episode ends with the promises of hygiene and of restored boundaries as Bloom reaches the museum: "Ah soap there I yes. Gate. Safe! (*U* 8:1192–93). But if the conclusion of the episode thus achieves clarity, as the syntactic confusion of Bloom's thoughts is followed by simple, even single-worded, sentences, this is not life; it leads merely to blank whiteness.

In this chapter I have argued that Joyce expands Stephen's moment of sentient thought into Bloom's ongoing aesthetic response to the urban environment. He does so, I have attempted to show, by developing Dujardinian bite-sized phrases that are produced by immediate sensory experiences and verbal associations. If I have celebrated here a mode of relation that is neither consumption, abstention, nor evaluation but rather an open and creative co-being, we might see Bloom in these passages as having advanced significantly from earlier moments in *Ulysses*. At the beginning of "Calypso," for example, Bloom rushes his transaction with

---

[62] Bloom does not yet know that Mina Purefoy is suffering through a "very stiff birth" at Holles hospital (*U* 8:284).

Dlugacz the porkbutcher in order to look at a woman like a piece of meat: "To catch up and walk behind her if she went slowly, behind her moving hams" (*U* 4:171–72). This moment suggests the crucial role of senses other than vision in collapsing the distance between the consuming subject and its objects. Yet if the lower sensory modalities undo the distinctions between bodies and between genders, sensory perception alone, in the absence of thought, leads to a dangerous submission. In contemplating musical appreciation in "Sirens," Bloom rejects the lure of pure sensation: "Cowley, he stuns himself with it: kind of drunkenness. Better give way only half way the way of a man with a maid. Instance enthusiasts. All ears. Not lose a demisemiquaver. Eyes shut. Head nodding in time. Dotty. You daren't budge. Thinking strictly prohibited. Always talking shop" (*U* 11:1191–94). The dominance of sensation here leads to a physical confinement, "daren't budge," and an eclipse of mental activity: the head "nodding in time" is "Dotty," a black mark on a musical stave. In this surrender to the consumption of music, language is figured as commercial commentary, "Always talking shop." Bloom's stream of consciousness, contrastingly, evades domination by consumption through coupling sensation and reflection, although, crucially, this is a reflection characterized by spontaneous processes of connection, elaboration, and distortion. Bloom's critique implies that the individual has the power to embrace an awareness in which thinking and feeling are unified. In modeling such a mode, he is an exemplary individual. There is, after all, to return to Ned Lenehan's characterization, a touch of the artist about old Bloom.

CHAPTER 4

Paris Reenvisioned: "Circe"

In July, 1920, Joyce returned to Paris at the invitation of Ezra Pound. Joyce threw himself into the composition of the "Circe" episode. As Jean-Michel Rabaté tells us, "Circe" was "an episode which he insisted he had to write in Paris."[1] Three days after he arrived, he wrote to Harriet Shaw Weaver that he was intending "to remain here three months in order to write the last adventure *Circe* in peace (?)" (*Letters I*, 142). Joyce, however, did not finish "Circe" in three months, nor did he leave Paris when he finished the episode. As Michael Groden observes, with "Circe" Joyce's mode of composition changed: "These episodes, especially 'Circe' and 'Ithaca,' took him much longer to write than he expected, and he found himself elaborating them far beyond his original intentions. His work on 'Circe' was crucial; he seems to have begun it as an episode similar in scope and length to the previous three, but by the time he had finished it, he had left the middle stage behind for new developments."[2] In the next chapter, we will trace the influence of the contemporary Parisian literary scene upon "Circe" and, consequently, of the episode's influence upon that scene. But here we will look at Joyce's grappling in a heightened way in "Circe" with a problem that had occupied him since his first period in Paris at the very beginning of his career.

In returning to Paris, Joyce returned to the scene of his first encounter with the full force of capitalism, and in "Circe," he constructs an episode that allows him to stage it, as well as his response to it, in extreme form.

---

[1] Rabaté, "Joyce the Parisian," 56.

[2] Groden, *Ulysses in Progress*, 52. Groden divides the composition of *Ulysses* into three stages: an early stage, beginning in 1914, in which Joyce produced variations of the interior monologue; a middle stage, in which Joyce engaged in more experimental forms, beginning with "Cyclops" in 1919; and a final stage from 1920 to the completion of the manuscript in 1922. As Groden himself has more recently noted, the subsequent recovery of additional manuscripts raises the possibility of a new account. Groden, "Joyce at Work on 'Cyclops': Toward a Biography of *Ulysses*," *James Joyce Quarterly* 44.2 (Winter 2007), 217–45, at 217.

The 1903 Paris Epiphany presented an encounter with a prostitution seamlessly operant within the workings of the boulevard; "Circe" presents Nighttown, the brothel district, a city unto itself. The Paris Epiphany featured an elliptical olfactory sensation that undid the calculations and objectifications of exchange and representation; "Circe," as we will see, features a powerful instantiation of the uncontainable and pleasurable body, one that defies not just the transactions of the brothel but also the limits of art.

That Joyce returned to the scene of a problem that galvanized his aesthetic suggests an answer to a critical crux concerning the episode. Critics have noted Joyce's new self-consciousness in writing "Circe." The enormous mass of the episode, which takes up a quarter of the Gabler edition, is in part due to its recasting of moments from the previous episodes of *Ulysses* and also from Joyce's previous writings, from the Epiphany to *Dubliners*.[3] We can understand this revisiting and reworking of material as Joyce's own emphatic reengagement with this problem and his use of Nighttown as the locus of the consummation of his efforts as a writer. "Circe" is a heightened and totalized world of exchange through which Joyce runs his oeuvre, grappling in intensified form with the conjunction of desire and capitalism in the city and developing a philosophy and an aesthetics to respond to it.

"Circe" takes the unusual form of a play script. As I hope to show, the episode's riotous series of fleeting visions, its logic of constant and uncontrolled motion, presents the ensnaring of human productive powers, as well as human reproductive powers, in structures of profit and possession. This appropriation leads to a creativity that is both hyperdeveloped and futile, a heightened and aberrant generativity. Critics have often interpreted "Circe" as exposing unconscious desires – Jeri Johnson, for example, writes: "This is Freud's 'Return of the Repressed' with a vengeance."[4] The desires that "Circe" explores are both those instrumentalized by structures of profit and those that resist those structures and, in doing so, are marked by guilt.

In the previous chapter, we looked at how Bloom's practice of sensual, digestive engagement erodes and opposes the logic of objectification, possession, and calculation of the city of consumer capitalism and, in

---

[3] Ronan Crowley summarizes this process succinctly: "Elements from his cutting-room floor, drawn from all stages of his career and from his published oeuvre, were pressed into new service." Ronan Crowley, "Fusing the Elements of 'Circe': From Compositional to Textual Repetition," *James Joyce Quarterly* 47.3 (Spring 2010), 341–61, at 345.

[4] *Ulysses*, ed. Johnson, 992.

doing so, undoes both individuation and gender. In Nighttown, gender binaries become newly salient not only as representative of the predominantly male use of female bodies in prostitution but also as emblematizing the positions of subject and object constructed by an exploitative system of profit. In this chapter, I do not read "Circe" as exploring the toll inflicted upon women by Nighttown, although I point to where the episode suggests it; I focus rather on the episode's representation of the instrumentalization of male desire in a commodified social world. The challenge that faces Bloom in Nighttown is the reappropriation of desire; his reappropriation defies the norms of profitable production, possession, and social propriety. It is expressed, in its most intense form, through an assertion about, and against, art. It is imbued with the energy of farce.

Zoe, the Womancity

The formal technique of "Circe" is exemplified in Bloom's encounter on the steps of Bella Cohen's brothel with Zoe Higgins, "*a young whore in a sapphire slip, closed with three bronze buckles, a slim black velvet fillet round her throat, [who] nods, trips down the steps and accosts him*" (U 15:1279–81). She touches his body, at the same time both arousing him and checking for physical ailments, and takes out of his pocket a potato, which Bloom calls "A talisman. Heirloom" (U 15:1313). Bloom's sensual perceptions form the entry and exit points to waking dreams; the episode's form is thus an expanded version of the stream of consciousness, one that exposes the interior processes of a musical and pictorial thinking. As she "*cuddl[es] him with supple warmth*," Zoe's embrace triggers Bloom's fantasy of opulent pleasure (U 15:1316). The "*oriental music*" generated by this pliable sensuality expands into the image of bountiful, cultivated nature: displays of cascading water, eyes enhanced with cosmetics, birds made of metal. Her "*sapphire slip*" transforms into "a sky of sapphire"; her "*bronze buckles*" become "*the bronze flight of eagles*"; her eyes "*ringed with kohol*" become "*shadows black of cedargroves*" around lakes; her "*tawny*" eyes leaping "*gazelles*" (U 15:1324–27). If Bloom's physical sensations are employed in the production of this vision, they also bring him out of it. Inhaling the odor of her breath, Bloom has a vision of the nature of their interaction: "*She bites his ear gently with little goldstopped teeth, sending on him a cloying breath of stale garlic. The roses draw apart, disclose a sepulcher of the gold of kings and their mouldering bones*" – the image of earthly paradise is replaced by an image of hoarded wealth and fallen male rulers (U 15:1339–41). In response to Zoe's question "And you know what thought did?" his thinking, prompted by a physical event, proceeds independently of his conscious volition, flashing up in a vivid image only to disappear again almost immediately.

Joyce names the formal technique of the episode "hallucination" in the Gilbert schema and "exploding vision" in the Linati schema. If "exploding" seems hyperbolic, the word's etymology sheds light upon its salience for the workings of the episode. While we usually understand the word in the senses of OED 4 and 5, "to expel or propel suddenly," "to cause (a substance) to undergo a rapid chemical or nuclear reaction that generates a violent release of energy in the form of intense heat, light, noise, and a powerful blast," its original sixteenth-century sense expresses more closely the workings of "Circe": "To condemn or decry; to drive off, banish" (OED 2a), and is explicitly related to the action "of an audience: "to drive (a performer) from the stage by clapping, booing, etc." (OED 2b). This theatrical sense is present in the Latin origins of explode: *ex plaudere*, to applaud away. It is from this root meaning that the word is associated with critique, as in OED 1a: "to reject or discard (something, esp. an opinion, proposal or custom)." This action of enthusiastic debunking is exemplified in the encounter with Zoe, where Bloom's reactions might be thought of as sequentially clapping and booing. The technique of "Circe" thus stages vividly the affects banished in Joyce's aesthetic terms, desire and loathing, affects central to Nighttown.

If, in "Lestrygonians," Bloom is initiated by Molly into a shared being, such encounters are banished from the stage of "Circe." The affectual conflict that accompanies the transformation of all relations into transactions is given clear expression in an early draft of the episode, "Circe 2," when Bloom sees Molly: "He wishes, unwishes, is cold, warm, knows, knows not, stands helpless, spellbound by her eyes and dress. Beneath her turreted turban a coin gleams on her brow. Her anklets are linked together by a fetterchain."[5] Molly, here, is clearly marked as a slave; Bloom too is bound by Nighttown, experiencing paralysis due to a succession of opposing responses.

By wavering between positive and negative images and references, the scene in which Bloom meets Zoe indicates both the yield and the cost of the wrongful cultivation of nature, the exploitation of human beings for

[5] *The Dublin Ulysses Papers by James Joyce*, Vol. 2, ed. Danis Rose (Dublin: House of Breathings, 2012), 22. In "Circe 2," Bloom experiences a more literal version of the invasive appeal Stephen met in Nighttown in *Portrait:* "the procuress pours into his ear a fetid husky message. The Procuress: Ten shillings a maidenhead. Fresh thing that was never touched Fifteen (Her mouldy sweat promises secret obscenities)" (23).

profit. This contradiction resonates in the passage's array of citations. Zoe represents Nighttown as a whole; she is described in the stage directions as the "womancity," a land of plenty, the Promised Land; her Hebrew words, "Schorach ani wenowach, benoith Hierushaloim" (*U* 15:1333–34), are taken from the Song of Solomon, "I am black, but comely, O ye daughters of Jerusalem."[6] Yet this fantasy conceals a critique, as it inverts a moment in William Blake's *The Four Zoas* (1795):

> Because the Lamb of God Creates himself a bride & wife
> That we his Children evermore may live in Jerusalem
> Which now descendeth out of heaven a City yet a Woman
> Mother of myriads redeemed & born in her spiritual palaces
> By a New Spiritual birth Regenerated from Death.[7]

Bloom's vision of Zoe is of a "City yet a Woman" but it is of a physical rather than a spiritual place, one linked not to redemption but to sale, and to an abundance that leads not to life but to death. Another opposing pair of citations echo in Bloom's melancholy observation in this encounter: "I never loved a dear gazelle but it was sure to . . ." (*U* 8:1323). The first is "The Fire Worshippers," Thomas Moore's story of the doomed lovers in *Lalla Rookh* (1817): "I never nurs'd a dear gazelle,/To glad me with its soft black eye,/But when it came to know me well,/And love me, it was sure to die!"[8] The second is Lewis Carroll's parody, "Tèma Con Vatiatiòni" (1869): "I never loved a dear Gazelle/Nor anything that cost me much:/High prices profit those who sell,/But why should I be fond of such?"[9] Carroll's version points to mercenary motivation of images of the exotic; Moore's *Lalla Rookh* was a tremendously lucrative presentation of Orientalist material. The tender relation of Moore's speaker to his pet gazelles is associated in this context with fatal enslavement. Carroll's satire on the line suggests another kind of deformation, as his financially focused speaker proclaims his own incapacity to love anything on sale above a certain price. The death that haunts Moore's speaker is superimposed with the comic failure reported by Carroll's speaker to transform his red hair, in the

---

[6] Gifford and Seidman, *Ulysses Annotated*, 470. Endowed with "Mammoth roses murmur[ing] of scarlet winegrapes" (*U* 8:1329), the womancity is a vivid expansion of Stephen's Temptress of the Villanelle, the utterly available female, "radiant, warm, odorous and lavish-limbed," whom he imagines while lying in bed, "staring at the great overblown scarlet flowers of the tattered wallpaper" (*P* 186, 186).

[7] Qtd. in Gifford and Seidman, *Ulysses Annotated*, 470.

[8] Thomas Moore, *Lalla Rookh: An Oriental Romance*, 2nd ed. (London: Longman, Hurst, Rees, Orme, and Brown, 1817), 188.

[9] Lewis Carroll, "Téma Con Variaziòni," *The Humorous Verse of Lewis Carroll* (New York: Dover, 1960), 198.

patently fake blue and green hues that result from the artificial hair coloring ("sure to die" – "sure to dye").[10] The citations thus cast Bloom in a positive and negative light, suggesting both his culpable experience of the death-dealing nature of prostitution (and his thriftiness), as well as his unhappy entrapment in a commodified world. As transformation is tied to the commodity, abundance meets failure and humor and pain coincide.

Zoe, named after the Greek for biological life, breathes death. Yet her breath has whiff of comedy. As its odor of garlic is described, oddly, as "cloying," the phrase scrambles a line uttered by Bottom to his fellow players in Shakespeare's *Midsummer Night's Dream*: "And, most dear actors, eat no onions nor garlic, for we are to utter sweet breath, and I do not doubt but to hear them say, it is a sweet comedy."[11] Bottom, delightfully bungling as ever, engages here in some false reasoning: if the actors' breath is sweet, he reasons, so is the comedy that they play. Yet his warning draws attention to the body's power to collapse illusion. Zoe's garlic breath drives off the exploding vision, revealing the morbidity that resides in the commodified human body. Yet her breath is thus sweet because it transforms the scene into a comedy in which Bloom escapes, if only temporarily. If his sense of smell allows him a glimpse of the nature of prostitution, it nonetheless subsequently leads him toward it: he enters the brothel, *"draw[n] by the odour of her armpits, the vice of her painted eyes, the rustle of her slip in whose sinuous folds lurks the lion reek of all the male brutes that have possessed her"* (*U* 15:2015–17). He trips on the threshold.

In "Circe," Bloom is caught up in a comedy of spectacles that collapse and reform over and over, an unending *Midsummer Night's Dream*. If we might define Shakespearian comedy in the briefest of terms as focused on the promise of regeneration achieved through happy marriage, "Circe" engages with the potential for generation within a context not of the bonds of love but of profit. In "Circe," the misconception typical of Shakespearean comedy is replaced with the logic of exchange. While rational thought provides no exit from the impasse of Nighttown's unreason, the episode offers a solution in terms of farce, a mode of humor that relies upon the

---

[10] And when I stained my hair, that Belle
    Might note the change, and thus admire
    And love me, it was sure to dye
    A muddy green, or staring blue:
    Whilst one might trace, with half an eye,
    The still triumphant carrot through. (Ibid., 199)
[11] Shakespeare, *A Midsummer Night's Dream*, ed. Burton Raffel (New Haven, CT: Yale University Press, 2005), IV.ii.42–44.

base realities of the body rather than the subtleties of the mind. According to Cuddon, "The basic elements of farce are: exaggerated physical action (often repeated), exaggeration of character and situation, absurd situations and improbable events (even impossible ones and therefore fantastic), and surprises in the form of unexpected appearance and disclosures."[12] Farce then does not merely lack the subtleties of intellectual wit, it is opposed to measure, reason, probability, and even established reality.

Farce is thus the means through which the physical world reasserts itself, in defiance of norms, meanings, and rational expectations. The form played a marginal role in the late Middle Ages when *farces* were the "stuffing" between religious and liturgical drama. Its practice of "pok[ing] fun at the foibles and vices of everyday life (particularly at commercial knavery and conjugal infidelity)"[13] is particularly salient to the modern world of Nighttown, a locus defined by the conjunction of unscrupulous profit and sexual waywardness. In response to a lifeworld totally colonized by commerce, farce's defiance of regulation through the uncontrollable body – its parts, emissions, and clothing – is not only disruptive of this space but makes possible a physical thinking that is opposed to the profitable but in league with pleasure. The mode of farce allows for an unconventional assertion of desire, and the explosion of subjectivity and gender identity; its transformative space becomes the place in which a new kind of creativity occurs.

Although we will go on to examine Stephen as both performing and witnessing the empty philosophy of Nighttown, at an odd moment in "Circe" he uncharacteristically inhabits the mode of farce. Hearing that he is just back from Paris, the prostitutes urge him to speak "parleyvoo" and, speaking an English rendered absurd by French syntax and French phrases, Stephen performs a confused version of heaven and hell in the cabarets of Pigalle, the Parisian instantiation of Nighttown. The adjective "parisian" appears, in small case, as a behavioral rather than geographical qualifier, referring to humorously exaggerated sexual antics enacted even more enthusiastically for single men from abroad, "parisian clowneries extra foolish for bachelors foreigns" (*U* 15:3886–87). Stephen describes the comic overturning of religious binaries: "Misters very selects for is pleasure must to visit heaven and hell show with mortuary candles" where "Angels much prostitutes like and holy apostles big damn ruffians"

[12] J. A. Cuddon, *The Penguin Dictionary of Literary Terms* (New York: Penguin, 2000), 330.
[13] Ibid.

(*U* 15:3888–902). In these clubs, spectator and spectacle blend together, as modest women strip while watching vampires debauch nuns with "dessous troublants," disordered underclothes, as Gifford has it, or, more literally, troubling nether regions.[14]

Stephen names here the neighboring nightclubs of Le Ciel and L'Enfer, or Heaven and Hell. Joel Schechter identifies the clubs as part of a new era in which eschatology becomes entertainment: "By 1900 the cabaret had become a competitive, commercial undertaking" [. . .] More and more cabaret became obsessed with death and its consequences. Cabaret du Ciel (Cabaret of Heaven) featured harp music, a master of ceremonies dressed in the robes of a priest, and a man costumed as an angel who sprinkled the audience with holy water. The programs consisted of a series of *tableaux vivants* depicting the pleasures of heaven. Offering an alternative to celestial bliss, Cabaret l'Enfer (Cabaret of the Infernal Regions) presented a glimpse of hell. The decorations that hung from the ceiling were sculptures of bodies writing in pain. An acrobat, dressed as Satan, performed a series of contortions, while his wife and her court, accompanied by deafening organ music, were consumed by multicolored flames. The artistic merits of these later cabarets is not an issue. [They] chose their bills of fare according to their commercial potential."[15]

L'Enfer's assertion of its unique status as a global tourist destination, "Cabaret unique au monde," is echoed in Stephen's declaration: "Perfectly shocking terrific of religion's things mockery seen in universal world" (*U* 15:3890–91). The nightclub caters not only to desire, with its "Attractions Diaboliques," but also to the opposing affect of guilt, staging the torments and metamorphoses of the damned, "Supplice des Damné" and "Les Métamorphoses des Damnés." These performances are placed side by side with beer, souvenirs, syrups, and liqueurs.[16] The title of the club's manager A. Alexander, "Directeur-Adminstrateur," combines artistic ambition with financial management.

In this new environment, the hell that terrified Stephen in Fr. Arnall's sermon in *Portrait* is offered purely for consumption, along with

---

[14] Gifford and Seidman, *Ulysses Annotated*, 514.

[15] Joel Schechter, *Popular Theater: A Sourcebook* (New York: Routledge, 2002), 185.

[16] Luc Sante observes that these cabarets were part of a new wave of tourist traps that used spectacle to accelerate consumption: "fully stage-managed experiences such as Le Ciel and L'Enfer and Le Rat Mort, which featured elaborately lurid façades, waiters in costume, ordinary beverages given the names of philters and potions and a lot of haunted house woo-woo. The professionals had taken charge." Sante, *The Other Paris* (New York: Farrar, Straus & Giroux, 2015), 141.

Figure 4.1   Cabaret de L'Enfer bill of fare, Joyceimages.com.

beverages.[17] Yet in contrast to this somewhat prosaic and clearly priced peddling of damnation, the scene Stephen presents defies any order. His invitation to "expense your evenings" rather than "spend your evenings" heralds a confounding assortment of goods: it is not clear how much anything costs, what is being sold, or to whom it is being sold. Here Stephen, uncharacteristically, entertains the gathering in Cohen's brothel and, caught up in a performance of a performance, his body is transformed into a puppet's: "*finny hands outspread, a painted smile on his face* [...] *Gabbles with marionette jerks*" (*U* 15:3877–81). This is his most warmly received artistic production: "Great success of laughing" he observes, without separating himself from the position of huckster (*U* 15:3900–01). This is one of the few moments in the episode when the women experience enjoyment as Stephen becomes an animated body for them. They laugh at his mincing enticements, his painted smile, and his doll-like twitches. If Stephen gives

[17] The *National Geographic Magazine* reports "le Café de l'Enfer may have been one of the world's first theme restaurants. According to one 1899 visitor, the café's doorman – in a Satan suit – welcomed diners with the greeting, 'Enter and be damned!' Hell's waiters also dressed as devils. An order for three black coffees spiked with cognac was shrieked back to the kitchen as: 'Three seething bumpers of molten sins, with a dash of brimstone intensifier!'" "Marais: Hell's Swells," *National Geographic Magazine*, August 2003, http://ngm.nationalgeographic.com/ngm/flashback/0308/index.html.

voice to the utter availability of everything for consumption in Paris, the terms in which he does so confuse the terms of exchange. "STEPHEN: Enter, gentleman, to see in mirror every positions trapezes all that machine there besides also if desire act awfully bestial butcher's boy pollutes in warm veal liver or omlet on the belly *pièce de Shakespeare*" (*U* 15: 3907–09). In earlier slang, the word "machine" was used for both penis and vagina (OED 9). Bella, in particular, enjoys the nonsense he utters, as he substitutes *Hamlet* with an omelet, turning one of the central works of the Western canon, associated by Stephen with his own artistic self-conception in "Scylla and Charybdis," into a meal of whipped eggs or, more probably, ejaculate. As art, meaning, gender, and sale become scrambled, the possibility for shared joy arises.

Throughout the episode, Bloom performs a heaven and hell show of his own in a repeating series of spectacles of empowerment and punishment. These exploding visions stage the aberrant productivity of a capitalist world in which the possibility of political and social transformation is tied to a domination of nature, manifested in a male use of female bodies in the production and transmission of wealth. Bloom's sexual desires, however, deviate into nonprocreative, nonheterogenital activities: voyeurism, masturbation, transvestitism, coprophilia. The farcical nature of these desires – their absurdity in the face of social conventions that dominate the episode – lends them a liberating power. While these activities could indeed be part of the bill of fare of any brothel, what is crucial to note is that the world of Nighttown and the brothel of Bella Cohen are constructed according to the polarities of male subject and female object. "Circe" uses heterosexual intercourse as an emblem for the generation of profit from human beings, as well as emphasizing its crucial role in the continuation of bourgeois dominance through the inheritance of property.

To understand the exploding visions of "Circe" it is necessary to explore Joyce's development of the form from textual precedents in a French nineteenth-century visionary literature that grapples with burgeoning materiality. "Paris Reenvisioned," accordingly, has four parts. The first examines the episode's indebtedness to Gustave Flaubert's *La Tentation de saint Antoine*, a novel written in the form of a play script, and argues that Joyce reworks the different relations to materiality depicted by Flaubert, from a world of divinely sanctioned essences, to his characters' fixation on objects of desire, to an impersonal identification with a shifting haeccity.[18] The second part examines how the "feast of pure reason"

---

[18] Flaubert worked on *La Tentation* throughout his career, publishing versions in 1849, 1856, 1872, and 1874.

Stephen experiences in Nighttown is inspired by the "paralogic" of
Gérard de Nerval's realist account of Pantin, the market/brothel district
of Paris, in *Les Nuits d'Octobre* (1852). This part goes on to contrast this
empty cogitation with Bloom's sentient thinking, modeled on Nerval's
"seepage of dreams" in *Aurélia, ou, le Rêve et la vie* (1855). The third part
turns to Arthur Rimbaud's amplification of Nerval's visionary form in
Une Saison en enfer (1873). It shows how in representing Bloom's
reformist speeches, Joyce draws on Rimbaud's reworking, in a time of
failed revolution, of the progressive language of the nineteenth century
in the mode of spectacle. Joyce redeploys Rimbaud's farcical oscillation
between hero and outcast; Bloom falls from power when he refuses to
adhere to the productive use of female bodies, either in marriage,
heterogenital sex, or prostitution. The fourth part argues for another
version of embodied art in Bloom's encounter with the brothel madam,
transformed into a nymph who abjures the commodity and desire.
Bloom asserts instead an interest in a nonidentical, non-gender-specific
sensuousness.

Flaubert and the Play of Desire

One of the most obvious sources for the form of "Circe" is Flaubert's *La
Tentation de saint Antoine*, a novel written in the form of a play script.[19]
Flaubert's novel offers Joyce the means with which to stage a generativity
that refuses control both through its play script form, which lends
increased vividness to the visions that appear, and its febrile referential-
ity. Scarlett Baron traces the texts' parallel intratextuality – as Antony's
visions enact the details from the Biblical passages he reads in opening
scene of the novel, so "Circe" reworks moments from the previous episodes
of *Ulysses*.[20] She also examines their common intertextuality: "The effect of
Joyce's telescoping of intertexts within his works is to open up an imaginary space behind the episode – a textual matrix of prior writings from
which its elements are derived and rearranged into a series of carefully
calibrated echoes. This effect almost exactly corresponds to Foucault's

[19] Tadié Benoît writes: "The parallel between *La Tentation* and 'Circe' has been a commonplace of
   comparative criticism of the two authors ever since Ezra Pound first drew attention to it: the
   masochism of Bloom and Anthony has been especially emphasized, as well as the recurrence of
   similar figures in their respective visions and, more generally, the dreamlike logic of both texts
   (Brunazzi, Mayoux)." Benoît, "The Room of Infinite Possibilities: Joyce, Flaubert, and the
   Historical Imagination," *Études Anglaises* 2/2005 (Tome 58), 131–40, 137.
[20] Baron, *'Strandentwining Cable,'* 146.

account of *La Tentation's* dizzyingly complex relation to other books."[21] She goes on to cite Foucault's observation that *La Tentation* "opens up the space of a literature that exists only within and through the network of the already written ... it is the dream of the other books."[22] As Baron observes, these texts' citational wealth does not diminish their originality.

I would suggest that this textual reworking of material is an instance of a modern productivity that in recombining material frees itself of any origins or sanction; Anthony's diabolically produced visions take on increased significance within the context of commodity capitalism. This question of the sanctioning of creative powers explains one of the oddest exploding visions of "Circe," in which Bloom sees the face of Sweny the chemist in a sun made of soap. The vision is based on the apparition of Christ in the sun that concludes *La Tentation*. In the previous passages, Anthony wishes to "be in everything – emanate with all the odours, – develop myself like the plants, – flow like water, – vibrate like sound – shine like light, – assume all forms – penetrate each atom – descend to the very bottom of matter, – be matter itself."[23] In contrast to such a dissolution of the self in endless shifting matter, Christ's sudden appearance in the final lines of the novel guarantees individual identity: "Even in the midst thereof, and in the very disk of the sun, beams the face of Jesus Christ. Anthony makes the sign of the cross and resumes his devotions. FINIS."[24] A personal God, smiling on Anthony, puts to rest the Devil's arguments that an infinite God is incapable either of personification or of any personal relation that would, logically, impinge on his absolute and ideal nature.[25] Appearing to and even for Anthony, Christ attests to the existence of particular substance, the reality of individual essence, which the Devil claimed was merely illusion. The rampant fantasies of the night are then merely that: empty images that provoke desire as they pull Anthony away from the reality of God's creation, a joyous scene in which individual essence is guaranteed by a personal God. Of course, this divine guarantee is rendered dubitable by the fantastical nature of the apparition. Anthony perceives the

---

[21] Ibid., 176.   [22] Ibid., 176–77.

[23] Gustave Flaubert, *La Tentation de saint Antoine* (Paris: Chapentier, 1876), 190. Here we might see Anthony as voicing the aims of contemporary speculative materialists. For example, Graham Harman in *Guerilla Metaphysics: Phenomenology and the Carpentry of Things* (Open Court, 2005), or Quentin Meillassoux in *After Finitude: An Essay on the Necessity of Contingency*, trans. Ray Brassier (New York: Continuum, 2008).

[24] Flaubert, *The Temptation of Saint Anthony*, trans. Lafcadio Hearn (New York: Modern Library, 1992), 191. "Tout au milieu, et dans le disque même du soleil, rayonne le face de Jésus-Christ. Antoine fait le signe de la Croix et se remet en prieure." Flaubert, *La Tentation*, 296.

[25] Flaubert, *The Temptation of Saint Anthony*, 167.

Christ-sun as he has perceived all of the previous visions; for the reader, it is yet another fantastical event in the medium of Flaubert's prose.

Adapting Flaubert's Christ-sun, Joyce sets it within an emphatically commercial context, indicating the shaping power of economic forces upon this new material abundance and the desires it arouses. Instead of closing the episode, the apparition features at the beginning of "Circe," after Bloom's encounter with Molly, who is dressed for a harem and newly commanding, "Go and see life. See the wide world" (U 15:330). In contrast to the end of the "Lestrygonians" episode, where the soap was associated with the gates of the museum and with the promise of freedom from the contamination of the street, here, the soap announces Bloom's entry into a realm governed by commerce. This realm is overseen by an entrepreneurial deity, Sweny. His price (for the soap and the lotion together) offers a far less stable definition of identity than a divinely created essence. As the soap recites its jingle, "We're a capital couple are Bloom and I./He brightens the earth. I polish the sky," the rhythms, rhymes and consonance bind it and Bloom together, as does the soap's assertion that they are a "capital couple" (U 15:338–39). The soap's vast hygienic potential, the salvation it offers in the place of Christian redemption, is available only for purchase.

This production that is free of divine sanction and dependent upon capital is explicitly situated within a context of exploitation. Just after Sweney's appeal for money, a brothel keeper offers Bloom a virgin girl: "THE BAWD: Ten shillings a maidenhead. Fresh thing was never touched" (U 15:359). A "rainbedraggled" Bridie Kelly appears, with whom Bloom once formed a capital couple. The transformative promise of the commodity, the creative engagement of human desire with the material world, is thus accompanied by the reality of exploitation. The guilt associated with this relation dogs Bloom in a series of encounters: Gerty MacDowell appears, now a prostitute, her virginity taken by Bloom's voyeurism: "([...] *shows coyly her bloodied clout.*) GERTY: With all my worldly goods I thee and thou. (*she murmurs*) You did that. I hate you" (U 15:373–76). This encounter maps all sexuality within exchange, as prostitution is expressed here as a garbled form of marriage; Gerty misquotes the Anglican Book of Common Prayer, "All my goods I thee endow." In Nighttown, erotic encounters must be accounted for.

Bloom thus experiences two very different kinds of guilt in Nighttown: The first is the guilt of participating in prostitution and increasing the suffering of Bridie Kelly, something that is implied but not stated in the episode. The second is what we might call a capitalist guilt, constructed around the notion that everything must be brought to account. The pleasure Gerty felt in displaying herself and her "bottom drawer" in "Nausicaa" is replaced in this scene by a mode of calculation in which her possibilities are reduced to the subject positions of virgin, wife, and prostitute. In the world of "Circe," which is mapped by exchange, behavior that does not conform to patterns of possession and profit is frowned upon and castigated. Bloom, looking but not buying, is punished. His voyeurism, as well his flirtation outside of marriage, and a list of other, less decorous practices such as masochism, masturbation, and coprophilia, cause outrage. According to Nighttown's law, women must be either rented or owned, in prostitution or marriage, and put to use, in sexual intercourse and in the production of children.

Bloom's repeated infractions of this order with his deviant desires are farcical in their physical indignity but also, and more importantly, farcical in their expression of a body that defies control, measure, and normative relations. His desires are not constrained by the poles of subject and object but occupy a more indeterminate relation to women: imaginative onlooker, flirt, subjected-subject, self-pleasurer, and enthusiast of human waste. These deviant proclivities might be summed up in the accusation leveled at Bloom later in the episode: "Adorer of the adulterous rump!" (*U* 15:2839). This rump evokes what J. M. Bernstein calls the "sensory rump": the contingent, the contextual, the nonidentical and variable that escapes the calculus of exchange.[26] Bernstein coins the phrase to explain Adorno's understanding of the contestatory power of art – a sanctuary for all that escapes the *ratio* of capitalism; Joyce presents in Bloom's deviant interests an embodied, lived form of aesthetic resistance.

We might turn to Rancière's and Foucault's understandings of Flaubert to draw out the different subject positions regarding materiality in Nighttown. Rancière identifies a pair of opposed relations to the material world in *La Tentation*, politicizing and historicizing Anthony's desire to merge with things. In his account, Flaubert's story of the third-century saint stages the effects of the unprecedented availability of objects of desire due to nineteenth-century French industrialism and a new media "which made words and images, dreams and aspirations, available everywhere to anybody."[27] These new forces, combined with the democratic upheavals of

---

[26] J. M. Bernstein, "'The Dead Speaking of Stones and Stars': Adorno's *Aesthetic Theory*," in *The Cambridge Companion to Critical Theory*, ed. Fred Rush (Cambridge, UK: Cambridge University Press, 2004), 144.

[27] Jacques Rancière, "Why Emma Bovary Had to Be Killed," *Critical Inquiry* 34.2 (Winter 2008), 233–48, at 235.

the nineteenth century, led to a free-floating desire in which the subject becomes loosened. Rancière celebrates this chaotic desire, as it suggests the possibility of a profoundly restructured social world. Flaubertian characters such as Emma Bovary, however, mistakenly fixate on these objects of desire, relating to them in terms of identity, which leads to narratives of suffering and downfall. Anthony, in *La Tentation*, is given a lesson by the Devil in a material life beyond individuation. The Devil makes Anthony "discover what life truly is when our sensations are released from the chains of individuality. With his help, the saint could discover strange forms of preindividual or impersonal life: 'inanimate existences, inert things that seem animal, vegetative souls, statues that dream and landscapes that think.' In such a world our mind loses all its conventional bearings. It bursts into atoms of thought that come into unity with things that have themselves burst into a dance of atoms."[28]

Foucault makes a similar observation regarding *La Tentation* when he notes that Anthony's desire for "mindless sanctity" comes to him from his reading: "He wished to be a saint through [. . .] dissolving himself into the images that come to him through the mediation of the Book [. . .] He wishes to be a dumb creature – an animal, a plant, a cell. He wishes to be pure matter. Through this sleep of reason and in the innocence of desires that have become pure movement, he could at last be reunited to the saintly stupidity of things."[29] If Foucault calls this sanctity, it is a deviant holiness: reading is the means by which Anthony conceives of giving up the spirit through which he is created in God's image. The willful nature of Anthony's language suggests this sinfulness: "J'ai envie de," "Je voudrais avoir," "I have a desire to," "I would like to have."[30]

Rancière identifies a conflict between Flaubert and his characters: he observes the democratic equivalence of any source of excitement for Emma and of any subject for Flaubert. This could lead to an end to the split between a male poetry of noble action and refined passions and a female realm of practical life, a development that threatens to extinguish art in consumption. Rancière sees Flaubert as devising the solution in an art that differs from the merely practical enjoyment of art as accessory, with its attendant desire to possess beautiful things. This art, which Flaubert himself engages in, is the representation of haecceity: "Literature tells the

---

[28] Ibid., 241.
[29] Michel Foucault, Introduction to *The Temptation of Saint Anthony*, trans. Lafcadio Hearn (New York: Modern Library, 2001), xliii.
[30] Flaubert, *La Tentation*, 296.

truth and makes us enjoy it to the extent that it releases those haecceities from the chains of individualization and objectification."[31]

Joyce resolves this conflict differently in Nighttown, as he identifies these "chains of individualization and objectification" as indeed the exploitative workings of capitalism. Instead of retaining for his own representational pleasure the savoring of a contingent, shifting, and non-identical matter, he grants this interest to Bloom – this is most vividly exemplified in a practice that he engages in with Molly, in Nighttown's off-stage, the literally obscene practice of coprophilia. Bloom offers this in a direct confrontation with a comic embodiment of the disinterested artwork, the Nymph who is a version of the commodity.

It takes a while to get there. Here, in this exploding vision, Bloom engages in another kind of subversion of possessive individualism and self-fashioning through consumption. The guilt of not marrying Gerty is replaced by the guilt of flirting with Mrs Breen, "Josie Powell that was. Prettiest deb in Dublin" (*U* 15:441–42). As they rehearse their flirtation, Bloom's costumes range from that of sophisticate, "*squire of dames, in dinner jacket with wateredsilk facings, blue masonic badge in his buttonhole, black bow and mother-of-pearl studs [...] Ladies and gentlemen, I give you Ireland, home and beauty*" (*U* 15:450–4), to cultivated imperial conqueror, "*a purple Napoleon hat with an amber halfmoon, his fingers and thumb passing slowly down to her soft moist meaty palm which she surrenders gently [...] tenderly, as he slips on her finger a ruby ring) Là ci darem la mano*" (*U* 15:465–69),[32] to sentimental grandee, "*oatmeal sporting suit, a sprig of woodbine in the lapel, tony buff shirt, shepherd's plaid Saint Andrew's cross scarftie, white spats, fawn dustcoat on his arm, tawny red brogues, fieldglassses in bandolier and a grey billycock hat) Do you remember a long, long time, years and years ago, just after Milly, Marionette we called her, was weaned and we all went together to Fairyhouse races, was it?*" (*U* 15:536–41). Sets of accoutrements capable of defining an entire love story are here donned and doffed at such speed that their power to create an identity is both illustrated and parodied. Joyce wrote to Frank Budgen: "I want to make *Circe* a costume episode also. Bloom for instance appears in five or six different suits" (*Letters I*, 148). Five or six is a modest estimate: Bloom's attire changes fantastically at least fifteen times. The

---

[31] Rancière, "Why Emma Bovary Had to Be Killed," 243.

[32] Bloom is linked several times in the episode to Napoleon: later he is dressed in "fur overcoat, with folded arms and Napoleonic forelock" (*U* 15:2721) and he himself appeals to Napoleon as an exculpatory figure: "Lapses are condoned. Even the great Napoleon when measurements were taken next the skin after his death ..." (*U* 15:3835–36).

clothes, like the other objects in the episode, repeatedly recast Bloom in a continuously shifting spectacle, one that in staging a series of fleeting subject positions both demonstrates the transformative potential of modern production and loosens its grip.

Bloom attempts to direct this transformative potential later in the episode, and the reception of his plans is marred by outrage at his deviant desires. To understand these scenes, we must trace their origins in the writings of Nerval and Rimbaud. But first it is necessary to examine the philosophy that lends the episode its structure, Stephen's "metaphysics in Mecklenburg Street," a thinking that resents the force of desire and that violently imposes form upon the sensual world. For this, too, Nerval offers Joyce a form.

Nerval, Paralogism, and the Seepage of Dreams

While Bloom encounters sensually the heaven and hell of Nighttown, Stephen, cerebral rather than sensual, enacts and observes its logic in abstracted form. In constructing this vision of unreason, Joyce draws not only on resources offered by Flaubert, the master stylist working assiduously in his study in Croisset, but also on Nerval, a writer from the same time whose experience and writing were profoundly affected by the material and social conditions of Paris. There is a deep history of Nerval in Joyce's writing. In the manuscript of *Stephen Hero*, Joyce writes and strikes out the French writer's name as he depicts a Stephen who closely echoes him:

> A certain extravagance began to tinge [Stephen's] life. He was aware that though he was nominally in amity with the order of society into which he was born, he would not be able to continue so. The life of an errant seemed to him far less ignoble than the life of one who had accepted the tyranny of the mediocre because the cost of being exceptional was too high. The young generation which he saw growing up about him regarded his manifestations of spiritual activity as something more than unseemly and he knew that, under their air of fearful amiableness, the representatives of authority cherished the hope that his unguided nature would bring him into such a lamentable conflict with actuality that they would one day have the pleasure of receiving him officially into some hospital or asylum. This would have been no unusual end for the high enterprise of youth often ~~leads~~ brings one to premature senility and ~~De Nerval's~~ a poet's boldness ~~was~~ is certainly proved an ill keeper of promises when it induces him to lead a lobster by a bright blue ribbon along the footpath reserved for citizens. (*SH* 184)

The passage links Nerval and Stephen by presenting their artistic development as inextricably related to their physical and social lives. If Nerval's reinvention of aesthetic practice as useless urban performance perhaps contrasts with Stephen's cerebral peripatetics in *Stephen Hero*, in walking a lobster Nerval shares much with Stephen's desire to resist the impulses of the city. As Nerval reimagines walking in the streets as a vividly incongruous aesthetic practice that opposes normal urban traffic, he offers a model for Stephen's own "extravagant" wandering and his efforts at authentic self-authorship that threaten to put him on the wrong side of institutions and officials. While this passage in *Stephen Hero* asserts that Stephen's "unguided nature," in his rejection of conventional social formation, risks a "boldness" that leads merely to insanity, it is in "Circe" that Stephen comes closest to a fearful madness. He does so in terms developed from Nerval.

Nerval produced, in his last four years, along with short stories, poems, and travel accounts, two works that explicitly contend with the experience of Paris and the fragility of identity that accompanies it, *Les Nuits d'Octobre* (1852) and *Aurélia ou, le Rêve et la vie*.[33] Nerval wrote these works at and immediately after the crowning of Napoleon III, as industrialization, urbanization, and commodification began to reshape the city.[34] In *Aurélia*, Nerval presents this shifting material abundance in a hallucinatory form; in *Les Nuits*, a realist account of Pantin, "the dark side of Paris," he devises a philosophy of unreason to characterize the transformative power of commerce.[35]

This philosophy is given concise expression when the narrator and his companion wander into a disreputable bar where they overhear a female ragpicker tell another that she was once "un vrai belle" over whom wealthy men fought duels:[36] "'That's the Good Lord's way of punishing you!' said someone near by. 'Where is he now, your Phaeton?' 'The Good Lord!' the ragpicker said in exasperation, 'The Good Lord is the Devil!'"[37] The ragpicker's comment provokes the intervention of "A scrawny fellow in a

---

[33] *Aurélia ou, le Rêve et la vie* was published posthumously in 1855.

[34] The World Exhibitions reached their height during this period.

[35] Gérard de Nerval, *Selected Writings*, trans. Richard Sieburth (London: Penguin Classics, 1999), 213. Nerval remarks "it was the chance reading of a piece of Dickens that set me off on these divagations!" (234); "La lecture d'un article de Charles Dickens est pourtant la source de ces divagations! . . ." Nerval, *Œuvres Complètes*, Vol. X.2, ed. Jean-Nicolas Illouz (Paris: Classiques Garnier, 2018), 81. Nerval's narrator refers to the essay "The Key of the Street," published in Dickens's review of the same name, although authored by his collaborator George Sala; it is the account of a night spent by the author in London on a pittance.

[36] Nerval suggests that Pantin is an Underworld through references to Dante's *Divine Comedy* and Mozart's *Don Giovanni*. As Dante is guided by Virgil, Nerval's persona is led by a "badaud" or idle onlooker, a man with an "absent-minded gaze" and "tall tales of adventures" (206). This Bloom-like guide is more pragmatic and more resistant to despair than his protégé: "'You're mistaken,' he replied. 'This is not Hell: this is at most Purgatory. Let's forge onwards'" (220).

[37] Nerval, *Selected Writings*, 226 (translation altered).

threadbare black suit, who had been asleep on a bench, woke up and staggered over towards us: 'If the Good Lord is the Devil, then the Devil is the Good Lord; it's always the same old story. This fine lady has just committed an egregious paralogism.'"[38] Yet what the philosopher deems to be illogical reasoning is the structure of Pantin. This transactional world is characterized by stark reversals of fate: the seedy bar displays demimondaines who, through investing in the wrong man or losing their allure, are now dealing in a corrupted abundance as ragpickers; the markets are populated by peasants who have become millionaires from trading, or rather "gambling," in sacks of beans.[39] In an environment where everything is permitted as long as it is profitable, being strays from essence and evil is indistinguishable from good. Philosophy in Pantin must take the form of paralogism: God is the Devil, and vice versa.

Nerval's scrawny scholar consoling himself in alcohol and philosophy is reimagined in "Circe" in the form of Stephen, who drunkenly observes the unreason of Nighttown. The episode climaxes (again) in his vision of a palindromic confrontation of political, social, and religious binaries, which he calls "the feast of pure reason." This exploding vision is sparked by an altercation with two English soldiers who are angered by his approaching the woman who accompanies them and his criticisms of King Edward as compromised by material concerns.[40] As their anger grows, a confrontation escalates between green and red, Irish and English, that enlists more and more historical, fictional, and archetypal figures until it becomes an Armageddon, the massive conflict that precedes the coming of the Antichrist. In a world made entirely fungible by commerce, the fervently held oppositions of politics and religion are madness. The world, in its historical embodiment, must end.

This syncretic end of the world features, as well as flying witches and raining dragons' teeth, a palindromic Black Mass offered over the pregnant belly of a naked Mina Purefoy *"goddess of unreason"* (U 15:4692).[41] Lynch

---

[38] Ibid.   [39] Ibid., 221–22.

[40] As Edward disappears into the role of consumer in "Lestrygonians," here he is absorbed by commerce. Stephen presents Edward, consecutively, as the developer of structures for the settlement of commercial disputes, an image of internalized oppression, an obsolete authority figure in the new age of commercial manipulation of consumer fears, and a penurious and lethal embodiment of greed. Most briefly: "He wants my money and my life, though want must be his master, for some brutish empire of his" (U 15:4568–70).

[41] The mass initiated by "Father Malachi O'Flynn: Introibo ad altare diaboli" (U 15:4698–99) completes a palindrome that frames the episode, as it mirrors Stephen's appearance in the first pages of the episode, at which he chants "with joy the introit for paschal time," introibo ad altare dei (U 15:73–74).

remarks that Stephen "likes dialectic, the universal language" (*U* 15:4726), and Stephen indeed understands the confrontation of Irish and English and of God and the Devil, or "Goooooooooood!" and "Doooooooooooog!" (*U* 15:4711–15), as constituting an ideal logic: "Reason. This feast of pure reason" (*U* 15:4735) he responds as Bloom urges him to abandon the confrontation with the soldiers. Yet the contradictory terms in this feast are not synthesized and sublated in a Hegelian dialectic; rather they mirror one another statically. "Pure reason," here, is an absurd confrontation of positive and negative oppositions, a feast for the eyes. Stephen's vision offers a liberation from the "nets" of nationality, language, and religion by exposing them as merely structural oppositions. This liberation is so thorough-going – this clash of all binaries is, as Stephen observes "a universal language," the confrontation of "The voices of *all* the damned" and "The voices of *all* the blessed" (*U* 15:4707–13) – that no meaning remains. This spectacle is a kind of madness.

Goethe's "Walpurgisnacht" is often cited as an intertext for "Circe" but this witches' festival comes to Joyce's episode not only from *Faust* (1808) but also through Nerval's reuse of Goethe to devise a hallucinatory mode of urban realism. At the age of nineteen, Nerval produced a literary translation of Goethe's *Faust* and, in *Les Nuits*, he invokes Goethe's text to figure the fantastical and lawless transformations of Pantin. The narrator remarks that a market girl has "the grace of a young debutante" at one moment and "shout[s] in a local accent" the next: "this sudden transition recalled the blonde witch in *Faust* who, while exchanging sweet nothings with her dancing partner, suddenly vomits up a red mouse."[42] Paris's most intense locus of exchange is thus expressed in terms of the festival on Brocken Mountain, an event that "surges maniacal magical song,"[43] where reproduction is disturbed, "the infant chokes, the mother bursts,"[44] and strange goods are produced for sale: Mephistopheles sends away a witch selling murderer's daggers and seducer's trinkets, "For only novelties excite."[45] Yet if "Walpurgisnacht" is an ostensible exception in *Faust*, it is the world of Pantin, a world that not only cannot be held separate from Paris but that embodies its values most vividly. In Georg Lukács's reading, Goethe is a dialectical historicist of the Hegelian mold, asserting the inevitable emergence of a better world through suffering and injustice:

[42] Nerval, *Selected Writings*, 222–23.
[43] Johann Wolfgang von Goethe, *Faust*, trans. Walter W. Arndt (New York: Norton, 1998), I. xxi.3955, 113.
[44] Ibid., I.xxi.3977, 113.   [45] Ibid., I.xxi.4413, 117.

"Goethe does nothing to mitigate the diabolical character of the capitalist form of this progress" but understands it as necessary for the subsequent emergence of an ideal, egalitarian society.[46] Faust's vision, according to Lukács, is of "the unceasing progress of the human species."[47] This vision is profoundly refuted by Nerval's paralogism, a refutation magnified by Joyce in "Circe" into the mirrored and static confrontation of godly and ungodly. Like Nerval's paralogism, the feast of pure reason Stephen observes is going nowhere. Philosophical thought is frozen. Wisdom is annihilated.

At the end of *Les Nuits*, the narrator swears off his effort to represent Paris: "This is the faithful history of the three October nights that cured me of my exaggerated notions of absolute realism – at least I have every reason to believe I have recovered."[48] Yet Nerval succumbs in his autobiographical work *Aurélia*, where the "awful mixture of comedy, dream and reality" of Pantin returns in an uncontrollable "seepage of dreams into life."[49] Published posthumously, *Aurélia* is Nerval's account of the wavering of his sanity. The text is "a series of visions which were perhaps insane or, more simply, the mere products of my illness."[50] Nerval's text associates his mental instability, his wavering between vision and reality, with a dismantled social and political world: "for us, born in an age of revolutions and upheavals which shattered all beliefs [...] things become quite difficult whenever we feel the need to reconstruct that mystic temple."[51]

---

[46] Qtd. in Inez Hedges, *Framing Faust: Twentieth Century Cultural Struggles* (Carbondale: Southern Illinois University Press, 2009), 84.

[47] Qtd. in Hedges, *Framing Faust*, 81.   [48] Ibid., 244.

[49] Ibid., 232, 269 (translation altered); "cet affreux mélange de comédie, de rêve et de réalité" (79); "l'épanchement du songe dans la vie réelle," Nerval, *Œuvres Complètes*, Vol. XIII, ed. Jean-Nicolas Illouz (Paris: Classiques Garnier, 2013), 51. Nerval's narrator in *Les Nuits* dreams of a tribunal of literary critics and philosophers who denounce him for bringing together the genres of realism, fantastical writing, and essay, not because they deviate from reality but because they lead to its dark side: "it's but a small step from *realism* to crime; for crime is, by its very nature, realistic. *Fantaisisme* [humorous writing] inevitably leads to the worship of monsters. *Essayisme* has landed this wayward mind on a rotting pallet in a dungeon." Nerval, *Selected Writings*, 241. "Du réalisme au crime il n'y a qu'un pas; car le crime est essentiellement réaliste. Le fantaisisme conduit tout droit à l'adoration des monstres. L'essayisme amène ce faux esprit à pourrir sur la paille humide des cachots" (Nerval, *Œuvres Complètes*, Vol. X.2, 90).

[50] Ibid., 270; "une série de visions insensées peut-être, ou vulgairement maladives" (Nerval, *Œuvres Complètes*, Vol. XIII, 52).

[51] Ibid., 290–91; "pour nous, nés dans des jours de révolutions et d'orages, où toutes les croyances ont été brisées [...] il est bien difficile, dès que nous en sentons le besoin, de reconstruire l'édifice mystique dont les innocents et les simples admettent dans leurs cœurs la figure toute tracée" (Ibid., 84–85).

Foucault refers fleetingly but repeatedly to Nerval's writings as one of the few eruptions in the nineteenth century of a life of "unreason" with the power to contest the conventional social order.[52] Foucault observes a "consecration of the sensible" in Nerval's writing; associating him with Hölderlin, Foucault argues that "The moment of the Ja-sagen, of the embrace of the lure of the sensible, was also the moment they retreated into the shadows of insanity."[53]

In a similar mechanism to Bloom's exploding visions, the material details of the objects Nerval encounters prompt his hallucinations, as we will see in the following passage. Building on Foucault's brief suggestions, I read the seepage of dreams in Nerval's *Aurélia* as exposing both the power of new material possibilities and also the guilt that accompanies their situation within relations of exchange. Paris as an environment of consumption is the locus for Nerval's struggles with sanity. In his account, the city manifests a magical and ominous abundance:

> I then proceeded towards Saint-Eustache, where I piously knelt at the altar of the Virgin while thinking of my mother. The tears I shed eased my soul and, upon leaving the church, I bought myself a silver ring. From there I went to my father's house to pay him a visit; as he was out, I left him a bouquet of daisies. I then wandered over to the Jardin des Plantes. The place was quite crowded and I stopped to watch a hippopotamus bathing in a pool. I then went to have a look at the osteological exhibits at the Museum of Natural History. The sight of the monsters on display got me thinking about the Flood and, as I made my way out to the gardens again, it was pouring with rain. I said to myself: What a shame! All these women and children are going to get drenched! . . . Then I said to myself: but things are far more serious! This is the beginning of the real Flood! The water was rising in the nearby streets; I ran down the rue Saint-Victor and, believing I might be able to stem the global tide, I threw the ring I had bought at Saint-Eustache into the deepest part of the water. It was roughly at this moment that the rain tapered off and a ray of sun burst forth.[54]

[52] Michel Foucault, *Madness and Civilization: A History of Insanity in the Age of Reason*, trans. Richard Howard (New York: Random House, 1988), 212.

[53] Michel Foucault, *History of Madness*, ed. Jean Khalfa, trans. Johathan Murphy (New York: Routledge, 2006), 351.

[54] Nerval, *Selected Writings*, 302–03. "Ensuite j'allai vers Saint-Eustache, où je m'agenouillai pieusement à l'autel de la Vierge en pensant à ma mère. Les pleurs que je versai détendirent mon âme, et, en sortant de l'église, j'achetai un anneau d'argent. De là, j'allai rendre visite à mon père, chez lequel je laissai un bouquet de marguerites, car il était absent. J'allai de là au Jardin des Plantes. Il y avait beaucoup de monde, et je restai quelque temps à regarder l'hippopotame qui se baignait dans un bassin. – J'allai ensuite visiter les galeries d'ostéologie. La vue des monstres qu'elles renferment me fit penser au déluge, et, lorsque je sortis, une averse épouvantable tombait dans le jardin. Je me dis: 'Quel malheur! Toutes ces femmes, tous ces enfants, vont rentrer mouillés! . . . '

Delusions aside, Nerval's actions are those of a man with ample means to enjoy what the city has to offer. His delusions are, I would argue, the expression of a heightened logic of exchange, according to which all things are fungible. Within this abundant world, physical objects are equivalent to the self, its emotions, and its sinful debt, as Nerval leaves flowers in his stead at his father's house, marks his tears with a silver ring, and casts the ring into the river to forestall the punishing flood. Nerval's struggle with insanity is coterminous with his relation to this material abundance; the abilities afforded by his money are accompanied by a profound personal guilt that has a societal amplitude, as suggested by the citywide proportions of the quasi-Biblical Flood that he senses approaching. That this guilt is sparked by social injustice is implied by his hyperbolic reaction to the prospect of women and children being exposed to the rainshower. If the silver ring marks the ease he gains by weeping at the memory of his dead mother, it is the sacrifice demanded of him by the sight of the material vulnerability of others. We can understand this payment as an altered form of the structure of commerce, which underlies Nerval's activities in the city.

Nerval's consumption and the sense of immense power associated with it are situated, in his account, in a shifting world that lacks foundational being. A scene in a workshop links this supernatural power to industrial production: the workmen tell Nerval that they use "the primordial fire which animated the first created beings" to make strange new creatures out of unknown metals of cinnabar red and sky blue. As they "seemed to have discovered the secrets of divine creation," the products of their artistry defy the boundary between natural and artificial: a workman tells him that things "which seem so natural to you, this animal which appears to be alive, are but the products of art raised to the highest level of our knowledge, and everyone should judge them accordingly."[55] This

---

Puis je me dis: 'Mais c'est plus encore! c'est le véritable déluge qui commence.' L'eau s'élevait dans les rues voisines; je descendis en courant la rue Saint-Victor, et, dans l'idée d'arrêter ce que je croyais l'inondation universelle, je jetai à l'endroit le plus profond l'anneau que j'avais acheté à Saint-Eustache. Vers le même moment, l'orage s'apaisa, et un rayon de soleil commença à briller" (Nerval, *Œuvres Complètes*, Vol. XIII, 102).

[55] Nerval, *Selected Writings*, 287–88. "'Ne créerait-on pas aussi des hommes?' dis-je à l'un des travailleurs, mais il me répliqua: 'Les hommes viennent d'en haut et non d'en bas: pouvons-nous créer nous-mêmes? Ici, l'on ne fait que formuler par les progrès successifs de nos industries une matière plus subtile que celle qui compose la croûte terrestre. Ces fleurs qui vous paraissent naturelles, cet animal qui semblera vivre, ne seront que des produits de l'art élevé au plus haut point de nos connaissances, et chacun les jugera ainsi.'" (79–80)

production then renders essence unknowable and the things of the world infinitely extendable in number and nature.

Later, Nerval identifies this unknowable world as subtended by a female principle that defies specific identification: if the doubling forms of the Virgin Mother and his mother shadow the syncretic exchange in the passage cited above, that same day he has a vision of his lost love, Aurélia[56]: "It seemed to me the goddess was appearing to me and saying: 'I am none other than Mary, none other than your mother, none other than the one you have always loved in every shape and manner.'"[57] This apparition's unique identity is never revealed; any identity is precluded by the generativity that pervades the text's events. A little later he perceives that: "Everything is alive, everything is in motion, everything corresponds." The location of this joyful vision is the Dubois clinic and its conclusive position in the text, at the end of the series of his troubled dreams, is the work of editors after his suicide.[58]

Rimbaud and Endless Farce

Joyce clearly draws on Nerval to construct the exploding visions of "Circe," as he creates around Bloom a shifting world of seemingly infinite abundance; in the following section, we will observe the crucial role of an ephemeral material presence that flows between individuals. But here, we will examine how in his comic rendering of Bloom's visions of heaven and hell, Joyce has recourse to the work of a French writer who reimagines Nerval's visions as farcical. The narrator of Arthur Rimbaud's *Une Saison en enfer* flaunts his rises and falls as a lamentable comedy: "An endless farce! My innocence would make me weep. Life is the farce we all play."[59]

---

[56] Shoshana Felman reads this apparition in psychoanalytic terms as embodying a female lack associated with the hero's castration: Aurélia is "a signifier of loss," finally "designat[ed] as a blank." Felman, *Writing and Madness (Literature/Philosophy/Psychoanalysis)*, trans. Martha Noel Evans and Shoshana Felman with Brian Massumi (Palo Alto, CA: Stanford University Press, 2003), 69–70. Against this castration, she argues, Nerval's character asserts his power in the "magic alphabet" of the material world: "The entire world is from then on a symbolic discourse, which the hero interprets according to his desires and fears ... which will allow the hero to affirm himself and vanquish the other" (72).

[57] Nerval, *Selected Writings*, 303. "Il me semblait que la déesse m'apparaissait, me disant: 'Je suis la même que Marie, la même que ta mère, la même aussi que sous toutes les formes tu as toujours aimée'" (Nerval, *Œuvres complètes*, Vol. XIII, 103).

[58] Nerval, *Selected Writings*, 307. "Tout vit, tout agit, tout se correspond" (107).

[59] Arthur Rimbaud, *Rimbaud: Complete Works, Selected Letters*, trans. Wallace Fowlie (Chicago: University of Chicago Press, 1966), 183. "Farce continuelle! Mon innocence me ferait pleurer. La vie est la farce à mener par tous," Rimbaud, *Complete Works*, 182.

Unlike *Aurélia*, in which Nerval is enmeshed in his own vicissitudes, in *Une Saison en enfer*, Rimbaud's persona gains power from a theatrical production of highs and lows. In "L'Alchimie du verbe," "The Alchemy of the Word," he announces: "I became a fabulous opera."[60]

Une Saison en enfer is written a generation after *Aurélia*, when the limits of industrial development had become brutally clear. Rimbaud wrote *Une Saison* following the violent obliteration of the nineteenth century's greatest effort at social and material transformation, the 1871 Paris Commune. Along with other artists, Rimbaud had declared his support for the radical experiment in socialist self-government by artisans and workers, which was violently suppressed after two months by the forces of the Third Republic. With the killing of 25,000 people in the streets, the attempt at an egalitarian reconfiguration of society was extinguished.[61] If Rimbaud's text is written at a historical moment of despair, it generates a sense of possibility through its scrambling of sense, texts, and relations. Rancière describes Rimbaud as writing in *Une Saison en enfer* "the great music of the nineteenth century," a "language of future harmonies" taken from the nineteenth century's own theories of itself: lectures by Flammarion, vaudevilles by Scribe, descriptions of World's Exhibitions, pamphlets by followers of Saint-Simon and Fourier on "cities of the future, the emancipation of women, the promotion of fertilizer, the development of byroads, workers' housing, future androgyny, efficient stoves and eternity by the stars" as well as prayer books, songs and fairytales, magically fused by the Cabala, hieroglyphs, and universal language into the language of the future.[62] These themes, familiar to readers of "Circe," are presented in *Une Saison* in a burlesque that is irreverent, disordered, and energetic.

"Circe" draws upon these spectacular highs and lows, reusing the deranged images and words of *Une Saison* in which Rimbaud's persona vacillates between hero and outcast, outlaw and respectable citizen. Some of Bloom's wildest exploding visions are expanded versions of scenes witnessed by the narrator in "Mauvais Sang," "Bad Blood":

---

[60] Ibid., 199. "Je devins un opéra fabuleux" (198).

[61] The "political imaginary" of the Commune lived on, according to Kristin Ross, in what she calls its spirit of "communal luxury": the Communards' "daily workings inverted entrenched hierarchies and divisions – first and foremost among those the division between manual and artistic or intellectual labor. The world is divided between those who can and those who cannot afford the luxury of playing with words or images." Kristin Ross, *Communal Luxury: The Political Imaginary of the Paris Commune* (New York: Verso, 2015), 50.

[62] Rancière, *The Flesh of Words*, 50, 51. Rimbaud's nature as a convert to a New Christianity, Rancière argues, means that the text is trapped in a recitation of the catechism; he is trapped in the "true hell: the new hell, that of parody" (54).

In cities the mud seemed to me suddenly red and black, like a mirror when the lamp moves about in the next room, like a treasure in the forest! Good luck! I cried, and saw a sea of flames and smoke in the sky; and on the left and on the right, every kind of richness flaming like a million thunderbolts. But debauchery and the companionship of women were denied me. Not even a friend. I saw myself in front of an infuriated mob, facing the firing-squad, weeping over the unhappiness they would not have been able to understand, and forgiving! – Like Joan of Arc![63]

Crammed together here are some of Bloom's most memorable scenarios in "Circe": the city in apocalypse, female adulation, public execution, the bloodthirsty mob, the noble scapegoat, the saintly victim. Rimbaud's braggadocious recasting of Nerval's fantasies of omniscience in *Aurélia*, "I intend to unveil all mysteries: religious mysteries or those of nature, death, birth, the future, the past, cosmogony, the void. I am the master of phantasmagorias. Listen . . . I possess every talent!"[64] is rendered even more farcical in Bloom's all-knowing performances: "CHRIS CALLINAN: What is the parallax of the subsolar ecliptic of Aldebaran? BLOOM: Pleased to hear from you, Chris. K. II. [. . .] BEN DOLLARD: Pansies? BLOOM: Embellish (beautify) gardens. BEN DOLLARD: When twins arrive? BLOOM: Father (pater, dad) starts thinking" (*U* 15:1655–71).

Rimbaud's language of political disillusionment provides a set of terms for Bloom's slide from social reform into mere performance. In "Nuit de l'enfer," "Night of Hell," Rimbaud's grandiose narrator offers a new kind of spectacle to replace political speeches. The narrator's assertions of omnipotence are associated with an art of fantastical and exploitative entertainment:

I possess every talent! – There is no-one here and there is someone. I would not like to expend my treasure. – Do you want negro songs, houri dances? Do you want me to disappear and dive after the *ring*? Do you? I will make gold and remedies.

Then trust in me. Faith provides relief and guides and cures. Come all, even the little children – and I will comfort you, and pour out my heart for

---

[63] Ibid., 179. "Dans les villes la boue m'apparaissait soudainement rouge et noire, comme une glace quand la lampe circule dans la chambre voisine, comme un trésor dans la forêt! Bonne chance, criai-je, et je voyais une mer de flammes et de fumée au ciel; et, à gauche, à droite, toutes les richesses flambant comme un milliard de tonnerres. Mais l'orgie et la camaraderie des femmes m'étaient interdites. Pas même un compagnon. Je me voyais devant une foule exaspérée, en face du peloton d'exécution, pleurant du malheur qu'ils n'aient pu comprendre, et pardonnant! – Comme Jeanne d'Arc!" (178).

[64] Ibid., 185, translation altered. "Je vais dévoiler tous les mystères: mystères religieux ou naturels, mort, naissance, avenir, passé, cosmogonie, néant. Je suis maître en fantasmagories. Écoutez! . . . J'ai tous les talents!" (184).

you – my marvelous heart! – Poor men, workers! I am not asking for
prayers. With your trust alone, I will be happy.[65]

This address substitutes radical politics with a conservative humanism
delivered in spectacular form. For this speaker, workers are not a political
collective but an audience, bonded together not by the struggle for the
construction of a better world but by feeling, as they grant "trust" to a
performance of humanity. The energy of transformation lives on as
spectacle, while pointing to its own inauthenticity. The subjectivity that
is to be consumed has already been dismantled: "Il n'y a personne ici et il y
a quelqu'un," "there is no one here and there is someone."

"Circe," too, features in great vividness the adulation of Bloom's marvelous heart by the people of Dublin, even as his radical calls for reform are
replaced by reactionary spectacles. Prompted by Zoe's retort to his dislike
of cigarettes, "Go on. Make a stump speech out of it" (U 15:1353), Bloom
embarks upon a set of progressive speeches that lead to his celebration
as "the world's greatest reformer" (U 15:1459). Dressed "in workman's
corduroy overalls, black gansy with red floating tie and apache cap," he begins
by envisioning a new automated mode of transport that would allow
greater efficiency and convenience. Yet he then associates automated
transportation with predatory capitalism: the "buccaneering Vanderdeck-
ens" (U 15:1369) are a stand-in for the businessman Cornelius Vanderbilt,
who famously amassed an enormous fortune in transport.[66] The transformative powers of industry become recast as a menace as Bloom associates Vanderdecken with the "phantom ship of finance" (U 15:1370), the
"[F]lying Dutchmen or lying Dutchmen" (U 15:1390), evoking a spectral
ship that presages disaster when it appears off the Cape of Good Hope.
Bloom figures workers in terms of the women of Nighttown, subject to "a
horde of capitalistic lusts upon our prostituted labor" (U 15:1394). Yet,
almost immediately, his critique collapses into spectacle. Now dressed in
the finery of civic power, he is unable to sustain the position of critic; as
the rhythms and alliterations of speechifying overpower the content of the
speech itself, his outraged criticisms gradually become entangled in merely
pleasurable sound, "purblind pomp of pelf and power" and "reign is rover

---

[65] Ibid., 185. "J'ai tous les talents! – Il n'y a personne ici et il y a quelqu'un: je ne voudrais pas répandre
mon trésor. – Veut-on des chants nègres, des danses de houris? Veut-on que je disparaisse, que je
plonge à la recherche de l'anneau? Veut-on? Je ferai de l'or, des remèdes. Fiez-vous donc à moi, la foi
soulage, guide, guérit. Tous, venez, – même les petits enfants, – que je vous console, qu'on répande
pour vous son coeur, – le coeur merveilleux! Pauvres hommes, travailleurs! Je ne demande pas de
prières; avec votre confiance seulement, je serai heureux" (184).

[66] "A household word for the 'buccaneering' financier." Gifford and Seidman, Ulysses Annotated, 471.

for rever and ever and ev... (*Prolongued applause*)" (*U* 15:1396–97).
Bloom is immediately subjected to one of the most lavish tributes of the
episode as he is celebrated by multitudes assembled from Dublin and
beyond, appearing dressed "*in a crimson velvet mantle trimmed with ermine,
bearing Saint Edward's staff, the orb and sceptre with the dove, the curtana.
He is seated on a milkwhite horse with long flowing crimson tail, richly
caparisoned, with golden headstall. Wild excitement*" (*U* 15:1442–46).

In a parody of World's Exhibitions and "cities of the future," Bloom
goes on to announce a personally branded Promised Land. Situated on
Irish land and built by Irish workers, the "new Bloomusalem [. . .] *is a
colossal edifice with crystal roof, built in the shape of a huge pork kidney,
containing forty thousand rooms*" (*U* 15:1544–49). The building evokes the
Crystal Palace of London but also, and even more closely, the 1867 World
Exposition Building in Paris, a 1600-foot-long ovoid building with a
glass and steel roof built on the Champs de Mars in the center of Paris.
The massive displacement of Parisian city dwellers by Haussmann's
urban developments is parodied here in the boxing up of Dubliners, with
the added twist that they are now marked as the private property of L. B.
In this "Nova Hibernia of the future," Bloom's bodyguards distribute
masses of gifts in a parody of utopian abundance, as the objects range
from useful commodities such as Jeyes' Fluid and rubber preservatives,
through treats like pork sausages and cigars, to the Christlike boons of
"*loaves and fishes*" to the postcapitalist amenity of "*season tickets available
for all tram lines*" (*U* 15.1544–84). The distributed objects also include
things of dubious worth: coupons for the suspect Hungarian lottery, 40
days' indulgences, counterfeit money, and reprints of the "*World's Twelve
Worst Books.*" Bloom's radically socialist declaration of "Free money, free
rent, free love and a free lay church in a free lay state" (*U* 15:1693) leads
merely to nonsensical, if popular, abundance.

An Art of Pleasurable Waste and Wasteful Pleasure

The crowds embrace Bloom's megalomaniac proposals to reshape the
world even when they depart from social justice and take the form of
absurd, fantastical, and even appropriative spectacle; their only condition is
that he exhibit an interest in reproductive sex. The new Bloomusalem as
well as Bloom's other regimes collapse not due to practical considerations
but following accusations made against Bloom of contraception, infantile
sexuality, masturbation, voyeurism, flirtation, heavy petting, masochism,
and coprophilia: Theodore Purefoy, "(*In fishingcap and oilskin jacket.*)

He employs a mechanical device to frustrate the sacred ends of nature" (*U* 15:1741–42); Alexander Dowie, "this stinking goat of Mendes gave precocious signs of infantile debauchery, recalling the cities of the plain, with a dissolute granddam (*U* 15:1755–57); a Crab, "(*In bush ranger's kit.*) What did you do in the cattlecreep behind Kilbarrack?" (*U* 15:1872–73); Gerty McDowell, "you saw all the secrets of my bottom drawer" (*U* 15:384); Josie Breen, "High jinks below stairs" (*U* 15:487); Martha Clifford, "Breach of promise. My real name is Peggy Griffin. He wrote to me that he was miserable" (*U* 15:765–66); Mary Driscoll, "He held me and I was discoloured in four places as a result. And he interfered twict with my clothing" (*U* 15:886–88); Mrs Yelverton Barry, "He wrote me an anonymous letter in prentice backhand [. . .] signed James Lovebirch" (*U* 15:1016–18); the Honorable Mrs Mervyn Talboys, "He implored me to soil his letter in an unspeakable manner" (*U* 15:1070–71); Mrs Bellingham, "Me too" (*U* 15:1075). Bloom admits guilt through his earnest denial of these alternatives to reproductive heterosexuality: "(*excitedly*) This is midsummer madness, some ghastly joke again. By heaven, I am guiltless as the unsunned snow!" (*U* 15:1768–69). He is repeatedly put to death for these urges.

It is important to acknowledge that there is nothing uncommercial as such in Bloom's deviant activities: one can suppose there are many brothels in which such doings are part of the standard bill of fare. Yet the brothel keeper's reaction to Bloom's confessions shows that they are outside the calculus of Nighttown. This is most clearly illustrated when Bello demands to hear of "the most revolting obscenity in all your career of crime" and Bloom admits to an extreme instance of his interest in wasteful pleasure: "BLOOM: (*docile, gurgles*) I rererepugnosed in rerererepugnant . . . BELLO: (*imperiously*) O, get out, you skunk! Hold your tongue!" (*U* 15:3042–59). Bloom's stuttering suggests a mixture of shame and erotic fixation, producing out of "repugnant" the terms "pug nose" and a reiterated "rere." Bello, who is capable of the cruelest treatment of women, cannot bear to hear about Bloom's coprophiliac sniffing. The "pug nose" Bloom admits to is the nose of a particularly flat-faced kind of dog, in which the nostrils are set in what looks like a head without a muzzle, suggesting an extreme openness to smell. The phrase is often used to refer to a short, thick human nose with an upturned tip, suggesting an expression indicating a powerful sense of disgust. Bloom's "most revolting obscenity" then is a "crime" neither against morals nor the law but against commerce and aesthetics: it is to revel in the valueless, or more precisely, to revel in that which contravenes value.

This book might seem to have its own pug nose in tracing the evolution of scenes in which intimate odors feature prominently in encounters between male and female figures: the Paris Epiphany, Stephen and Emma Clery's encounter in the library colonnade at the end of *Portrait*, and Bloom's encounter with Josie Breen in "Lestrygonians." In these scenes, the material characteristics of bodily smell evade the evaluative categories that regulate urban space as an arena of consumption. The particulate, invasive, and ambiguous nature of these smells undoes both individual boundaries and gender distinctions. These scenes, I have argued, are instances of a somatic aesthetics situated within the world of commerce but possessed of the power to reinstate other pleasures within it. In these encounters, desire becomes decoupled from transaction and associated instead with an intimate, aesthetic relation. I have also traced how, alongside these scenes, Joyce has presented, through characters such as Cranly, Lynch, and Bloom, informal critiques of the emphasis eighteenth-century accounts of classical aesthetics placed on the autonomous artwork, with its ideal, closed forms. These two strains come together at the climax of "Circe," when Bloom discusses his interest in excreta with Bella Cohen's next avatar, an "art masterpiece" Nymph, a conversation that revisits the questions Joyce posed about art in Paris in 1903.

Before turning to that conversation, we might borrow some language from Lee Edelman to tease out the significance of the deviant activities in which Bloom engages. Bloom's desires here are not queer desires: they are desires of a man for a woman.[67] Yet they are directed away from hetero-genital sex. The larger context of *Ulysses* offers an explanation for this redirection of desire: "Could never like it again after Rudy," Bloom muses in "Lestrygonians," thinking of the death of his baby son and the subsequent hiatus in sexual intercourse between him and Molly (*U* 8:610). Yet this avoidance is recast in "Circe" as a refusal of the positions of client, husband, and father. Edelman associates the figure of the child with "reproductive futurism" and the normalizing imperatives of reproductive ideology; in "Circe," child-making is central to the operation of capital.[68] Bloom's desires deviate from the production and the reproduction of wealth.

---

[67] For explorations of Bloom's queer tendencies see, for example, Jennifer Levine, "James Joyce, Tattoo Artist: Tracing the Outlines of Homosocial Desire" in Joe Valente, *Quare Joyce* (Ann Arbor: University of Michigan Press, 1998), 101–20, and Barry McCrea, *In the Company of Strangers: Family and Narrative in Dickens, Conan Doyle, Joyce, and Proust* (New York: Columbia University Press, 2011).

[68] Lee Edelman, *No Future: Queer Theory and the Death Drive* (Durham, NC: Duke University Press, 2004).

At Bloom's most glorious and even tyrannical moments in Bloomusalem, he is celebrated as a father. Despite having the Man in the Macintosh shot for saying his name is Higgins, as well as striking his enemies dead, Bloom is adulated as a paterfamilias, "([. . .]*Babes and sucklings are held up.)* THE WOMEN: Little father! Little father!" (*U* 15:1588–91). The episode's celebration of reproduction, and its connection to the accumulation and maintenance of wealth, is made clear when Bloom gives birth to octuplets, having remarked: "O, I do so want to be a mother" (*U* 15:1817). They appear, fully grown, in a wealthy, cultured setting, already functioning as captains of industry: "*immediately appointed to positions of high public trust in several different countries as managing directors of banks, traffic managers of railways, chairmen of limited liability companies, vicechairmen of hotel syndicates*" (*U* 15.1828–32). The octuplets' "*valuable metallic faces*" obscure their humanity while their names are amalgams of body parts and precious metals rather than markers of identity: "Nasodoro, Goldfinger, Chrysostomos, Maindorée," etc. (*U* 15.1827–28). Bloom is lauded and showered with tokens of wealth: "*General commotion and compassion. Women faint. A wealthy American makes a street collection for Bloom. Gold and silver coins, blank cheques, banknotes, jewels, treasury bonds, maturing bills of exchange, I. O. U's, wedding rings, watchchains, lockets, necklaces and bracelets are rapidly collected*" (*U* 15:1811–15). Yet, although the doctor uses the pregnancy to plead on his behalf, "I appeal for clemency in the name of the most sacred word our vocal organs have ever been called upon to speak. He is about to have a baby" (*U* 15:1809–10), this miraculous ability to give birth lacks the masculinist agency required to save Bloom.

Bloom's disinterest in taking up the male role in procreative sexuality finds expression in a slur. A "deadhand" writing on a wall denounces him as a "cod" (*U* 15:1871) and, at the end of their strange encounter, Bella Cohen too uses the term to denounce Bloom: "I know you, canvasser! Dead cod!" (*U* 15:3495). Cod is, in slang, a scrotum. It is also a joke, a hoax, a leg-pull, a parody, and a burlesque (OED 5.2). Bloom's unused reproductive organs are thus at the center of the farce of "Circe," emblems of unproductive enjoyment. In contrast, Blazes Boylan enacts a policy of possession and use through heterogenital penetration of Molly: "I have a little private business with your wife, you understand?" (*U* 15:3764–65). As Bello Cohen puts it, "there's a man of brawn in possession there [. . .] Wait for nine months, my lad!" (*U* 15:3136–42). Bloom's response to their copulation is to take pleasure in watching: "Show! Hide! Show! Plough her! More! Shoot!" (*U* 15:3815–16). In Bloom's pointless imperatives, which merely describe Boylan's actions, Molly's body is figured as soil to be cultivated. Boylan's forceful planting of seed is associated with accumulation as his gun-like "Shoot!" is enacted under the banner of "More!" This successive showing and hiding of heterogenital intercourse is a miniature of the episode's exploding visions.

Bloom, in contrast, under the domination of the sadistic Bello, is marked as an article of trade produced by the brothel, "stamped, of course, with my houseflag" (*U* 15:2979–80). Quantification and containment are stressed as the means of maximizing control in his objectification: "Tape measurements will be taken next your skin. You will be laced with cruel force into vicelike corsets of soft dove coutille, with whalebone busk" (*U* 15:2974–76). Bello makes literal this objectification: "you are unmanned and mine in earnest, a thing under the yoke" (*U* 15:2965–66). Bloom thus assumes the position of a prostitute but, like Stephen speaking parleyvoo, he enacts this role as a farce. His pleasures undermine the terms of his instrumentalization: "BELLO: "Pander to their Gomorrahan vices. BLOOM: (*bends his blushing face into his armpit and simpers with forefinger in mouth*) O, I know what you're hinting at now!" (*U* 15:3121–25). This is also a burlesque of literary styles. Bello's subjugation of Bloom becomes a parodic attack on possessive individualism as he describes what is happening at 7 Eccles St.: "A man and his menfriends are living there in clover [. . .] (*cuttingly*) Their heelmarks will stamp the Brusselette carpet you bought at Wren's auction. [. . .] Pages will be torn from your handbook of astronomy to make them pipespills. And they will spit in your ten shilling brass fender from Hampton Leedom's. BLOOM: Ten and six. The act of low scoundrels. Let me go. I will return" (*U* 15:3174–91). If Bello's provocations awaken a masculine sense of proprietorship in Bloom, it appears only in clichéd form, "*Bloom clenches his fists and crawls forward, a bowieknife between his teeth*" and disappears almost immediately, when "*he bites his thumb*" (*U* 15:3295–02).

In contrast to such possessive individualism and instrumentalization, Bloom's desires defy the profitable and productive operations of the brothel. If Edelman suggests an alternative force to reproductive futurity in the form of a death drive that he identifies with the violence of wounding, fracturing, disfiguration, and "lifeless machinery," Bloom models in Cohen's brothel a deviation from reproductive desire that undermines the conventional boundaries of the person, as well as the oppositions of subject and object.[69] He does so through curious pleasure.

[69] Edelman, *No Future*, 27, 38.

This deviant enjoyment is opposed to the mode of bounded subjects and objects. It is explicitly named during Bello's interrogation as an interest in bodily waste. However, and crucially, this interest is not purely material but also relational. Bello accuses Bloom of sitting down to urinate when wearing a dress for the school play *Vice Versa*; while Bloom's dress is part of an officially sanctioned transvestitism, his seated micturition crosses the lines of conventional gender behavior.[70] But Bloom explains that he adopted the pose in search of knowledge of universal but individually embodied pleasures: "Science. To compare the various joys we each enjoy" (*U* 15:3019). Bloom is interested in an expansion of pleasure not through instrumentalizing women but rather through coming closer to their experience. He is motivated not by greed but by sensual curiosity; he displays, as Bello alleges, "womanish care," but more crucially, and intimately, as he sits on "the smoothworn throne" he approaches a different inhabitation of the physical world. This interest, as we will see, is presented in a more intense form in Bloom's encounter with the Nymph at the climax of the episode.

The Nymph occupies the insecure position of a magazine illustration that has been "Given away with the Easter number of *Photo Bits*: splendid masterpiece in art colours" (*U* 4:369–70) and that Bloom has framed and hung above his and Molly's bed. She is thus situated at the border of commerce and art, embodying the question of the survival of art in consumer capitalism. With a pained stress on her otherworldly status – she addresses Bloom as "Mortal!" – she thanks Bloom for saving her from her previous commercial – or, in her word, "evil" – environment: a commercial publication, packed with sensational stories, advertisements for intimate gadgets, and soft pornography. She asserts her separate status from this corruption as an object preserved for private use, "I was hidden in cheap pink paper that smelt of rock oil" (*U* 15:3248).

Despite having taken her from this sordid environment and set her high on the wall, Bloom still relates erotically to the Nymph. If this is an embarrassment to her as an aspiring artwork, Joyce had long doubted the possibility of excluding desire from the sphere of art. In 1903, in "The Paris and Pola Commonplace Book," Joyce questioned the generic status of the sculpture a contemporary sculptor made of his wife: "Spicer-Simson has made a bust of his wife. Is it lyrical, epical or dramatic?" Joyce defines these terms in the same notebook as, respectively, art "whereby the artist

---

[70] Gifford notes of the play based on Thomas Anstey Guthrie's 1882 novel: "The central theme of the farce is father against son played out when the father's spirit inhabits the son's body, and vice versa." Gifford and Seidman, *Ulysses Annotated*, 504.

sets forth the image in immediate relation to himself [. . .], to himself and to others, [and] to others" (*OCPW* 103). The question insinuates that in at least one, if not all, of these cases this relation is one of desire.

Joyce's dramatic mode helps us to understand the aesthetic nature of Bloom's deviant interests in the bedroom. To see this, however, we must refer to Stephen's fuller articulation of this mode of art in *Portrait*: "The dramatic form is reached when the vitality which has flowed and eddied round each person fills every person with such vital force that he or she assumes a proper and intangible aesthetic life" (*P* 180). This vague but suggestive definition, which goes beyond conventional theatrical scenarios, is realized in "Circe," not in Bloom's direct relation to the Nymph but rather to Molly, in the space beneath the Nymph's frame. If this dramatic art might seem to be a positive refutation of the fifth aesthetic question Joyce framed in Paris, "Why are not excrements, children and lice works of art?" this aesthetic consists not exactly in the scatological but rather in simple, intimate material sensations.

These sensations rework and invert the terms eighteenth-century aesthetics used to describe classical art. These terms feature in Bloom's praise of the Nymph, which combines his thoughts of marble goddesses in "Lestrygonians" with a reference to Keats's *Endymion*: "Your classic curves, beautiful immortal, I was glad to look on you, to praise you, a thing of beauty, almost to pray" (*U* 15:3267–68). Keats's aesthetic, within the context of *Photo Bits*, sounds like a solid investment: "A thing of beauty is a joy forever/Its loveliness increases; it will never/Pass into nothingness."[71] Yet the nymph elliptically hints that this praise, "during dark nights," has been very different, and Bloom responds, "Yes, yes. You mean that I. . . . Sleep reveals the worst side of everyone" (*U* 15:3272–73). As a remedy, he ponders "that English invention, pamphlet of which I received some days ago, incorrectly addressed. It claims to afford a noiseless, inoffensive vent" (*U* 15:3274–76). Bloom's "praise" is then directly opposed to "a thing of beauty [that] is a joy forever"; his expression of flatulence is at most a passing joy and one that we might assume is neither beautiful nor ideal.

Yet this is not yet the art that "Circe" stages; that art occurs between bodies. In contrast to the Nymph's self-designation as an ideal form, an autonomous and closed body, "(*loftily*) We immortals, as you saw today, have not such a place and no hair there either. We are stonecold and pure. We eat electric light" (*U* 15:3392–93), Bloom lists pleasures associated

---

71 Gifford and Seidman, *Ulysses Annotated*, 491.

with crude bodily realities from the scatological to the masturbatory: "Soiled personal linen, wrong side up with care"; "That antiquated commode. It wasn't her weight"; "that absurd orangekeyed utensil that only has one handle. (*The sound of a waterfall is heard in bright cascade.*)"; "She climbed the crooked tree and I. A saint couldn't resist it"; "Done. Prff!"; "Enemas too I have administered. [. . .] With Hamilton Long's syringe, the ladies' friend"; "*Pecavi!* I have paid homage on that living altar where the back changes name. (*with sudden fervour*) For why should the dainty scented jeweled hand, the hand that rules . . .?" (*U* 15:3288–3407). If some might call Bloom deviant in this set of sordid activities, and if bodily emissions are central to his experiences of wasteful pleasure and pleasurable waste, these instances are centered not on a fascination with a particular kind of taboo matter but rather with an interpersonal experience, an experience situated at the boundaries of the individual. This is a joy that Bloom names directly as "Science. To compare the various joys we each enjoy" (*U* 15:3019).

To understand the significance of these relations, we might turn to the vocabulary of Julia Kristeva. Kelly Anspaugh argues that Joyce's "excremental vision" is centered on a purgation of the abject, a term he takes from Kristeva: "That Bloom, however, is also subject to abjection is suggested by the nightmare episode 'Circe,' where Joyce's excremental hero is put on trial for his many copro-crimes."[72] Anspaugh argues that what "is represented is *precisely* Bloom's repressed guilt over his coprophiliac tendencies, and by extension perhaps Joyce's own ambivalence."[73] Anspaugh quotes Kristeva: "refuse and corpses *show me* what I permanently thrust aside in order to live. These bodily fluids, this defilement, this shit are what life withstands, hardly and with difficulty, on the part of death. There, I am at the border of my condition as a living being. My body extricates itself, as being alive, from that border. Such waste drops so that I might live."[74] Kristeva's concept of abjection is a powerful and an influential one; theorizing a prelinguistic and presubjective relation to the mother, she holds that in order to establish an ego and enter the differentiated field of language, this primary unity must be rejected, or abjected. This repressed maternal body returns in the form of the troubling matter Kristeva discusses in the passage Anspaugh quotes earlier. Yet for Kristeva these are secondary phenomena, reminders of an

---

[72] Kelly Anspaugh, "Powers of Ordure: James Joyce and the Excremental Vision(s)," *Mosaic: An Interdisciplinary Critical Journal* 27.1 (March 1994), 73–100, at 89.
[73] Ibid., 90.   [74] Ibid., 85.

abjected presubjective, preobjective state. The abject primarily makes itself felt in a manipulation of language, in "literary utterance."[75] When she discusses Joyce and the abject, Kristeva talks not of Bloom's coprophilia and the outrage he encounters because of it but rather Molly's monologue in "Penelope," reading it somewhat idiosyncratically as to do with a struggle of "one woman with another."[76]

If neither Bloom nor shame over nonstandard sexual practices feature in Kristeva's discussion of the abject, we might reframe Kristeva's terms to describe Bloom's situation in "Circe." The abject has to do with "what disturbs identity, system, order. What does not respect borders, positions, rules."[77] In the world of Nighttown, individual identity is turned to profit, as the person is cast either in the position of subject or object in a system of exploitation. To be "at the border of [one's] condition as a living being" – not vis-à-vis death but vis-à-vis another individual – takes on an important power in resisting the circumscribed subject, the possessive individual.[78] If Bloom is punished for this in Nighttown, he feels not guilt but joyful resistance. Anspaugh cites Clive Hart's more positive view that "both Bloom and Joyce enjoy the things in Celia which so troubled Swift, and happiness seems to lie in an untroubled recognition of what is to be enjoyed."[79] It is the nature and significance of this joy in "Circe" that I want to explore further here.

This joy is articulated most forcefully when, at the climax of the chapter, Bloom thinks of the warmth of Molly's bottom: "It overpowers me. The warm impress of her warm form. Even to sit where a woman has sat, especially with divaricated thighs, as though to grant the last favours,

---

[75] Julia Kristeva, *Powers of Horror: An Essay on Abjection* (New York: Columbia UP, 1982), 22.

[76] "If that monologue spreads out the abject, it is not because there is a woman speaking. But because, from afar, the writer approaches the hysterical body so that it might speak, so that he might speak, using it as springboard, of what eludes speech and turns out to be the hand to hand struggle of one woman with another, her mother of course, the absolute because primeval seat of the impossible – of the excluded, the outside-of-meaning, the abject. Atopia" (22).

[77] Ibid., 4.

[78] Suzette Henke uses Kristeva with the grain, so to speak, in a feminist/psychoanalytic mode; she writes that Kristeva's account of "radical psychic and aesthetic differences between the logocentric, symbolic register of the father and pre-Oedipal, semiotic attachment to the mother [. . .] is crucial to this study, since I have suggested that, for Joyce, the locus of psychic desire is often matrifocal and that the absence of primordial maternal bonding evinces a state of infantile abjection necessarily carried over into adult life." Suzette Henke, *James Joyce and the Politics of Desire* (London: Routledge, 2015), 9. If Henke explores Joyce's "forging of new psycho-sexual subject-positions in a controversial new discourse of desire," I focus on these new subject-positions not in an abstracted phallogocentric hegemony but in a not-unrelated social world structured by capitalism (10).

[79] Clive Hart, "The Sexual Perversions of Leopold Bloom," 1974, qtd. Anspaugh, 82.

most especially with previously well uplifted white sateen coatpans. So womanly, full. It fills me full" (*U* 15:3424–27). Although, given the preceding activities, we might be tempted to associate this position with defecation, "to grant the last favours" euphemistically refers to a woman's engaging in sexual intercourse with a man. Yet Bloom is focused neither on an act nor a substance; rather he is "overpowered" by the sensory traces of a woman's body: the secondhand heat and the negative space created by her form. This occupation of another person's shape, the sensation of her body temperature, allows something close to a sharing of physical experience, a surmounting of the boundaries between persons. In contrast to an external, visual assessment of a woman's form, or an objectification in sexual congress, this is an attempt to be inside another person, or more precisely to have another person's sensations fill him up: "It fills me full." This relation upends the appropriative logic of the phrase that refers to a woman "grant[ing] the last favors," as she gives away the last of what she has to give; Bloom now mimics a figurative version of that position ("as if") and in doing so, is "filled" himself, although in a gentle suffusion, a permeation of warmth. Nothing has been taken yet a feeling of plenitude results.

If this might be understood in terms of Bloom, the "new womanly man" (*U* 15:1798–99), in the context of "Circe" it is takes on a different significance. Bloom's joy here is to come into contact with the sensuous, nonidentical pleasure of a particular seated woman, and of Molly, especially. This constitutes a shift from the sentient thinking that features in the earlier episodes of *Ulysses* and the waking dreams of this episode; here, we see an expanded sensual curiosity. The terms of the episode suggest that we can understand this inquisitiveness about sensation as scientific. In contrast to a normal understanding of science as a system of general principles generated through empirical observation, Bloom's "Science. To compare the various joys we each enjoy" (*U* 15:3019) is the knowledge of the particular. It is what Alfred Jarry calls a "science of exceptions," which we will explore in this book's final chapter. Bloom's curiosity runs against the calculus of Nighttown, undoing its logic of subject and object, its stable possessions, positions, and identities.

This transient and relational exploration of pleasure offers a version of the original sense of *aesthesis*, gratifying physical sensation. A profoundly desublimated art, it inverts the principles attributed to Greek classical statuary by neoclassical aesthetic theorists. Instead of a beautiful statue, whose "curves are beauty," here Bloom experiences curves in the negative, as impress rather than form, and as a sensation that is material but necessarily ephemeral. This transient warmth is very different from the ageless grace of Greek statues. Winckelmann celebrates the marble forms' appearance of being "inflated by a gentle breath."[80] He understands this as a spiritual beauty: "This beauty is like an idea conceived without the aid of the senses, which might be generated in a lofty understanding and in a happy imagination, if it could rise in contemplation near to divine beauty; so great is the unity of form and outline, that it appears to have been produced not with labour, but awakened like a thought, and blown out with a breath."[81] Menninghaus explains how such beauty warded off the realities of the body that were held to be repellent by scholars such as Winckelmann and Schiller: "Such imaginary orality and airiness of the statue – its beautiful stony form as an effect of 'breathing' and 'blowing' – realizes disgust's avoidance: through a consequent sublimation of all materiality and scripturality on and beneath the skin of the beautiful."[82] The beautiful Greek statue is then an empty shell rather than a full body.

In "Penelope," Molly complains about Bloom's interest in her bottom, "where we haven't 1 atom of any kind of expression in us all of us the same 2 lumps of lard" (*U* 18:1403–04); in the context of "Circe" this interest is not objectifying but materializing, as it is focused on sensation rather than use. Bloom's sensual art is a desublimation that does not merely reject the ideal and embrace the realities of the body but that consecrates an intimate, shared experience that is disallowed by the exchanges of Nighttown. If for Schiller and Winckelmann, the taboo on body openings in the ideal forms of statuary holds the promise of a restoration of wholeness and cohesion to society, in the exploitative system of Nighttown, however, it is precisely that wholeness and cohesion that has to be attacked. The open body, its emissions and emanations, but even more so another's experience of those emissions and emanations, are crucial to countering the calculations of that system.

That this is a turn from thought into a less-cerebral awareness of feeling is indicated by the reiterated words with which Bloom refers to his sensations of heat and plenitude: "The warm impress of her warm form [. . .] full. It fills me full." Yet this cognitive flatline is in fact Bloom's escape from the exploding visions provoked by Zoe's "supple warmth" at the beginning of the episode. In contrast to that suggestive heat, here Bloom experiences simple warmth. If thought is enmeshed in the episode's

---

[80] Johann Winckelmann, *The History of Ancient Art: Among the Greeks* (London: John Chapman, 1850), 93.
[81] Johann Winckelmann, *Writings on Art*, ed. David Erwin (London: Phaidon, 1972), 132.
[82] Menninghaus, *Disgust*, 56.

workings – the associations and deformations of sentient thinking leading
into and out of the exploding visions – this sensual curiosity leads not to
fantasy but to a closeness that pushes at the boundaries of identity. We
might return to Cuddon's definition of farce as constituted by "exaggerated physical action (often repeated), exaggeration of character and situation, absurd situations, and improbable events (even impossible ones and
therefore fantastic), and surprises in the form of unexpected appearance
and disclosures."[83] This reassertion of the body effects a farcical rebellion
against the established reality of Nighttown, against the measure and
reason of its business as usual. While Bottom exhorts his fellow player to
"utter sweet breath" in order to stage a "sweet comedy," the repugnant
smells and embarrassing positions explored by the "Adorer of the adulterous rump!" (U 15:2839) break into the waking dreams of Nighttown,
disrupting its (para)logic.

  This farcical interruption finds its most literal instance when the
Nymph responds to Bloom's description of the "overpowering" sensation
of Molly's "warm impress" by transforming into a nun and declaring a ban
on physical craving:

THE NYMPH: [. . .] The apparitions of Knock and Lourdes. No more desire. (*she
    reclines her head, sighing*) Only the ethereal. Where dreamy creamy gull
    waves o'er the waters dull.
    (*Bloom half rises. His back trouserbutton snaps.*)
THE BUTTON: Bip!
    (*Two sluts of the Coombe dance rainily by, shawled, yelling flatly.*)
THE SLUTS: O, Leopold lost the pin of his drawers/He didn't know what to do,/
    To keep it up,/To keep it up.
BLOOM: (*Coldly*) You have broken the spell. The last straw. (U 15:3436–49)

The Nymph/nun's injunction against desire combines the neoclassical
aesthetic ideal of sublimated airiness with Catholic apparitions, the insub-
stantial appearances of holy bodies. She also invokes Joyce's Paris poem in
which a bird flying over waters allegorized sensual control. Yet in the most
farcical of retorts, Bloom's trousers fall down. Nearby prostitutes understand it as another of Bloom's empathic cross-gender physical experiences,
casting Bloom in the song of the harlots in "Lotus Eaters": "O, Mairy lost
the pin of her drawers/She didn't know what to do [. . .]" (U 5:281–84).
The spell now broken, Bloom manifests a new agency: retrieving his
potato from Zoe, protecting Stephen amidst the worst of Nighttown,
and going on to see a vision of Rudy, which we will discuss in the next

[83] J. A. Cuddon, *The Penguin Dictionary of Literary Terms*, 330.

chapter. But we'll leave him here. With the potato, he turns away from the realm of prostitution – nature petrified as a commodity and turned into "*a sepulcher of the gold of kings and their moldering bones*" (*U* 15:1341) – to an object that is worthless in commercial terms but precious to him as it is imbued with memories of his mother.[84]

What relation does this spell-breaking have with the visionary mode inherited from Flaubert, Nerval, and Rimbaud? The personae of Nerval's *Aurélia* and Rimbaud's *Une Saison en enfer* remain trapped within their waking dreams. In Flaubert's *Tentation*, Anthony is rescued at the last minute by the intervention of a somewhat less than credible God-Sun. However, Bloom's interest in basic physical sensations recalls the saint's attraction to matter in the moments right before that divine reinstitution of essences. Anthony witnesses life at a cellular level[85] and desires to merge with unconscious material being: to "be in everything – emanate with all the odours, – develop myself like the plants, – flow like water, – vibrate like sound, – shine like light, – assume all forms, – penetrate each atom, – descend to the very bottom of matter, – be matter itself" (190). This yearning to lose himself in material being is inspired by the Devil: to recall Rancière's words, the Devil makes Anthony "discover what life truly is when our sensations are released from the chains of individuality." While Bloom indeed attempts to release himself from these chains of individuality, the life he wishes to experience is neither preindividual nor impersonal but interpersonal. If Anthony's final vision is the apotheosis of the rampant fantasies of the night, Bloom's intimate and even intraindividual sensation is at odds with the exploding visions he has hitherto encountered. This sensation affords him to a new sense of connection. Bloom achieves a joyful sensation of relation at a much more modest scale than Nerval, who at the ecstatic verge of insanity declares that "Everything is alive, everything is in motion, everything corresponds." Yet is this a bathetic end to the progressive energies of the nineteenth century that Flaubert, Nerval, and Rimbaud stage so powerfully and that "Circe"

---

[84] Catherine Gallagher shows that the potato is neither pure nature nor bankable product: "The potato is a threshold phenomenon: [it] threatens to turn culture into nature and to overwhelm meaning with matter." Catherine Gallagher, "The Potato in the Materialist Imagination" in *Practicing New Historicism* (Chicago: University of Chicago Press, 2000), 112–13. She writes that in Ireland in the eighteenth century, the "potato represented a presocial state of isolation in which the poor were cut off from civilization and undifferentiated both from each other and from nature" (114); aside from these cultural associations, the potato also was linked to the unpredictability and "intractability of nature" (133).

[85] "tiny globular masses, no larger than pinheads, with cilia all round them. They are agitated with a vibratite motion" (190).

rehearses in the mode of spectacle? Is this transformative potential lost or denied in the episode, in favor of this basic, interpersonal relation? Does the episode suggest that human connection is more important? The most accurate answer might be that "Circe" shows us that disregard for human connection is the main obstacle to the realization of this transformative potential.

This chapter has traced Joyce's multiple reenvisionings of Paris in "Circe." It showed how Joyce projects onto and identifies in Dublin the massive transformations of urban life by capitalism that were spectacularly instanced in Paris. In doing so, it explored how Joyce reworks the forms and themes nineteenth-century Parisian visionary literature developed in order to give voice to the shifting world that results from those transformations, due to the power of their material possibilities and also to the destabilization of the social and political world that results from the situation of those immense powers in a capitalist system of exchange. Furthermore, it has shown how Joyce reenvisions in "Circe" his own early representations of the Paris boulevard, picturing with increased intensity not only consumer capitalism's erosion of human relations but also a permeating, undefinable corporeality that undercuts the calculus of consumption. Ultimately, however, "Circe," stages something more than reworked visions; in its farcical theater, intimate and ephemeral sensations cross the boundaries between individuals and between genders. Joyce comes closer to realizing a dramatic art; this is, in "Circe," an art of material co-being.

CHAPTER 5

Paris Profanely Illuminated: Joyce's Walter Benjamin

This chapter explores the "Circe" episode's relation to 1920s Paris. It traces both Joyce's absorption of contemporaneous influences in writing the episode and also the episode's impact on the Parisian scene. It situates "Circe" at the origins of the Surrealist movement, of which it is both father and child. It shows Joyce's reception, upon arrival in Paris, of the first Surrealist play, Guillaume Apollinaire's *Les Mamelles de Tirésias*, and argues for the influence of "Circe" on the first Surrealist novel, Louis Aragon's *Le Paysan de Paris*. In tracing the development of the mode of sentient thinking, it reexamines the reception of Surrealism by Walter Benjamin. While critics have often drawn ideas from Benjamin to describe Joyce's works, here I consider them as coevals, inhabiting a shared material, social, and literary space. For Joyce, Aragon, and Benjamin, nonrational, sensual modes of engagement enable the possibility of experience within the realm of exchange, the recovery of historical experience within that realm, and the conception of transformative political energy. Benjamin's development of the exploding vision allows us to understand the implications of Joyce's sentient thinking: Benjamin's image-body space is a sensory experience that eradicates thought in the political aim of eradicating bourgeois subjectivity. Benjamin's further reconception of this image-body space in the *Passagen-Werk* offers us a means with which to respond to Joyce's new textual mode in *Finnegans Wake*.

Writing around Joyce

In his 1928 "Curriculum Vitae," Benjamin writes: "I have been planning a book on the three great metaphysicians of our day: Franz Kafka, James Joyce, and Marcel Proust."[1] Heyward Ehrlich asks what Benjamin means,

---

[1] Walter Benjamin, *Selected Writings: 1931–1934*, trans. Rodney Livingstone et al., ed. Michael Jennings, Gary Smith, and Howard Eiland (Cambridge, MA: Belknap, 2005), 78 (translation altered). "Daneben besteht der Plan eines Buches über die drei großen Metaphysiker unter den Dichtern der Gegenwart: Franz Kafka, James Joyce, Marcel Proust." Benjamin, *"Lebenslauf,"*

observing that "the full Joyce–Benjamin connection awaits definition. [...] Was Benjamin familiar with the term 'metaphysical' in Anglo-American criticism to describe Donne and the 17th century English poets [...]? [Or did he see Joyce as] reach[ing] beyond the common sense view of physical reality into the super-sensual concerns of the realms of mind, memory, and language?"[2] As I hope to show here, Benjamin's naming of Joyce as a "Metaphysiker" signals his sense of Joyce's engagement with the fundamental questions of being in the modern world, an inquiry, which we have seen Joyce engage in explicitly in his early turn to Aristotle, that explores the essential attributes of identity, substance, causality, time, and space. As Benjamin intuits, Joyce shifts this exploration of being from philosophy into literature and into the contemporary world.

Benjamin was hampered in his intention to write about Joyce by his knowledge of English. As Robert Weininger notes: "for the best-educated Germans, the classical languages, Latin and, to a lesser degree, Greek, remained the primary foreign languages well into the twentieth century; English had replaced Greek by 1901 only at the *Realgymnasien* and *Ober-realschulen,* not at the humanistic *Gymnasien* traditionally attended by the educated establishment. Thus most German intellectuals, such as Alfred Döblin, the author of *Berlin Alexanderplatz,* were forced to wait until the first German translation [of *Ulysses*] appeared in 1927."[3] The novel remained a "mysterious specter" until Georg Goyert's translation, which had a huge impact on German literary circles – reviewed fourteen times in 1927 and thirty-four in 1928.[4] Howard Eiland and Michael Jennings note the inclusion of a copy of Goyert's *Ulysses* in a list of Benjamin's library compiled in 1933.[5]

Benjamin's explicit engagements with Joyce's work take place in various literary reviews: reviews of Joyce by other writers, Benjamin's reviews of works by other writers on Joyce and, passingly, in Benjamin's reviews of contemporary novelists. In the absence of Benjamin's sustained engagement with Joyce's text, Döblin's 1928 review of *Ulysses* was particularly important in shaping his perception of the novel; Benjamin's subsequent comments on *Ulysses* evoke its terms. Döblin criticizes the contemporary

---

Gesammelte Schriften, Vol. VI, ed. Hermann Schweppenhäuser and Rolf Tiedemann (Frankfurt am Main: Suhrkamp, 1991), 219.

[2] Heyward Ehrlich, "Joyce, Benjamin and the Futurity of Fiction," in *James Joyce, Walter Benjamin and Magical Urbanism,* ed. Enda Duffy and Maurizia Boscaglia (Amsterdam: Rodopi, 2011), 187.

[3] Robert Weininger, *The German Joyce* (Gainesville: University of Florida Press, 2012), 24.

[4] Ibid., 25.

[5] Howard Eiland and Michael Jennings, *Walter Benjamin: A Critical Life* (Cambridge, MA: Belknap, 2016), 704, note 15.

predominance of novels with ordered, bounded narratives, which he associates with "private individuals, citizens who earn money, pay taxes, walk down the street," and celebrates the representation of a new kind of depersonalized urban experience: "To the experiential image of a person today also belongs the streets, the scenes changing by the second, the signboards, automobile traffic. The heroic, the importance altogether of the isolated event and the individual person, has receded substantially, overshadowed by the factors of state, parties, and the economic system. Much of this was already true, but now a person is truly no larger than the waves that carry him. A part of today's image is the disconnectedness of his activity, of his existence as such, the fleeting quality, the restlessness."[6]

Benjamin subsequently adopts these terms in his negative review of Hans Henny Jahnn's 1929 novel *Perrudja*. Benjamin takes up Döblin's praise of the representation of a depersonalized and contingent existence, writing that, in contrast to Jahnn, Joyce's "loosening of syntax" constructs a wide-open, diverse world. Calling Joyce the "main representative of the so-called interior monologue," Benjamin writes that "the narrow, monomaniacal world which Jahnn creates through identifying with his protagonist is as far from Joyce's as Jahnn's verbal uncertainty is from the linguistic powers of the Irishman."[7] In posthumously published notes from the context of his writings on narration and the novel (dated between 1928 and 1935), Benjamin connects the future of narration to a departure from clearly defined interiority and to the cultivation of a new looseness and objectivity. He writes about the death to storytelling that is private life, "every intimate, conventional, egoistical, personal discretion is an apoplectic fit that robs the storyteller of his ability to speak"; the novels of the day are too "poorly ventilated," he complains and calls for "new inaccuracy in an argot of storytelling" that would follow "film, superimpositions, photomontage," praising the "big city dialect stories" of Hemingway and Joyce, as well as the Russian and Polish novelists Boris Pilniak and Antoni Slonimski.[8]

---

[6] Alfred Döblin, "*Ulysses* by Joyce," *The Weimar Republic Sourcebook*, ed. Anton Kaes, Martin Jay, and Edward Dimendberg (Berkeley: University of California Press, 1994), 514.

[7] "Nun bringt die Form des sogenannten monologue intérieur, deren Hauptvertreter Joyce ist, freilich ebenfalls eine Auflockerung der Syntax zustande, die an sich der expressionistischen bei Jahnn ähnelt. Nur ist eben die Welt des Verfassers, der sich mit seinem Helden identifiziert(,) in ihrer monomanischen Enge ebensoweit von der von James Joyce entfernt wie seine sprachliche Unsicherheit von der Sprachkraft des Iren." Benjamin, *Gesammelte Schriften* (henceforth cited as *GS*) VI:140, (my translation).

[8] "Die Heutigen sind zu schlecht ventiliert: durch jede, noch die schlichteste Erzählung geht ein großer Luftzug [...] Nichts tötet den Geist des Erzählens so gründlich ab, wie die unverschämte Ausdehnung, die in unser aller Existenz das 'Private' gewonnen hat und jede intime, konventionelle, egoistische, persönliche Diskretion ist wie ein Schlaganfall, der dem Erzähler ein Stück seiner Sprachfertigkeit raubt (und nicht nur, wie man meinen möchte) ein Thema" (*GS* II.3:1282).

Despite these statements of admiration for Joyce and of intention to produce a critical work on him, Benjamin told Bertolt Brecht in November 1930 that he had only heard of Joyce. Benjamin's denials of his knowledge of *Ulysses* may have had something to do with Brecht's impressive ad hoc rhetorical powers and with the complexities of their relationship. Erdmut Wizisla provides the minutes for a meeting for the planned journal *Krise und Kritik*. Brecht calls Joyce's and Döblin's "methodological improvements" a kind of "creative construction": "What would personally interest me would, for example, be to show that James Joyce and Döblin are to be related to certain other improvements of creative construction. Thinking as a productive force."[9] Brecht continues: "The type represented by James Joyce and Döblin in general regards thinking as method and separates itself from the purely private personal. Döblin, who is progressive, and above all Joyce, already see their method of thinking as something transportable (*Transportables*). This is very obvious. Joyce does not open himself up, he does not express himself simply, but he sets up machinery, which incidentally he is continually changing, and which is saleable and as such can be transported. He is already selling machines. He adopts points of view." Benjamin replies: "This interests me more than you could possibly have wished; from a depth of ignorance, I don't know Joyce, have only heard about him and have formed a certain very inadequate impression that doesn't immediately coincide with what you are saying. I would be very interested to learn more. May I remind you that you once formulated this topic differently and very acutely? Is there a technical obligation, a standard in literature? And where is a technical obligation, a standard in Joyce and Döblin?"[10]

Much later, in a 1937 review, Benjamin returns to this notion of literary form as apparatus for thought, something already implied in his 1928 reference to Joyce as a metaphysician. The review covers works by Helmut Anton, Hansjörg Garte, Oskar Walzel, Alain Stendhal, Hugo von Hofmannsthal, Hermann Blackert and, finally, Herman Broch's *James Joyce and die Gegenwart* (*James Joyce and the Present*). Benjamin finds that Broch's study does not advance understanding of Joyce: his methodology yields "happy ideas" but is limited by its failure to understand Joyce's technical position in terms of contemporary novelistic production.[11]

---

[9] Erdmut Wizisla, *Walter Benjamin and Bertolt Brecht: The Story of a Friendship* (New Haven, CT: Yale University Press, 2009), 196.

[10] Ibid., 197.

[11] "Die Auseinandersetzung mit dem Werk von James Joyce wird durch die Schrift *Brochs* wohl nur wenig gefördert werden. [...] Diesem Versuch dienen eine Reihe mehr oder minder glücklicher

Yet Benjamin commends Broch's central thought: "'das Dichterische in die Sphäre der Erkenntnis zu heben,' eine gerade unserer Zeit zufallende Aufgabe sei"; "'to elevate the poetic into the sphere of knowledge,' a task which falls urgently to our time." *Erkenntnis,* translated here as knowledge might be also translated as insight, discovery, perception, and cognition.

I will argue here that despite Benjamin's failure to produce a critical work on Joyce, and his distance from the actual text of *Ulysses,* Benjamin had already grappled with and employed one of Joyce's "machines for thinking," to adopt Brecht's phrase. The form he explores is not the stream of consciousness, which is mentioned most frequently in reviews, but the exploding vision of the "Circe" episode. In the "First Sketches" for the *Arcades Project,* entries in the *Passagen-Werk,* and in his essay "Surrealism: Last Snapshot of the European Intelligentsia," written between mid-1927 and the end of 1929, Benjamin reworks and extends this form of sentient thinking, which he received not directly from Joyce but through Aragon, conceiving of it as a means for the realization of the political potential of the past in the profane illumination. This sentient thinking sidesteps conscious cognition and operates through "eines nicht bewußten Wissens," "a not conscious knowledge," that Benjamin pushes to an extreme in his conception of the image-body space. Conceiving of a material transformation of individuals, Benjamin departs from the "technical obligation" that machines for thinking would involve insight, discovery, perception, and cognition, rather than, merely, sensation. This radical notion is itself overturned in Benjamin's writing, however, in the form of an image of fertile textual materiality and a mode of nonexpository writing that helps us understand how to approach Joyce's *Finnegans Wake.*

Benjamin and Joyce came close to meeting in Paris. One of their common connections in the city was Adrienne Monnier, the owner of the bookstore Les Amis des Livres on the Rue de l'Odéon and the close friend of Sylvia Beach, owner of the neighboring bookstore, Shakespeare & Co. Joyce met Monnier, along with Sylvia Beach, soon after he arrived in Paris in 1920. Momme Broderson reports that Benjamin came to know Monnier at the beginning of 1930.[12] Monnier counts "among the citizens of Odéonia" her close friends "Paul Valéry, Valery Larbaud, André Gide, Léon-Paul Fargue, Paul Claudel, Jules Romains, Ernest Hemmingway,

Einfälle [...] Hätte sich der Verf[asser] die Mühe genommen, die technische Position von Joyce innerhalb der heutigen Romanproduktion zu bestimmen, so hätte er einen Beitrag zur Lösung dieser Aufgabe geleistet" (*GS* III:517).

[12] Momme Broderson, *Walter Benjamin: A Biography* (New York: Verso, 1998), 172.

and James Joyce"; in addition, she notes that "other writers of several
nationalities – were friendly passers-by [. . .] they too became citizens of
Odéonia" and among these honorary citizens we can count Benjamin.[13]
Many of the figures Monnier names connect Benjamin and Joyce. For
example, Fargue was especially influential in the French translation of
Ulysses; Benjamin considered him "the greatest living poet in France."[14]
Gisèle Freund, having met Joyce in 1936 at a dinner party given by
Monnier, photographed him in advance of the publication of *Finnegans
Wake* in spring of 1938 and the spring of 1939.[15] Freund had photographed Benjamin in 1937 in the Bibliothèque Nationale, where in
1903 Joyce had read Aristotle and Pseudo-Aristotle and transcribed his
aesthetic essay and notes. Benjamin writes that the *Passagen-Werk* began
under the blue sky of its ceiling.[16] It also began, by Benjamin's own
admission, in an encounter with a novel inspired by Joyce.

As Monnier's comments suggest, Joyce and Benjamin occupied positions of different status in the Paris literary scene. Joyce was a resident of
the city and the well-known writer of *Portrait* and *Dubliners* and of the
strikingly innovative and even obscene episodes of *Ulysses* in the *Little
Review*. As is well known, he met Beach and Monnier shortly after his
arrival in 1920 and was patronized by them in the form of publication and
promotion. Famously, Beach was the first publisher of *Ulysses*; Larbaud's
lecture in December 1921 on the yet-unpublished novel took place in
Monnier's Les Amis des Livres. Benjamin, on the other hand, was a

---

[13] Adrienne Monnier, *The Very Rich Hours of Adrienne Monnier: An Intimate Portrait of the Literary
and Artistic Life in Paris between the Wars*, trans. Richard McDougall (New York: Scribner, 1976),
3. Monnier writes of Benjamin, whom she consulted in 1934 on the meaning of the German
swastika (365). Monnier was to provide crucial aid to Benjamin, accompanying him to a police
station to secure a lodging certificate and "certificate of good life and morals" on May 29,
1940 (393).

[14] Qtd. in Eiland and Jennings, *Walter Benjamin: A Critical Life*, 336. Fargue told Benjamin a story of
Joyce's meeting with Proust, which Benjamin records in his "Pariser Tagebuch" (Dec '29–Feb '30).
The encounter is an important addition to the meeting reported by Ellmann, which took place on
May 18, 1922, at a reception given by the Englishman Sydney Schiff and his wife Violet at the
Hotel Majestic in Paris, where Joyce and Proust reportedly spoke of their physical ailments, of
liking truffles, and of not having read one another's work (*JJ* 508–09). Benjamin's account of their
meeting *chez* Fargue emphasizes class politics: Fargue invited them to dinner at his house, despite
his fear of having to keep the conversation going which, in Fargue's words "'seemed like lifting a
100-pound load. So I had invited two beautiful women to moderate the collision (*Zusammenstoß*).
But that didn't prevent Joyce from swearing high and low when he left to never set foot in a room
where there was a danger of meeting this figure.' And Fargue mimicked the outrage that trembled
through the Irishman when Proust with gleaming eyes solemnly declared of some imperial or
princely aristocrat, 'C'était ma première altesse!'" (*GS* IV.1, 569–70, my translation).

[15] Gisèle Freund, *Three Days with Joyce* (New York: Persea, 1985), 17.

[16] Qtd. Broderson, *Walter Benjamin: A Biography*, 234.

periodic visitor in Paris and at the fringes of its literary world. If Joyce could hang back – Monnier describes him as sitting quietly at a soirée "with his wings folded"– Benjamin was eager for contact and dismayed by the difficulty of forming connections with Parisians.[17] As Eiland and Jennings report, much of Benjamin's social interaction during his first extended stay in Paris, in 1926, was due to two Germans, Franz Hessel and Thankmar von Münchhausen, with whom Benjamin carried out an "exploration of the Parisian demimonde."[18] During a longer stay the next year, Benjamin wrote to Hugo von Hofmannsthal that "It is extraordinarily rare to achieve the kind of empathy with a Frenchman that would make it possible to converse with him for more than fifteen minutes."[19] Yet for Benjamin, as for Joyce, the Parisian literary scene was a powerful influence. In the next chapter, we will consider Joyce's responses to Apollinaire's literary montages as well as to the absurdist work of the former lover of Fargue, Alfred Jarry. But, here, we will look at Joyce's relation to the earliest works of Surrealism by Apollinaire and Aragon, and at its signal importance for Benjamin.

Apollinaire's Mechanical Children

A couple of weeks after arriving in Paris, as he was working on the beginnings of the "Circe" episode, Joyce remarked on the number of current Parisian Homeric adaptations: "Odyssey is very much in the air here. Anatole France is writing *Le Cyclope*, G. Fauré the musician an opera *Penelope*. Giraudoux has written Elpenor (Paddy Dignam). Guillaume Apollinaire *Les Mamelles de Tirésias*. I hope during the week to have definite news about translations of novel and play."[20] Joyce's succinct overview of this seam of Parisian artistic production points to his connection to Monnier. He focuses his attention, in this account, on the work of Apollinaire, whose play *Les Mamelles de Tirésias* was first staged in 1917, having been written in 1903.

Apollinaire's play features a marriage driven by accumulation, as, having dispatched her bosoms, Thérèse-become-Tirésias goes off to fight for the interests of Zanzibar, while her/his husband stays at home to produce children to harvest the riches found in the territories.[21] This gender

---

[17] Monnier, *The Very Rich Hours*, 113.   [18] Eiland and Jennings, *Walter Benjamin*, 252.
[19] Qtd. Eiland and Jennings, *Walter Benjamin*, 280.   [20] Letter to Stanislaus, *Letters III*, 10.
[21] "Chaste citizens of Zanzibar/Who no longer have children/Know that the fortune and the glory/
    The forests of bananas and the herds of elephants/Belong by right/In the near future/To those who

mobility features, as we have seen, in "Circe" where Bella Cohen, the brothel madam, becomes Bello, who resembles the cocky Tirésias: "I feel as manly as the devil, I am a stallion from head to hooves, now I'm a bull, now I'm a bull-fighter."[22] Meanwhile, the deserted husband engages in the production of children on an industrial scale, giving birth to 40,050 children in a single day. The unnamed husband declares at the opening of the second act: "Ah! The mad joys of paternity/40049 children in a single day/My happiness is complete."[23] This joyful fecundity is enmeshed in commerce: dressed as a woman, the husband understands his multitudinous offspring, scattered on the stage, in the wings, and in the auditorium, as a mechanically extendible source of financial profit: "Ah yes it's simple as a periscope/The more children I have/The richer I'll be/and the better I'll be able to feed myself."[24] Bloom himself gives birth to multiple children in "Circe," remarking with a levity reminiscent of Apollinaire's play: "O, I do so want to be a mother" (*U* 15:1817). His octuplets appear, fully grown with "valuable metallic faces" already functioning as "managing directors of banks, traffic managers of railways, chairmen of limited liability companies, vicechairmen of hotel syndicates," only to disappear again; their production is predicated upon the episode's logic of constant motion, its riotous series of fleeting visions (*U* 15:1831–32). Joyce's playscript episode realizes the ambition Apollinaire declared in the program for his stage play to exploit the illusionistic capacities of the theater: "It is right that the dramaturge uses/all mirages he has at his disposal/as Morgane did on Mont Gibel/it is right that he makes crowds and inanimate objects speak/if it pleases him/and that he adheres no more to the passage of time than to space."[25]

To trace these connections is not to undercut the argument of the previous chapter: Gustave Flaubert's *La Tentation de saint Antoine*, Gérard

---

in order to take them will have had [made] children"; "Chastes citoyens de Zanzibar/Qui ne faites plus d'enfants/Sachez que la fortune et la gloire/Les forêts d'ananas les troupeaux d'éléphants/ Appartiennent de droit/ Dans un proche avenir/À ceux qui pour les prendre auront fait des enfants." Guillaume Apollinaire, *Les Mamelles de Tirésias*, in *L'Enchanteur pourrissant*, ed. Michel Décaudin (Paris: Gallimard, 1972), 158.

[22] 10. "Je me sens viril en diable, je suis étalon de la tête aux talons, me voilà taureau, me voilà torero." Ibid., 136.

[23] "Ah! c'est fou les joies de la paternité/40049 enfants en un seul jour/Mon bonheur est complet." Ibid., 147.

[24] "Eh oui c'est simple comme un périscope/Plus j'aurai d'enfants/Plus je serai riche et mieux je pourrai me nourrir." Ibid.

[25] "Il est juste que le dramaturge se serve/De tous les mirages qu'il a à sa disposition/Comme faisait Morgane sur le Mont-Gibel/Il est juste qu'il fasse parler les foules les objets inanimés/S'il lui plait/Et qu'il ne tienne pas plus compte du temps/Que de l'espace." Ibid., 130.

de Nerval's *Les Nuits d'Octobre* and *Aurélia, ou, le Rêve et la vie,* and Arthur Rimbaud's *Une Saison en enfer* have been understood as crucial precursors for Surrealism in general and for Apollinaire in particular. As Apollinaire's biographer Laurence Campa observes: "Born into the end of poetic symbolism, [Apollinaire] was indebted to his predecessors, Rimbaud, Verlaine, Mallarmé, and above all Nerval."[26] Apollinaire's text, however, departs from its precedents in explicitly ascribing capitalist aims to its own productivity. In 1917, when he invents the term Surrealist, Apollinaire announces a "new spirit" in art in which it associates itself with material progress. He uses the term for *Les Mamelles de Tirésias,* having devised it one month earlier to describe Jean Cocteau, Sergei Diaghilev, Pablo Picasso, and Erik Satie's multimedia ballet, *Parade.* Apollinaire describes his own play as much as *Parade* when he writes in the program notes for the ballet that its assemblage of diverse elements leads to "a sort of surrealism in which I see the point of departure for a series of manifestations of that new spirit which, finding now the opportunity to show itself, will not fail to seduce the elite and promises to modify the arts and the conduct of life [*moeurs*] from top to bottom in universal joyousness, for it is only good sense, after all, that they keep pace with scientific and industrial progress."[27] Apollinaire strikes a conservative note here, with his interest in appealing to the privileged and influential, his emphasis on "good sense," and his identification of art with the technological developments associated with industry. Is this a celebration or a parody? "Il m'est impossible de décider si ce drame est sérieux ou non," Apollinaire writes in his preface to his play. The heralding of the birth of Surrealism, then, is marked by an ambiguity regarding its relation to established power and material interests.[28]

[26] "Né à la poésie dans le symbolisme finissant, il était redevable à ses prédécesseurs, Rimbaud, Verlaine, Mallarmé, et surtout Nerval." Laurence Campa, *Guillaume Apollinaire* (Paris: Gallimard, 2016), iii (my translation).

[27] "De cette alliance nouvelle, car jusqu'ici les décors et les costumes, d'une part, la chorégraphie, d'autre part, n'avaient entre eux qu'un lien factice, il est résulté, dans *Parade,* une sorte de surréalisme où je vois le point de départ d'une série de manifestations de cet esprit nouveau, qui, trouvant aujourd'hui l'occasion de se montrer, ne manquera pas de séduire l'élite et se promet de modifier de fond en comble les arts et les mœurs dans l'allégresse universelle, car le bon sens veut qu'ils soient au moins à la hauteur des progrès scientifiques et industriels." Qtd. in Catherine Miller, *Jean Cocteau, Guillaume Apollinaire, Paul Claudel et le groupe des six: rencontres poético-musicales autour des mélodies et des chansons* (Brussels: Editions Mardaga, 2003), 139.

[28] Shattuck describes Apollinaire's association with Alfred Jarry in 1903, during the period in which he wrote *Les Mamelles,* and, without making the connection to the play, of Jarry's "convincing Apollinaire of the significance of a special form of humor and distortion in art." Roger Shattuck, *The Banquet Years: The Origins of the Avant Garde in France, 1885 to World War I: Alfred Jarry, Henri Rousseau, Erik Satie [and] Guillaume Apollinaire* (New York: Vintage Books, 1968), 262.

"Circe," as we have seen, grapples with the turning of human generativity to profit. Bloom's occupation of the female position of child-bearing contributes to the episode's parody of the production and reproduction of wealth. These children and, more especially, Rudy have indeed something to do with those of *Les Mamelles*. The husband makes a child out of newspapers:

> Let's make a journalist first of all: that way I'll know everything, guess what's left over, and invent the rest. (He puts the torn-up newspapers in the empty cradle.) What a wonderful journalist this one will be: eye-witness reporting, think pieces, et cetera. (He takes the bottle of ink and pours it into the cradle.) He needs to have blood drawn from the inkwell. (He puts the enormous pen-holder in the cradle.) He needs a backbone. (He pours the paste-pot into the cradle.) Some brains, so he won't have to think. A tongue, to drool more. (He puts the scissors into the cradle).[29]

This child of reconstituted print media fulfills the husband's need for the economic power granted by knowledge of social and political intrigues. This composite child is also, however, the figure for a new kind of textuality. Born, already at the age of majority, of text and editorial tools come to life, he embodies a mode of writing that is drawn from its immediate social and material context and one that will become explicitly celebrated in Apollinaire's theory of literary montage. This odd child, we will see, resembles the mysterious Rudy at the end of "Circe," constructed from diverse fragments from the text of *Ulysses*. In this play-script episode, Joyce too is moving toward a new kind of textuality.[30] This new textuality will become, increasingly, the mode of Joyce's response to the problem of art within capitalism, a problem that, as I argued at the beginning of the last chapter, Joyce became freshly aware of on returning to the city in which he had so powerfully encountered it. To develop an approach to this new textuality, we must pursue the influence of Joyce's sentient thinking.

---

[29] "Faisons d'abord un journaliste, comme ça je saurai tout, je devinerai le surplus, et j'inventerai le reste. (Il se met a déchirer des journaux, son jeu doit être très rapide.) Il faut qu'il soit apte à toutes les besognes, et puisse écrire pour tous les partis. (Il met les journaux déchirés dans le berceau vide.) Quel beau journaliste ce sera: reportage, articles de fond, et cetera. (Il prend la bouteille d'encre et la verse dans le berceau.) Il lui faut un sang puise dans l'encrier. (Il met un énorme porte-plume dans le berceau.) Il lui faut une épine dorsale. (Il verse le pot à colle dans le berceau.) De la cervelle pour ne pas penser. Une langue pour mieux baver. (Il m et les ciseaux dans le berceau.)" Apollinaire, *L'Enchanteur pourrissant*, 148.

[30] See also Finn Fordham, "'Circe' and the Genesis of Multiple Personality," *James Joyce Quarterly* 45.3–4 (Spring–Summer 2008), 507–20.

Aragon's Waking Dreams

In 1920, Aragon embarked on an ambitious new novel, *La Défense de l'Infini*. His biographer, Philippe Forest, likens this mysterious and complex book to *Finnegans Wake*: "The project of *The Defense of Infinity*, according to the title given to the work, is characterized by its inordinate design and its ambition of absorbing absolutely everything in a sort of *work in progress* of which no one could really say what would have been the ultimate limits."[31] Forest goes on to describe the work as "a mass of fragmentary texts, surrounded by a thick fog" which Aragon preferred not to dispel.[32] Aragon abandoned the project in 1927 and destroyed the manuscript the following year, but Forest likens to "Circe" Aragon's subsequent account of his plan for the novel: "the crowd of characters would all meet, each by the logic or illogic of his destiny, in an immense brothel, where criticism and confusion would operate between them [...] a collapse of all morals in an immense orgy."[33]

Forest's comparisons are not ungrounded: Aragon himself writes in his 1969 memoir, *Je n'ai jamais appris à écrire*, "Maybe, because it happens that I talked so much about Joyce, one could believe that I had drawn the brothel as a perspective on society (or understood as a critique of society) from *Ulysses*, from the 'Circe' episode."[34] Aragon is circumspect about this influence, although he notes, elsewhere in his memoir, that in April 1921, at the recommendation of the poet John Rodker, he read the installments of *Ulysses* in the *Little Review*.[35] He writes that he didn't read the whole novel until Auguste Morel's French translation appeared in 1929. Yet Beach reports that Aragon "spoke excellent English without an accent" and was a frequent visitor to Shakespeare & Co. and Les Amis des Livres.[36] Beloved by both Beach and Monnier, it is hard to believe that he waited

---

[31] "[L]e projet de *La Défense de l'infini*, selon le titre donné à l'ouvrage, se caractérise tout dans une sorte de *work in progress* dont personne ne peut dire véritablement quelles auraient été les limites ultimes." Philippe Forest, *Aragon* (Paris: Gallimard, 2016), 274.

[32] "un amas de textes en morceaux," ibid.

[33] "Toute cette foule des personnages allait se retrouver, chacun par la logique ou l'illogisme de son destin, finalement dans une sorte d'immense bordel, où s'opéreraient entre eux la critique et la confusion, je veux dire la défaite de toutes les morales, dans une sorte d'immense orgie." Ibid.

[34] "Peut-être, parce qu'il se trouve que j'ai parlé tantôt de Joyce, le bordel comme perspective sociale (ou comme critique de la société s'entend), pourra-t-on croire que j'avais puisé cela dans *Ulysses*, en l'épisode de Circé." Louis Aragon, *Je n'ai jamais appris à écrire*. ed. Albert Skira (Paris: Editions d'Art, 1969), 50.

[35] Aragon, *Je n'ai jamais appris*, 21.

[36] Noel Riley Fitch, *Sylvia Beach and the Lost Generation: A History of Paris in the Twenties and Thirties* (New York: Norton, 1983), 44.

eight years to read the rest of *Ulysses,* published at great personal cost by Beach amidst celebration and scandal. Aragon even recounts his own attempts to win André Breton over to *Ulysses,* commenting that despite the scandal surrounding the obscenity trial of the *Little Review,* he failed to "share with my friends the interest I had in this work."[37]

If "Circe" resembles Aragon's *La Défense de l'Infini,* it resembles far more closely "Le Passage de l'Opéra," the larger section of *Le Paysan de Paris,* a novel Forest notes that Aragon wrote, beginning in 1924, in the "margins of and intervals between" the manuscript of *La Défense.*[38] In this text, a locus of prostitution associated with a mass of objects becomes the place of confrontation with capitalism and commodification, a confrontation that takes the form of waking dreams. Aragon takes up the exploding visions of "Circe" in "Passage de l'Opéra" but he develops them in a number of ways. He uses this form to stage not just the recovery of experience within relations of exchange but the recovery of historical experience. In Louis, Aragon presents a protagonist who is cognizant of his implication in structures of instrumentalization, as well as subject to them. He understands the prostitutes as active subjects in contesting the rationalizations of exchange. He presents the "error of the senses" as capable of altering the modern sense of existence.

It might be, correctly, observed that "Le Passage de l'Opéra" bears some similarities to a chapter of the novel Aragon completed in 1920, *Anicet ou le panorama,* in which the protagonist tells a somewhat tedious Arthur Rimbaud of his encounters in the "Passage de Cosmoramas." However, the modes of the two texts are profoundly different. *Anicet* emphasizes "intangible realities": its Rimbaud refuses to eat, as he refuses the "a priori forms of sensual perception." His "dérèglement de tous les sens" is an abstract and absurdist distortion of reality: "it was mere child's play for me to perceive to the world as I pleased, giving *n* the most diverse values."[39] Similarly, Anicet's tale of the arcade is a testament to his imaginative force, his ability to "transform at will" the world into "Beauty." His refusal of the senses is so profound that he discovers at the end of his adventure that

---

[37] "Je n'arriverai pas, même avec le scandale qui fut cette année-là la publication par *Little Review* de fragments de *Ulysses* et le procès qui en fut mené à New York contre cette revue, à faire partager à mes amis l'intérêt que je portais alors à cette œuvre." Aragon, *Je n'ai jamais appris,* 22.

[38] My translation. Forest, *Aragon,* 274.

[39] Louis Aragon, *Anicet or The Panorama.* trans. Anthony Melville (London: Atlas Press, 2016), 23. "ce fut au contraire un amusement pour mon esprit que d'envisager le monde en donnant à *n* les valeurs le plus diverses." Louis Aragon, *Anicet ou le panorama* (Paris: Éditions de la Nouvelle Revue Francaise, 1921), 11.

the sexual adventuress Lulu is not in fact a girl of sixteen but a "vieille impudique" of fifty, whom he strangles. This whimsical violence is part of the novel's ironic tone. Anicet's attitude is that of a carefree man about town; the arcade is where "my sensibility was satisfied."[40] The novel goes on to become a *roman à clef* and a novel of initiation as Anicet joins a secret society, whose members are disguised versions of Bréton, Max Jacob, Jean Cocteau, Paul Valéry, and Picasso, and faces the challenges of perilous missions, thefts, and assassinations in the quest of an alluring and unattainable ideal, Mirabelle.

In contrast, Aragon abandons these modes in "Le Passage de l'Opéra" in favor of a realist account of the arcade. The solitary Louis wanders in the gloomy passages used by prostitutes to solicit and entertain clients. The text itself takes a wandering form as he observes the women, their clients, the business owners, and the strange objects in the arcade's cafés, baths, stores, and tiny theatre. But most crucially, rather than transforming the world at will, Louis has a series of waking dreams that are triggered by his sensory and sensual perceptions. These waking dreams and the sensations associated with them lead Louis to a profound empathy with the victims of commerce and an awareness of his complicity in those transactions.

"Le Passage de l'Opéra" is committed so firmly to the sensations of the actual world that Aragon faced criticism from the early Surrealists. In 1924, Aragon founded Surrealism with André Breton and Philippe Soupault. In his memoir, Aragon writes of the scandalized reaction of the early Surrealists to the descriptive mode of "Le Passage de l'Opéra," a mode he specifically adopted in defiance of the traditional novelistic norms they still, tacitly, supported:

> I was seeking [...] a new kind of novel that would break all the traditional rules governing the writing of fiction, one that would be neither a narrative (a story) nor a character study (a portrait) [...] I was writing this novel-that-was-not-a-novel – or at least I thought of myself as writing it – to *demoralize* my [surrealist] friends, who were so busy proclaiming themselves the enemy of the novel in every form while still indulging in reading matter such as Lewis' *The Monk* or Restif de la Bretonne [...] I have written precisely what must inevitably have seemed intolerable to my intimates who were also my judges: that is to say, I adopted a descriptive tone.[41]

---

[40] Aragon, *Anicet*, 36; "où se complait ma sensibilité," Ibid., 26.
[41] Qtd. in Simon Watson Taylor, introduction to *Paris Peasant* (Boston: Exact Change, 1995), xix–ii (original italics).

He goes on to describe the outburst of indignation and criticism that "Le Passage de l'Opéra" provoked when he first presented the piece to an "assembled company of a dozen or so comrades,"[42] reflecting that this experience thrust him on the path of "surrealist realism."[43] As Aragon notes, this realism uses close attention to sensory experiences in order to resist the categories of individual character and narrative. This sensual awareness is key to the contestatory and liberatory power of the text's visions.

Aragon describes the Passage de l'Opéra at the moment of its imminent demolition to clear a new route to the Boulevard Haussmann.[44] His preoccupation with the soon-to-be-destroyed Passage allows him to relive the more extensive nineteenth-century period of demolition during the reign of Napoleon III, under the direction of Baron Haussmann, that facilitated a massive program of urban renewal motivated by social control and capitalist expansion. The demolition of the Passage de l'Opéra will benefit the large stores "who count upon this tunneling to produce a renewed flow of traffic and an indeterminable multiplication of their profit."[45] It will erase the paradoxical sociality of the Passage de l'Opéra, which is simultaneously urban and domestic: "a quiet stay-at-home public."[46] Louis contemplates the effects of the demolition on the subjectivities of the inhabitants of this area of Paris: "One might ask if a good part of the human river which carries incredible floods of dreams and languor from the Bastille to the Madeleine may divert itself through this new channel, and thus modify the ways of thought of a whole district, perhaps of a whole world."[47] This slow-moving "fleuve humain," with its "flots de

---

[42] Qtd. in Taylor, xiii.

[43] "I have never in my life unleashed such consternation. There was total silence, broken only by coughs, the scraping of chairs, exchanged glances, scowls [. . .] and the torrent of indignant words. I would blush to repeat them. The outburst was so utterly unexpected, so out of all proportion, that I did not even derive any pleasure from it." Qtd. in Taylor, xiii–iv.

[44] While description is the key mode of "Le Passage de l'Opéra," it lacks an object against which it can be confirmed: "I had taken the precaution of choosing a landscape that would very quickly become unverifiable for the simple reason that the passage was about to be demolished in favor of an access way to the Boulevard Haussmann." Qtd. in Taylor, xii.

[45] Aragon, *Paris Peasant*, 26 (translation altered); "qui escomptent du percement une recrudescence de passage et la multiplication indéterminée de leur chiffre d'affaires." Aragon, *Le Paysan de Paris* (Paris: Gallimard, 1953), 35.

[46] "Public tranquille, casanier." Aragon, *Le Paysan de Paris*, 34 (my translation).

[47] Aragon, *Paris Peasant*, 14 (translation altered); "On peut se demander si une bonne partie du fleuve humain qui transporte journellement de la Bastille à la Madeleine d'incroyables flots de rêverie et de langueur ne va pas se déverser dans cette échappée nouvelle et modifier ainsi tout le cours des pensées d'un quartier, et peut-être d'un monde" (22).

rêverie et de langueur," will cease to exist in the swift, rationalized flow of the "new channel" to the Boulevard Haussmann.

In Aragon's representation, the Passage de l'Opéra slows the rapid, streamlined exchanges of the neighboring auction house, the Hôtel des Ventes. As its "passions filter through the sieve" of the Passage de l'Opéra, "nervous gamblers" and "watchmen" "gradually turn into men."[48] The arcade is thus not a space outside of the workings of commerce but rather one that while facilitating its operations counteracts their dehumanizing effects through sensuality. It is described as both an enchanted spectacle ("les féeries du lieu") and a natural space, a lair ("cet antre"). This last animalistic metaphor suggests that the arcade retains some vestiges of nature, that it is a retreat that offers safety and physical closeness.

In the Passage de l'Opéra, commerce and eros push against one another. The concierge of the arcade remarks: "There is a to-ing and fro-ing in there, a dust . . . You see some funny people, pretty women and some less pretty."[49] Louis describes them, disturbingly, as aging, unsubtle, and mechanical, yet he nonetheless recognizes a life in them that is absent from the bourgeois women who display themselves as instruments of reproduction: "Old whores, set pieces, mechanical mummies, I love that you feature in this habitual decor, as you are still lively lights compared to those mothers of families that one meets on the public parks."[50] While the women in the Passage sell their bodies for profit, they nonetheless take physical pleasure in their encounters there. This constrained sensuousness results in what Louis calls "the stammerings of sensual pleasure."[51] This swaying is communicated in a convoluted sentence that I translate literally here: "It does not seem to be a concern distant to caresses which leads

---

[48] Ibid., 42 (translation altered); "L'Hôtel des Ventes laisse filtrer un peu de ses passions dans le crible du passage de l'Opéra. Mais la hantise y transforme ceux qui s'en échappent, et ce n'est qu'à leur entrée dans cet antre que ces joueurs inquiets, ces guetteurs fiévreux portent encore sur leur visage le reflet flambant des enchères: en avançant dans ces galeries enchantées ils se prennent aux féeries du lieu et deviennent à leur tour des hommes" (54–55).

[49] Ibid., 20 (translation altered); "Il y a un va-et-vient là-dedans, une poussière . . . On voit des drôles de gens, des jolies femmes, et des moins jolies" (28–29). In his introduction, Aragon writes of the revelatory potential of parapraxis and then observes: "Il y a dans le trouble des lieux de semblables serrures qui ferment mal sur l'infini. Là où se poursuit l'activité la plus équivoque des vivants, l'inanimé prend un reflet de leurs plus secrets mobiles" (20); "There is in the confusion of places similar locks which cannot be bolted fast against infinity. Wherever the living pursue particularly ambiguous activities, the inanimate may sometimes assume the reflection of their most secret motives" (13, translation altered).

[50] Ibid., 35; "Vieilles putains, pièces montées, mécaniques momies, j'aime que vous figuriez dans le décor habituel, car vous êtes encore de vivantes lueurs au prix de ces mères de famille que l'on rencontre dans les promenades publiques" (46).

[51] Ibid., 40. "balbutiement de la volupté" (52).

into this kingdom this changing population of women who grant to sensual pleasure a perpetual right over their comings and goings."[52] This "va-et-vient" is also the mode of the novel itself, which repeatedly presents and retracts fantastical scenes.

In one of Louis's most vivid waking dreams in the arcade, he is attracted by a mechanical noise, "une sorte de bruit machinal et monotone," to the display window of a cane shop, in which the canes have turned to seaweed.[53] In their midst swims a woman:

> At first, I thought I must be dealing with a siren in the most conventional sense of the term, for I certainly had the impression that the lower half of this charming specter, who was naked down to a very low waistline, consisted of a sheath of steel or scales or possibly rose petals. But by concentrating my attention on the swaying that held her in the streaks of the atmosphere, I suddenly recognized this person, despite the emaciation of her features and distraught appearance. It was in the equivocation of the insulting occupation of the Rhineland and the drunkenness of prostitution that I met Lisel, on the banks of the river Saar, who had refused to follow the rest of her people after the disaster and who sang through the nights on the Sophienstrasse the songs her father had taught her, a hunting captain from the Rhine.[54]

Lisel is an undefinable thing. Part human, part mechanism, part of the natural space of the arcade as she silently mouths hunting songs, she appears to be far away yet is just behind the window.[55] Aided by the sensations of to-ing and fro-ing that accompany her appearance, Louis realizes that she is not a "mere" prostitute, "a siren in the most conventional sense," but someone who has suffered the violence and loss of the inter-Allied occupation of the German Rhineland after the Armistice. This swaying movement, "balancement," allows Louis to recall the ambivalence

---

[52] Ibid., 35. "Il ne semble pas qu'un souci étranger aux caresses entraîne dans ce royaume tout ce peuple changeant de femmes qui concède à la volupté un droit perpétuel sur ses va-et-vient" (46).
[53] Aragon, Le Paysan de Paris, 30; "a mechanical and monotonous noise" (22, translation alterered).
[54] Ibid., 22–23 (translation altered); "J'aurais cru avoir affaire à une sirène au sens le plus conventionnel de ce mot, car il me semblait bien que ce charmant spectre nu jusqu'à la ceinture qu'elle portait fort basse se terminait par une robe d'acier ou d'écaille, ou peut-être de pétales de roses, mais en concentrant mon attention sur le balancement qui le portait dans les zébrures de l'atmosphère, je reconnus soudain cette personne malgré l'émaciement de ses traits et l'air égaré dont ils étaient empreints. C'est dans l'équivoque de l'occupation insultante des provinces rhénanes et de l'ivresse de la prostitution que j'avais rencontré au bord de la Sarre la Lisel qui avait refusé de suivre le repli des siens dans le désastre, et qui chantait tout le long des nuits de la Sofienstrasse des chansons que lui avait apprises son père, capitaine de vénerie du Rhin" (31–32).
[55] Aragon, Paris Peasant, 22; "Sa petitesse semblait plutôt ressortir de l'éloignement, et cependant l'apparition se mouvait tout juste derrière la vitre" (31).

he himself felt, "the equivocation of the insulting occupation of the provinces of the Rhine and of the drunkenness of prostitution."[56]

Louis attempts to situate this encounter in a sublimated realm, as if the shop window were the frame of a work of art: "The Ideal," he cries at her, "finding nothing better to say in my confusion."[57] Yet the display is overtaken by a "convulsion générale" and the concierge arrives to move Louis on. The next morning, he finds in another window of the same shop a Meerschaum pipe "whose bowl depicted a siren," fallen on silesia fabric, its head crushed to dust. Louis's vision of Lisel was thus triggered by the sight of an odd, no longer fashionable object, itself half fleshly white, lying on textile from an equally war-torn, formerly Prussian province.[58] However sympathetic his witnessing of her experience, Louis has contributed to the violence that has crushed her. In this exploding vision there is no place for neutral observation.

While Louis is a guilty party, he too is turned to profit as his sexual acts are made visible to unseen voyeurs. Louis understands himself, also, as situated between these forces of calculation and sensuality. In the final lines of "Le Passage de l'Opéra," he describes himself as the contingent product of conflicting forces in terms that recall Lisel's equivocal swaying: "I am at one and the same time sunrise and sunset. I am a limit, a characteristic (or a line, *un trait*). Let all things mingle in the wind: those are the only words on my lips. And it is a ripple that surrounds me, seemingly the invisible waves of a frisson."[59] At the end of his adventures

---

[56] Ibid., 22 (translation altered); "l'équivoque de l'occupation insultante des provinces rhénanes et de l'ivresse de la prostitution" (31).

[57] Ibid., 23; "Idéal! [. . .] ne trouvant rien de mieux à dire dans mon trouble" (32).

[58] "one of the pipes in a rack, a meerschaum whose bowl depicted a siren, had broken, as if it had been condemned to be a target in some seedy shooting gallery at a fair. From the end of this pipe's illusionistic stem there still protruded the twin curve of a charming breast: a little white dust that had fallen on the silesia fabric of an umbrella testified to the erstwhile existence of a head crowned with flowing hair," Aragon, *Paris Peasant*, 24; "une pipe d'écume qui figurait une sirène, et qui, au râtelier, sans qu'on s'en aperçut, s'était brisée comme dans un vulgaire tir forain, et qui tendait encore au bout de son tuyau d'illusion la double courbe d'une gorge charmante: un peu de poussière blanche tombée sur la silésienne d'un parapluie attestait l'existence passée d'une tête et d'une chevelure" (33).

In a moment that resembles Stephen's Black Mass in "Circe," the failure of abstract thought is given emblematic presence in *Le Paysan* when an allegorical figure referred to as "the sentiment of futility" plays on an accordion: the word "Pessimism" is progressively spelled out letter by letter only, once having appeared, to disappear, letter by letter, again. Louis too begins again, "Let me retrace my steps" (49); "Je reviens sur mes pas" (63).

[59] Ibid., 111; "Je suis du même coup l'occident et l'aurore. Je suis une limite, un trait. Que tout se mêle en vent, voici tous les mots de ma bouche. Et ce qui m'entoure est une ride, l'onde apparente d'un frisson" (136).

in the Passage, Louis represents himself not as a person but as a transient material effect.

In the prologue to Le Paysan de Paris, Aragon valorizes this capacity of the senses to produce new social worlds:

> To each error of the senses correspond strange flowers of reason. Admirable gardens of absurd beliefs, forebodings, obsessions and frenzies. Unknown, ever-changing gods take shape there ... New myths spring up beneath each step we take. Legend begins where man has lived, where he lives. All that I intend to think about from now on is these despised transformations. Each day the modern sense of existence becomes subtly altered. A mythology ravels and unravels.[60]

This "error of the senses" underlies the pattern of raveling and unraveling that structures Aragon's novel. While these sensual visions recover the past for its characters, they are also capable of recreating the temperament of society, "le sentiment moderne de l'existence." It is this power, we will see, that proved so profoundly compelling to Benjamin.

Benjamin's Profane Illumination and Image Space

This close engagement with Aragon's Le Paysan de Paris allows us to reexamine the criticisms Benjamin directed at it and to trace its impact on his writing. In 1935, Benjamin wrote to Theodor Adorno of the foundational importance of the novel for the Passagen-Werk: "It opens with Aragon – the paysan de Paris. Evenings, lying in bed, I could never read more than two to three pages by him because my heart started to pound so hard that I had to put the book down. What a warning! What an indication of the years and years that had to be put between me and that kind of reading. And yet the first preliminary sketches for the Arcades originated at that time."[61] As Benjamin confesses the impact Aragon's

---

[60] Ibid., 10 (translation altered). "A toute erreur des sens correspondent d'étranges fleurs de la raison. Admirables jardins des croyances absurdes, des pressentiments, des obsessions et des délires. Là prennent figure des dieux inconnues et changeants ... Des mythes nouveaux naissant sous chacun de nos pas. Là où l'homme a vécu commence la légende, là où il vit. Je ne veux plus occuper ma pensée que de ces transformations méprisées. Chaque jour se modifie le sentiment moderne de l'existence. Une mythologie se noue et se dénoue" (15).

[61] Walter Benjamin to Theodor Adorno, May 31, 1935, in The Correspondance of Walter Benjamin, 1910–1940, ed. Gershom Scholem and Theodor Adorno, trans. Manfred R. Jacobson and Evelyn M. Jacobson (Chicago: University of Chicago Press, 1994), 488. "Da steht an ihrem Beginn Aragon – der Paysan de Paris, vom dem ich abends im Bette niemehr als zwei bis drei Seiten lesen konnte, weil mein Herzklopfen dann so stark wurde, daß ich das Buch aus der Hand legen musste. Welche Warnung! Welcher Hinweis auf die Jahre und Jahre, die zwischen mich und solche

novel had for him, he locates his encounter with it in an erotic space between waking and dreams. The affective, physical, and transformative mode of reading he describes and eschews here, intimately related to Aragon's sensual mode of engagement, are of enduring importance for Benjamin. Aragon's novel, and Benjamin's encounter with it, point the way to the most important concerns in the *Passagen-Werk*: the arcade as a crucial locus of critical reflection upon the workings of capitalism; the prostitute as a key figure of modern commodification; the recovery of threatened or submerged experience from the obsolete commodity; and, what will be of central focus here, the necessity of moving through nonrational, sensual modes of engagement in order to gain access to that experience.

Benjamin's acquaintance with Aragon's writing began in May 1925, when Willy Haas, the editor of *Die Literarische Welt*, "entrusted Benjamin with a series of reports on developments in French culture, a task eagerly accepted. While retaining his older interests in Gide and Giraudoux, Benjamin began immersing himself in the 'questionable books of the Surrealists,' with an eye to an article for the journal; he read André Breton's 'Manifesto of Surrealism' and initiated a long engagement with the world of Louis Aragon by reading *Une Vague de rêves*."[62] Although the Prologue and "Le Passage de l'Opéra" had appeared in issues of *La Revue* in June and September of 1924, *Le Paysan* was not published until September 1926.[63] It was probably during his second extended stay in Paris, in 1927, that Benjamin met Aragon, whom he met again on returning to the city in December 1929.[64]

Benjamin was primed to understand the political potential of Aragon's mobilization of sensation. As Michael Jennings notes, Benjamin had read Erich Unger's 1921 *Politik und Metaphysik* and called it the "most significant piece of writing on politics in our time."[65] Jennings points to the similarity of Unger's principles to Benjamin's: they were both convinced

Lektüre gebracht werden mussten. Und doch stammen die ersten Aufzeichnungen zu den Passagen aus jener Zeit." (*GS* V.2:1117).

[62] Eiland and Jennings, *Walter Benjamin: A Critical Life*, 236.   [63] Forest, *Aragon*, 216.

[64] Benjamin published translations of Aragon's work in *Die Literarische Welt*, no. 23 (June 8, 1928), pp. 3–4, and no. 24 (June 15, 1928), pp. 7–8. Broderson, *Walter Benjamin: A Biography*, 293–94, note 71.

[65] Qtd. Michael Jennings, "Toward the Apokatastatic Will: Walter Benjamin's Late Theological Politics," in *Walter Benjamin and Theology* (New York: Fordham University Press, 2016), 99. Jennings cites Benjamin, *The Correspondence of Walter Benjamin 1910–1940*, 127. Jennings also footnotes Margarete Kohlenbach, "Religion, Experience, Politics: On Erich Unger and Walter Benjamin," in *The Early Frankfurt School and Religion*, ed. Raymond Geuss and Margarete Kohlenbach (Basingstoke: Palgrave Macmillan, 2005), 64–84.

that the Kantian model of experience and knowledge was inadequate; they shared a distrust of "rationalist activism," democracy, and pragmatic, discursive political practices; and they "saw in the mind/body problem a determinative analogy for any understanding of politics."[66] Jennings outlines the centrality of sensory modes to Unger's *Politics and Metaphysics*: "At the core of Unger's book lies a radical theory of the reformation of the human sensorium [. . . T]he distant intervention of *Geist* in the corporeal world 'according to the manner of the body' is conceivable only if nature – what he calls the 'naturally given elements of the psychophysiological phenomenon' – is itself 'modifiable.' And this modifiability itself can only, in turn, be based on a reformation of the concept of *Anschauung* – of an intuition based on observation of the phenomenal world. Unger calls for the creation of what he calls a 'pure sensuousness' – 'reine Sinnlichkeit' [. . .] The reconstruction and reformation of the human sensorium is, in *Politik und Metaphysik*, thus the key to a reconsideration of the very concept of experience and, more importantly, an expansion of the field constituted by the possible objects of experience."[67] Jennings connects Benjamin's exploration of the reformation of the sensorium through modern media such as cinema to his interactions with the G-Group, which included Laszlo Moholy-Nagy, Mies van der Rohe, El Lissitsky, and Hans Richter, as well as intellectuals such as Ernst Schoen.

We can see the direct relevance of Unger's notion of a transformed sensorium for Benjamin's reading of Aragon's novel, in which sensual experiences become the mode in which a historical–political consciousness awakens. This requires stripping away some of Benjamin's criticisms of *Le Paysan*. In the "First Sketches" of the *Passagen-Werk*, begin in the middle of 1927, Benjamin asserts the distance of his thinking from Aragon's:

> Delimitation of the tendency of this project with respect to Aragon: whereas Aragon persists within the realm of dream, here the concern is to find the constellation of awakening. While in Aragon there remains an impressionistic element, namely the "mythology" (and this impressionism must be held responsible for the many vague philosophemes in his book), here it is a question of the dissolution of "mythology" into the space of history. That of course can happen only through the awakening of a not-yet-conscious knowledge [eines nicht bewußten Wissens] of what has been. [H°, 17][68]

[66] Ibid., 99.   [67] Ibid., 100.
[68] Benjamin, *The Arcades Project*, trans. Howard Eiland and Kevin McLaughlin (Cambridge, MA: Belknap, 2002), 845. "Abgrenzung der Tendenz dieser Arbeit gegen Aragon: Während Aragon im Traumbereich beharrt, soll hier die Konstellation des Erwachens gefunden werden. Während bei Aragon ein impressionistisches Element bleibt – die, Mythologie'– und dieser Impressionismus ist

As we have seen in reading Louis's exploding vision of Lisel, this awakening is exactly what Aragon represents. Aragon's myth has none of the negative features Benjamin associates with the term as he uses it later: erroneous accounts of the world, the fallacy of an all-powerful fate, the misapprehension of the mere advancement of capitalism as qualitative progress in human society. Aragon's depiction of Lisel as a siren resembles Benjamin's own use of mythological characters as critical and suggestive representations of modern urban figures.[69] Yet, as Aragon makes clear himself, myth in his novel is most importantly a historically contingent structure of perception rather than a lexicon of imagery. It is precisely this structure, the ebb and flow of the text in its images and the experiences they afford, that affords the text its critical energy.

Aragon does indeed engage in "vague philosophemes" in *Le Paysan,* quoting Hegel and Kant to somewhat obscure ends. Forest notes that Aragon's philosophical musings were considered laughable by his associates but argues that they must be considered as poetic: "It is impossible to reconstruct from *Le Paysan* a coherent conceptual system."[70] The crucial thinking of the novel occurs not through its theoretical ruminations but through the form of sentient thinking adapted from "Circe." These visions, and the characters who partake of them, directly inform Benjamin's thinking in a passage of the "Prostitution, Gambling" section of the *Passagen-Werk,* written between the fall of 1928 and end of 1929.[71]

> Rites de passage – this is the designation in folklore for the ceremonies that attach to death and birth, to marriage, puberty, and so forth. In modern life, these transitions are becoming ever more unrecognizable and impossible to experience. We have grown very poor in threshold experiences. Falling asleep is perhaps the only such experience that remains to us. (But together with this, there is also waking up.) And, finally, there is the ebb and flow of conversation and the sexual permutations of love – experience that surges over thresholds like the changing figures of the dream. "How mankind loves to remain transfixed," says Aragon, "at the very doors of the

---

für die vielen gestaltlosen Philosophen des Buches verantwortlich zu machen – geht es hier um Auflösung der, Mythologie' in den Geschichtsraum. Das freilich kann nur geschehen durch die Erweckung eines nicht bewußten Wissens vom Gewesenen" (*GS* V.2:1014).

[69] See, for example, Benjamin's likening of cashiers to Danae in the *Passagen-Werk* (*Arcades Project,* 82), or his allusions to Baudelaire's, Daumier's, and Larmartine's use of Homeric characters to characterize and satirize contemporary figures.

[70] "On peut rire d'Aragon, bien sûr. [...] Aragon lit la philosophie de Hegel – ou bien de Schelling – comme il lit la poésie de Musset, de Racine – ou celle de Rimbaud et de Lautréamont. C'est-à-dire qu'il la lit en poète. Et c'est pourquoi il la transforme de telle sort qu'il devient impossible de reconstituer à partir du *Paysan de Paris* un système conceptuel cohérent." Forest, *Aragon,* 222.

[71] *GS* V.2:1073–74, 1262.

imagination!" *Paysan de Paris* (Paris, 1926, p. 74.3). It is not only from the thresholds of these gates of imagination that lovers and friends like to draw their energies; it is from thresholds in general. Prostitutes, however, love the thresholds of these gates of dream. The threshold must be carefully distinguished from the boundary. A *Schwelle* <threshold> is a zone. Transformation, passage, wave action are in the word *schwellen*, swell, and etymology ought not to overlook these senses. On the other hand, it is necessary to keep in mind the immediate tectonic and ceremonial context which has brought the word to its current meaning. Dream House [02a, 1][72]

Here, Benjamin presents the key structure of *Le Paysan*'s waking dreams, while distancing it from Aragon and setting it within an anthropological frame. Taken out of the context of Aragon's novel, and removed from the lair of the Passage de l'Opéra, this association of the prostitute with a transformative dream energy is surprising. Yet Benjamin's invocation of these threshold zones at the gates of dream recall Aragon's celebration of the "error of the senses [to which] correspond strange flowers of reason." The structure of Aragon's novel underlies the experiences and motions presented here: falling asleep and waking up, ebb and flow, and, most important, *wiegen*, wave action. The erotic energy of the Passage de l'Opéra's visions lurks in *schwellen* (to distend, tumefy, intumesce).[73] In these transformative threshold experiences, Benjamin rephrases Aragon's "mythology that ravels and unravels," the "despised transformations" that, in the absence of traditional rites of passage and in the depersonalizing rationality of economic development, allow the modern sense of existence to be felt and also to take on new qualities.

The historical and social content yielded by this wavering zone is not discussed in this entry. Benjamin indeed wavers in his understanding of the agency associated with sensuality. Although, here, he understands

---

[72] Benjamin, *Arcades Project*, 494. "Rites de passage – so heißen in der Folklore die Zeremonien, die sich an Tod, Geburt, an Hochzeit, Mannbarwerden etc. anschließen. In dem modernen Leben sind diese Übergänge immer unkenntlicher und unerlebter geworden. Wir sind sehr arm an Schwellenerfahrungen geworden. Das Einschlafen ist vielleicht die einzige, die uns geblieben ist. (Aber damit auch das Erwachen.) Und schließlich wogt wie der Gestaltenwandel des Traums über Schwellen auch das Auf und Nieder der Unterhaltung und der Geschlechterwandel der Liebe. 'Qu'il plaît à l'homme' sagt Aragon, 'de se tenir sur les pas des portes de l'imagination!' (Paysan de Paris) Es sind nicht nur die Schwellen dieser phantastischen Tore, es sind die Schwellen überhaupt, aus denen Liebende, Freunde, sich Kräfte zu saugen lieben. Die Huren aber lieben die Schwellen dieser Traumtore. Die Schwelle ist ganz scharf von der Grenze zu scheiden. Schwelle ist eine Zone. Wandel, Übergang, Fluten liegen im Worte 'schwellen' und diese Bedeutung hat die Etymologie nicht zu übersehen. [O2a,1]" (*GS* V.1:617–18).

[73] In *Arcades Project* (991 n.4), Eiland and Jennings note that "*Schwelle*, cognate with the English word 'sill,' has the root sense of 'board,' 'structural support,' 'foundation beam.' According to current information, [*Schwelle*] is etymologically unrelated to *schwellen*," a point that Benjamin resists.

prostitutes as "enjoy[ing] the thresholds of these gates of dream" at both the borders of sleep and through the variations of sexual interaction, in another entry in the "Prostitute, Gambling" section, also written between the fall of 1928 and the end of 1929, Benjamin represents the prostitute as a passive instrument, "adaptable and obedient" to "the will to pleasure":

> In prostitution, one finds expressed the revolutionary side of technology (the symbolic side, which creates no less than discovers). "As if the laws of nature to which love submits were not more tyrannical and more odious than the laws of society! The metaphysical meaning of sadism is the hope that the revolt of man will take on such intensity as to summon nature to change its laws. [. . .]" Emmanuel Berl, "Premier Pamphlet" [. . .]. And in fact: the sexual revolt against love not only springs from the fanatical, obsessive will to pleasure; it also aims to make nature adaptable and obedient [suited] to this will. [O2, 3][74]

The prostitute is understood here as a product of human labor rather than a laborer herself, as the object rather than the subject of transformative erotic enjoyment. Her body is a site for others' expression of freedom, as well as for their pleasure. As revolution puts all seemingly natural conditions in question, so love and "nature," the logic goes, are deconstructed in prostitution, as in sadism. Read most generously, this is an image of a bold experimentation that opposes a social order in which inequity and suffering are naturalized. Susan Buck-Morss interprets it in this vein: "Benjamin saw prostitutes as distorted images of the material, physical desire for sensual happiness which [. . .] his negative theology affirmed."[75] Yet when Benjamin recruits Emmanuel Berl as accomplice for the conception of the prostitute's body as the material through which the limits of nature and society would be defied, he turns away from the experiential possibilities of the previous passage.[76]

---

[74] Benjamin, *Arcades Project*, 493. "In der Prostitution kommt die revolutionäre Seite der Technik zum Ausdruck (die schaffende, obzwar gewiß auch deren entdeckende, die symbolische). 'Comme si les lois de la Nature, auxquelles l'amour se soumet, n'étaient pas plus tyranniques et plus odieuses que celles de la Societé! Le sens métaphysique du sadisme est l'espoir que la révolte de l'homme prendra une intensité telle qu'elle mettra la nature en demeure de changer ses lois[. . .]' Emmanuel Berl: Premier Pamphlet (Europe No 75 p405/406). In der Tat: die sexuelle Revolte gegen die Liebe entspringt nicht nur einem fanatischen, besessenen Lustwillen, sie geht auch darauf aus, die Natur ihm gefügig und angemessen zu machen. O2,3" (*GS* V.1:616–17).

[75] Susan Buck-Morss, "The Flâneur, the Sandwichman and the Whore: The Politics of Loitering," *New German Critique* 39 (Autumn 1986), 99–140, at 137.

[76] In a more general sense, Benjamin sees the individual prostitute as an instance of commodified femininity: "Prostitution opens a market in feminine types" (*Arcades Project* 515); "Die Prostitution zieht einen Markt der weiblichen Typen auf" (*GS* V.1:641). She is further divested of subjectivity as Benjamin remarks: "Love for the prostitute is the apotheosis of empathy with the commodity" (375); "Die Liebe zur Prostituierten ist die Apotheose der Einfühlung in die Ware" (*GS* V.1:637).

In Benjamin's "Surrealism" essay, which he later described as "an opaque screen placed before the *Passagen-Werk*," this shift also occurs in his thinking regarding the Surrealist artist.[77] The essay begins with a positive image in which the Surrealists resemble the prostitutes at the gates of dream. Here Benjamin names the sensory elements of Aragon's text but without accounting for how they lead to insight: "Life seemed worth living only where the threshold between waking and sleeping was worn away in everyone as by the steps of multitudinous images flooding back and forth [. . .] Image and language take precedence [. . .] Not only before meaning. Also before the self. In the world's structure, dream loosens individuality like a bad tooth. This loosening of the self by intoxication is, at the same time, precisely the fruitful, living experience that allowed these people to step outside the charmed space of intoxication."[78] He names this experience, which he holds to have been discovered by the Surrealists, "profane illumination": "a materialistic, anthropological inspiration, to which hashish, opium, or whatever else can give an introductory lesson"; Benjamin goes on to criticize the Surrealists for remaining within this dream space: "This profane illumination did not always find the Surrealists equal to it, or to themselves, and the very writings that proclaim it most powerfully, Aragon's incomparable *Paysan de Paris* and Breton's *Nadja*, show very disturbing symptoms of deficiency."[79]

In a radical move that combines dream energy and revolutionary technology, Benjamin extends the exploding visions of Aragon's novel into a means for the transformation of bourgeois society, which he presents as technological action upon physical matter:

> The collective is a body, too. And the *physis* that is being organized for it in technology can, through all its political and factual [objective] reality, be produced only in that image space to which profane illumination initiates us [uns heimisch macht]. Only when in technology body and image space so interpenetrate that all revolutionary tension becomes bodily collective

[77] Benjamin, *Correspondence*, 348. The essay was first published in *Die Literarische Welt* in February 1929.

[78] Benjamin, *Selected Writings: 1927–1934*, ed. M. P. Bullock and M. W. Jennings (Cambridge, MA: Harvard University Press, 1999), 208; "Das Leben schien nur lebenswert wo die Schwelle, die zwischen Wachen und Schlaf ist, in jedem ausgetreten war, wie von Tritten massenhafter hin und wider flutender Bilder, die Sprache nur sie selbst, wo Laut und Bild und Bild und Laut mit automatischer Exaktheit derart glücklich ineinandergriffen, dass für den Groschen 'Sinn' kein Spalt mehr übrigblieb. Bild und Sprache haben den Vortritt" (*GS* II.1:296).

[79] Ibid., 209. "Dieser profane Erleuchtung hat den Sürrealismus nicht immer auf ihrer, seiner Höhe gefunden, under gerade die Schriften, die sie am kräftigsten bekunden, Aragons unvergleichlicher 'Paysan de Paris' und Bretons 'Nadja' ziegen da sehr störende Ausfallserscheinungen" (Ibid., 297).

innervation, and all the bodily innervations of the collective become revolutionary discharge, has reality transcended itself to the extent demanded by the *Communist Manifesto*.[80]

Individual consciousness is rendered redundant here as the body politic is understood as a natural material, a *physis*, that is manipulated, or "organized." This technological organization of *physis* is a solution to the problem bourgeois subjectivity presents for the communist transformation of society. Just as the "dream loosens individuality like a bad tooth," when this image space reorganizes the *physis*, individual cognition is overwhelmed. The once-unconscious transformative dream energies – the stuff of the profane illumination – are turned into a somatically and subjectively determinant flow that stimulates collective physical animation, a "leibliche kollektive Innervation."

This scenario of total social transformation pushes to an extreme the space of the Surrealist novel: "the one hundred percent image space . . . this will still be a space of images and, more concretely, a body space."[81] This is a violent space: It is "the space, in a word, in which political materialism and physical creatureliness share the inner man, the psyche, the individual, or whatever else we wish to throw to them, with dialectical justice, so that no limb remains untorn."[82] Benjamin attributes a paradoxical power to this space, which "can no longer be measured by contemplation": as it "uns heimisch macht," it makes us at home or turns us into natives.[83] The familiar tone of Benjamin's use of the first-person plural jars amusingly with this new collective being inimical to (bourgeois) understanding.

As an image of "collective physical animation," Benjamin closes his essay by populating this image space with Surrealists as mechanical dolls: "For the moment, only the Surrealists have understood [the *Communist*

---

[80] Ibid., 217–18. "Auch das Kollektivum ist leibhaft. Und die Physis, die sich in der Technik ihm organisiert, ist nach ihrer ganzen politischen und sachlichen Wirklichkeit nur in jenem Bildraume zu erzeugen, in welchem die profane Erleuchtung uns heimisch macht. Erst wenn in ihr sich Leib und Bildraum so tief durchdringen, das alle revolutionäre Spannung leibliche kollektive Innervation, alle leiblichen Innervationen des Kollektivs revolutionäre Entladung werden, hat die Wirklichkeit so sehr sich selbst übertroffen, wie das kommunistische Manifest es fordert" (Ibid., 309–10).

[81] Ibid., 217; "den hundertprozentigen Bildraum [...] wird dieser Raum noch Bildraum, und konkreter: Leibraum sein" (Ibid., 309).

[82] Ibid.; "der Raum mit einem Wort, in welchem der politische Materialismus und die physische Kreatur den inneren Menschen, die Psyche, das Individuum oder was sonst wir ihnen vorwerfen wollen, nach dialektischer Gerechtigkeit, so daß kein Glied ihm unzerissen bleibt, miteinander teilen" (Ibid., 309).

[83] Ibid., 217; "Dieser Bildraum aber ist kontemplativ überhaupt nicht mehr auszumessen" (Ibid., 309).

Manifesto's] present commands. They exchange, to a man, the play of human features for the face of an alarm clock that in each minute rings for sixty seconds."[84] Indistinguishable in their collective response, their faces are replaced with automated features. In the place of subjectivity is a mechanical expression of agitation, as they become functional objects at the threshold between sleep and waking.

Benjamin's image-body space radicalizes the exploding visions of Joyce's "Circe," replacing the passive sensations that prompted insight with a totally determining image space that abolishes individual consciousness in favor of collective revolutionary action. The violence of this conception is problematic, and more so in the absence of any clear agent. Might this massive reconstruction of society be engineered by political actors? In providing a gloss on the image-body-space, Sigrid Weigel writes that it "dissolv[es] the boundary between subject and òbject. The reader can no longer be distinguished from the agent, nor the one who deciphers an image from the one who represents or in actuality *is* an image: actor and audience merge."[85] Yet it is difficult to discern a mutual transformation in Benjamin's account; the profane illumination is ascribed agency and so, more evidently, is technology. Benjamin writes of the unconscious utopian energies of industrial capitalism, a concept that met with intense criticism from Adorno as rejecting the nature of collective politics and the dialectical role of the commodity in producing the practical transformative know-ledge the proletariat uses to transform society. Yet, the alternative is also problematic: the massive deconstruction of the subject in the image-body space might indeed be the work of political agents who set violent technology in place. This is, of course, to read in the light of subsequent historical atrocities.

Obviating this problem, Benjamin goes on to resituate the image-body space in the space of the arcade, as the idiosyncratic and spontaneous workings of its obsolete objects on the individuals who encounter them. As Winfried Menninghaus writes: "The 'dream kitsch' of the 19th century was for Benjamin a – if not *the* – main repository of the energy represented

---

[84] Ibid., 218. "Für den Augenblick sind die Sürrealisten die einzigen, die seine heutige Order begriffen haben. Sie geben, Mann für Mann, ihr Mienenspiel in Tausch gegen das Ziffęrblatt eines Weckers, der jede Minute sechzig Sekunden lang anschlägt" (Ibid., 310).

[85] Sigrid Weigel, *Body and Image-Space: Re-Reading Walter Benjamin* (London: Routledge, 1996), 19. Weigel's gloss takes on a marked circularity: "the image space becomes indistinguishable from the body collective to the extent that the reality of the latter is produced in an image-space which in turn refers to the corporeal materiality of the collective as its matrix" (19).

by this image space."[86] This action of the objects in the Arcades is suggested in some of the first sketches cited earlier, in which Benjamin distinguished his project from Aragon's work: "Arcades" and "The Arcades of Paris," an essay and a set of short fragments that date, respectively, from the summer or fall of 1927 and from "1928 or, at the latest, 1929."[87] Benjamin describes the possibility of a sensual engagement within the space of commodities that yields knowledge that is opposed to rational thought. This knowledge is explicitly associated with the unrealized transformative potential of the industrial revolution: "Here was the last refuge of those infant prodigies that saw the light of day at the time of the world exhibitions."[88] They prompt, Benjamin announces, "die Erweckung eines nicht bewußten Wissens vom Gewesenen," which is translated as "the awakening of an unconscious knowledge of what has been" but might be rendered, more literally, as "the awakening of a *not conscious* knowledge of what has been."[89]

We can trace this utopian awakening, too, to *Le Paysan de Paris*. Benjamin's account of the effects of the objects of the arcades would seem to multiply profoundly the possibilities Aragon imagined, adding a cohesive if unspecific utopian potential to the specific historical and sociological insights gained, for example, by Louis with Lisel, prompted by his chance encounter with an old Meerschaum pipe. Yet in the final section of *Le Paysan de Paris*, written in 1926, Aragon ascribes a far more radical utopian power to the concrete object. Aragon later describes the essay, titled "The Peasant's Dream," as offering "a materialism which is not achieved in the final pages of the book, but only *promised*."[90] Here, Aragon indicates the far-reaching potential of material objects: "The fantastic, the

---

[86] Winfried Menninghaus, "On the 'Vital Significance' of Kitsch; Walter Benjamin's Politics of 'Bad Taste,'" in *Walter Benjamin and the Architecture of Modernity*, ed. Andrew Benjamin and Charles Rice (Melbourne: Re.Press, 2009), 55.

[87] Eiland and Jennings's note, *Arcades Project*, 873. Benjamin's notes were for an essay that was to be titled "Pariser Passagen: Eine dialektische Feerie," "Paris Arcades: A Dialectical Fairyland," which retains the theatrical, oneiric sense of Aragon's text; *féerie*, Eiland and Jennings note, "being the name also of a popular nineteenth century French theatrical genre that involved allegorical figures and dreamlike décor" (*Walter Benjamin*, 873). Benjamin also expressed this sense of a performative, visionary space when he described the *Passagen-Werk*, on January 20, 1930, as "the theater of all my struggles and all my ideas" (*Correspondence*, 359).

[88] Benjamin, *Arcades Project*, 883. "Hier war die letzte Unterkunft der Wunderkinder [. . .] auf Weltausstellungen das Tageslicht erblickten" (*GS* V.2:1044).

[89] Benjamin, *The Arcades Project*, 845.

[90] Aragon, *Je n'ai jamais appris à écrire*, 55: "le materialisme qui ne sera point atteint aux dernière pages du livre, mais seulement *promis*" (Aragon's italics).

beyond, dream, survival, paradise, hell, poetry, so many words signifying the concrete."[91] The antithesis of abstraction, truth, and logic, the concrete is the matrix of all possibilities, the realm of the marvelous. Aragon ends *Le Paysan de Paris* with an imperative that is writ large in Benjamin's "Surrealism" essay: "Force to its farthest limit the idea of the destruction of the person, and go beyond that limit."[92]

In a gentler conception of such a destruction, Benjamin writes, in "Arcades," that utopian knowledge manifests itself through mechanical performance. It consists of a mimetic relation to the heterogeneous objects and printed matter found in the Passage de l'Opéra, which are invested with a strange, shifting life: "the merchandise on display is unintelligible, or else has several meanings [. . .] these insistent letterings want to say more [. . .] If a shoemaker's shop should be neighbor to a confectioner's, then his festoons of bootlaces will resemble rolls of licorice. [. . .] Combs swim about, frog-green and coral-red, as in an aquarium; trumpets turn into conches, ocarinas to umbrella handles; and lying in the fixative pans from a photographer's darkroom is birdseed."[93] These unstable patterns of likeness require the viewer to perceive them. "No one ought to enter this shop with preconceived ideas" Benjamin's speaker remarks and, in response to the objects in this space, he engages in depersonalized mimicry:

> There is no thing here that does not, where one least expects it, open a fugitive eye, blinking it shut again; and should you look more closely, it is gone. To the whispering of these gazes, the space lends its echo. "Now what," it blinks, "can possibly have come over me?" We stop short in some surprise. "What, indeed, can possibly have come over you?" Thus we gently bounce the question back to it.[94]

---

[91] Aragon, *Paris Peasant*, 205; "Le fantastique, l'au-delà, le rêve, la survie, le paradis, l'enfer, la poésie, autant de mots pour signifier le concret" (248).

[92] *Paris Peasant*, 205; "Poussez à sa limite extreme l'idée de destruction des personnes, et dépassez-la" (249).

[93] Benjamin, *Arcades Project*, 871–72. Benjamin's language here becomes sonically delightful: "die ausliegende Ware ist undeutlich oder vieldeutig [. . .] diese eindringlichen Buchstaben wollen noch mehr sagen [. . .] Ist ein Schusterladen Nachbar einer Confiserie, so werden seine Schnürsenkelgehänge lakritzenähnlich. [. . .] Froschgrün und korallenrot schwimmen Kämme wie in einem Aquarium, Trompeten werden zu Muscheln, Okarinen zu Schirmkrücken, in den Schalen der photographischen Dunkelkammer liegt Vogelfutter" (*GS* V.2:1041–42).

[94] Ibid., 878; "Da ist kein Ding, das nicht ein kurzes Auge wo man es am wenigsten vermutet, aufschlägt, blinzelnd schließt, siehst du aber näher hin so ist es verschwunden. Dem Wispern dieser Blicke leiht der Raum sein Echo: 'Was mag in mir, so blinzelt er, sich wohl ereignet haben?' Wir stutzen. 'Ja, was mag in dir sich wohl ereignet haben?' So fragen wir ihn leise zurück" (*GS* II.2:1050).

The multiple reflections in the mirrored space constitute a social space in which individual identity disappears. Critical thought here consists of zetetic echoing. This physical mirroring only slightly deforms the sensory impression created by its object – in the German, Benjamin's question departs only by changing the pronouns and beginning with "*Ja.*" This question might be more literally translated as "What might have happened in me? [...] Yes, what might have happened in you?" although this rendering does not capture the odd convolution of the original: "Ja, was mag in dir sich wohl ereignet haben?" Benjamin repeats here the scenario of Louis, facing Lisel in the vitrine with the mirrored ceiling, but he resists the temptation to invoke the ideal. Instead, Benjamin conceives of a persona that is a machine for a material kind of thinking.[95]

With the *Passagen-Werk*, Benjamin attempts to transform the reader into a machine for thinking. As Menninghaus writes, with this huge collection of diverse textual fragments, Benjamin attempts to bring about in the reader "the (Surrealist) 'explosion' [...]. The problem of presentation in *The Arcades Project* was to simulate this 'striking' (*Zustoßens*) by means of its own literary form."[96] The reader now is to be subjected to sensations more powerful than expository discourse; instead of the language of rational activism, he or she is to undergo a material transformation. Yet, this "explosion" is now idiosyncratic ... We might bring this ambition to the last image of "Circe," an image that is related to the offerings of Paris and one that both models and prompts a new kind of thinking.

Rudy

The exploding visions of "Circe" end, as Benjamin's early drafts for the *Passagen-Werk* begin, in "infant prodigies" and random material that is invested with a mysterious life. The "Circe" episode closes with Bloom's vision of Rudy:

> (*Silent, thoughtful, alert he stands on guard, his fingers at his lips in the attitude of secret master. Against the dark wall a figure appears slowly, a fairy boy of*

---

[95] Benjamin's discussion turns to the experience of the city as he describes the flaneur as "driven by a clockwork mechanism," "von einem Uhrwerk getrieben" – "bei altem Spielzeug eine Spieluhr," "a music box of long ago"; through this mechanical action, he gains a "gefühltes Wissen" a "felt knowledge" of the streets, a combination of sensory data and dead facts gleaned from reading accounts of Paris of the past. Benjamin, *Arcades Project*, 880; *GS* V.2:1054.

[96] Menninghaus, "On the 'Vital Significance' of Kitsch," 55.

eleven, a changeling, kidnapped, dressed in an Eton suit with glass shoes and a
little bronze helmet, holding a book in his hand. He reads from right to left
inaudibly, smiling, kissing the page.)

BLOOM: (*Wonderstruck, calls inaudibly*) Rudy!

RUDY: (*Gazes, unseeing, into Bloom's eyes and goes on reading, kissing,*
smiling. He has a delicate mauve face. On his suit he has diamond
and ruby buttons. In his free left hand he holds a slim ivory cane
with a violet bowknot. A white lambkin peeps out of his waistcoat
pocket.)   (U 15.4955–67)

Bloom's vision of his dead baby as an eleven-year-old boy is a kind of wish
fulfillment but Rudy here has not come back to life; he remains in a
separate space, blind to Bloom and deaf to his call.

Rudy bears a striking resemblance to the mechanical dolls Benjamin
describes on sale in the Parisian arcades, at the beginning of "The Arcades
of Paris." If Rudy is not named as an automaton, unseeing and unhear-
ing, he acts like one, bearing a notable similarity to those described by
Benjamin: "They are the true fairies of these arcades (more salable and
more worn than the life-sized ones): the formerly world-famous Parisian
dolls, which revolved on their musical socle and bore in their arms a doll-
sized basket out of which, at the salutation of the minor chord, a lambkin
poked its curious muzzle."[97] It seems too much to say that Joyce
wandered through the Parisian arcades and was inspired by the same
dolls as Benjamin, although it is possible. It also might be too much to
say that Benjamin read the final paragraph of "Circe" and was inspired to
think again about the contents of the Passage de l'Opéra, although this is
certainly possible.

If not chronologically the last, Rudy comes at the end of our exploration
in this chapter of a series of literary experiments with mechanical creatures
associated with the transformative powers of capitalist modernity. Some
have suggested a new world of possibilities that lacks foundational being;
in Nerval's *Aurélia*, in the previous chapter, workmen use "the primordial
fire which animated the first created beings" to make strange new creatures
out of unknown metals, in a generativity that intensifies the text's ground-
lessness. Some have embodied the possibility of resisting the worst

---

[97] Benjamin, *Arcades Project*, 874. "Sie sind die wahren Feen dieser Passagen – käuflicher und
gebrauchter als die lebensgroßen – die einst weltberühmten pariser Puppen, die auf dem
singenden Sockel sich drehten und auf den Armen ein Körbchen hatten, aus dem in den
werdenden Mollakkord ein Schäfchen die witternde Schnauze streckte" (*GS* V.2:1045).

of capitalist modernity: Lisel, a singing half-human mechanism, is one of the prostitutes Aragon sees as the last vestiges of sensitivity in a world of commercial traffic, countering commerce with sensual pleasure. Some have been products of the effort to create a new social world by abandoning the cognition associated with the false rationality of capitalism: Benjamin's revolutionary collective, and his alarm-clock Surrealists, produced by the image-body space's eradication of individual and inner life. Some have embodied, perhaps ironically, the effort to remake the human being to maximize profit: Apollinaire's child of reconstituted print media grants knowledge of social and political intrigues that lead to commercial gain, and Bloom's octuplets, born fully grown with "valuable metallic faces," are leaders of business and captains of industry.

Rudy is by far the most ambiguous figure in this series. He is touched by death. A changeling, he is an inhuman substitution for a stolen child. His face resembles that of another dead child Bloom has seen: "A dwarf's face, mauve and wrinkled like little Rudy's was. Dwarf's body" (*U* 6.326–27). His lambkin recalls the Agnus Dei medal worn by Bloom's mother, Ellen Bloom, bearing the representation of Christ in the form of a lamb to be sacrificed. But if the lamb symbolizes redemption, it appears here as part of a commodity. Its redemptive power is further compromised by Stephen's joke about "Mr Lamb from London," a former customer of Cohen's brothel, who in marrying one of the girls who works there "takest way the sins of our world" (*U* 15:3638). Yet Rudy is also animated by lively elements: by shoeing Rudy in glass slippers, Joyce invokes the realm of fairy tales, invested as they are with trust in the benevolence of nature; he mixes it with the artifice of mythology, as Rudy's fragile head is protected by an Achaean bronze helmet. For readers who no longer believe in fairy tales and myth, however, is there a promise of salvation or rebirth in Rudy? It inheres in his ambiguity, his material suggestiveness.

In this, Rudy signals a shift from an encounter between textual figures to an encounter between readers and text. The mechanical creatures we've looked at have been associated with efforts around the beginning of Surrealism "to elevate the poetic into the sphere of knowledge." We've traced a set of explorations of the felt knowledge of *Erkenntnis*, in which insight, discovery, perception, and cognition are intertwined. Bloom's encounter with Rudy works in a different way to the exploding visions of "Circe," where Bloom's sensations trigger fantasies and then release his attention again; looking upon Rudy, however, Bloom remains immobile. Surrounded by stage directions that focus on actions and objects,

Bloom calls out the sole word of the scene, his son's name. Suggestive but inscrutable, Rudy lives on, beyond his father, in a strange kind of life. He is the only kind of new life that is possible in Nighttown, one that is not compromised by exchange.

Rudy is a new machine for thinking, specifically by both being unintelligible and in offering several meanings. Rudy prompts us, too, to repeat the words associated with him. As we repeat them we see that, reading and kissing a book, Rudy is himself a textual creature. Rudy is assembled from previous moments of *Ulysses*, many of which are fantasy purchases from former times: Bloom's image, in "Hades," of Rudy had he survived, "Walking beside Molly in an Eton suit" (*U* 6.76); the ring given to Mrs Breen by Bloom in "Circe" that replays the title of the erotic novel, *Ruby, Pride of the Ring*: "*(tenderly, as he slips on her finger a ruby ring) Là ci darem la mano*" (*U* 15.468–69); even Molly's "new violet garters" in "Ithaca" (*U* 17.2092). As a collection of old and compromised materials, Rudy is the embodiment of a new kind of text. Exemplifying a fertile textual materiality, he is a harbinger of *Finnegans Wake*, as well as of Benjamin's *Passagen-Werk*.

Let us assume for a moment that Joyce's Rudy inspired Benjamin's description of the mechanical dolls of the Parisian arcade. For Benjamin, these dolls surpass the "mechanical mummies" Aragon praises in the Passage de l'Opéra as they "more salable and more worn"; they have a superior ability to stimulate desire and, as a consequence or a cause, a greater accumulation of material history in their forms. Precisely because of this accumulation, that registers as decline and obsolescence, they are invested with transformative power, even though it appears as a purely mechanical autonomy in the routine emergence of something that merely seems to be natural and alive. The dolls' worn forms refuse calculation, instrumentalization and conceptual domination. They are, to use again Bernstein's phrase, the sensory rump, left over from the rationalizations of reason. The concrete, Aragon writes, can signify almost anything, "the fantastic, the beyond, dream, survival, paradise, hell, poetry." It "has no other form of expression than poetry."[98] In our readings of Joyce, we have explored how the poetic proceeds through the material relations between words, phrases, and images, in pun, association, and distortion. This is the mode of reading prompted by Rudy; it is also the mode of Joyce's

---

[98] Aragon, *Paris Peasant*, 202–03.

Finnegans Wake as well as Benjamin's mode of nonexpository writing. If it might be too much to say that the image of Rudy enacts a reformation of the human sensorium, we can say that he places readers in an echoing, whispering space in which they become engaged in repetitive questioning rather than abstracted insight. This is a transformative space because it is where preconceived ideas are useless. With this comes new possibilities of being for readers, the possibility of a new sense of existence.

Kevin

CHAPTER 6

Paris Compounded: Finnegans Wake

In the previous chapters, I have examined a series of encounters in Joyce's writing between men and women. I have argued that Joyce develops increasingly innovative narrative forms in which transactional relations are countered through an aesthetic practice occurring between characters. In the Paris Epiphany, an observer purports to objectively categorize and judge women on the street but in registering their intimate smells he is implicated in a shared embodiment that undoes any classification. In *Finnegans Wake*, I will argue here, Joyce scrambles the encounters between characters, creating ambiguous interchanges between archetypal and historical figures of various numbers, genders, and sexual orientations, in a host of different relations and configurations. The densely ambiguous verbal texture that results involves the reader in an aesthetic practice, not just with the text itself but with other readers. The *Wake* thus becomes the means for what I call an aesthetic sociality.

The central event of the *Wake* is the encounter known as the "Crime in the Park." It is replayed throughout the text in numerous forms. However, instead of descriptions of events and even clear indications of the subjects and objects involved, polysemantic word clusters undo any objective identification. As the washerwomen launder in the river the dirty linen of HCE, Humphrey Chimpden Earwicker, in I.8, they speak of the crime: "Well, you know, when the old cheb went futt and did what you know. Yes, I know, go on. [. . .] Or whatever it was they threed to make out he thried to two in the Fiendish park. He's an awful old reppe."[1] Despite their assertions of knowledge, the women's exchange is utterly unclear. Dirt is the nature of their speech, in terms of the content of their gossip, the stains they release from the clothing, and the muddled, muddied phrases they

---

[1] James Joyce, *Finnegans Wake*, introd. John Bishop (London: Penguin, 1999), 196.6–11. Hence abbreviated as *FW*, followed by reference to page and line numbers.

discharge. The numeric puns, "threed," and "thried to two," layered on the First-Draft Version, "Or whatever it was *they try to make out* he ~~did~~ tried to do in ~~the~~ Phoenix park," suggest one man, two women, and three men, in an increasing scale of involvement.[2] This set of permeations is played out in iterations of the scene at other moments in the book: in the double female presence are superimposed the binary oppositions of virgin and prostitute, and of young and old woman, but also the mirror images of HCE's daughter Issy and his wife ALP, Anna Livia Plurabelle; these possibilities are complicated even further by the opposing figures of HCE's two sons, Shem and Shaun, complements who exchange identities and are also mediated by an interlinking figure who transforms them into a militant triad.[3] The washerwomen's densely polysemantic discussion offers no clarification about HCE's objectionable relations with others, as possibilities of exhibitionism, voyeurism, flirtation, masturbation, defecation, urination, and abstention teem shamefully and comically in their speech: "What did he do a tail at all on Animal Sendai? And how long was he under lough and neagh? It was put in the newses what he did, nicies and priers, the King fierces Humphrey, with illysus distilling, exploits and all [. . .] O, the roughty old rappe! Minxing marrage and making loof" (*FW* 196.18–24). This short last sentence suggests a range of deviant sexual behaviors from bestiality to micturition, from engagement with boldly flirtatious women (and pet dogs) to promises of marriage, and from making love, loo, oof (slang for money) to, most literally, loof, in the sense of using the palm of the hand, as well as, despite everything, remaining aloof.

In the washerwomen's dialogue, the Paris Epiphany's encounter between male observer and female bodies is reversed, and its undermining of a distanced judgment of commercial behavior is intensified. As the washerwomen release the filth from HCE's underclothes, they engage in sentient thinking: their knowledge is acquired through physical work on smells, textures, and sights. They register their own vulnerability in this matrix by talking of the hungry children they neglect in order to work. They explicitly name their own bodies as painfully generating knowledge: "I know by heart the places he loves to saale, duddurty devil! Scorching my hand and starving my famine to make his private linen public"

---

2 James Joyce, *A First-Draft Version of "Finnegans Wake,"* ed. David Hayman (Austin: University of Texas Press, 1963), 123.
3 See Vincent Cheng's *Joyce, Race and Empire* (New York: Cambridge University Press, 1995) for a postcolonial reading of this triadic configuration.

(*FW* 196.14–16). HCE's crime is both of staining and selling, as the women's exchange situates it not just in a matrix of sexual possibilities but also of economic relations, "he loves to saale."

Other critics have understood the washerwomen's work as an aesthetic practice. As Margot Norris observes, I.8 "reverses the forcible dissociation of art from manual labor that Max Horkheimer and Theodor Adorno find figured in Odysseus's stratagem in the sailors' encounter with the sirens in their *Dialectic of Enlightenment*."[4] The washerwomen sing a "'seductive sirens' song that is nonetheless coterminous with their labor"; Joyce "asks us to listen with proletarian interest, like sailors with unsealed ears, who hear in the beauty of the text's lyricism a work song of the kind rarely heard in high art, that they can recognize as their own."[5] In contrast to what Norris sees as Joyce's idealized female figures, instanced in the Bird Girl Stephen Dedalus observes on Sandymount Strand, she argues that in I.8 Joyce finally understands the material circumstances of the women he represents, not just the washerwomen but the main figure of their discourse, ALP. Against "nineteenth-century aestheticism: the Baudelairean enterprise of finding flowers in evil, gold in mud," Norris continues, Joyce "retrieve[s] the speech and feelings of the repressed washerwomen [and] labor and ugliness assert themselves in art, the institutional site for discourses of beauty."[6] Norris understands I.8 as an act of desublimation, "the specific strategy Peter Bürger identifies with the self-critical capacity of the historical avant-garde."[7]

In my reading, the washerwomen are not only instances of a new relation of art to labor but also a development of Joyce's ongoing interest in a somatic art that works within and against commercial space. They exemplify a new stage in this interest: as the washerwomen work on the dirty clothes, they perform a kind of art that elicits a new type of aesthetic practice in readers. Theirs is one of many scenes in the *Wake* of a *collective* attention to matter of dubious value and unstable status: the feasting of the mourners around and on the corpse of Finnegan/HCE; the work of the scholars on ALP's letter found in the midden heap; and, as we will examine at a little more length, the soldiers' responses to the excreting

---

[4] Margot Norris, *Joyce's Web: The Social Unravelling of Modernism* (Austin: University of Texas Press, 1992), 139.
[5] Ibid., 139. [6] Ibid., 143.
[7] Ibid., 142. Norris refers here to Peter Bürger's *Theory of the Avant-Garde* (Minneapolis: University of Minnesota Press, 1984).

body of the Russian General.[8] These scenes emblematize the text itself as a waste product that asks us to be its washerwomen. With this seemingly easy metaphor, I gesture toward a more radical sense of a collective aesthetic performance. *Finnegans Wake* not only resembles works of the historical avant-garde; in this chapter, I will show that it draws upon specific moments in the Parisian avant-garde to conceive of a new kind of collaborative art. In the *Wake*, Joyce shifts from representing a city, as he did in *Ulysses*, to staging a *ville énorme* with a set of references so profoundly compacted, diverse, and contradictory that it elicits an ideal community to read it.

He Could Not Tell What He Did Ale

Since the publication of *Finnegans Wake*, scholars have established references and thematic structures as interpretative principles for readers familiar with the text and as intimidating codes for newcomers. The relatively straightforward excerpt from I.8 cited earlier exemplifies the work's massively eclectic nature, as it obscures itself with slang, archaic diction, and a mess of terms drawn from the church calendar, maps of Japan, legal writs, the biography of Oscar Wilde, the history of British naval charts, popular sayings, and the *Odyssey*, as well as the illicit distilling of whiskey, German black horses, Swiss cents, and waterclosets.[9] It also indicates something both of the generativity of the *Wake* and of the creativity it demands of its readers. If Joyce's final, weighty volume looks like a Yeatsian monument of intellect that must be studied with the spirit, understanding *Finnegans Wake* in the Parisian context in which Joyce wrote it allows us to see more clearly its unageing nature and to understand this nature as inhering in the demands the *Wake*'s material qualities make on the senses. To complete the work of situating the *Wake* in 1920s and 1930s Paris is beyond the scope of this chapter, or indeed of a single volume. Joyce's composition

---

[8] As Vincent Cheng observes, "The references to elimination and excrement in *Finnegans Wake* are, of course, legion and ubiquitous, since they are so much at the very core of the proto-mythical stories of *Finnegans Wake*: such as HCE's fall in Phoenix Park when he peeps at the girls peeing (while the three soldiers peep at the peeper peeping at the pee-ers; we have a queue of peepers and pee-ers, minding their pees and queues); or Buckley shooting the Russian General after the latter has shat on the grass [. . .] or the prankquean's wet raining and reigning with her 'wit foreninst the dour' (FW 21.16) – and so on." Vincent Cheng, "'Goddinpotty': James Joyce and the Language of Excrement," in *The Languages of Joyce*, ed. R. M. Bolletieri Bossinelli et al. (Amsterdam: John Benjamins, 1993), 85–102, at 93–94.
[9] See Roland McHugh, *Annotations to Finnegans Wake*, 4th ed. (Baltimore, MD: Johns Hopkins University Press, 2016) and www.finwake.com/1024chapter8/1024finn8.htm.

of *Finnegans Wake* is doubtless overdetermined; the abundance of its textual references has been discussed by works such as Roland McHugh's *Annotations*, James Atherton's *The Books at the Wake*, as well as a host of philological and genetic studies.[10] Here I would like to explain the fundamental structure of the *Wake*, and some of its most important tropes, with reference to the works of two of the most crucial figures of the early 1920s Parisian literary scene: more briefly, Guillaume Apollinaire, the impresario of the avant-garde and the instigator of literary montage, and, at more length, Alfred Jarry, the notorious originator of a *philosophie de merde* and the object of renewed notoriety in 1921 and 1922. I explore these relations not to provide further interpretive principles or intimidating codes but rather to shed light on the *Wake*'s appeal to readers.

Montage was one of the dominant modes of the Parisian avant-garde of the early twentieth century. Bürger writes that "montage may be considered the fundamental principle of avant-gardiste art. The 'fitted' (*montierte*) work calls attention to the fact that it is made up of reality fragments; it breaks through the appearance (*Schein*) of totality."[11] Montage, thus understood, is the means through which the beautiful appearance of the traditional artwork is defied and art becomes integrated into the praxis of life outside of the academy and the museum. The striking new collages by the Synthetic Cubists of newspaper clippings, paint, texts, photographs, and found objects were inspirational to Apollinaire, who wrote admiringly of Picasso and originally intended to publish his 1918 collection *Calligrammes* under the title, "*Moi, aussi, je suis peintre,*" "I too am a painter." In "Zone," the opening poem in his 1913 collection *Alcools*, he announces a new poetics of everyday urban ephemera: "You read handbills catalogues advertisements that sing out loud and clear/ There is where poetry is this morning and for prose there are the newspapers."[12] He realizes this program in *Caligrammes* with a compositional method that relies on found textual and verbal materials of the city. "Lundi Rue Christine," "Monday Christine Street," collages fragments of

---

[10] James Atherton's, *The Books at the Wake: A Study of Literary Allusions in James Joyce's "Finnegans Wake"* (Carbondale: Southern Illinois University Press, 2009); I will refer to several works of genetic criticism but cite here *Genetic Joyce Studies* as the central journal: www.geneticjoycestudies.org.

[11] Bürger, *Theory of the Avant-Garde*, 72.

[12] Guillaume Apollinaire, *Alcools: Poems by Guillaume Apollinaire*, trans. Donald Revell (Middletown, CT: Wesleyan University Press, 1995), 3 (translation altered). "Tu lis les prospectus les catalogues les affiches qui chantent tout haut/Voilà la poésie ce matin et pour la prose il y a les journaux" (2).

conversations overheard in a café: "He says to me sir would you care to see what I can do in etchings and pictures/All I have is a little maid."[13]

In 1920, Joyce expressed urgent interest in Apollinaire's *Les Mamelles de Tirésias*, and he was surely also aware of *Calligrammes*, which was published in 1918 to great acclaim just after Apollinaire's death. Joyce had captured the cadences of urban speech from the beginning of his writing; Apollinaire's montage poems model the direct capture of that prose from the urban context and its release from overt authorial or narrative framing and syntactical ordering. Eugène Jolas records Joyce's declaration that *Finnegans Wake* was composed by many ordinary voices: "'Really, it is not I who am writing this crazy book,' he said in his whimsical way one evening. 'It is you, and you, and you, and that man over there, and that girl at the next table.'"[14] Jolas provides an example of Joyce's amused notation of a Swiss waitress's misprision, and remarks that Joyce "retained all such scraps of conversation."[15] If, as Harriet Shaw Weaver later reported, Joyce declared after finishing *Ulysses*: "I think I will write a history of the world," it is fitting that everyone tells that history (*JJ* 537). Collage, or montage (to retain Bürger's term), offers Joyce a means of intensifying his breakdown of the epic form by moving to an even more radical mode of inclusivity.[16]

The earliest passage Joyce wrote for *Finnegans Wake* models a new, indiscriminate acquisitiveness. Joyce wrote the Roderick O'Conor sketch in March 1923, and it forms the conclusion of II.3, the "novel's central chapter."[17] David Hayman remarks that the sketch, added to the manuscript of the *Wake* only in September 1938, remains remarkably unchanged: "'Roderick' appears today much as he did in 1923."[18] Alone, after his guests have departed, King Roderick swallows the dregs of their drinks: "he finalized by lowering by his woolly throat with the wonderful midnight thirst was on him, as keen as mustard, he could not tell what he

---

[13] Ibid., 55. "Il me dit monsieur voulez-vous voir ce que je peux faire d'eaux-fortes et de tableaux/Je n'ai qu'une petite bonne" (54).

[14] Eugene Jolas, Klaus H. Kiefer, and Rainer Rumold, *Eugene Jolas: Critical Writings, 1924–1951* (Evanston, IL: Northwestern University Press, 2009), 400.

[15] Ibid., 401.

[16] Apollinaire describes Picasso as transforming the epic mode in the manner of both infant tyrant and artistic innovator: "He is a newborn babe who rearranges the universe for his personal convenience and to facilitate understanding with his fellowmen. His cataloguing has an epic grandeur." Apollinaire, *Les Peintres Cubistes* (Paris: Éditions Figuière, 1913), 67.

[17] David Hayman, *The "Wake" in Transit* (Ithaca, NY: Cornell University Press, 1990), 39.

[18] David Hayman, "Male Maturity: Chapters II.3," in *How Joyce Wrote "Finnegans Wake": A Chapter by Chapter Genetic Guide*, ed. Luca Crispi and Sam Slote (Madison: University of Wisconsin Press, 2007), 295.

did ale, that bothered he was from head to tail, and, wishawishawish, leave it, what the Irish, boys, can do, if he didn't go, sliggymaglooral reemyround and suck up, sure enough, like a Trojan, in some particular cases with the assistance of his venerated tongue, whatever surplus rotgut, sorra much, was left by the lazy lousers of maltknights and beerchurls in the different bottoms of the various different replenquished drinking utensils left there behind them on the premisses" (*FW* 381.26–35). Joyce announced his writing of the passage in a letter to Sylvia Beach the following day, commenting: "*Il lupo perde il pelo ma non il vizio*, the Italians say. The wolf may lose his skin but not his vice or the leopard cannot change his spots" (*Letters I*, 202). This vice is Joyce's persistent interest in consumption, in characters who are pervaded by their environment, and in prose forms that capture that pervasion. Yet the *Wake* gives us a more extreme version of that condition: if Bloom moves through the verbal and physical matter of the city like a mackerel in the sea, Roderick indiscriminately fills himself with liquid. This too is a response to commerce: the castle of the (soon-to-be) last High King of Ireland, who will become a vassal of Henry II, is also the contemporary public house of HCE. Roderick's swallowing of the dregs of commercial beverages, "whether it was chateaubottled Guiness's or Phoenix brewery stout it was or John Jameson and Sons or Roob Coccola or, for the matter of that, O'Connell's famous old Dublin ale that he wanted like hell," bypasses the value of the goods (*FW* 382.03–06). Furthermore, this haphazardly gathered mess is not inert. In "Lestrygonians," Bloom imagines the possibilities of excessive consumption: "Dinner of thirty courses. Each dish harmless might mix inside. Idea for a poison mystery" (*U* 8:870–71). The alcoholic contents of the belly of King Roderick, "such as it was, fall and fall about," are subject to an uncontrollable mutation; if the *Wake* is a history, it is a "yeastyday" (*FW* 4.21).

Roderick mimics Joyce's own mode of consuming dregs, as Joyce gathers leftover scraps of *Ulysses* in a notebook, later known as "Scribbledehobble," for his new *Work in Progress*.[19] Hayman writes that "between the completion of *Ulysses* early in 1922 and the composition in March 1923 of the first passage for the gestating work, Joyce's preparations were largely exploratory and recuperative, a long and elaborate fishing expedition."[20] Additionally, studies by Hayman and other genetic scholars of Joyce's many notebooks of fragmentary "new" material for the *Wake* show that Roderick's intake also parallels Joyce's assemblage of fragments of

---

[19] See Hayman's description of "Scribbledehobble" in *The "Wake" in Transit*, 18–25.   [20] Ibid., 8.

works of high and low literature, which are "replenquished," both relinquished and replenished, in his text.[21]

It is crucial to note that the fermentational quality of Wakean prose distinguishes it from Apollinaire's montages. The *caligrammes* operate through elliptical phrases, which can be read in different combinations; "Lettre-Océan," for example, offers the reader fragments such as: "on the left bank in front of Iéna Bridge," "Long live the Republic," "I have seen thousands of keys," etc.[22] Joyce crafts sentences that maximize polysemy, both undoing and generating meaning through the combination of multiple and often contradictory fragments. The *Wake* thus resembles more closely the work of Jarry; I will argue here that this post-Symbolist adversary of both the conventions of art and the principles of bourgeois capitalism offered crucial strategies to Joyce.

Joyce and Jarry have an uncanny overlap of interests: Jarry points the way for Joyce to develop to the full his existing interests in allusion, scatology, materialism, and the identity of opposites. In the extraordinarily dense and fertile verbal texture of the *Wake*, as well as in its overall cyclical structure, Joyce realizes what Jarry theorizes and performs at powerfully emblematic moments. Attention to Joyce's references to Jarry in *Finnegans Wake*, as well as in his earliest notebooks, and comparison of the thematic content of the *Wake*'s key scenes and its densely allusive circular form to the thematics and structures of Jarry's work allows us to concretize our sense of the *Wake* as an avant-garde text. Understanding Joyce's relation to Jarry enables us to situate within a specific literary and historical moment aspects of the *Wake* that have been often seen as timeless: Joyce's use of as archetypal figures such as Christ and Caesar and his deployment of the medieval *coincidentia oppositorum* and Viconian cycles.[23] Joyce's relation to Jarry allows us to understand his use of these tropes in the *Wake* as part of a project to undermine the bourgeois process of valuation. Additionally, it reveals linguistic features often thought to be projected upon the *Wake* by poststructuralist theory – such as the free play of the signifier – to be part of that project. Jarry helps Joyce to develop in the *Wake* his exploration of

---

[21] See *The Finnegans Wake Notebooks at Buffalo*, ed. Vincent Deane, Daniel Ferrer, and Geert Lernout (Turnhout, Belgium: Brepols Publishers, 2001).

[22] I discuss Joyce's radio montage passage in *Finnegans Wake* in relation to Apollinaire's famous *caligramme* "Ocean Lettre" in "*Finnegans Wake*'s Radio Montage: Man-Made Static, Collective Reading and the Avant-Garde," *James Joyce Quarterly* 52.2 (special issue on "Joycean Avant-Gardes," ed. Catherine Flynn and Richard Brown) (Winter 2015), 287–306.

[23] It is clear that Joyce associates the names Giordano Bruno, Nicholas of Cusa, and Giambattista Vico with these features in the *Wake* and, especially in the case of Vico, draws upon their texts; however, I will argue that his particular deployment of them is inspired by Jarry.

intimate and even obscene bodily processes as a counter to the objectifications of capitalist exchange and transaction; as Joyce does so, he produces a
new aesthetics of readerly interaction, a riotous response.

I'm Enormously Full of That Foreigner

Fullness, as we will see, is of central importance in Jarry's work and in
Joyce's reception of him: a personal, corporeal fullness, a textual fullness,
and a metaphysical fullness. Joyce mentions Jarry by name in a passage in
III.2:

> He's the sneaking likeness of us, faith, me altar's ego in miniature and every
> Auxonian aimer's ace as nasal a Romeo as I am, for ever cracking quips on
> himself, that merry, the jeenjakes [. . .] He has novel ideas I know and he's a
> jarry queer fish betimes, I grant you, and cantanberous, the poisoner of his
> word, but lice and all and semicoloured stainedglasses, I'm enormously full
> of that foreigner, I'll say I am! (*FW* 463.6–15).

As Jean-Michel Rabaté observes of the passage, in these lines "we hear
Joyce speaking in the voice of Shaun just then praising in a mocking
manner his estranged brother, the writer, who appears closer to Jarry than
to Joyce's brother Stanislaus. Like Jarry, this foreigner did in fact poison
himself with absinthe and other drinks, was rather cantankerous and
queer, but had 'novel ideas' all the time!"[24] In addition to these references,
the passage also evokes Jarry's tiny frame and the peculiar nasal, monotonous vocal delivery he affected, although the phrase "as nasal a Romeo as
I am" also suggests Joyce's recognition of Jarry as a writer of equal stature,
"as noble a Roman as I am."[25] Jarry's eccentric lifestyle is suggested here,
including his survival on a diet of fish he caught himself, his odd humor,
and his related preoccupation with scatology, "for ever cracking quips on
himself, that merry, the jeenjakes." A page earlier, Jarry's release from the
army is suggested as Juan describes his twin's return, dressed in "mufti," in
terms that condense Jarry's 1901 novel *Le Surmâle, The Supermale*, which

[24] Jean-Michel Rabaté, "Joyce and Jarry 'Joyeux,'" *Papers on Joyce* 10/11 (2004–2005), 187–97, at
193. Rabaté points to the shared "joyicity" of their names: the homonym *je ris* would not have been
missed by the foreigner in Paris who emphasized the *joie* in Joyce. Joyce, Rabaté argues, expresses
fascination with Jarry's "meteoric trajectory": "You rejoice me! Faith, I'm proud of you, french
davit!" (464.36); Ibid., 193.

[25] Another reference to Jarry's stylized manner of speaking is identified by William Anastasi in the
phrase "me innerman monophone," a few lines earlier in the long passage (*FW* 462.15–16).
William Anastasi's series *me innerman monophone*, a commentary on the presence Jarry in the
work of James Joyce, is featured in William Anastasi, *Pataphysical Society: Jarry, Joyce, Duchamp, and
Cage*, ed. Aaron Levy and Jean-Michel Rabaté (Philadelphia: Slought Books, 2005).

features a race in which the protagonist invisibly overtakes a five-person cycle and a high-speed train: "th'athlate! [...] not on one foot either or on two feet aether but on quinquisecular cycles after his French evolution and a blindfold passage by the 4.32" (*FW* 462.28–35).[26]

Joyce declares that he is "enormously full of that foreigner," who is himself "borrowing all before him" (*FW* 463.25). This fullness is *énorme* in two senses: it is huge in extent, and it deliberately flouts normativity. Juan, the lascivious alter ego of Shaun, emphasizes this disgusting association in the next page: "Mark my use of you, cog! Take notice how I yemploy, crib! Be ware as you, I foil, coppy! It's a pity he can't see it for I'm terribly nice about him" (*FW* 464.03–06).[27] Juan or Joyce's declaration calls attention to a larger arc of influence: this action of copying a copier with coprophiliac tendencies is evident in a passage Joyce added to *Ulysses* after his arrival in Paris. The "Calypso" scene in which Bloom reads in the privy bears striking similarities to a scene in Jarry's posthumously published novel, *Gestes et opinions du Docteur Faustroll, pataphysicien: roman néo-scientifique*, in which a bishop reads while defecating in an outhouse. Bishop Mendacious reads the real-life novelist Pierre Loti, "a mass-market author [who was] something of a *bête noire* for Jarry."[28] This borrowing is signaled in "Circe" when Bloom's aspirations to produce a little something to sell are met with Philip Beaufoy's righteous anger: "A plagiarist. A soapy sneak masquerading as a *littérateur*. It's perfectly obvious that with the most

---

[26] This reference to *Le Sûrmale* finds a greater relevance to II.2 though association with Jarry's 1903 "*La Passion considérée comme course de côte*," "The Passion of Christ Considered as an Uphill Bicycle Race": in the chapter, Joyce has Jaun pass through the Stations of the Cross by rolling downriver in a barrel; see William York Tindall, *A Reader's Guide to Finnegans Wake* (New York: Farrar, Strauss, and Giroux, 1967), 237–39. Furthermore, "aether" is a crucial term in Jarry's pataphysics: Aethernity, or "Éthernité" is the title of Book VIII of Jarry's *Exploits and Opinions of Doctor Faustroll, Pataphysician in Collected Works of Alfred Jarry II: Three Early Novels* (London: Atlas, 2006).

[27] Tributes to Jarry also appear in other places in the *Wake*: Rabaté points to the footnote written by Issy, the psychotic daughter of the family: "(1) Gosem pher, gezumpher, greeze a jarry grim felon! Good bloke him!" (*FW* 278 F 1), associating this joy with a dangerous *jouissance*.

[28] Ben Fisher, *The Pataphysicians Library: An Exploration of Alfred Jarry's Livres Pairs* (Liverpool: Liverpool University Press, 2000), 204. Edmund Gosse's contemporaneous characterization of Loti's writing is useful in illustrating the opposition of Loti's style to Jarry's: "At his best Pierre Loti was unquestionably the finest descriptive writer of the day. In the delicate exactitude with which he reproduced the impression given to his own alert nerves by unfamiliar forms, colours, sounds and perfumes, he was without a rival. But he was not satisfied with this exterior charm; he desired to blend with it a moral sensibility of the extremest refinement, at once sensual and ethereal. Many of his best books are long sobs of remorseful memory, so personal, so intimate, that an English reader is amazed to find such depth of feeling compatible with the power of minutely and publicly recording what is felt." Edmund Gosse, "Pierre Loti," *Encyclopædia Britannica Eleventh Edition* (New York: Encyclopaedia Britannica, 1910).

inherent baseness he has cribbed some of my bestselling copy, really gorgeous stuff, a perfect gem, the love passages in which are beneath suspicion" (*U* 15.822–25).[29] While Bloom "envies kindly" Beaufoy's financial success with "Matcham's Masterstroke," Jarry is virulent in his attack on Loti, collapsing the sentimental vagueness of Loti's story "Tante Claire nous quitte" in a parody entitled, punningly, "Mort de Latente Obscure," in which the aunt's refined, ethereal death is likened to the passage of a turd. Many of the details of the "Calypso" passage are to be found in Jarry's text, beginning with Bloom's nimble entry into the outhouse, "he jumped nimbly into the designated pit [...] victualled with a thousand varied matters suitable to encourage a crap."[30] Joyce intermingles in one sentence Bloom's reading and defecation: he "read, restraining himself, the first column and, yielding but resisting, began the second" (*U* 4:506–07); Jarry punctuates the bishop's bowel movement with quotations from Loti's text: "'heuh heuh ... *Bitter tears ... the doctor says that she will not last* [pass] *the night* ... Off with you, frog! Down into the shades below. – *Her life is drawing to a close* [...] LATENT OBSCURE HAS LEFT US!!! thanks be to God,' exclaimed the bishop, getting up."[31]

Whether the scene in "Calypso" signals Joyce's cultural elitism has been a matter of dispute. While Jarry is certainly guilty of the aggression of which some critics have accused Joyce, Jarry models for Joyce an identification of text and turd, not only thematically but also in the passage of foreign matter through the body of the text. Joyce's borrowing from Jarry reiterates a mode of textual reworking in which literature becomes matter to be processed, matter that becomes *énorme*, invested with its own life. This mode reaches full realization in *Finnegans Wake*. If Bloom, like Jarry's bishop, uses the short story as toilet paper, it is not till the *Wake* that the used pages speak back from the latrine as they do in Jarry's novel: "'*We rise and descend like ghosts*,' panted the leaves in their successive service."[32]

[29] Beaufoy is a pseudonym of real-life Philip Bergson, the author of a *Tit-Bits* piece according to David Pierce in John Simpson, "Philip Beaufoy and the Philosopher's Tone," *James Joyce Online Notes*, www.jjon.org/jioyce-s-people/beaufoy.

[30] 77, 78; "Il sauta allégrement dans le puits désigné." *Œuvres Complètes I*, ed. Michel Arrivé (Paris: Bibliotheque de la Pléiade, 1972), 707; "il entra dans son cabinet, avitaillé de mille sortes de choses propres à exciter à cagar" (706).

[31] 79, 80; "hen... hen ... *Larmes amères ... le médecin déclare qu'elle ne passera pas la nuit* ... T'en iras-tu, grenouille! dans les ténèbres inférieures? – *Elle va finir sa vie* [...] LATENTE OBSCURE NOUS A QUITTÉS!!! Merci, mon Dieu, exclama l'évêque en se levant" (*Œuvres Complètes*, 707–08).

[32] *Faustroll*, 80; "*Nous montons et descendons comme des fantômes*, haletèrent les feuilles en leur service successif" (*Œuvres Complètes*, 708).

We will examine active waste in the representation of another act of defecation in the *Wake's* densest chapter, II.3.

Joyce's encounter with Jarry was overdetermined. At the beginning of the 1920s, Jarry was, like Joyce's Shem the penman, "an odious and still today insufficiently malestimated notesnatcher" (*FW* 125.21–22). Roger Shattuck notes that Jarry was raised from relative obscurity during the Dadaist demonstrations of 1921 and 1922 when Charles Chassé "published a book violently contesting Jarry's authorship of *Ubu roi* in favor of one of the surviving Morin brothers, an artillery officer. Chassé as much as accused Jarry of plagiarism and, to boot, challenged the literary merit of the supposedly purloined text. The mixed outburst of protest and welcome which greeted this attack resounded through every literary quarter."[33] Shattuck's account leaves out the particular form of this case of plagiarism: Jarry may have staged, in addition to his own, the outrageous and obscene plays penned by his schoolboy friends at the Rennes lycée in their tradition of mocking their infamously inept and extraordinarily rotund physics teacher, "Père" Félix-Frédéric Hébert.[34] Jarry had staged *Ubu roi* to massive impact in 1907; Chassé's accusations cast it as the unoriginal and insignificant work of *potaches*, filthy-minded schoolboys. In doing so, however, Chassé overlooks the anti-authoritarian power of resolutely juvenile and joyful obscenity, a mode that, as we will see, Joyce embraces in his earliest ideas for the *Wake*.

The debate sparked by Chassé's accusations led to the republication of *Ubu roi* and *Faustroll*. Joyce, however, already knew of Jarry's work. As William Anastasi observes, "Joyce had access to Adrienne Monnier's library, which had all of the published and much of the unpublished Jarry."[35] Furthermore, Joyce was well acquainted through Les Amis des Livres with Léon-Paul Fargue, who had become Jarry's friend in 1892 at the Lycée Henri IV in Paris and was, by his own account, his lover.[36] Fargue was, as a schoolboy, "already familiar with the art and writing of his day, and he even had some literary connections. It may have been he who introduced Jarry to the work of the new generation of writers, the

---

[33] Roger Shattuck, *The Banquet Years:* 223.
[34] See Alastair Brotchie, *Alfred Jarry: A Pataphysical Life* (Cambridge, MA: MIT Press, 2011) and Keith Beaumont, *Alfred Jarry: A Critical and Biographical Study* (New York: St. Martin's, 1984).
[35] William Anastasi and Michael Seidel, "Jarry in Joyce: A Conversation," *Joyce Studies Annual* 6 (1995), 39–58, at 46.
[36] Jill Fell, *Alfred Jarry* (London: Reaktion, 2010), 29.

Symbolists, although a number of his other friends shared this enthusiasm."[37] Fargue's pet name, Ablou, is intertwined with Haldern, "a Breton form of Alfred" in the title of Jarry's 1895 play about murderous sexual fate, *Haldernablou*, showing "the beast doubly coupled."[38] Brilliant and garrulous, Fargue was an excellent explicator of Jarry's work; Fell notes that he "late in life, could still quote large chunks of *Ubu roi* by heart."[39]

Joyce also encountered Jarry through an Irish source. In 1906, W. B. Yeats had attended the second of the two performances of *Ubu roi*, at the opening of which the protagonist advanced and declaimed the distorted expletive "*Merdre!* causing the audience to erupt into two opposing factions."[40] In his 1922 memoir, *The Trembling of the Veil*, Yeats narrates this infamous gesture of artistic provocation that defied theatrical and public propriety, coining an extraordinarily powerful phrase to describe it:

> The players are supposed to be dolls, toys, marionettes, and now they are all hopping like wooden frogs, and I can see for myself that the chief personage, who is some kind of King, carries for sceptre a brush of the kind that we use to clean a closet [i.e. a toilet]. Feeling bound to support the most spirited party, we have shouted for the play, but that night at the Hôtel Corneille I am very sad, for comedy, objectivity, has displayed its growing power once more. I say, "After Stephane Mallarmé, after Paul Verlaine, after Gustave Moreau, after Puvis de Chavannes, after our own verse, after all our subtle colour and nervous rhythm, after the faint mixed tints of Conder, what more is possible? After us the Savage God."[41]

Ubu's pronouncement attacks a revered topos of French patriotism, one embedded in its military and literary history. *Merdre!* deforms the famous declaration of *Merde!* by Napoleon's General Cambronne on receiving the order to retreat in the battle of Waterloo. What became known as "le mot de Cambronne" was understood as a glorious and patriotic victory-in-defeat, which Victor Hugo celebrates in *Les Misérables* (1862): "To thunder forth such a reply at the lightning-flash that kills you is to conquer! [. . .] to be Irony itself in the tomb, to act so as to stand upright though fallen, to drown in two syllables the European coalition, to offer kings privies which the Cæsars once knew, to make the lowest of words the most lofty by entwining with it the glory of France, insolently to end

[37] Brotchie, *Pataphysical Life*, 40.
[38] Maurice Marc LaBelle, *Alfred Jarry: Nihilism and the Theater of the Absurd* (New York: New York University Press, 1980), 20.
[39] Fell, *Alfred Jarry*, 59.   [40] *Œuvres Complètes*, 355.
[41] W. B. Yeats, *The Collected Works of W.B. Yeats Vol. III: Autobiographies*, ed. William H. O'Donnell and Douglas N. Archibald (London: Touchstone, 1999), 266.

Waterloo with Mardigras, to finish Leonidas with Rabelais, to set the crown on this victory by a word impossible to speak, to lose the field and preserve history, to have the laugh on your side after such a carnage, – this is immense!"[42] Having thus situated Cambronne's verbal feat, Hugo celebrates this paradoxical triumph over physical reality through the creative use of base expression, "Borne down by numbers, by superior force, by brute matter, he finds in his soul an expression: *'Excrément!'* We repeat it, – to use that word, to do thus, to invent such an expression, is to be the conqueror!" Ubu's *Merdre!* lacks every element of this noble irony; holding a toilet brush, he declares not a triumph over base matter but a slurred plunge into it. Jarry's Ubu is, as Yeats observes, in shocking contrast to recent poetic practice. Yeats sees in Jarry's play an offensively unmitigated – and distastefully comic – materiality that routs Symbolist poetry, understood as invested in subtle tonalities and complex meanings beyond the physical. No longer transmuting filth into worth but celebrating filth itself, Jarry opposes Baudelaire's self-designation as a "parfait chimiste" that makes gold out of mud in the last lines of one of his unfinished projects for an epilogue to the 1861 edition of *Les Fleurs du Mal:* "Tu m'as donné ta boue et j'en ai fait de l'or."[43] If Baudelaire resisted the valuations of the Second Empire, Jarry resists valuation entirely. Yeats's phrase "Savage God" indeed casts Ubu as a violent idol of collapsed values.

In the three plays of the *Ubu* cycle, Ubu stands for not for cultivation but for undifferentiating acquisition. Charles Grivel reads Ubu's distended gut as signaling this: "Ubu is abdominal . . . he is and he has his stomach."[44] As Elizabeth Menon points out, Jarry's drawings of Ubu resemble caricatures of Louis-Philippe from the 1930s.[45] In a hyperbolic parody of bourgeois materialism, when Ubu becomes king, in *Ubu roi*, he collects taxes from all, including noblemen, and then progresses to extracting bodily fluids. His favorite utensil, apart from "la machine à décerveler," the debrainer, is an apparatus for extracting excrement, named again with the characteristic distortion, "un pompe à merdre." Accumulating both cerebral and excremental matter, Ubu parodies the action of *prendre profit.*

---

[42] Victor Hugo, *Les Misérables*, trans. Isabel F. Hapgood (New York: Crowell & Co., 1887), 38a.

[43] Baudelaire, *Œuvres Complètes* I, 292. Emily Cohen notes that Baudelaire hates Belgium because "All that is left of Toilette is the toilet." Emily Cohen, "Mud into Gold: Baudelaire and the Alchemy of Public Hygiene," *Romantic Review* 87.2 (March 1996), 239–256, at 239.

[44] Charles Grivel, "Les representations jarryesque," *Revue de Sciences Humaines* LXXIIIV/203, 5–28, at 11.

[45] Elizabeth K. Menon, "Potty-Talk in Parisian Plays: Henry Somm's *La Berline de l'émigré* and Alfred Jarry's *Ubu roi*," *Art Journal* 52.3 (Autumn, 1993), 59–64.

This collapse of money and body is expressed in the combination of the words *finance* and *physical* in Ubu's declaration, used by Jarry as one of the "Prolegomena" for his obscure apocalyptic drama *César-Antechrist* (1895), "When I have taken all the Phynance, I will kill everyone in the world and go away."[46] Ubu's further escalation of greed is articulated in the second of the Ubu plays, *Ubu cocu*, in the description of him as a "barrel that rolls"; he describes himself as the "isomorph" of the "barrel's hyperphysical body."[47]

Inseparable from Ubu's indiscriminate acquisitiveness is a disruptive polysemy. Despite Ubu's base materiality, Jarry was deeply influenced by Symbolism. Beaumont points to the Symbolist works in the fictional Dr Faustroll's library and observes, "Jarry's encounter with Symbolism had a determining influence both upon his thought and upon his style in prose as well as in verse – the idiosyncratic syntax and slightly precious vocabulary of Mallarmé tempering a natural ebullience and verbal inventiveness nourished on Rabelais."[48] Furthermore, the Symbolist deployment of language to suggest a multiplicity of meanings, especially by Mallarmé, was particularly important for Jarry. Yet, predictably, as Beaumont points out, "For all his numerous pronouncements on the subject, his own conception of 'Beauty' was clearly radically different from theirs. Nor did he share the widespread mystical belief that behind the phenomena of the visible world there lay some hidden 'meaning' or 'correspondence' with an ideal world, or some mysterious 'essence', which it was the task of poetry to reveal. It is this, ultimately, which causes him to part company with Mallarmé."[49] This rejection of essence and of transcendentals is broadcast with *Ubu roi*'s scandalously unbeautiful Rabelaisean opening.

While Mallarmé has been cited as an influence for Joyce, Jarry's material disruption of language in the service of an obscene attack on social structures and hierarchies provides a robust source of inspiration for the *Wake*.[50] Jarry, as Beaumont notes, develops the Symbolist practice of

---

[46] *Caesar-Antichrist* in *Collected Works of Alfred Jarry I: Adventures in Pataphysics*, trans. Paul Edwards and Antony Melville. Ed. Alastair Brotchie and Paul Edwards (London: Atlas, 2001), 104. "Quand j'aurai pris toute la Phynance, je tuerai tout le monde et je m'en irai."

[47] Jarry, *The Ubu Plays: Ubu Rex, Ubu Cuckolded, Ubu Enchained*, trans. Cyril Connelly and Simon Watson Taylor (New York: Grove, 1968), 87, 88.

[48] Beaumont, *Alfred Jarry*, 56. Jarry perhaps suggests a route for Joyce to Rabelais. In 1927, Joyce reported that he had only read Sainéan's book on Rabelais' vocabulary. See Jacob Korg, "Polyglotism in Rabelais and Finnegans Wake," *Journal of Modern Literature* 26.1 (Fall 2002), 58–65.

[49] Beaumont, *Alfred Jarry*, 82.

[50] David Hayman, in *Joyce et Mallarmé: stylistic de la suggestion* (Paris: Lettres Modernes, 1956), traces Joyce's development of "la conception mallarméenne de la suggestion" (12). Hayman argues that this influence leads Joyce to a depersonalized representation of the universe: "L'auteur doit

suggestive allusion to what sounds to a reader of Joyce to be a Wakean level: "This concept [of suggestive allusion], pushed to its logical extreme, gives rise to an element of indeterminacy: the meaning attributed to and the response evoked by, a poem or even a particular word may differ with each individual reader. Implicit in this ideal of suggestion is therefore the possibility of a *deliberate* ambiguity, or 'polysemy.'"[51] Beaumont points to Jarry's own declaration of his intention to "create in the highway of sentences a crossroads of all the words."[52] The declaration is found in the preface to *Les Minutes de sable mémorial*, a title emblematic of this project in offering multiple permutations of meaning.[53]

This indeterminacy is part of Jarry's philosophy of pataphysics, which he describes, fittingly, in a range of contradictory ways. It is: "the science of the particular"; "of the laws governing exceptions"; it describes "a universe which can be seen, and which perhaps should be seen, in the place of the traditional one"; it is "the science of imaginary solutions which symbolically attributes to the lineaments of objects the properties described by their virtuality."[54] Both Gilles Deleuze and Jean Baudrillard link Jarry's pataphysics to a metaphysical fullness exemplified by Ubu's hyperphysical body. Deleuze understands pataphysics as an instance of a metaphysics beyond metaphysics; Père Ubu's "fat being" defies the nothingness that constitutes being as understood by Heidegger: "what defines the loss of Being is the forgetting of forgetting, the withdrawal of withdrawal, whereas withdrawal and forgetting are the manner by which Being shows itself or is *able* to show itself. [. . .] Thus, it is the culmination of metaphysics in technology that makes possible the overcoming of metaphysics, i.e. pataphysics."[55] In contrast to the normal unfolding of particular being through its difference from other beings and its difference from its own non-being,

---

disparaître, cédant la place à la voix des instincts et des émotions les plus impersonnelles – se transformant en microcosme, reproduction fidèle de l'univers. Ainsi, toute sa recherche expérimentale dans *Dedalus*, dans *Ulysse* et dans *Finnegans Wake* tendait vers un même but" (67); "The author must disappear, giving way to the voice of the most impersonal instincts and emotions – transforming into a microcosm, a faithful reproduction of the universe. Thus, all his experimental research in *Stephen Dedalus*, in *Ulysses* and in *Finnegans Wake* tended towards the same goal" (my translation).

[51] Beaumont, *Alfred Jarry*, 68. Beaumont's italics.

[52] Qtd. in Beaumont, *Alfred Jarry*, 68. "Suggérer au lieu de dire, faire dans la route des phrases un carrefour de tous les mots." *Les Minutes de sable mémorial*, in *Œuvres Complètes I*, 171.

[53] Beaumont reckons eighteen different permutations of the semantic possibilities of *minutes*, *sable*, and *mémorial* (68).

[54] *Faustroll*, 145–46.

[55] Gilles Deleuze, "An Unrecognized Precursor to Heidegger: Alfred Jarry," *Essays Critical and Clinical*, trans. Daniel W. Smith and Michael A. Greco (Minneapolis: University of Minnesota Press, 1997), 93.

Ubu with his mechanisms of appropriation is all-encapsulating. There is nothing that Ubu is not.[56]

With Ubu's hyperphysicality Jarry reimagines the *coincidentia oppositorum* familiar to Joyce from Giordano Bruno and Nicholas of Cusa. The irreverent and subversive linguistic and literary deployment of the unity of contraries in Jarry's Ubu trilogy and other texts makes them compelling models for *Finnegans Wake*. As J. Mitchell Morse observes, "Joyce uses Nicholas of Cusa's ideas, as he does Giordano Bruno's and Giambattista Vico's, without necessarily accepting them. What interests him is not the coincidence but the coinci*dance* of contraries, in which they weave infinitely varied patterns without losing their contrariety, though in the whirl they may often be indiscernible."[57] This dance is readily apparent in Jarry's *César-Antechrist*, where the poles of Ubu's cycle of rise and fall are superimposed in the play's strange collapsed apocalypse, as God the Father says of the Antichrist in the final act, "this is my son the beloved, in whom I am well pleased."[58] This eschatological undoing of oppositions is accompanied by a semiotic disturbance: the "baton-a-physique" or "physick-stick," which Ubu carried in *Ubu roi*, becomes animated and, "turning on its extremities," physically demonstrates the coincidence of opposite poles.[59] Looking on are signs rather than characters in any psychological sense: "The Templar," identified with the positive cross on his chest, and "Fess," which in the language of heraldry signifies recumbence and accordingly is a minus sign. Their conversation celebrates the undoing of these oppositions: "in you I look upon my reflection."

This odd exchange gives a sense of the densely allusive character of *César-Antechrist*, which combines religious imagery, heraldry, scientific jargon, mathematical notation, and philosophical exchange as well as allusions to an array of literary texts. The strange work also thematizes its own teeming verbal texture in ways that anticipate *Finnegans Wake*. As the Templar cries out, "Uprooted phallus do not leap about so," Jarry alludes to Lautréamont's *Les Chants de Maldoror*, "in which a hair left by God in a brothel leaps noisily about and threatens to betray His patronage of this establishment."[60] The "uprooted phallus" announces an emphatically material and unstable language. The Templar tells Fess he is the

---

[56] Baudrillard has a perversely opposite reading: "Pataphysics: philosophy of the gaseous state. [. . . Ubu] convinced everyone of nothingness and constipation." Jean Baudrillard, "Pataphysics," trans. Drew Burk, 1000 Days of Theory, www.ctheory.net/articles.aspz?id=569.

[57] J. Mitchell Morse, "Burrus, Caseous, and Nicholas of Cusa," *Modern Language Notes* 75.4 (April 1960), 326–34, 332–33.

[58] *Collected Works I*, 192.   [59] Ibid., 140.   [60] Ibid., 53.

"burgeoning emblem of germination, (and yet if that were so you would be damned, bourgeois), but of spontaneous germination, vibrio and volvox" – two micro-organisms that reproduce by fission and in doing so defy the ordered accumulation and inherited wealth of bourgeois tradition.[61]

In *Faustroll*, Jarry names this creative fission using the language of Lucretian materialism: "the unforeseen beast Clinamen" is a spinning painting machine, which "swayed and turned in infinitely varied directions and followed its own whims" and "ejaculated onto the walls of its universe."[62] This random production figures Jarry's textual process in which fragmentary and opposing allusions intersect, producing what Linda Klieger Stillmann calls the "exceptional, the unexpected, [...] the easily ignored [and] the arbitrary.[63] Clinamen is also evident in Ubu's simpler sonic deformations. In *Ubu roi*, the captain takes Ubu away in chains while issuing the order: "Amenez le grand foc, prenez un ris aux huniers," "Haul down the main job, take a reef in the topsails." Ubu replies "Ceci n'est pas mal, c'est même bon! Entendez-vous, monsieur l'Équipage? amenez le grand coq et allez faire un tour dans les pruniers," "That's a good one. That's not bad at all. Did you hear that, Mister Crew? Boil down the main rib; roast beef and oxtails!" which can be more literally translated as "Take the big cock and make a tour in the plum trees."[64] The linguistic swerve finds its most emblematic exemplification in "Merdre!" which displays the ease with which conventions and ideals are shattered, as language is deformed through obscenity and mispronunciation.

No Dung on the Road?

In *Finnegans Wake*, Joyce brings Jarry's pataphysical aesthetics to a new level of intensity, staging collapsing cycles of power through heterogeneous, deformative, and superimposed collage.[65] The *Wake* is all swerve. Joyce mobilizes dynamic assemblages that host the identity of contraries

---

[61] Ibid., 55.

[62] *Faustroll* in *Collected Works of Alfred Jarry II: Three Early Novels*, trans. Alexis Lykiard, Simon Watson Taylor and Paul Edwards, ed. Alastair Brotchie and Paul Edwards (London: Atlas, 2006), 195.

[63] Linda Klieger Stillmann, "Modern Narrative Techniques: Jarry, the Pre-Text," *SubStance* 11.36 (1982), 72–81, at 78.

[64] *Œuvres Complètes I*, 397; *The Ubu Plays*, 72.

[65] The contemporary avant-garde writer Steve McCaffery proposes a subtly contradictory poetics based on Jarry's clinamen: "Envisioned will be a materialist poetics formed around the mobility of the single grapheme in partly – or entirely – aleatoric configurations. It will be a poetics that *deliberately* introduces error into linguistic systems of constraint to indicate the interplay of chance and necessity." He points to the poets Raymond Roussell and Jean-Pierre Brisset as exemplary

and undo every kind of authority.[66] This deformative generativity is dependent on montage and allusion to undo the unit of the word. As Steve McCaffery notes when commenting on Jarry, clinamen is a product of citation: it "inheres implicitly in Derrida's notion of iterability and the *force de rupture* virtual in any sign."[67] Iteration is "basic to any event of citation, for any sign when placed between quotation marks 'can break with every given context, engendering an infinity of new contexts in a manner which is absolutely illimitable.'"[68]

Joyce's notes show that he was thinking about Jarry at the time he wrote the very first sketches for the *Wake*. In the VI.B.3 notebook, which Danis Rose dates between March and July of 1923,[69] Joyce makes reference to Jarry in the middle of a long set of notes based on *Ireland: Its Saints and Scholars*: "(a) round stuff/ (merde) (b) uttered what follows / (c) Was habe ich / Ihnen getan? / (M.F) (d) oneilles/ merdre (Ubu Roi)/ (e) Quiet person/ surprised by savage/ rudeness answers (//)."[70] The editors note: "Two words taken from Jarry's *Ubu Roi*. 'Oneilles' is used a number of times (act 3, sc iv, v, vii, viii; act 4, sc. Vii; act 5, sc. I) as a comic distortion of *oreilles* (ears). The play opens famously with the exclamation 'Merdre!' a distortion of *merde* (shit) – from Père Ubu. Possibly connected with (a). The crossing through 'oneilles' is probably the accidental result of an interlinear stroke following the last unit."[71]

The previous page, right after a sudden a reference to Lewis Carroll, "Curioser/Mathematics Dodgson,"[72] follows an anecdote Joyce dictated to Nora on 14 March 1923: Saint Kevin goes to an island on a lake on which he builds a hut, inside of which he scoops a hole which he fills with water from the lake. He then sits in this pond and "Meditates with burning zeal on the sacrament of baptism or regeneration by water."[73] We might

---

practitioners of such a poetics. Steve McCaffery, *Prior to Meaning: The Protosemantic and Poetics* (Evanston, IL: Northwestern University Press, 2001), 25–26.

[66] We might surmise here that Jarry's clinamen is closer than Joyce's text to Lewis Carroll's portmanteaux; if the English nonsense tradition seems relevant to but at a remove from the *Wake*, we might think of Jarry as the intermediary link. Jarry was indeed familiar with Carroll and attempted to write a novel called *Navigations dans le miroir*, which Beaumont observes is "obviously inspired" by Lewis Carroll's *Through the Looking Glass* (85). Beaumont also claims Jarry was familiar with the writing of Edward Lear, as evidenced in his characters' journey around Paris by sea in a sieve in *Faustroll*, a reference to Lear's Jumblies (183).

[67] McCaffery, *Prior to Meaning*, 19.   [68] Derrida quoted in Ibid.

[69] Danis Rose, *The Textual Diaries of James Joyce* (Dublin: Lilliput Press, 1995), 25.

[70] VI.B.3.046. *The Finnegans Wake Notebooks at Buffalo* VI.B.3, 48. The last sentence on that page might read "Quiet person surprised by Jarry's rudeness answers," as the initial letter lacks the emphatic curves of the other iterations of initial S, although in Yeats's powerful phrase, Jarry's Ubu is indeed a Savage.

[71] Ibid.   [72] VI.B.3.045 (b) 47.   [73] VI.B.3.045 (a) 47.

surmise that the monastic, hermetic life described by *Ireland: Its Saints and Scholars*, with its emphasis on the three "virtues of obedience, poverty, and chastity" evokes, by a kind of counterimage, Ubu's life of vice: his disobedience, greed, and talk of buggery. More concretely, Kevin's immersion in a set of concentric circular containers evokes the polar opposite of this labor of self-purification: Ubu's refuge in the watercloset in *Ubu cocu*, where he communes with Conscience and intensifies his own avarice in what might be thought of as a regeneration through excremental immersion. This citational swerve leads to Joyce's noting of two of the most important verbal distortions of *Ubu roi*: *merdre* and *oneilles*. These terms are crucial models for the workings of *Finnegans Wake* in exemplifying a verbal swerve associated with deviant scatology and distorted aural experience.

That Jarry was in Joyce's mind offers an explanation of Joyce's recording, in the same notebook, a scatological scenario that is named twenty-six times in the *Wake* and forms the center of its densest chapter, a story called by critics: "How Buckley Shot the Russian General."[74] The story is based on an anecdote by John Joyce. Ellmann records Joyce's own rendering of it in Switzerland in 1915:

> Buckley, he explained, was an Irish soldier in the Crimean War who drew a bead on a Russian general, but when he observed his splendid epaulettes and decorations, he could not bring himself to shoot. After a moment, alive to his duty, he raised his rifle again, but just then the general let down his pants to defecate. The sight of his enemy in so helpless and human a plight was too much for Buckley, who again lowered his gun. But when the general prepared to finish the operation with a piece of grassy turf, Buckley lost all respect for him and fired. (*JJ* 398)

Joyce only began to write this scene in 1937. In the 1923 notebook, however, he is already imagining it as a reciprocal, circular scenario: "So Buckley shot the Russian General but who shot B_."[75] Joyce associates this moment of scatological overthrow with *merdre*'s original target, "le mot de Cambronne," which appears in distorted forms, "cabronne" and "combrune" (*FW* 352.21 and 352.22). In the previous notebook, which Rose dates from "late Oct 1922-Jan 1923" Joyce made the note: "mere de Dieu / – – Cambronne."[76] The notebook's editors observe: "i.e. 'mère de Dieu / 'Merde!' de Cambronne.' In French, *mère de* (mother of) and *merde*

[74] Clive Hart, *Structure and Motif in "Finnegans Wake"* (Evanston, IL: Northwestern University Press, 1962), 218.
[75] VI.B.3.082.   [76] Rose, *Textual Diaries*, 25.

(shit) sound the same."[77] Joyce assembles, thus, within a space of a few months, an iconic scenario and an iconic expletive with which to echo Jarry's Ubu.

Immediately after his telegraphic question about Buckley and the Russian General, Joyce pens a little rhyme, which we can see as, among other things, announcing a scatological textuality. Leaving the rest of the page blank, he writes: "The turd swiftsure/Flew down the sewer/& the Sluicehounds/Flushfleshed after."[78] The poem replaces human characters with material substances, switching themes from the overthrow of authority to a literal fall and pursuit. If this interest in turds seems adolescent, we can understand this schoolboy scatology in terms of Jarry's *potache* productions: the mobilization of excremental slapstick for anti-authoritarian ends. As Jarry modeled for Joyce an identification of turd and text, this image of fascinated pursuit might be interpreted as an allegory of a new kind of reading. When Joyce borrowed Jarry's jakes scene in "Calypso," he repeated the triad of a human figure, a reworked text, and processed matter; this scene is situated within the sewage system, in which readers are multiple, anonymous, and shifting. The "Sluicehounds" dynamic embodiment is suggested by their "Flushfleshed" response: their flesh is water; their form is motion. To provide another contrast: as he walks along Grafton Street in "Lestrygonians," Bloom thinks of himself as digested and disgorged by the city, "Feel as if I had been eaten and spewed" (*U* 8.495); in *Finnegans Wake*, any sense of individuality disappears. The text is a digestive tract from which characters cannot be extricated and in which readers themselves become activated.

Before returning to this concept of collective readership, let us first consider the textual conditions that give rise to it. *Finnegans Wake* undoes essences, hierarchies, and valuations and, as it does so, it repeatedly identifies its language as excremental matter. Take, for example, the scene of HCE's naming. In the most reductive version of the "plot," HCE is proprietor of the public house and, accordingly, purveyor of beverages and entertainment in the form of radio and television.[79] Capitalism is the last in a series of forms of order and rule, which he embodies: throughout the *Wake*, he is not just the purveyor of goods but also the conqueror of lands, in the form of various historical personages, all of which are subjected to

---

[77] VI.B.10.010 (h).   [78] VI.B.3.083

[79] See Finn Fordham, "Early Television and Joyce's "Finnegans Wake": New Technology and Flawed Power," in *Broadcasting in the Modernist Era*, ed. Matthew Feldman, Erik Tonning, and Henry Mead (London: Bloomsbury, 2014), 39–56.

confusion and deformation through various forms of obscenity. In I.2, Earwicker is announced to be an "occupational agnomen" (*FW* 30.03), an honorific related to his activities as the keeper of an ostensibly commercialized public space, a turnstile on a road. The chronicler–narrator of I.2 locates his naming, despite reports of his Anglo Saxon or Viking origin, according to the dubious inverted-Talmudic authority of the "Dumlat" at a quasi-feudal moment at the dawn of capitalism. At news of approaching royalty, he runs from the "prefall paradise peace" of cultivating the garden behind his "mobhouse," an alehouse or madhouse: "Forgetful of all save his vassal's plain fealty to the ethnarch Humphrey or Harold stayed not to yoke or saddle but stumbled out hotface as he was" (*FW* 30.19–22). "Plain fealty" was never less plain: "Humphrey or Harold" is decked out in a multicolored array of clothing that proclaims loyalty to every kind of historical order associated with the English monarchy and the British Empire. Yet the exchange between "majesty" and "Haromphreyld" is an irrational transaction. Meaning to ask about the poor state of the roads, as the money both stamped with and collected in his name fails to be spent on what he has decreed, the king asks instead, perhaps rhetorically, about the best use of bait, a question that runs into its answer and thus casts its asker as simultaneously subject and subjected, as user and taker of bait: "asking substitutionally to be put wise as to whether paternoster and silver doctors were not now more fancied bait for lobstertrapping honest blunt Haromphreyld answered in no uncertain tones very similarly with a fearless forehead: Naw, yer maggers, aw war jist a cotchin on thon bluggy earwuggers" (*FW* 31.6–11). Joyce borrows the phrase "fearless forehead" from Erigena, as quoted in Fitzpatrick's history *Ireland and the Making of Britain*: "I am not so browbeaten by authority nor so fearful of the assault of less able minds as to be afraid to utter with fearless forehead what true reason clearly determines and indubitably demonstrates.'"[80] Yet HCE's response, described in terms borrowed from this loyal Northern Irelander, follows neither the logic nor the expository forms of reason but instead combines ingenuous informality with subversive obscenity. In his reply, majesty is identified with creepy-crawlies (yer maggers/earwuggers), as the deformed pronoun (thon for those) slides into the Irish Gaelic for arse, *an thón*, presenting HCE as engaged in an intimate examination of feces. The King too evades the grasp of logic, just as he is released from the constraint of paying at the turnpike. HCE's answer prompts not his anger but his

[80] McHugh, *Annotations*, 31. Benedict Fitzpatrick, *Ireland and the Making of Britain* (New York: Funk & Wagnalls, 1921), 48.

smiles and, after much digressive narrative framing, the king declares: "we have for surtrusty bailiwick a turnpiker who is by turns a pikebailer no seldomer than an earwigger!" (*FW* 31.26–28). Maintaining syntax but not logic, the shifting terms have the cadence of meaning rather than the substance. The twisting sequence of baili/wick/turn/piker/turns/pike/ bailer/wigger suggests the movement of a burrowing worm as he gives HCE the name Earwicker, after the insect that penetrates into the head through the ear. But this meaningless or overly meaningful materialized language is also a kind of carefully worked waste matter. This exchange at the turnpike, then, is not of sense or of cents but of twisted and pleasurable turd-worms.

The narrator gestures toward this production of waste when he declares doubt about the authority of the documents on which this account is based: "Comes the question are these the facts of his nominigentilisation as recorded and accolated in both or either of the collateral andrewpaul-murphyc narratives. Are those their fata which we read in sibylline between the *fas* and its *nefas*? No dung on the road?" (*FW* 31.33–32.01). Following this question without a question mark, right and wrong, possible and impossible, destiny and counterdestiny, law and crime are the poles with which this record is associated, although none of them govern it. Dung here is the possibility of words without or with too much value, of words that escape order. "No dung" is at the same time an unconvincing assertion of an excremental absence and Nothung, the broken sword that the foolish and fearless Siegfried shreds, melts, and recasts to slay the giant hoarder Fafner and to smash Wotan's spear, causing the downfall of the Gods.[81] This carefully crafted word-waste reworks in comic terms Stephen's climactic rejection of his mother's ghoul in "Circe" when he cries "Shite!," an outburst so out of character that Bloom asks, "What?" (*U* 15:4223–25), and then smashes the lamp, exclaiming "Nothung!" (*U* 15:4242). If Stephen's deformed expletive is inspired by the opening profanity of *Ubu roi*, it lacks its impact, perhaps because of the years since *Ubu roi*'s debut but also because "Circe" features waste matter in other far more inventive ways.[82] In contrast to the Circean outburst, the no

---

[81] According to David Hayman, Joyce inserted the phrase "No dung on the road" in the mid-thirties when he revised two copies of *transition* no. 2 for publication with Faber. David Hayman, *James Joyce Archive* 45, p. x.

[82] Ronan Crowley observes the first appearance of the Wonderworker, subsequently called "Hamilton's Long Syringe, the ladies friend" (*FW* 15.3399–400) in a notebook Joyce began in Paris in the summer of 1920: "the first of two drafts of 'Circe' now at the National Library of Ireland, MS 36,639/12 (hereafter the Paris copybook), contains the earliest reference to the device

dung/Nothung of the *Wake* emblematizes an ongoing process of verbal deformation. Resisting all order, this texture is both resistant to and rich with meaning.

In these turd-words, the King and his servant HCE are in a mutual relation of confused, pleasurable desire. They merge into one another. That HCE is already king is suggested by his names: Harold – the last Anglo-Saxon king of England – and Humphrey – Duke of Gloucester, the Lord Protector and Plantagenet heir presumptive. "Humphrey or Harold" becomes "Haromphreyld" (*FW* 31.8–9) and, as the three-page paragraph twists onward, he becomes through an act of popular textual interpretation both ruler and everyman: "all holographs so far exhumed initialed by Haromphrey bear the sigla H.C.E. and while he was only and long and always good Dook Umphrey for the hunger-lean spalpeens of Lucalizod and Chimbers to his cronies it was equally certainly a pleasant turn of the populace which gave him as sense those normative letters the nickname Here Comes Everybody" (*FW* 32.13–19). The equalizing and inclusive effect of this moniker is swiftly and repeatedly reversed in the next sentence: "An imposing everybody he always indeed looked, constantly the same as and equal to himself and magnificently well worthy of any and all such universalization, every time he continually surveyed, amid vociferatings from in front of *Accept these few nutties!* and *Take off that white hat!*, relieved with *Stop his Grog* and *Put It in the Log* and *Loots in his* (bassvoco) *Boots*" (*FW* 32.19–24). While HCE's everyman status is "imposing," this laudatory "universalization" is undermined by his role as an indiscriminating consumer of a mishmash of popular culture. Absorbing the Evergreen Touring Company of Liverpool's *Royal Divorce*, Moore and Burgess Minstrells, *Puss in Boots*, Benedict's *Lily of Killarney*, the Dublin Horse Show or the more titillating "all horserie show" (*FW* 32.35), being heckled all the while, his preeminence is reduced to sartorial superiority, "on every point far outstarching" (*FW* 33.08). This preeminent stiffness is accompanied by whispers of scandal, and HCE lives through another of the cycles of downfall in a farce that centers on his body as an uncontrollable and unknowable site of desire and shame.

Jarry offers in Ubu a prototype for HCE: a fallen king with a scandalous, hyperphysical body that undoes opposites as it embodies them. The third play of the Ubu cycle, *Ubu enchaîné*, follows Ubu's downward

known to survive in the genetic dossier of *Ulysses*." Ronan Crowley, "That English invention: The Wonder Worker in nighttown," *James Joyce Online Notes*, www.jjon.org/joyce-s-environs/wonder-worker-ii.

trajectory from King to servant to convict to galley slave. Despite this decreased status, Ubu now dominates from below. At the end of the play he is offered command of the slave galley in which everyone imitates him but he remains steadfast in an attitude of controlling inferiority: "Even though you've chucked me out of this country and are taking me God knows where as a passenger in this galley, I still remain Ubu Enchained, Ubu slave, and I'm not giving any orders ever again. That way people will obey me all the more promptly."[83] The poles of kingship and slavery, tyranny and freedom, power and submission become indistinguishable from one another. This collapse is expressed vividly when Ubu is flogged and declares: "this lash obeys the curves of my strumpot [belly]. Why, I'm as good as a snake-charmer."[84] The gaoler's infliction of violence upon Ubu is seen as evidence of defeat; Ubu's passive body, receiving the violence, dictates the blows. If this in some ways makes sense, it is also absurd, typifying the utter strangeness of the play. While the earlier plays in the Ubu cycle attack bourgeois society, especially its values of acquisition and status, *Ubu enchaîné* escalates this attack into an exploration of anarchy.[85] At the play's most extreme, freedom in *Ubu enchaîné* is freedom from sense.

The incoherence that is played out at the level of plot and dialogue in Jarry's writing characterizes both the verbal textual and the archetypal protagonist of *Finnegans Wake*. As HCE comes to us in a disparate mass of linguistic and literary material, both his status and his relation to others is confused and contradictory. The shameful uncontrollability of his body is paralleled and amplified by the collision and merging of the elements of this textual material. If the general outline of the *Wake* gestures toward the cyclicality of Vico's history, this verbal multidirectionality undoes the terms of that cyclical order in a manner similar to Jarry's *Ubu enchaîné* and *César-Antechrist*.

The verbal mishmash of Buckley and the Russian General in II.3 is an anti-authoritarian mobilization of excremental slapstick that leads to the explosion of identifiable, directional action. The story is told by Butt to Taff, shifting avatars of Shem and Shaun, whose dialogue is broadcast from

---

[83] *Ubu Plays*, 148. "Si vous m'avez mis à la porte de ce pays et me renvoyez je ne sais où comme passager sur cette galère je n'en suis pas moins resté Ubu enchaîné, esclave, et je ne commanderai plus. On m'obéit bien davantage," *Œuvres Complètes* I, 462.

[84] *Ubu Plays*, 123. "Cette lanière obéit à toutes les courbes de ma gidouille. Je me fais l'effet d'un charmeur de serpents," *Œuvres Complètes* I, 441.

[85] Several of Jarry's friends were anarchists and the Palais Bourbon was bombed by anarchists in 1893. See Shattuck, *The Banquet Years*, 20–22.

a radio or television switched on at the request of the customers in HCE's public house. This account of a scandalous body thus airs in a space in which commerce is superimposed on sociality. Toward the end of his analysis of the dialogue's nuances, Fordham remarks in passing on the problematic nature of Butt and Taff's exchanges of "commodity tokens" (*FW* 354.21) as well as "words, information, money (16), insults (1.6), punches (303), places (462), pens or pans (610). This may well engage with theories of exchange and economics generally, of the symbolic value of money, of labor, the value of value, but if so, it is not clear what it is, at least not to me yet. [...] After all, nothing really adds up in the *Wake*. Because the form of everything changes so rapidly, it does not seem like the monetary world where the value of objects relies on a measure of constancy or predictability."[86] Indeed it does not. Butt and Taff's account of scatological downfall is an extreme instance of Joyce's textual undoing of relations of transaction. Here, in HCE's public house, the material characteristics of language and somatic events undermine the values and categories that regulate transactional exchange. Butt/Buckley/Shem/Shaun's declaration, "I shuttm, missus, like a wide sleever! Hump to dump! Tumbleheaver!" (*FW* 352.14–15), evokes a phrase that recurs throughout the *Wake*, "and the duppy shot the shutter clup," which Hart associates with "putting up the shutters, closing the shop – a symbol of death and the coming of a new age."[87] This closing of shop is not merely a symbol of the end of a temporal continuum; it indicates an attack on the rules of exchange through a language of fertile waste. Taff, looking on, declares a collapse of opposites that is simultaneously a confusion of the terms of war and commerce: "Ah, you were shutter reshottus and sieger besieged. Aha race of fiercemarchands counterination oho of shorpshoopers" (*FW* 352.25–26). Butt is the teller retold; he conquers but is conquered. In a mingling of national stereotypes, fieldmarshals and shooters, and merchants and shoppers, turn into one another.

At the climax of his story, Butt utters a key word that emblematizes the *Wake*'s ardurous and ordurous polysemy: "I gave one dobblenotch and I ups with my crozzier. Mirrdo! With my how on armer and hits leg an arrow cockshock rockrogn. Sparro!" (*FW* 353.19–21). The single word "Mirrdo!" has elicited a wide range of responses. McHugh offers the Italian *mirdo*, I take aim, as well as the Spanish expletive, *mierda!* William Sayer

---

[86] Finn Fordham, "I Shuttm!" Fordham, *Lots of Fun at "Finnegans Wake"* (New York: Oxford University Press, 2007), 89–174, 145.
[87] Hart, *Structure and Motif*, 213.

identifies Rabelais' distortion of the French *merde* into "an oath '*par la mer Dé*; ('by the Mother of God')" as well as hearing "echoes of English *mired,* Italian *mèrda* and *mirando* meaning 'wonderful, marvelous,' and Rabelais' *mirifique,* used to describe the voluptuous effects of the gosling [with which Gargantua wipes himself after defecating]."[88] Various critics have associated Butt's exclamation with *le mot de Cambronne,* which features twice in the preceding page in distorted form, "cabronne!" and "combrune" (*FW* 353.21, 22). We can add to these Jarry's *Merdre!* Accordingly, and with apologies for excremental puns, we must hear in the exclamation *Mirrdo!* the observation "Mere dough!" and the imperative to readers to engage in their own transformations, "More do!"

This polysemic announcement is immediately followed by an interpolated account of the splitting of the atom. As critics have often noted, this "*abnihilisation of the etym*" defies singular meaning; it is both an annihilation and creation *ex nihilo.* The "etym" or atom is also an etymon, a primary word or morpheme but the singular event of Rutherford's scientific breakthrough is presented in a concatenation of verbal deformations more evocative of the everyday event of Lucretius's clinamen, "*by the grisning of the grosning of the grinder of the grunder*" (*FW* 353.22–23). The scissiparity and merging of pataphysical atoms is encapsulated in the fission and fusion of "*general uttermosts confussion*" (*FW* 353.25). This is not a singular event but a total condition that is characterized by disordered and spontaneous erotic associations, "*moletons skaping with mulicules,*" amidst a movement between economic and social opposites, "*coventry plumpkins fairlygosmotherthemselves in the Landaunelegants of Pinkadindy*" (*FW* 353.26–29). This "skaping" or escaping from bonds is at the same time an act of creation, as *skape,* in Norwegian, is to create.[89] The splitting of the atom indeed leads to a creative fusion in which Butt and Taff merge like Jarry's contraries. The stage direction describes them as speaking in unison, as master and slave, slave-wager and foreman, in both a feudal and a free state: "*desprot slave wager and foeman feodal unsheckled, now one and the same person*" (*FW* 354.07–08). Losing their individual identities, Butt and Taff form a communist collectivity: "*with a commonturn oudchd of fest man and best man astoutsalliesemoutioun palms it off like commodity tokens against a cococancancacanotioun*"

---

[88] William Sayers, "The Russian General, Gargantua, and the Writing of 'Wit's Waste,'" *Joyce Studies Annual* (2008), 146–62, at 152.

[89] McHugh, *Annotations,* 353.

(*FW* 354.19–21). This concatenation is a collaborative, erotic, scatological dance of contrary concepts.

We are now "In alldconfusalem" (*FW* 355.11). This is the *Wake*'s version of the New Bloomusalem of "Circe," which parodied the nineteenth-century commercial appropriation of the utopian abundance of the Promised Land.[90] In the *Wake*'s *ville énorme*, matter escapes measure, identities shift, and words swerve to evade conclusive identification. If any interpretation fails to capitalize on the rich semantic suggestions in the passage, this is precisely the point. Joyce pushes to their extreme Jarry's verbal and textual innovations to reimagine the city that Baudelaire described in *Le Spleen de Paris, petits poèmes en prose*. Baudelaire's prose poetry presents, often in figural terms, the innumerable relations and sensations of the city as an overwhelming environment in which the self disappears. In the *Wake*, Joyce recreates that disappearance of individuality in dynamic and seductive sensory stimulation in order to resist the economic structure of the modern metropolis.

Butt's shooting of the Russian General emblematizes a new stage in the evolution of Joyce's sentient thinking. In the words that pass through the air of HCE's public house, the *Wake* further refines the somatic aesthetic that I have traced in preceding chapters of this book. This embodied art is coincident with a sentient thinking that is engaged in at increasing degrees of consciousness by Joyce's characters. It begins with ambiguous bodily odors, sensed by the male observer of the female figures in the Paris Epiphany, by Stephen with Emma Clery in the library colonnade at the end of *Portrait*, and by Bloom with Josie Breen on the street in "Lestrygonians." In "Circe," Bloom remembers a more ephemeral bodily emission when he describes his sensation of Molly's body heat. In HCE's public house, the audience and the readers encounter words that are both conceptual and material. This is an active fullness, to repeat a phrase from our exploration of Jarry. In this melding and merging verbal texture, the collision of elements produces unexpected effects. While Bloom, in "Lestrygonians," can ponder a mystery novel in which poison is created by the mingling of a particular set of foods in the belly, it is our interaction with the contents of *Finnegans Wake* that results in the emergence of events; the text becomes a kind of digestive tract in which we, as readers, are active, responding to it with association, pun, and sonic transformation.

---

[90] McHugh notes that the Crimean War "began over a dispute over the key to the church of Bethlehem" (355).

While the aesthetic encounters we have examined in previous chapters center on digestion and the lower sensory modalities of smell, taste, and touch, the passage that follows Butt and Taff's univocal speech after the abnihilisation prescribes synesthesia as an interpretive approach. A shifting relation of sense impressions is suggested in the scrambling of temporally ordered causality: "*All the presents are determining as regards for the future the howabouts of their past absences which they might see on at hearing could they once smell of tastes from touch*" (*FW* 355.02–07). These elusive past absences are accessible only by a synesthetic effort in which sight and sound, the qualities of language, are granted by the senses of smell, taste, and touch. Accordingly, the terms of accounting float free, defied by the sentences in which they appear: "*To ought find a values for. The must overlistingness. When ex what is ungiven*" (*FW* 355.05–06). The libidinal nature of this proximate relation is indicated in the fragmentary directional phrase before the paragraph ends in distorted assertions of silence and blankness, "*As ad where. Stillhead. Blunk.*" (*FW* 355.01–07).[91] The fragmentary phrase resembles a recurrent motif in the *Wake* that Hart lists as "ad lib. (Vico's fourth Age is performed 'ad lib.'; the regeneration which takes place during it is expressed in the close correspondence of the two last statements of the motif: 'ad libidinum, ad liptum,' whereby the sexually regenerative power of tea is emphasized) 283.15, 287.26, 302.22, 441.09, 541.28."[92] Here, desire moves in multiple directions, gesturing toward the fecundity of material perceptions. The relation into which we are asked to enter is not that of knowledge, nor of identification, but of desire in a physical encounter with a text. Yet precisely because of its fecundity, the sentient thinking prompted by the *Wake* extends beyond the individual reader's encounter with it to a collective engagement.

Aesthetic Sociality

At the debut of Jarry's *Ubu roi*, the audience split into two violently opposing factions. Some accounts have it that Jarry organized these factions, and that some of his friends even shouted in support of both sides.[93] Yeats's account indicates a response governed by social criteria, as he feels the need to support "the more spirited party." The spectrum of reactions from staged response through sympathetic participation to furious outrage speaks to the power of art to shape social relations. Linda Klieger Stillman

---

[91] McHugh gives *stilhed* as Danish for silence.   [92] Hart, *Structure and Motif,* 212.
[93] Beaumont, *Alfred Jarry,* 99–104.

criticizes Jarry's semioclasm as a merely textual affair: "an act of theoretical violence with no evident practice-political application, a public inutility, one cannot hope to actually smash anything. Pataphysics is weak and tactical."[94] Whether or not Stillman is correct about Jarry, I would like to argue that the play of meaning in *Finnegans Wake* has a social application in the collective reception it elicits.

This eliciting occurs in number of ways. Thematically, the text models and summons group readings with its scenes of collective feasting, reading, and interpretation. After Butt and Taff's dialogue, for example, HCE's bar erupts in a barrage of opposing responses to the performance. The massive and perplexing plenitude of these and other voices in the *Wake* leads us to feel that we cannot read it alone. It is arguably the most intimidating work in modernist literature and it is also, maybe because of that, one of the most popular works among reading groups and, not incidentally, among nonacademic reading groups. This phenomenon perhaps illustrates the success of Joyce's stated project for the *Wake*: when asked "'But are there not levels of meaning to be explored?' Joyce responded, 'No, no [...] it's meant to make you laugh'" (*JJ* 703). Yet his response is somewhat reductive: the comic effect of the *Wake* depends upon readers' awareness of its undoing of straightforward expression through simultaneously invoking different and contradictory levels of meaning.

To argue that these multiple levels of meaning prompt what I call an aesthetic sociality, I will (briefly) draw on some opposing positions on the nature of aesthetics. We might first turn to the democratic aesthetics of John Dewey. In *Art as Experience* (1934), Dewey writes: "the conditions that create the gulf which exists generally between producer and consumer in modern society operate to create also a chasm between ordinary and esthetic experience."[95] As Martin Jay summarizes, "For Dewey, the full potential of aesthetic experience and its political counterpart would be realized only if three fundamental changes were effected. First, art had to leave the elite world of museums," second, it would have to cast aside "the Kantian notion that it was inherently contemplative and spectatorial" and, third, it would have to involve the "whole body."[96] Dewey calls for an art that is coincident with experience, understood as "active and alert commerce with the world; at its height it signifies complete interpenetration of

[94] Linda Klieger Stillman, *Alfred Jarry* (Woodbridge, CT: Twayne Publishers, 1983), 116.
[95] John Dewey, *Art as Experience* (New York: Perigee Books, 1934), 8.
[96] Martin Jay, "Somaesthetics and Democracy: Dewey and Contemporary Body Art," *Journal of Aesthetic Education* 36.4 (Winter 2002), 55–69, at 56.

self and the world of objects and events [...] Even in its rudimentary forms, it contains the promise of that delightful perception which is esthetic experience."[97] This delightful perception must be complete: Dewey identifies consummation as an essential element of experience, which contrasts with the inchoate incompleteness of mere activity. Aesthetic experience brings a unified balance to this completeness, "intensif [ying] the sense of immediate living."[98] Dewey imagines this aesthetic experience as taking numerous forms, including "singing, dancing, and oral story-telling to an immediate audience."[99] Yet the democratic power of these lived art forms is perhaps undercut by the possibility of the passive reception of individually performed, readily consumed, consummated works. Dewey's concept of aesthetic experience, however, allows us to think about the nature and potential of *Finnegans Wake* reading groups. The *Wake* denies the consummation Dewey desires in the aesthetic experience: if completion and fulfillment are an essential part of the aesthetic experience for Dewey, the *Wake* never supports such a relation. This is, in fact, the core of its aesthetic nature.

Put differently, it is the *Wake*'s articulation of this impossibility of consummation that ensures its aesthetic status. It does so, paradoxically, through features Adorno associated with hermetic modernist art. In contrast to what Adorno understood as the false abolition of art by the culture industry – the degeneration of aesthetics in consumable products that offer themselves readily for subjective projections that are themselves desires and attitudes standardized by the market – modernist art separates itself from the world of exchange and resists its transactions through a sensory excess that undermines conceptual domination. Art is the realm of the nonidentical – what cannot be said but must be interpreted. Art, as Adorno remarks in *Aesthetic Theory*, assumes the expression of incomprehensibility. If his aesthetic theory thus might readily describe *Finnegans Wake*, as characterized here, Adorno refuses, however, a collective reception. In contrast to Dewey, art for Adorno offers itself only to isolated reading and listening.

Adorno has an immediate interlocutor in this characterization of art's reception: Walter Benjamin, with his theory of an art that through advances in reproductive technology replaces individual (and bourgeois) contemplation with mass reception. To replace contemplation, Benjamin proposes the mode of distraction, best exemplified in the film audience

[97] Dewey, *Art as Experience*, 18–19.   [98] Dewey, *Art as Experience*, 5.
[99] Dewey, *Art as Experience*, 236.

that cultivates a "heightened presence of mind" in order to "parry the shock effect of the film."[100] If Benjamin cites Dada as offering moral shock effects that precede this physical shock, his terms nonetheless come from his own discussion in the *Passagen-Werk* of Baudelaire's experience of modernity. Yet, as has been frequently observed, this mode of distraction is easily co-opted by forces other than the progressive ones Benjamin imagined. Furthermore, as Jürgen Habermas observes, and claims Benjamin himself recognized, "The experience of the shock is not an action, and secular illumination is not a revolutionary deed."[101] Habermas endorses Adorno's criticisms of the lack of dialectical mediation of Benjamin's claims about culture and adds his own criticism that, despite Benjamin's efforts, historical materialism is incompatible with Benjamin's understanding of political change as a cycle without progress.[102]

However, Habermas recognizes another potential for social transformation in Benjamin's writing, one that speaks to the possibilities of *Finnegans Wake*. Habermas points to Benjamin's notion of the mimetic nature of language. Rather than a means for the generation of new meanings, as orthodox Marxists might feel, language for Benjamin is a repository of our expressions of connection to nature, both to our own bodies and to the world around us. This mimetic capacity, the compulsion to become similar, is "the source of that wealth of meaning poured out of language over the world – a world not humanized but for this process – by needs set free in the socio-cultural patterns of existence."[103] Habermas explains, somewhat surprisingly, Benjamin's understanding of the history of art "from the cultic to the postauratic work of art, as a history of attempts to reproduce an image of these non-sensuous similarities or correspondences, yet simultaneously to break the spell which was once upon this mimesis."[104] This spell is the entrapment of "streams of semantic energies" in limiting behaviors and attitudes: magical practices, primal fears of a vengeful Nature, and myths of human powerlessness and unfreedom.[105] For Habermas, these semantic energies offer the means to advance beyond mere economic and political progress (Habermas is sanguine about these possibilities) to achieve a mass experience of happiness with spiritual and sensual content. "Semantic materialism" becomes the means to infuse

[100] Walter Benjamin, "The Work of Art in the Age of Its Reproducibility," in *Walter Benjamin: Selected Writings*, Vol. 3, 1935–1938, ed. Howard Eiland and Michael W. Jennings (Boston: Belknap, 2002), 119.
[101] Jürgen Habermas, "Consciousness-Raising or Redemptive Criticism: The Contemporaneity of Walter Benjamin," *New German Critique* 17 (Spring 1979), 30–59, 56.
[102] Ibid., 52, 55. [103] Ibid., 49. [104] Ibid., 50. [105] Ibid., 50.

happiness into the otherwise "joyless reformism" of what indeed sound like joyless modes of communicative reason: "discursive will formation" and "administrative decision-making structures."[106]

We might combine elements of each of these theorists' accounts to articulate the unusual aesthetic potential of group readings of *Finnegans Wake*. In both refusing and oversupplying meaning, the *Wake* is a repository of sensory wealth. It offers both a record of linguistic forms and a parallel to our experience of nature. It refuses subjective projections; instead, its materialized language encourages the identification of patterns and the articulation of connections made visible by its readers' own, different cultural and economic situations. If Benjamin argued for the disintegration of culture into "goods which can become objects of possession for mankind," *Finnegans Wake* offers itself for ordinary appropriation but not through a mode of distraction or of contemplation but rather through material perception articulated in collective, heterogeneous discussion.

It is the difficulty with which the heterogeneity of these collective receptions is sustained that qualifies successful versions of this experience as an aesthetic sociality. The differentiated articulation of responses to the *Wake* demands the activation of qualities Habermas describes as harbored in the classical bourgeois work of art. During a brief period of secular society, before it was consumed by capitalism, art was:

> the refuge for a satisfaction, even if only virtual, of those wants that have become, as it were, illegal in the material process of life in bourgeois society. I refer here to the need for a mimetic relation with nature, external nature as well as that of one's body; the need for solidarity in living with others, indeed for the happiness of a communicative experience, exempt from imperatives of purposive-rationality (*Zweckrationalitiit*) and giving scope to imagination as well as spontaneity.[107]

Habermas's formulations here are strikingly similar to those of Benjamin's notion of restored semantic potential. An aesthetic sociality involves the creative fostering of these conditions; spontaneity, imagination, and communication beyond means-end calculation are the social demands made by collective readings of the *Wake*. In achieving these conditions, the aesthetic sensitivity that begins in an individual response to the material features of the text extends to others' readings. Readers come to know one another through seeing what they see and hearing what they hear. This requires

[106] Ibid., 58.   [107] Ibid., 42.

more than merely taking turns at speaking; it relies on a sensuous aware-ness of others' physical presences – their facial expressions, their physical postures, their breathing. The text itself tests interactions not by providing a criterion of correctness but rather by always providing an occasion for a different interpretation. In contradistinction to Dewey's notion of a con-clusive art, the aesthetic sociality of *Finnegans Wake* reading groups depends upon their lack of closure. The conditions I describe here are, it is important to emphasize, ideal conditions. They are attained through a collective effort around and through the text. Members of group readings know when these conditions are met; they know when their readings are heard, and the text, if they are honest, tells them when they refuse to hear. Engaged in fully, this aesthetic sociality becomes the means through which interpretive frameworks come into question in an experience of co-being, co-creation, and of the various joys we each enjoy.

Afterword

With *James Joyce and the Matter of Paris*, I have presented Joyce as a person embedded in an early, burgeoning moment of consumer capitalism. Here he writes as an aspiring member of a community of literary artists who set their efforts within and against that moment in cultural history. In this effort, and over the long course of his career, I have followed him successively reframing his style, reconfiguring the strategies of his Parisian literary milieu so as to resist and reorient those external, deforming pressures of commercialism. What comes of this shared endeavor is a somatic art, one that assimilates and metabolizes, unmakes and remakes those forces of transaction and calculation into a new medium of human interaction. From his 1903 representation of women on a city street to the *ville énorme* of *Finnegans Wake*, he finds ways to figure the recovery and sustenance of spontaneity, imagination, and joy in personal interactions.

What I have called the matter of Paris is our matter too. We live in an environment even more intensively structured by transaction, one in which interpersonal relations are increasingly supplanted by relations of exchange. At this moment, Joyce's innovative use of verbal art to explore the significance of embodiment offers readers crucial resources to counter the dominance of mediatized spectacle, to resist the ever-greater streamlining of language in the furtherance of transaction. In attending to the proximate senses with increasingly demanding modes of writing, Joyce resists what Benjamin calls the "penny-in-the-slot called meaning" and, in doing so, he gives readers something that they need more. The subtle acoustics of repeated and shifting sounds, the living body of language through which he presents embodied being: here is an excess that, in making demands on us, gives us so much more in return. For Joyce's verbal art does more than heighten our attunement to sensory experience. It requires us to grapple with our own ability to think and to feel and, I propose here, to think and feel with one another's thoughts and feelings. For grappling with my own in this book, I am grateful to you. As Joyce would say, appropriately in somebody else's language: muchibus thankibus.

Index